THE USE AND ABUSE OF SACRED PLACES
IN LATE MEDIEVAL TOWNS

MEDIAEVALIA LOVANIENSIA

Editorial Board

Geert H.M. Claassens – Jean Goossens
Carlos Steel – Werner Verbeke

SERIES I / STUDIA XXXVIII

KATHOLIEKE UNIVERSITEIT LEUVEN
INSTITUUT VOOR MIDDELEEUWSE STUDIES
LEUVEN (BELGIUM)

THE USE AND ABUSE OF SACRED PLACES IN LATE MEDIEVAL TOWNS

EDITED BY

Paul TRIO
and
Marjan DE SMET

LEUVEN UNIVERSITY PRESS
2006

© 2006 Leuven University Press / Presses Universitaires de Louvain / Universitaire Pers Leuven, Blijde-Inkomststraat 5, B-3000 Leuven/Louvain (Belgium).

All rights reserved. Except in those cases expressly determined by law, no part of this publication may be multiplied, saved in an automated data file or made public in any way whatsoever without the express prior written consent of the publishers.

ISBN 90-5867-519-X
ISBN 978-90-5867-519-4
D/2006/1869/1
NUR: 684-684

CONTENTS

Introduction

Paul TRIO
Introduction   vii

Low Countries

Marjan DE SMET
Heavenly Quiet and the Din of War: Use and Abuse of Religious Buildings for Purposes of Safety, Defence and Strategy   1

Jan KUYS
Weltliche Funktionen spätmittelalterlicher Pfarrkirchen in den nördlichen Niederlanden   27

Jacoba VAN LEEUWEN
Praise the Lord for this Peace! The Contribution of Religious Institutions to the Ceremonial Peace-Proclamations in Late Medieval Flanders (1450-1550)   47

Brigitte DEKEYZER
For Eternal Glory and Remembrance: On the Representation of Patrons in Late Medieval Panel Paintings in the Southern Low Countries   71

German Regions

Jenny Rahel OESTERLE
The Liturgical Dimension of Royal Representation   103

Gabriela SIGNORI
   Sakral oder Profan? Der Kommunikationsraum Kirche   117

British Isles

Jens RÖHRKASTEN
   Secular Uses of the Mendicant Priories of Medieval London   135

Emilia JAMROZIAK
   St Mary Graces: A Cistercian House in Late Medieval London   153

Sheila SWEETINBURGH
   Mayor-Making and Other Ceremonies: Shared Uses of Sacred Space among the Kentish Cinque Ports   165

Karen STÖBER
   The Role of Late Medieval English Monasteries as Expressions of Patronal Authority: Some Case Studies   189

Conclusion

Koen GOUDRIAAN
   Conclusion   209

List of contributors   227
Index librorum manu scriptorum   231
Index locorum   232
Index nominum   241
Index operum   246

INTRODUCTION

by
Paul TRIO

Secular authorities used ecclesiastical buildings and lands for non-religious or only partly religious purposes from the beginning of the Middle Ages. One of the many reasons for treating ecclesiastical property in this way was that in the Middle Ages, religious spaces – and particularly those outside the closed world of the monasteries – were not always considered a completely different world, but were often seen as part of the space where more secular activities and events were commonplace. We need not look far for an initial explanation of this phenomenon. Ecclesiastical and secular societies often intertwined and were less strictly separated than is the case today; secular society in the Middle Ages was permeated by ecclesiastical and religious acts and customs, as surely as the secular world had invaded the ecclesiastical and religious world.

During the course of the twelfth and thirteenth centuries, there was already a long tradition of ecclesiastical buildings and lands being used by urban society as a whole, by specific parts in particular, and by the central authorities. Indeed, did not church towers, with their donjon-like structure, often function as the ultimate place of refuge from attacking enemies? An example of this is the church of St Donatian in Bruges. Galbert provides us with a realistic description, in which he tells us how some of the persons involved in the murder of Charles the Good in 1127 had fled there. However, as urbanization took hold, this development gained momentum, and important changes – in comparison to earlier, more agrarian society – followed in its wake. Indeed, it would be very interesting if the present research could help to discover these trends in medieval towns.

The situation in the Low Countries was quite special, since some of its regions, such as Flanders, Brabant, Zeeland and Holland, were among the most urbanized in Europe, equalled only by those in Northern Italy. It is likely that the high level of urbanization in some parts of the Low Countries entailed a very specific interpretation of the role and use of ecclesiastical spaces and lands in those regions. With the urbanization of the Low Countries, came an early and strongly growing economy that first manifested itself in the textile industry, and later mainly in the so-called art industries. The use of certain monastic complexes, by the guilds for instance, as a meeting place is a result of this development. Moreover, the Low Countries were the scene of a typical urban socio-religious civil culture that developed parallel to their economic expansion. Initially this development was strongest in the South, and later shifted to the North. The typical 'burgher culture' manifested itself in many ways: plays, pageants, processions, chambers of rhetoric, *etcetera*. Ecclesiastical buildings and lands also offered accommodation to some of these expressions of urban culture. Finally, it should be clear that the typical political-institutional organization of the late medieval Low Countries, with its strongly democratic nature and its vigorous – though rapidly declining – urban autonomy, led to some very particular developments with regard to the use of religious buildings by secular organizations. The fact that some of the following papers concern towns situated outside the territory of the Low Countries should enable us to understand better what we believe to be the very specific nature of the Low Countries.

Those who choose late medieval ecclesiastical buildings as their subject of research must clearly define what precisely is to be understood as such. To avoid a too narrow delimitation of the subject, the editors of this book have opted for a practical definition: all buildings and lands within the immediate jurisdiction of an ecclesiastical institution. This institution might be a monastery or abbey, a church fabric, a chapter or a cathedral. *De facto*, hospices and hospitals were semi-ecclesiastical institutions and, theoretically, only their place of worship (church or chapel), with or without its own graveyard, fell within the competence of an ecclesiastical institution, while the rest of the buildings or lands of the urban charitable institutions – with some exceptions – in general ultimately came under the control of the urban government. Indeed, one should ask oneself whether, because of this special status, these semi-ecclesiastical institutions were attributed different functions and roles with regard to the urban and central authorities.

The contributors to this volume try to explain why these ecclesiastical buildings and lands were used for secular or semi-secular activities. For the initial stages of urban development and for quite some time afterwards, the explanation seems to be a very practical one. Indeed, initially, there were few large public and sturdy – *i.e.* stone – buildings of a purely secular nature to be found in the developing towns. As a result, the tower of the urban parish church often functioned as a watchtower to warn the population in the event of fire or the attacks of enemies. Later, the typical belfries assumed this function. Sturdy and large buildings built from stone could accommodate archives, fire fighting equipment and weapons, and the population might find protection there from hostile intruders. When the urban authorities did not have such 'ideal space' of a secular nature at their disposal, they might select an ecclesiastical building, usually part of one of the many monastic complexes that populated the town.

However, this practical explanation sometimes seems insufficient in the later Middle Ages, when the town government and all its diverse hierarchical administrative structures had sufficient accommodations of its own. Nevertheless, even then, towns continued to make use of ecclesiastical buildings. This raises the question whether there were any particular advantages attached to using ecclesiastical space, or whether there was an additional symbolic meaning present. Was it possible, for instance, that such an ecclesiastical space stood a better chance of remaining intact in the event of revolt or invasion, hence offering better protection for the town's archives? It is also quite striking that the textile trades preferred to have their meetings at the Begards, the male counterpart of the Beguines, who usually engaged in the textile industry to earn a living. Whenever the ruler visited, and when he had no residence of his own in town, the authorities usually selected the most important ecclesiastical institution for his accommodation. Undoubtedly, this choice was made because of the available space, certainly when the ruler was travelling with his retinue, and this retinue – or part of it – also required accommodation. However, there were probably other reasons of a more political-ecclesiastical nature that influenced this choice. From this perspective, it would be very interesting to examine whether the urban authorities had different preferences than the central authorities.

Apart from the use of ecclesiastical property for specific meetings of, for example, the Golden Fleece or a visit to the patron saint's church on the occasion of a Joyous Entry, most church buildings – and particularly places of prayer – regularly played a role in secular society, even though these places also usually had a religious meaning/function. Gravestones or tombs, church furniture such as paintings, sculptures, stained glass windows *etcetera* could also represent the social position and status of the donor and his family, for instance by the presence of coats of arms. Apart from a religious image, commemorative tableaux usually also contained a representation of the founders or donors and their immediate family, recognizable by a legend and their armorial bearings. In addition, certain groups within a town, such as guilds (of merchants, crafts, archers and rhetoricians) and confraternities clearly manifested their presence within the church building in which they had their altar or chapel. Beautiful and very clear examples of this are the group portraits of the members of confraternities of the Holy Sacrament and of Jerusalem confraternities, several of which were painted in the sixteenth century by Peter Pourbus and John Scorel. The urban authorities might also wish to make their presence visible. The church of St Martin of Ypres, for example, possessed a tapestry with the names and coats of arms of the aldermen who had been murdered in 1303. This valuable piece was displayed every year on St Andrew's Night (29 November), when a Requiem Mass commemorated the murder. Throughout the Middle Ages, this was the way in which the town's magistrate chose to emphasize the predominance of the urban elite in the town's government, the same elite to which the murdered aldermen had belonged. This manifestation of political representation was clearly directed against any possible claims by the lower social classes, including the urban proletariat. Especially during the reigns of the Burgundian dukes and their Habsburg successors, the donation of royal stained glass windows to numerous urban places of worship became a very popular method of emphasizing the importance of the dynasty and its political supremacy. The coats of arms of the knights who had been present at a gathering of the Order of the Golden Fleece usually remained in place in the church where the meeting had been held for a long time afterward. The coats of arms of the knights of the Golden Fleece who were assembled in 1559 can still be admired even now in the cathedral of St Bavo in Ghent, where the meeting was held.

Numerous series of royal portraits that have decorated many monasteries or abbeys indicate that not only the urban authorities, but the rulers too enjoyed displaying their authority and prestige inside the actual church buildings. Some remain today: for example, the series of the Counts of Flanders in the Major Seminary in Bruges dating from 1480 and the following years. This series of portraits was originally part of the important Cistercian abbey of Ten Duinen (Dunes Abbey, Koksijde).

Apart from the specific temporary or long-lasting adaptations of church buildings and ecclesiastical lands to more secular activities, the participation of the clergy – secular as well as regular – in these adaptations will also be discussed. Were they involved in the adaptation of the building and in the profane ceremonies that took place there, or did they stay on the sidelines, merely as passive onlookers?

Certain religious services were always accompanied by an element of charity. During the Late Middle Ages in particular, the number of commemorative services, such as funerals and annual masses, increased, and most of these entailed distributions to numerous institutions (monasteries, hospitals *etcetera*) and to needy individuals. Indeed, every parish church had its table of the poor, a table at the back of the church where occasionally money or help in kind (bread, meat, fish, clothes, shoes *etcetera*) was distributed to the needy. Although in medieval times this was not strictly speaking a religious activity, this custom was never considered foreign to or inadmissible in the House of God. Indeed, the beneficiaries were expected to attend the services, at the end of which the distributions took place. In this way, their prayer and their partaking of Communion would contribute to the salvation of the donors' souls.

Since the general assumption was that every believer – and no person was allowed to call himself a non-believer – attended mass on Sundays and several feast days, apart from other sacraments such as confession during Lent, the parish church was the ideal place to announce secular matters to all concerned. For instance, certain matters concerning the buying and selling of moveable and immovable property were proclaimed in the local parish church. In the county of Flanders, the so-called 'kerkgeboden' (church commands) were the medium by which parishioners learned about the seizure or confiscation of property in lieu of unpaid rent. Only after this seizure had been proclaimed in the parish church three times, could the mortgaged property pass into the hands of the creditor.

Of special importance was the right of asylum, which allowed criminals or persons who were being persecuted to escape the judicial power of the urban or central authorities. This ecclesiastical protection originated earlier, but it was still used frequently in the Late Middle Ages. However, the right to asylum was often violated by the secular authorities, usually resulting in a long legal battle before reconciliation was reached. How did the application of this right of asylum evolve? A study of this might shed light on the relationship between the Church and its functionaries, and the civilian population and its authorities.

In this short introduction, I have tried to show the richness of the subject within the geographical context of the late medieval towns of the Low Countries in particular, and of the surrounding countries in general. Of course, the subject is not a new one, especially not abroad, judging by the existing number of studies. With regard to the territory of the Low

Countries, only some – usually quite local – partial studies exist. As a result, the study of this subject could only benefit from being placed within a general comparative context.[1]

Katholieke Universiteit Leuven / K.U. Leuven Campus Kortrijk

---

[1] This book is the result of a colloquium that was organized at the Kortrijk Campus of the Katholieke Universiteit Leuven on 4-5 December 2003, within the context of two current research projects. The first is the project "Stadscultuur in de laatmiddeleeuwse Nederlanden" (Urban culture in the late medieval Low Countries), Section 4: "Urban Devotion". This project is a cooperative effort of the Nederlandse Onderzoekschool Mediëvistiek (Dutch Research School for Medieval Studies) and a number of Flemish Universities. The second is the VNC project "De interactie van Kerk en wereldlijke overheden bij de godsdienstige hervormingen in de Nederlanden tussen 1370 en 1560" (The interaction between the Church and the secular authorities with regard to the religious reforms in the Low Countries between 1370 and 1560). We would like to thank the Nederlandse Onderzoekschool Mediëvistiek, the NWO (Nederlandse Organisatie voor Wetenschappelijk Onderzoek) and the FWOV (Fonds voor Wetenschappelijk Onderzoek – Vlaanderen) for their financial support for this colloquium.

Marjan DE SMET

HEAVENLY QUIET AND THE DIN OF WAR: USE AND ABUSE OF RELIGIOUS BUILDINGS FOR PURPOSES OF SAFETY, DEFENCE AND STRATEGY

Introduction

Ideally, the world of the *bellatores* never invaded the peaceful domain of the *oratores* – ideally. In reality, religious and ecclesiastical persons, institutions and places often became involved in, and suffered the consequences of, the violence that riddled late medieval society. The peaceful atmosphere within monasteries and churches was often brutally shattered by soldiers and swordsmen, cannons and fire.

In what follows, we will concentrate on the way in which urban religious buildings – mainly churches and monasteries – functioned within the town's defensive system or figured in its strategies, and on the (ab)use that was made of them by secular authorities. Our 'Low Countries' include – roughly speaking – the territory of present-day Belgium, the Netherlands, and the Northern French region of French Flanders; our 'Late Middle Ages' range from *circa* 1350 to as far as 1570/80, this rather late finishing point being the result of the fact that, at that time, quite some towns in our regions were in the hands of Calvinist governments, and quite some urban religious traditions came – temporarily or permanently – to an end or were reformed. Thematically, we will focus on the use that was made of religious buildings; when talking about 'religious buildings', we will also occasionally include such semi-religious institutions as leper houses, hospices and hospitals, where the care-givers were usually nuns or monks, and which often disposed of a chapel or altar. There were several ways in which religious institutions or persons could become caught up in violent activities: monks or priests could serve as army chaplains, messengers, spies, negotiators, or even soldiers. Monasteries or abbeys could – willingly or unwillingly – support the war effort by establishing rents or issuing loans, by contributing money, horses, wood, food, *etcetera*, bishops and popes could command armies and wage war... None of these various aspects will be discussed here. Nor will we touch upon the 'usual' destruction churches, chapels, monasteries and abbeys suffered at the hands of mobs or soldiers during wartime all over the Low Countries, including the damages incurred during the Iconoclastic Furies of the 1560s.[1] Our attention will go to the buildings and their inhabitants, and their relationship with the secular authorities – mainly the urban authorities, occasionally the central authorities.

More in particular, we will discuss the different uses of religious buildings we found in our data, in peacetime as well as in times of revolt and war, and afterwards. It will not always be possible to maintain the distinction between the situation in times of peace and in times of war, since plans made in the former period tended to become reality in the latter. For the more peaceful periods, we will mainly focus on the various secular functions of the so-called 'church-belfries', *viz.* as a watch tower, as a bell tower, and as an archival depot. Also the general use made of religious buildings to store, repair or fabricate weapons will be discussed. For periods of wartime, we will concentrate on the demolition by the town's defenders of strategically ill-situated religious buildings, and its consequences. Particular attention will be paid to the consequences of two sixteenth-century conflicts: the Guelders War and the Dutch Revolt. Finally, the important role of monasteries and churches as venues for peace negotiations or victory celebrations will be considered.

This paper is based on information and examples found in secondary literature. For this initial survey of the subject, no archival research was done, but hopefully it will lead to an increased awareness that texts by urban and ecclesiastical authorities or institutions with regard to the 'military functions' of religious buildings, might contain important information about the relationship between the late medieval towns and the urban religious institutions. Our data were mainly found in numerous town histories, and studies concerning war and warfare. Interesting works of the latter type are, for instance, the acts of the 1996 colloquium in Spa, *Verwoesting en wederopbouw van steden, van de Middeleeuwen tot heden* ('Destruction and reconstruction of towns, from the Middle Ages to the present'),[2] Van Autenboer's article concerning the destruction and

---

[1] For France, the works by H.S. Denifle, *La désolation des églises, monastères et hôpitaux en France pendant la Guerre de Cent Ans* (Brussels, 1965 (anastatic reprint of Paris, 1897-1899)) and Idem, *La désolation des églises, monastères, hôpitaux en France vers le milieu du XVe siècle*, 2 vols. (Paris, 1897-1899), provide a wealth of information concerning the destruction of ecclesiastical and religious buildings during wartime. We suspect the same might be true for the study by V. Carrière, *La désolation des églises au diocèse de Luçon pendant la seconde moitié du XVIe siècle (documents inédits)* (Paris, 1947), though we did not have the chance to consult it.

[2] *18ᵉ Colloque international / 18ᵈᵉ Internationaal Colloquium. Spa, 10-12.IX.1996. Destruction et reconstruction de villes, du Moyen Age à nos jours / Verwoesting en wederopbouw van steden, van de Middeleeuwen tot heden. Actes / Handelingen*, Gemeentekrediet. Historische Uitgaven in -8°, vol. 100 (Brussels, 1999).

reconstruction of large parts of Mechelen in the late sixteenth century,[3] the article by Gaier with regard to the military destiny of the abbey of St Lawrence in Liège,[4] the – not very recent – study by Van der Does about the Guelders commander-in-chief, Maarten van Rossum,[5] and many other.

In Peacetime

In the Middle Ages, the religious persons, institutions and buildings in the towns, though fully integrated within urban life, still remained separated from certain of its aspects, through customs, laws and privileges. The clergy dressed differently, fell under Canon instead of Civil Law, was exempt from certain taxes; churches were – in principle – sacrosanct, places of refuge and asylum. Yet when the safety of the town was at stake, churches and monasteries could, to a large extent, be incorporated within the town's defensive system, and even fulfil a vital function in it. This is hardly surprising, since they tended to be higher and/or more sturdily built that the majority of the surrounding buildings; this made them eminently suited for certain important functions, also in peacetime.

One part of the church – usually the main parish church, but not necessarily so – in particular often had a vital function within the urban defensive system: the church tower. In many towns of the Low Countries, these towers doubled as town belfries, often until the town erected a – secular – belfry of its own. This was the usual scenario in the county of Flanders, where most of the powerful towns did indeed, after a while, have their own belfry. However, in many cases, the church tower retained this function throughout the Middle Ages, or even throughout the *Ancien Régime*; this type of 'church-belfries' is, for instance, frequently found in the duchy of Brabant.[6]

The three main functions of belfries – including the church-belfries – were the following: first of all, they were observation posts for the town's guardsmen, whose job it was to watch out for fires and approaching enemies. Many examples of church towers functioning as watch towers can be found in the Low Countries, in towns such as Antwerp, Ghent,

---

[3] E. Van Autenboer, 'Mechelen in de 16de eeuw: schade wordt toegebracht en hersteld', *Handelingen van de Koninklijke Kring voor Oudheidkunde, Letteren en Kunst van Mechelen*, 89 (1985), pp. 197-242.

[4] C. Gaier, 'Le destin militaire de l'abbaye Saint-Laurent de Liège', in: R. Lejeune (ed.), *Saint-Laurent de Liège. Eglise, abbaye et hôpital militaire. Mille ans d'histoire* (Liège, 1968), pp. 219-224.

[5] J.C. van der Does, *Maarten van Rossem. De glorieuse Geldersche legeraanvoerder* (Utrecht, s.d).

[6] M. Heirman, *Langs Vlaamse belforten en stadhuizen* (Louvain, 2003), pp. 11-13.

Haarlem, Courtrai, Mechelen, Louvain, Utrecht, ...[7] Secondly, the church tower often housed the town's alarm bell or tocsin, which raised all members of the urban community in times of fire or other danger. Again, many

[7] Some examples of church towers that served as observation posts: Antwerp: even though the Gothic church was already under construction, the tower of the Romance church of Our Lady remained standing until *circa* 1475, since the town needed it as an observation post (J. Lampo, *Vermaerde Coopstadt. Antwerpen in de Middeleeuwen* (Louvain, 2000), p. 82); Ath: two watchers stood on the bell tower of the church of St Julian (J. Dugnoille, 'Les initiatives des échevins d'Ath dans la gestion de la cité sous l'Ancien Régime', in: *L'initiative publique des communes en Belgique. Fondements historiques (Ancien Régime) / Het openbaar initiatief van de gemeenten in België. Historische grondslagen (Ancien Régime) / 11ᵉ colloque international / 11ᵈᵉ internationaal colloquium. Spa, 1-4 sept. 1982. Actes / Handelingen*, Gemeentekrediet van België, Historische uitgaven, Series in -8°, vol. 65 (S.l., 1984), pp. 223-239, 229); Breda: the fire watchmen were stationed on the tower of the Great Church (G.J. ter Kuile, Jr., 'Over oude straten, pleinen, huizen, over leven en bedrijf', in: *Geschiedenis van Breda*, vol. 1: *De Middeleeuwen* (Schiedam, 1976 (anastatic reprint)), pp. 230-255, 246); Brussels: the fire watchmen were stationed on the tower of the church of St Nicholas (M. Vanhamme, *Bruxelles: de bourg rural à cité mondiale* (Antwerp / Brussels, 1968), p. 27); Courtrai: the night watchmen stood on the tower of the church of St Martin (F. De Potter, *Geschiedenis van de stad Kortrijk*, vol. 1 (Brussels, 1975), p. 300; N. Maddens, 'De Nieuwe Tijd', in: N. Maddens (ed.), *De geschiedenis van Kortrijk* (Tielt, 1990), pp. 147-363, 221); Ghent: the town's guardsmen used the tower of the church of St Nicholas, certainly from 1321/22 onwards, until the fifteenth century. Even though the town's belfry was completed around 1380, in 1436 the urban guardsmen were still positioned on the church of St Nicholas (B. Baillieul e.a., 'De Late Middeleeuwen', in: B. Baillieul & A. Duhameeuw (eds.), *Een stad in opbouw. Gent vóór 1540* (Tielt, 1989), pp. 137-316, 153; F. De Potter, *Gent van den oudsten tijd tot heden. Geschiedkundige beschrijving der stad*, vol. 1: 2 (Roeselare, 1995 (anastatic reprint)), pp. 382, 488 and 552, and *Ibidem*, vol. 3: 1 (Roeselare, 1995 (anastatic reprint)), pp. 164 and 168; D. Nicholas, 'In the Pit of the Burgundian Theater State. Urban Traditions and Princely Ambitions in Ghent, 1360-1420', in: B.A. Hanawalt & K. L. Reyerson (eds.), *City and Spectacle in Medieval Europe*, Medieval Studies at Minnesota, vol. 6 (Minneapolis / London, 1994), pp. 271-295, 281; M. Boone, 'Openbare diensten en initiatieven te Gent tijdens de Late Middeleeuwen (14ᵈᵉ-15ᵈᵉ eeuw)', in: *L'initiative publique des communes en Belgique*, pp. 71-114, 94; G. Van Doorne, 'Architectuur als visuele taal van de stedelijke cultuur', in: J. Decavele (ed.), *Gent. Apologie van een rebelse stad. Geschiedenis, kunst, cultuur*, Mercatorfonds (Antwerp, 1989), pp. 373-395, 375); Gorinchem: the watchmen were in 1514 positioned on the church tower, amongst other places (R. Fruin (ed.), *Informacie up den staet faculteyt ende gelegentheyt van de steden ende dorpen van Hollant ende Vrieslant om daernae te reguleren de nyeuwe schiltaele, gedaen in den jaere MDXIV* (Leyden, 1866), p. 409); Haarlem: the church tower functioned as observation post (C.L. Verkerk, 'De parochie Haarlem en de religieuze stichtingen binnen haar grenzen', in: *Deugd boven geweld. Een geschiedenis van Haarlem, 1245-1995* (Hilversum, 1995), pp. 63-87, 66); Louvain: by day, the watchmen were positioned on the church of St Peter, at night on the tower of the church of St Michael (R. Van Uytven, 'Stedelijke openbare diensten te Leuven tijdens het Ancien Régime', in: *L'initiative publique des communes en Belgique*, pp. 21-43, 28; G. Spiessens, 'De Antwerpse Stadsspeellieden (1415-1794)', *Bijdragen tot de geschiedenis*, 58: 1-4 (1985), pp. 103-126, 115; G. Huybens, 'Vier eeuwen muziek in en voor de stad Leuven', *Bijdragen tot de geschiedenis*, 68 (1985), pp. 113-126 (theme issue: *De Brabantse stad. Zevende colloquium, Brussel, 13-15 september 1984*), 116; E. Van Even, *Louvain dans le passé &*

examples can be found: Brussels, Ghent, Louvain, ... [8] Thirdly, the town's most important documents, charters and privileges were often kept there in a special strongroom, in an iron chest, so that these documents,

dans le présent. Formation de la ville – événements mémorables – territoire – topographie – institutions – monuments – oeuvres d'art (Louvain, 1895), p. 372); Mechelen: the guardsmen were positioned on the towers of the churches of St Rumold (attested since 1356) and of Our Lady (attested since 1485) (R. Van Uytven, 'De Mechelse burgers tegenover hun politieke meesters: de heerlijkheid Mechelen en haar meesters – de bestuursorganen van de stad – de heerlijkheid en vrijheid van Walem', in: Idem (ed.), *De geschiedenis van Mechelen. Van Heerlijkheid tot Stadsgewest* (Tielt, 1991), pp. 58-67, 63; J. Schoeffer, *Historische aanteekeningen rakende de kerken, de kloosters, de ambachten en andere stichten der stad Mechelen*, vol. 1: *Opkomst en bloei der stad Mechelen met zijne parochie kerken en kapellen*, Algemeen Rijksarchief en Rijksarchief in de Provinciën. Reprints, vol. 52 (Brussels, 1996 (anastatic reprint of Mechelen, s.d.)), pp. 33-34 and 123; Heirman, *Langs Vlaamse belforten*, p. 47; J.B. David, *Geschiedenis van de stad en de heerlykheid van Mechelen* (Kortemark / Handzame, 1985 (anastatic reprint of Louvain, 1854)), p. 200); Utrecht: the church tower, for instance the tower of the Buurkerk, was used as refuge and observation post (H.L.P. Leeuwenberg, 'Steden en hun kerken', in: M. van Rooijen (ed.), *Steden en hun verleden. De ontwikkeling van de stedelijke samenleving in de Nederlanden tot de negentiende eeuw* (Utrecht / The Hague, 1988), pp. 81-104, 92; W.H. Vroom, *De financiering van de kathedraalbouw in de middeleeuwen, in het bijzonder van de dom van Utrecht* (Maarssen, 1981), p. 345 (with bibliographic references)).

[8] Some examples of church towers that housed unconsecrated town bells: Antwerp: until 1475, the bronze tocsin called 'Orida' (from the Latin 'horrida', terrible), hung in the Romance tower of the church of Our Lady; afterwards, it was transferred to the new Gothic tower (*Musea Antwerpen: Museum Vleeshuis: Collectie: Kunstambachten: De stormklok Orida*. http://museum.antwerpen.be/vleeshuis/); Brussels: several of the town bells hung in the tower of the church of St Nicholas (A. Henne & A. Wauters, *Histoire de la ville de Bruxelles*, vol. 1 (Brussels, 1968 (anastatic reprint of Brussels, 1845)), pp. 166-167; Heirman, *Langs Vlaamse belforten*, p. 24); Courtrai: *circa* 1520, the town bells were transferred from the belfry to the church of St Martin, because they endangered the stability of the former building (Heirman, *Langs Vlaamse belforten*, p. 117); Ghent: before the completion of the belfry in the middle of the fourteenth century, the town's bells hung in the tower of the church of St Nicholas, and the great bell of the church of St John was used to announce celebrations (De Potter, *Gent*, vol. 1: 2, p. 488; Van Doorne, 'Architectuur', p. 375; Heirman, *Langs Vlaamse belforten*, p. 81); Lier: during the fifteenth century and once more in 1505, some of the bells from the town's belfry were moved to the tower of the church of St Gummarus (Heirman, *Langs Vlaamse belforten*, p. 41); Louvain: the town bells hung in the chapter tower until 1542, when they were transferred to the main tower of the church of St Peter; after the fire of 1462, they were moved to the tower of the church of St Michael for some years; in 1570, when the tower of the church of St Peter had partly collapsed, the tower of the church of St Michael once more became the town's belfry (Huybens, 'Vier eeuwen', p. 116; Van Even, *Louvain*, pp. 343-344 and 372); Mechelen: from 1326 onwards, the town's bells hung in the tower of the church of St Rumold (David, *Geschiedenis*, p. 200; Heirman, *Langs Vlaamse belforten*, pp. 47 and 167); Tienen: the tower of the church of St Germanus functioned as the town's belfry (J.-B. Nys, *Récits historiques et légendes tirés des annales de la ville de Tirlemont* (Brussels, 1900), p. 145); Utrecht: the tower of the Buurkerk housed the town's *banklok* or tocsin, and several other unconsecrated bells (Leeuwenberg, 'Steden', p. 92; Vroom, *De financiering*, p. 345). In Mechelen, the Franciscan monastery apparently had the care

which represented the legal basis for the town's very existence, freedom and rights were kept – relatively – safe from theft, violence or fire, protected by metal, stone, and the sacred nature of the building in which they were kept.[9]

of the town's alarm bell (J. Baetens, 'Minderbroederskloosters in de Zuidelijke Nederlanden. Kloosterlexicon. 47. Mechelen', *Franciscana*, 44 (1989), pp. 3-62, 21). From what happened in Montreuil-sur-Mer, a Northern French town, it becomes clear that keeping the tocsin was also a matter of prestige: after the town's belfry had collapsed in 1377, the tocsin hung in the Benedictine abbey for fifteen years, and the monks were very upset when the reconstruction of the belfry was undertaken (L. Danhieux, 'Het belfort, een symbool', in: G. Dehulster e.a., *Brugge. Belfort en beiaard. Tentoonstelling in het Provinciaal Hof, Markt, Brugge (14 augustus 1984-9 september 1984)* (Bruges, 1984), pp. 9-27, 13-14).

[9] The archivist S. Muller Fzn. came to the same conclusion: in many of the smaller towns, the oldest parish church was used to keep the town's archive safe, because these buildings were – relatively – fire-resistant, and because they were sacrosanct places (F.W.J. Koorn, 'De bewaring van de stadsprivileges. Aspecten van de middeleeuwse en vroegmoderne archiefzorg in Haarlem', in: D.P. Blok e.a. (eds.), *Datum et actum. Opstellen aangeboden aan Jaap Kruisheer ter gelegenheid van zijn vijfenzestigste verjaardag*, Publicaties van het Meertens Instituut, vol. 29 (Amsterdam, 1998), pp. 265-276, 271; see also P.J. Blok, *Geschiedenis eener Hollandsche stad*, vol. 2: *Eene Hollandsche stad onder de Bourgondisch-Oostenrijksche heerschappij (met een kaart)* (The Hague, 1912), p. 4; H. ten Boom, 'Rotterdam aan de vooravond van de Reformatie. I: De Rooms-katholieke Kerk en haar instellingen', *Rotterdams Jaarboekje*, Series 9, 1 (1983), pp. 199-237, 212; Leeuwenberg, 'Steden', p. 92; R. Van Uytven, 'Wereldlijke overheid en reguliere geestelijkheid in Brabant tijdens de Late Middeleeuwen', in: *Colloque 'Sources de l'Histoire religieux de la Belgique' (Bruxelles, 30 novembre – 2 décembre 1967) / Colloquium 'Bronnen voor de religieuze geschiedenis van België' (Brussel, 30 november – 2 december 1967)* (S. l., 1967), pp. 169-271, 186). Some examples of churches as archive deposits: Alkmaar: the town's privileges were kept in the church; in 1517, when the Guelders-Frisian troops destroyed all archival documents kept in the town hall, only these privileges were saved (Koorn, 'De bewaring', p. 271); Amsterdam: until the nineteenth century, the town's privileges and valuable documents were kept in the so-called 'Iron Chapel' in the Old Church, a room with heavy vaults, small windows and an iron door; according to Koorn, this room probably was first used as an archive deposit after 1578; before that period, the charters would have been kept somewhere else in the church (H. Brugmans, *Geschiedenis van Amsterdam*, vol. 1: *Middeleeuwen 1100/1544*, Aula-paperback, vol. 10 (Utrecht / Antwerp, 1972), p. 140; Koorn, 'De bewaring', p. 271); Bergen op Zoom: the town's charters and seals were kept in a room in or adjacent to the parish church, probably in the tower, in a chest; only in 1573 the town council decided to transfer the chest to the town hall, because of the dangerous situation (W.A. van Ham, *Macht en gezag in het Markiezaat. Een politiek-institutionele studie over stad en land van Bergen op Zoom (1477-1583)* (Hilversum, 2000), p. 250); Breda: certainly already during the fifteenth century, the town's most important documents were kept in a large chest which was stored in the collegiate church ((Father) Placidus, 'Geschiedenis der katholieke Kerk te Breda', in: *Geschiedenis van Breda*, vol. 1: *De Middeleewen* (Schiedam, 1976 (anastatic reprint)), pp. 123-182, 141); Brussels: the town's privileges were possibly kept in the church of St Nicholas (Heirman, *Langs Vlaamse belforten*, p. 24); Courtrai: in the treasury of the church of St Martin, the most important archives of the town were kept, and this during a long period of time (F. De Potter, *Geschiedenis der stad Kortrijk*, vol. 3 (Brussels, 1975 (anastatic reprint of Ghent, 1875)), p. 81); Delft: certainly during the fifteenth century, the church of St Hippolyte served as the archival depot for the *Hoogheemraadschap* (polder district)

of Delfland; in 1450, the town of Delft did not allow the *Hoogheemraadschap* to remove its privileges, and this was the beginning of an 'archival war' which lasted for four years (D.P. Oosterbaan e.a., *De Oude Kerk te Delft gedurende de Middeleeuwen* (The Hague, 1973), p. 88); Deventer: the county's archival chest was kept in the church, above the chapter house (B.H.D. Hermesdorf, *Rechtsspiegel. Een rechtshistorische terugblik in de Lage Landen van het herfsttij* (Nijmegen, 1980), p. 20); Haarlem: the important privileges of the town were kept in the church of St Bavon, in a chest above the sacristy (certainly in 1428) (L. van den Bergh-Hoogterp e.a., 'Artistiek centrum in het graafschap Holland', in: *Deugd boven geweld. Een geschiedenis van Haarlem, 1245-1995* (Hilversum, 1995), pp. 110-138, 126; Koorn, 'De bewaring', pp. 265-266); Herentals: the urban charters were kept in the church of St Waltrude until the completion of the belfry in the middle of the sixteenth century (Heirman, *Langs Vlaamse belforten*, p. 37); Leyden: at least since 1408, the town's privileges were kept in the church of St Peter, beneath the tower; before, they had been kept in the town hall; after the collapse of the church in 1512, the documents were once more kept in the town hall (Koorn, 'De bewaring', p. 271; Blok, *Geschiedenis*, vol. 2, p. 4); Lier: the town's privileges were kept in the church of St Gummarus, until they were burned during the Iconoclastic Fury of 1580 (Heirman, *Langs Vlaamse belforten*, p. 41); Louvain: the Joyous Entry of 1356 made Louvain the depository for the Brabant charters; they were kept in the tower of the church of St Peter, which functioned as the town's belfry; there were three keys: one for the duke, one for the town of Louvain, and one for the town of Brussels; according to Van Even, the Brabant charters remained there until 1407, when they were transferred to Nivelles; the town's charters were also kept in the church of St Peter, in a chest with twelve keys, first in the tower, afterwards in a vaulted room of the chapter; in 1499, the town's charters were transferred to the town hall, only to be returned to the church that same year. From 1571 onwards, they would remain in the town hall (J.A. Torfs, *Geschiedenis van Leuven, van den vroegsten tijd tot op heden* (Tienen, 1984 (anastatic reprint of Louvain, 1899)), p. 144; Van Even, *Louvain*, pp. 276 and 337; Heirman, *Langs Vlaamse belforten*, pp. 163-164); Maastricht: the urban charters were kept in het church of Our Lady, according to a document of 1513 (J. van Herwaarden, 'Steden en hun verleden', in: M. van Rooijen (ed.), *Steden en hun verleden. De ontwikkeling van de stedelijke samenleving in de Nederlanden tot de negentiende eeuw* (Utrecht / The Hague, 1988), pp. 9-32, 28; A. Kessen, *De historische schoonheid van Maastricht* (Amsterdam, 1947³), p. 41); Rotterdam: the town's seal, privileges and important charters were kept in a chest in the church of St Lawrence (Koorn, 'De bewaring', p. 271); Schiedam: 1344: a copy of the town's staple privilege was kept in a chest in the church (Hermesdorf, *Rechtsspiegel*, p. 20); 's-Hertogenbosch: the original privileges were kept in the town's chest, in the church of St John; they staid there until they were moved to the town hall to protect them from the Iconoclastic Fury (A. Schuttelaars, *Heren van de raad. Bestuurlijke elite van 's-Hertogenbosch in de stedelijke samenleving, 1500-1580* (Nijmegen, 1998), p. 2; J. Scheerder, *De beeldenstorm* (Haarlem, 1978²), p. 66); Utrecht: since the middle of the fifteenth century, the town's statute book was kept in the library of the Buurkerk (Leeuwenberg, 'Steden', p. 92). In quite some towns, the town's charters were kept in one of the urban monasteries: Dordrecht: the most important charters were kept in the Franciscan monastery, the other in the town hall; also the charters of the polder district were kept in the monastery, in the sacristy behind the main altar (in 1407) (P.A. Henderikx, *De oudste bedelordekloosters in het graafschap Holland en Zeeland. Het ontstaan van bedelordekloosters voor ca. 1310 te Dordrecht, Middelburg, Zierikzee en Haarlem, alsmede enige aspecten van de plaats van deze kloosters in het stedelijk leven en daarbuiten gedurende de Middeleeuwen*, Hollandse Studiën, vol. 10 (Dordrecht, 1977), pp. 169-170); Ghent: during the fourteenth century, before the belfry was completed, the town charters were sometimes – apparently mainly in times of unrest, revolt or war – kept safe in the Franciscan monastery; when this was the case, the monastery was sometimes guarded by the town's watchmen; an entry in the *Memorieboek* from the year 1401 tells

Because of their vital function for the town's safety, many urban governments were prepared to take upon them the construction and/or reparation costs of these 'church-belfries', effectively becoming the owners of these towers.[10] Remnants of this situation survive to this day. For instance: to this day, the town of Antwerp still owns the tower of the Cathedral of Our Lady, and pays for its restauration, since it served as the town's belfry for centuries; the rest of the building is owned by the church fabric. The same is true for the cathedral of Mechelen.[11]

Our data contain hardly any objections from religious persons against this use of religious buildings by the secular authorities. Of course, many studies have pointed out that most church buildings served different kinds of secular uses, as long as certain sacred areas were respected. Also, the church towers, which often played such crucial parts in the town's defence, were apparently not included in the immunity of the church.[12]

---

us that 'in that year, the privileges of this town were fetched from the Friars Minor, where they had been for a long time, and that they were taken from there and put in the vault under the belfry'; these valuable documents were also sometimes stored in the monastery of the Carmelites (P.C. Vander Meersch (ed.), *Memorieboek der stad Ghent. Van 't j. 1301 tot 1793*, vol. 2, Maetschappy der Vlaemsche bibliophilen. 2nd Series, vol. 15 (Ghent, 1852), p. 136; De Potter, *Gent*, vol. 1: 1, pp. 312-313 and vol. 4: 1, pp. 229-230; S. Van Ruysevelt, 'De Franciscaanse kerken. De stichtingen van de dertiende eeuw. Gent', *Franciscana*, 24 (1969), pp. 123-145, 129-130); Groningen: the 'landkiste', the county's chest, was sometimes kept by the Franciscans (F.J. Bakker, *Bedelorden en begijnen in de stad Groningen tot 1594*, Groninger Historische Reeks, vol. 3 (Assen / Maastricht, 1988), p. 82.

[10] According to Hermesdorf, *Rechtsspiegel*, p. 10, in many towns of the Low Countries, the church tower was communal property. Some examples of towns sharing in its construction or maintenance costs: Haarlem (Verkerk, 'De parochie Haarlem', p. 66); Louvain: the town paid for the maintenance of the church tower which served as the town's belfry (Van Even, *Louvain*, p. 337; Heirman, *Langs Vlaamse belforten*, p. 163); Rotterdam: during the fifteenth and sixteenth centuries, the town repeatedly contributed to the construction and reparation of the tower of the church of St Lawrence (ten Boom, 'Rotterdam aan de vooravond', p. 222); Tongeren: in 1314, there was an agreement between the town and the chapter of Our Lady, concerning the concerted reconstruction of the burned-down tower; the bells would be recast, and the town would supply the bell cords (Hermesdorf, *Rechtsspiegel*, p. 10); Utrecht: reparations of the tower of the Buurkerk were paid for by the church fabric, except for the costs concerning the town bells; those were paid for either by the town, or jointly by the town and the church fabric (Vroom, *De financiering*, p. 345).

[11] Heirman, *Langs Vlaamse belforten*, pp. 13 and 155; *Monumentenwacht Vlaanderen: Nieuwsbrief: Antwerpse kathedraal maakt werk van onderhoud, december 1998.* http://www.monument.vlaanderen.be/mowav/nl/antwerpsekathedraal.html. The town of Mechelen still owns the tower of the church of Saint Rumold, despite the fact that the town made no major financial contribution to its construction, as was the case in other towns. In fact, the tower was largely financed with money from papal indulgences (Heirman, *Langs Vlaamse belforten*, p. 167).

[12] W. Nolet & P.C. Boeren, *Kerkelijke instellingen in de Middeleeuwen* (Amsterdam, 1951), p. 102.

Apart from a part of a church or monastery fulfilling the function of the town belfry, there is second 'military' function urban religious buildings could have in peacetime: they could serve as a storage room or as a construction space for military implements and weapons. Supposedly, this type of buildings was often thought to be eminently suited for such purposes because of their sturdy construction – as has been mentioned before –, the presence of spacious rooms, and probably also often because of their central situation within town, far from any possible attackers, and at the same time easily accessible to the town's defenders. Some examples will clarify this. The fourteenth-century Ghent magistrates used the tower room of the church of St Nicholas for storing the bows of the town's archers.[13] For a long time, gunpowder was stored in the treasury of the church of St Martin in Courtrai.[14] In Amsterdam, at the beginning of the sixteenth century, the town erected a *bushuis* (gun house) on the grounds of the convent of St Paul.[15] In 1381 the trebuchet of the town of Deventer was kept in the church.[16] In Haarlem in 1533 the Dominicans allowed the town to establish an artillery storage room on their lands in town, on condition that 'there will be no noise made there that could disturb the friars in their dormitory or in their library', and on condition that the town would support the friars' claim that they had the right to preach in the hospice of St Gangulf on All Saints' Day.[17] Also, the abbey of St Peter in Ghent served in 1381 as a construction area for war engines; in 1413, the abbey was also mentioned as a depot for artillery.[18]

---

[13] De Potter, *Gent*, vol. 3: 1, p. 168: 'Jtem den ghenen die de boghen af holpen van den turre S. Niclaus ende droughen jn ser Gerards Dievelshuus ende weder up den turre' ('Item to those who have helped to carry the bows from the tower of St Nicholas and into the house of Sir Gerald the Devil, and back into the tower' (*Town Accounts* of 1336-1337)).

[14] De Potter, *Kortrijk*, vol. 3, p. 81: 'ghegheven meester Godevaerte den temmerman ende sinen ghesellen van dat sy tghehanc ende rec maecten in de tresorie vander stede in de kerke van St. Maertins in Curtrike, omme tdonderbos pouder vander stede te hanghene' ('given to master Godevaert the carpenter and his journeymen, for making the hanger and rack in the town's treasury in the church of St Martin in Courtrai, where the town's gunpowder will be hung' (*Town Accounts* of 1393)).

[15] Brugmans, *Geschiedenis*, vol. 1, p. 193.

[16] M. Carasso-Kok, 'Der stede scut. De schuttersgilden in de Hollandse steden tot het einde der zestiende eeuw', in: M. Carasso-Kok & J. Levy-van Halm (eds.), *Schutters in Holland. Kracht en zenuwen van de stad* (Zwolle, 1988), pp. 16-35, 19.

[17] S.P. Wolfs, *Middeleeuwse dominicanenkloosters in Nederland. Bijdrage tot een monasticon* (Assen, 1984), p. 81; Henderikx, *De oudste bedelordekloosters*, p. 109.

[18] 'Item [betaelt] van den engienen die men maecte sente Pieters, in den cloestre' ('Item, [paid] for the engines made in the monastery of St Peter' (*Town Accounts* of 1381, fol. 252 v°)) and 'Item, betaelt Boudeyn van Lokeren van donderbus poeder te maken, te wegen en van de enginen te voeren St-Pieters' ('Item, paid to Boudeyn van Lokeren for

In two cases, an additional use of the spacious terrains of religious institutions within the town walls was found, though only when war was imminent or in times of war. With a diet mainly based on corn, mills were strategically important facilities in a medieval town. In case of a siege, the windmills and watermills surrounding the town could become inaccessible to the townspeople. In 1383, during the siege of Ypres by the English and Ghent armies, the Franciscan monastery within the walls put part of its land at the town's disposal to build a mill, since the mills in the suburbs could no longer be used. This proof of goodwill was highly appreciated by the urban authorities.[19] In Groningen, in 1568, the authorities ordered the inhabitants of the Olde Convent to put their horse mill (which was possibly situated on the grounds of the monastery) into working order; they even paid for the repairs, since the mill would function as a backup in case of a siege.[20]

In Wartime

In case of war, the 'suburbs' of a town, situated outside the city walls, were not only extremely vulnerable to passing, attacking or besieging armies, they also became a liability. Indeed, in a period when artillery became increasingly more powerful and sophisticated, any structure situated within the field of fire from the town's ramparts not only offered the enemy shelter against the volleys of the town's defenders, but also offered that enemy a base of operation for a protracted siege or a bombardment, effectively obstructing the defenders' field of fire. Large and sturdy buildings in particular, such as stone churches or monasteries that were situated outside the town walls, caused many a town government in the Low Countries to worry about the town's safety in case of a siege. The phenomenon was very common in the Late Middle Ages; most towns would have at least one monastery – often more – situated outside the town walls, but 'within range', or even adjacent to the walls, so it is hardly surprising that, in the fourteenth, fifteenth and sixteenth centuries, when many wars were fought on the territory of the Low Countries, quite some towns tried to get rid of these 'liabilities'.

---

the preparation of gunpowder, for weighing and for bringing the engines to St Peter' (*Town Accounts* of 1413, fol. 22 v°)) (J. Huyttens, 'Recherches sur l'organisation militaire de la ville de Gand au Moyen-Age', *Messager des sciences historiques, ou Archives des Arts et de la Bibliographie de Belgique* (1858), pp. 413-452, 445).

[19] P. Trio & W. Simons, 'Achtergronden bij het ontstaan van de tuindagprocessie: bronnen en situering', in: R. Vinckier (ed.), *Ieper Tuindag. Zesde Eeuwfeest. Een bundel historische opstellen* (Ypres, 1983), pp. 107-128, 123.

[20] Bakker, *Bedelorden*, p. 176.

When there was no urgent reason for preparing the town's defensive system, there was room for discussion, negotiation and compromise. Sometimes the town magistrate won, sometimes the friars, monks or nuns of the 'offending' monastery, who were usually loath to leave their home while they were still uncertain about whether they would receive a suitable compensation if their monastery were to be demolished. For example, in 1543, the Brussels' authorities planned to tear down the monastery of the Rich Clares which leaned against the town wall, in order to renew the town's fortifications. Protest mainly came from the nuns of the hospital of Saint John, who were expected to move out of their hospital, since the Rich Clares would find a new home there.[21] The hospital nuns' most important argument for refusing was, that they were not willing to bear the considerable expenses for the equipment of a new hospital, in order that the Rich Clares, a rather 'useless' order, could find a new home in their monastery. The plan failed – for the time being; the idea was rekindled in 1551/52, when some engineers, who had been asked for advice by the regent, Mary of Hungary, once more suggested the demolition of the monastery. Fortifications were being built south of the town, and the site of the monastery was needed. Again, protest from the order that was supposed to make room for the expelled Rich Clares – now the nuns of the hospital of St Peter – caused the project to be cancelled, since they produced written proof that their location in town had been guaranteed. All this happened in a period when the war against France occasionally flared up, and there was a hectic urge to fortify the town each time French troops came near Brussels: the demolition plans of 1543 were the result of the advance of French troops as near as Binche, and also the plans of 1552 were the result of a French threat. Still, the Rich Clares could – apparently relatively easily – stave off the demolition of their monastery, probably thanks to their good relations with the authorities. By the late seventies of the sixteenth century, however, the town was controlled by a Protestant committee, supporters of William the Taciturn, and the Spanish army under the command of Don Juan was advancing. A commitee in charge of the fortifications advised the destruction of the churches of St Giles, Obbrussel and Molenbeek, the rubble of which would be recycled in the newly to be constructed fortifications, and also used for the reinforcement of that part of the walls where the monastery

---

[21] We often see this domino-effect when urban authorities promised the inhabitants of a monastery that was about to be demolished accommodation in some monastery within the city walls, the occupants of which had to move out, sometimes to again another monastery. In the case of Brussels in 1543, the hospital nuns were supposed to move to the house of the Friars of the *Wolfsgracht*.

of the Rich Clares was situated. The proposal was accepted by the Three Members of Brussels in 1577. In 1580, after the Prince of Orange and the General States had left Brussels for Antwerp, fleeing the approaching armies of Don Juan, the monastery of the Rich Clares was finally destroyed for urgent military reasons, and a ravelin was erected there.[22] A similar process of 'trial and failure' can, for instance, also be found in Kampen. Thrice – in 1493, 1495 and 1522 – was decided that the monasteries of St Michael and of the Augustinian nuns represented a hazard for that town's defence. Pleas from – amongst others – the Prior of Windesheim and the town of Zwolle (daughters of its burghers were present in both convents), caused the demolition to be postponed. Clerical supporters of the nuns even kneeled before the council, with bent knees, folded hands and weeping eyes.[23] Both buildings were demolished only in 1581, when the religious communities had already been abolished.[24] In Liège, the abbey of St Lawrence was a thorn in the side of the town's military authorities, situated as it was close to the walls. During the years 1467 and 1468, it was more than once suggested that the only way to safeguard the town was to demolish the abbey buildings; undoubtedly, the fact that the monks sympathized with Louis of Bourbon did not help their cause. Still, in 1467, the monks could stave off the destruction of their abbey.[25] They had a close shave in 1468. On 28 October, the district of St Margaret was burned down to deprive the Burgundian army of any possible shelter; afterwards, the Liégeois inhabitants set fire to the district of St Lawrence. Again, the abbey was spared, thanks to the eloquent plea of the abbey's representatives (amongst whom was the chronicler Adrian of Oudenbosch).[26]

---

[22] Henne & Wauters, *Histoire*, vol. 1, pp. 357-358; M.-J. Juvyns, 'Le couvent des Riches Claires à Bruxelles (1343-1585)', *Franciscana*, 20 (1965), pp. 141-163, 157-159; H.R. Roggen, *De Clarissenorde in de Nederlanden*, Instrumenta Franciscana, vol. 1 (Saint Trond, 1995), pp. 88-89.

[23] 'Den raad en meente toe voete vallende myt geboechden knyen, myt gevolden handen en schreyende ogen' (J. Don, 'Kerkelijk leven te Kampen in de Middeleeuwen', *Kamper Almanak* (October 1954/55), p. 234). However, the town authorities laid down before a notary that if these monasteries were to be troubled or attacked by the citizens of Kampen or by enemies, the town would not have the responsibility to intervene.

[24] T. van Mierlo, 'Ontwikkeling van het stadsbeeld tot circa 1800. Een 'cyraet van olde antiquiteit'', in: H.J.J. Lenferink (ed.), *Geschiedenis van Kampen*, vol. 1: *'Maer het is hier te Campen'*, Uitgave van de IJsselakademie (Kampen, 1993), pp. 13-56, 38; M. Schoengen, *Monasticon Batavum*, vol. 1: *De Franciscaansche orden*, Verhandelingen der Nederlandsche Akademie van Wetenschappen, Afdeeling Letterkunde. Nieuwe reeks, vol. 45 (Amsterdam, 1941), p. 124; Don, 'Kerkelijk leven', pp. 225-242, 234-235.

[25] Gaier, 'Le destin', p. 220.

[26] *Ibidem*, p. 221.

Protection of a noble patron might considerably increase a religious institution's chances to survive when threatened with destruction by the town's authorities. In Arras, for instance, in 1347 the threat of an English attack caused the French king to authorize the destruction of the suburbs, without the town having to pay indemnities. However, the cathedral of St Vaast and the cloister were explicitely exempted.[27] In 1425-1426 Philip the Good, Duke of Burgundy, offered his protection to various monasteries in Holland which, because of their location outside the town walls, were at risk.[28] At the end of the sixteenth century the women's monasteries near Utrecht survived longer than the men's monasteries because of family protection.[29] In 1468 the Liège authorities did not order the – from a strategical point of view dangerously situated – abbey of St Lawrence to be destroyed, possibly because the town might afterwards need to appeal to the good relationships between the abbey and the Duke of Burgundy.[30]

Without the compelling argument of immediate danger to back up their request, the authorities could hardly refuse to offer some kind of compensation.[31] As we have seen before, this compensation could take the form of a vacated monastery within the city walls. For instance: the abbey of Notre Dame des Près in Douai was demolished to secure the town against French invasions in 1475. Its inhabitants received from Mary of

[27] P. Bougard, 'France et Bourgogne (1340-1526)', in: P. Bougard, Y.-M. Hilaire & A. Nolibos (eds.), *Histoire d'Arras*, Collection Histoire des villes du Nord – Pas-de-Calais, vol. 10 (Dunkirk, 1988), pp. 77-95, 77-78.

[28] The monasteries he took under his protection were the Regulars' monasteries near Gouda (1425) and Amsterdam (1426), and the Carthusian monasteries near Amsterdam and Geertruidenberg (1426). His protection was also extended to monasteries who had remained loyal to Bishop Zweder of Culemborg (R.R. Post, *Kerkgeschiedenis van Nederland in de Middeleeuwen*, vol. 2 (Utrecht / Antwerp, 1957), p. 66). During the war between the duke and Ghent in the middle of the fifteenth century, the abbey of Ename for a while enjoyed the safeguard of both warring parties; only in 1453 were the monks obliged to flee to the nearby town of Audenarde, as a result of threats by the Ghent army, which did indeed destroy the abbey shortly afterwards (Audenarde, Municipal Archives, Fund of the St Walburga Church: De Rantere, *Kroniek*, entry for the year 1453).

[29] C.A. van Kalveen, 'De vijf adellijke vrouwenkloosters in en om de stad Utrecht', in: E.S.C. Erkelens-Buttinger e.a. (eds.), *De kerk en de Nederlanden. Archieven, instellingen, samenleving. Aangeboden aan prof. dr. C. Dekker bij zijn afscheid als rijksarchivaris en als hoogleraar in de archiefwetenschap alsmede de paleografie van de 14e tot en met de 17e eeuw aan de Universiteit van Amsterdam* (Hilversum, 1997), pp. 152-167, 165.

[30] Gaier, 'Le destin', p. 221.

[31] According to A. Rigaudière, indemnification was the rule in France by royal ordinance, but there, as elsewhere, the rule was hardly ever followed and litigation usually led to either the discouragement of the interested parties, or a symbolic compensation (A. Rigaudiere, *Gouverner la ville au Moyen Age*, Collection 'Historiques' (Paris, 1993), pp. 431-432).

Burgundy the beguinage within the walls (the last beguines had to move to the beguinage of Wetz).³² The town could also offer a piece of land, and the money to rebuild the monastery, or help the community move to a location further removed from town. The location held by the Franciscan Tertiaries of the convent of St Mary in Bethlehem near Utrecht represented a constant threat to the town; already in 1493 were there negotiations in which the town proposed to either relocate the sisters to within the town walls, or to move the convent to a distance of half a mile from the town. However, the Tertiaries refused to move, and only in 1575 can they be found within the town walls.³³

However, if a quick destruction was warranted by the threat of war, the religious community was often entirely dependent on the goodwill of the urban government or of a noble patron. The monastery of the Gulielmites, situated outside the city walls of 's-Hertogenbosch was demolished in 1542 for strategic reasons (it was too close to the walls) by the urban authorities by command of the Court of Brabant. Pleas from the monks did not avail, even when they promised to burn down their own monastery at the first sight of the enemy. It was destroyed. Compensation failed to materialize, litigation dragged on.³⁴ When in 1485 the Ghent armies

---

³² M. Mestayer, 'Des communautés religieuses florissantes', in: M. Rouche (ed.), *Histoire de Douai*, Collection Histoire des villes du Nord – Pas-de-Calais, vol. 9 (Dunkirk, 1985), pp. 61-71, 66; A. Salamagne, 'La défense des villes des Pays-Bas à la mort de Charles le Téméraire (1477)', in: P. Contamine & O. Guyotjeannin (eds.), *La guerre, la violence et les gens au Moyen Age*, vol. 1: *Guerre et violence*, Comité des travaux historiques et scientifiques (Paris, 1996), pp. 295-307, 303. The town's decision was taken on 12 March 1475, but the actual demolition began only in 1477.

³³ Schoengen, *Monasticon Batavum*, vol. 1, p. 185.

³⁴ The monastery was rebuilt at the Windmolenberg, within the city walls (Schuttelaars, *De heren*, pp. 175-176; W. Heijting, 'Het Wilhelmietenklooster Baseldonk te 's-Hertogenbosch', in: *Een vrije universiteitsbibliotheek. Studies over verleden, bezit en heden van de bibliotheek der vrije universiteit* (Assen, 1980), pp. 221-254, 231-232; T.E.A. Bosman, C.J.A. van den Oord & A. Vos, 'Beschenken of besteken? Een bronnenonderzoek naar relaties en geschenken in 's-Hertogenbosch 1550-1650', *Bijdragen tot de Geschiedenis*, 68 (1985), pp. 205-226 (theme issue: *De Brabantse stad. Zevende colloquium, Brussel 13-15 september 1984*), 214; J. van de Ven, 'Het boekbedrijf van de broeders van het gemene leven te 's-Hertogenbosch in de zestiende eeuw', in: A.-J.A. Bijsterveld, J.A.F.M. van Oudheusden & R. Stein (eds.), *Cultuur in het laatmiddeleeuwse Noord-Brabant. Literatuur – boekproductie – historiografie* ('s-Hertogenbosch, 1998), pp. 55-63, 58; R. De Beer, 'Manuscriptproductie en randversieringen in Noord-Brabant. De karakteristieken van de kloosters', in: Bijsterveld, van Oudheusden & Stein (eds.), *Cultuur*, pp. 64-74, 67; M. Schoengen, *Monasticon Batavum*, vol. 3: *De Benedictijnse orden, benevens de Carmelieten en Jesuïeten*, Verhandelingen der Nederlandsche Akademie van Wetenschappen, Afdeeling Letterkunde, Nieuwe Reeks, vol. 45 (Amsterdam, 1942), p. 64. The monks' offer to burn down their own monastery when necessary was not unusual. In times of need, for instance, the inhabitants of the suburbs of Liège and the monks of the monastery of St Lawrence and of the Carthusian monastery burned down their own buildings (Gaier, 'Le destin', p. 224).

appeared before the walls of Audenarde, the town governor and magistrate had the leper house destroyed for strategic reasons. However, since the town's financial situation was far from good, there was never a chance of complete restitution, and there is no evidence to suggest that the town gave aid to the homeless community.[35] A piece of land belonging to the begards of Zoutleeuw was confiscated by the town in 1506, 'because of the war'; their demands for compensation remained unanswered.[36]

Nor were the evicted inhabitants always welcome to rebuild within the town walls. Indeed, the Late Middle Ages was also the period in which many town governments issued legislation to stem the unlimited increase in ecclesiastical institutions and property within their towns.[37] The inhabitants were, of course, allowed to take shelter within the city walls for as long as the danger outside had not abated, but once it had, they were sometimes even forced to leave the town. In 1510, during the Guelders War, the Windesheim monastery near Zwolle was burned down by the town government. The nuns took shelter in the town, but in 1516, when they intended to settle in a town house, the urban authorities ordered them to return to their burned-down monastery. Support was promised, but never given.[38] In Antwerp, after the destruction of their monastery in 1542 and after immediate danger had passed away, the Carthusians, who had fled into the town, were not allowed to stay there nor were they allowed to rebuild their monastery where it had stood before, close to the walls. An agreement between the monks, the regent and the urban authorities solved their plight: with some help from the Antwerp government,

---

[35] E. Vanderstraeten, *Recherches sur les communautés religieuses et les institutions de bienfaisance établies à Audenarde depuis le XIIe jusqu'à la fin du XVIIIe siècle*, Algemeen Rijksarchief en Rijksarchief in de Provinciën, Reprints, vol. 5, 2 vols. in 1 (Brussels, 1995 (anastatic reprint of Audenarde, 1858 and 1860)), vol. 2, p. 90. Another example of a monastery that was destroyed for strategic reasons: Zoutleeuw: because the Guelders armies, assisted by the French and the Liège armies, were plundering the surrounding area, the military authority of Zoutleeuw in 1507 had the monastery of the Scholars demolished (everything except the dormitory and refectory), because the monastery was situated on a hill from which the enemy – if he were to take the monastery – could dominate the entire town (P.V. Bets, *Zout-Leeuw, beschrijving, geschiedenis, instellingen*, vol. 2 (Tienen, 1888), p. 173). Some French examples can be found in Rigaudière, *Gouverner*, pp. 425, 430-432.

[36] Bets, *Zout-Leeuw*, vol. 2, p. 185.

[37] F. Prims, *Geschiedenis van Antwerpen*, vol. 7: *Onder de eerste Habsburgers (1477-1555). 3de boek: Geestelijke orde* (Antwerp, 1940), p. 246.

[38] M. Schoengen, *Monasticon Batavum*, vol. 2: *De augustijnsche orden benevens de Broeders en Zusters van het Gemene Leven*, Verhandelingen der Nederlandsche Akademie van Wetenschappen, Afdeeling Letterkunde. Nieuwe reeks, vol. 45 (Amsterdam, 1941), pp. 222-223.

they built an new monastery in Lier, where they were welcomed in town.[39] The Antwerp beguines of Sion were only in 1544, two years after the destruction of their beguinage, allowed to settle within the town.[40]

Of course, in many cases the town did not abandon the inhabitants of demolished monasteries and, indeed, they were often allowed to settle within the town walls. After the monastery of Thabor near Mechelen had a second time been destroyed for military reasons in 1578, the magistrate of that town allowed the nuns to settle in a town house.[41] The inhabitants of the monastery of Ternonnen near Antwerp received help from the town's magistrate, and they too were allowed to settle within town.[42] In 1484, the town of Audenarde set fire to the monastery of Sion to prevent that the Ghent army would find shelter there, as they had before. The nuns took shelter in the town, and in 1488 they were given some land near the Burgundian castle were they could rebuild their monastery since the old one, outside the Eine Gate, had been burned to the ground.[43] Also the Frisian town of Leeuwarden allowed around 1500 two of its religious houses – of the Franciscans and of the beguines – within the town's jurisdiction to move to large fallow terrains within the town walls.[44]

Some monasteries suffered demolition more than once, when a religious order had dared to rebuild at exactly the same spot as before.[45] In

---

[39] Prims, *Geschiedenis*, vol. 7: 3, pp. 246-247; H. Delvaux & H. De Grauwe, 'Chartreuse de Sainte-Catherine près d'Anvers, puis à Lierre', in: *Monasticon belge*, vol. 8: *Province d'Anvers. Second volume* (Liège, 1993), pp. 673-729, 710.

[40] Prims, *Geschiedenis*, vol. 7: 3, p. 210.

[41] J. Schoeffer, *Historische* aanteekeningen, vol. 2: *Alle de voormalige of nog hedendaags bestaande Mans en Vrouw Kloosters*, Algemeen Rijksarchief en Rijksarchief in de Provinciën. Reprints, vol. 53 (Brussels, 1996 (anastatic reprint of Mechelen, s.d.)), p. 327.

[42] Prims, *Geschiedenis*, vol. 7: 3, pp. 218-219. Some additional examples: Bruges: after the destruction of their monastery in 1578, the Annuntiates found a new home within the city walls, as did the Carthusians (J.A. Van Houtte, *De geschiedenis van Brugge* (iconography by L. Devliegher & A. Vandewalle) (Tielt / Bussum, 1982), p. 368); Roermond: 1483: the convent of the Franciscan Tertiaries was demolished in 1483, for reasons of strategy; the convent was moved to within the town walls (Schoengen, *Monasticon Batavum*, vol. 1, pp. 169-170).

[43] De Rantere, *Kroniek*, entries for the years 1484 and 1488.

[44] M. Schroor, 'Leeuwarden tussen middeleeuwen en nieuwe tijd', in: R. Kunst e.a. (eds.), *Leeuwarden 750-2000. Hoofdstad van Friesland* (Franeker, 1999), pp. 78-105, 94.

[45] For instance: Kampen: the leper house of St Catherine and Mary Magdalen had been burned by the urban authorities in 1543, because they expected Maarten van Rossum to attack the town; the hospital was rebuilt at exactly the same location, but in 1572, it was once more destroyed (Don, 'Kerkelijk leven', p. 238); Zwolle: the monastery of the Regular nuns of Windesheim was destroyed for strategic reasons in 1510, and, after it had been repaired by the nuns, once again in 1524 (Schoengen, *Monasticon Batavum*, vol. 2, pp. 222-223).

some cases, the town did not allow such a thing to happen. In other cases, the precautionary actions of the town authorities took the form of a 'razing' of the surrounding area, together with a severe prohibition to build any 'lasting' edifice within a certain range, effectively creating a *non aedificandi*-zone.[46] In Antwerp, after the attack by Maarten van Rossum in 1542, the urban authorities decided to replace the old town walls by a more modern type of fortification. Moreover, Charles V ordered all permanent buildings within the range of 717 metres from the town walls to be destroyed, and from that moment onwards only wooden constructions were allowed within 287 metres from town. As a consequence, the Carthusian monastery, the monastery of Ternonnen and the beguinage, which were all in ruins, could not be rebuilt at their original location.[47] Also around Mechelen, a circle was drawn: all buildings within that circle had to be destroyed within two weeks; outside that limit, only wooden or loam buildings were allowed.[48]

Often, there was also an additional profit to be had from the demolition of a monastery. Indeed, more than once, the rubble was recycled by the town in newly-erected fortifications.[49]

One might wonder whether the destruction of a religious building – usually a monastery, but also often a church – for strategic reasons by

---

[46] See also: Rigaudiere, *Gouverner*, p. 433.

[47] Prims, *Geschiedenis*, vol. 7: 3, pp. 218-219 and 246; H. Soly, 'De groei van een metropool', in: K. Van Isacker & R. Van Uytven (eds.), *Antwerpen. Twaalf eeuwen geschiedenis en cultuur* (Antwerp, 1986), pp. 84-92, 87-88; P.J. Goetschalckx, *Geschiedenis van het Bisdom van Antwerpen*, vol. 1: *Aartspriesterschap Antwerpen*, vol. 1 (Ekeren-Donk, 1915), pp. 227-228; Delvaux & De Grauwe, 'Chartreuse', p. 710.

[48] Van Autenboer, 'Mechelen', p. 203.

[49] Some examples: Antwerp: 1543: in return for the rubble from the demolished Carthusian monastery, the Antwerp government built two of the cells of the new Carthusian monastery in Lier; the rubble was used for the town's fortifications (Prims, *Geschiedenis*, vol. 7: 3, p. 247); the material of what was left of the church of St Willibrord after the attack by Maarten van Rossum was used in the construction of the bastion near the Red Gate (Goetschalckx, *Geschiedenis*, p. 228); Courtrai: 1578: the rubble from the Groeninghe Abbey was used in the new fortifications (Maddens, 'De Nieuwe Tijd', p. 280; De Potter, *Kortrijk*, vol. 3, p. 371); Douai: 1477: the *Tour des Dames* was erected with the materials from the abbey *des Près* (Salamagne, 'La défense', p. 303); Mechelen: 1578: when the beguinage was destroyed, the large stones were destined to be recycled in the new bastions near the Water Gate, the Brussels Gate and the Neckerspoel Gate, and near the water mill; the bells were melted down and made into cannons (Schoeffer, *Historische Aanteekeningen*, vol. 1, p. 283; H. Installe, 'Verwoesting en wederopbouw te Mechelen in de zestiende eeuw', in: *Destruction et reconstruction de villes,* pp. 155-184, 161; Van Autenboer, 'Mechelen', p. 202). This recycling of building materials happened everywhere, for instance also in France: in 1358, the collegiate church of St Aignan, situated in the suburbs of Orléans, was destroyed for strategic reasons, and its stones were reused in the ramparts (Rigaudiere, *Gouverner*, p. 425).

secular authorities, was always readily accepted by the ecclesiastical authorities. Sacred, sacrosant buildings were being destroyed! To answer that question, more detailed archival research would be necessary. Indeed, the literature only very rarely mentions any permission being given or denied. We have found two instances where permission was granted by an ecclesiastical authority. In 1581, the destruction of the monasteries of Vrouwenklooster and Oudwijk near Utrecht was justified by an old privilege, granted in 1254 by Bishop Henry of Vianden to the town of Utrecht, stating that it was allowed to tear down ecclesiastical buildings situated in the fields around the town in times of acute danger.[50] In a brief from 1473, Pope Sixtus IV granted the town of Nijmegen permission to move the monastery of the Observant Franciscans within its walls for reasons of military safety.[51] Destruction did not automatically imply desecration. The church of the Carthusian monastery of Antwerp, for instance, which had been demolished in 1542, remained consecrated.[52]

As we have mentioned before, magistrates or military commanders had less qualms to resort to the time-honoured technique of the 'scorched earth' when danger was imminent. This technique – consisting of the methodical destruction of all buildings in the immediate vicinity of a fortification, so as to deny attackers any form of shelter – had indeed been used time and again in the previous centuries,[53] but our material shows a distinct increase in its use during the sixteenth century. Why precisely is unclear: maybe simply more records were kept, and urban histories usually pay much attention to the hectic sixteenth century; the sixteenth century was also a very bellicose century in our regions with, for instance, the Guelders War, the war between France and the Holy Roman Empire, the Revolt of the Low Countries against the King of Spain, *etcetera*. Also, new types of artillery were introduced, and towns began to redesign their fortifications, often according to Italian military design.[54] All this might have caused the increase in demolished monas-

[50] Van Kalveen, 'De vijf adellijke vrouwenkloosters', p. 165.
[51] Schoengen, *Monasticon Batavum*, vol. 1, p. 152; H.D.J. van Schevichaven, *Penschetsen uit Nijmegen's verleden*, Arnhemse herdrukken. Herdrukken van zeldzame en belangrijke werken op het gebied der Nederlandse topografie, vol. 7 (Arnhem, 1966), p. 268.
[52] Prims, *Geschiedenis*, vol. 7: 3, p. 247.
[53] Gaier, 'Le destin', p. 220. The technique was not only an old one, but apparently also an accepted one: in 1466, Captain Jean de Haynin was amazed that the defenders of Dinant had failed to burn down the suburbs of the town, thus allowing the Burgundian army to install its artillery there, which resulted in the defeat of the town.
[54] At the end of the fourteenth century, it became clear that the increasingly more frequent use of gunpowder weapons would alter siege techniques and fortification

teries we have found in our data. We would now like to take a closer look at two sixteenth-century conflicts that – directly or indirectly – caused quite some religious buildings to be destroyed: the Guelders War and the Dutch Revolt.

First of all, the Guelders War. This war between the Duke of Guelders and the Burgundians – and afterwards the Habsburgs – was a struggle for power in the duchy of Guelders. It ended in 1543 with the Treaty of Venlo, favourable to the Emperor Charles V. But in 1542 the war was still undecided, and Maarten van Rossum became the scourge of Brabant. Van Rossum was a commander-in-chief in the service of the Duke Charles of Guelders († 1538), and his successor, William II the Rich, and his expeditions within the duchy of Brabant earned him the reputation of being the 'Guelders Attila', some say deservedly, others say erroneously. Sev-

---

constructions. There were experiments with additional gunports in the walls and the addition of new fortifications to the existing defensive structures, but by the end of the fifteenth century, it was recognized that the traditional medieval fortifications could not provide adequate defense against a gunpowder weapon attack. 'A more elaborate system of fortifications was needed, a system whose walls could withstand the constant impact of stone or metal canonballs while at the same time offering its own forceful gunshot bombardment against those besiegers' (K. Devries, *Medieval Military Technology* (Lewiston (N.Y.), 1992), pp. 268-269). The answer was found in Italy, where a system of artillery fortifications originated that would come to be known in all of Europe as the *trace italienne*. A description of it was first found in Leon Battista Alberti's *De re aedificatoria* (*Ibidem*, p. 269). For a description of this type of fortification, we refer to F. Tallett, *War and Society in Early-Modern Europe, 1495-1715*, War in Context (London / New York, 1992), pp. 34-35: 'It comprised a number of different elements. Fortress walls were redesigned: stripped of crenellations and projections, which splintered dangerously, they were sloped backwards to present a glancing surface to artillery shot; they were constructed of earth and rubble and faced with brick ... the better to absorb the impact of shot; and they were made much lower and thicker than ever before. Fortress layout was altered to allow the defenders to subject the besiegers to the maximum amount of return fire. The crucial development here was the introduction of the angle bastion, a huge triangular-shaped projection, open to the sky in its fully developed form, which served as a gun platform, allowing counter-bombardment of the enemy guns. A series of mutually supporting bastions added to the curtain wall at carefully measured intervals, with guns concealed in their sides, provided effective flanking fire, and ensured that there was no 'dead' ground in front of the fortress which was not swept by the defenders' guns. Attacking troops could thus not penetrate to the fort without passing through a barrage of fire'. Although the superiority of the *trace italienne* was quickly and universally recognized, it was not immediately introduced in all parts of Europe. Adapting the existing fortifications to the new principles was very expensive, and towns usually only introduced the *trace italienne* when it became really indispensable. 'It was deployed rapidly throughout the Habsburg possessions in Italy and then in the Low Countries, initially by Charles V who spent lavishly on securing his borders with France, and subsequently by both the Spanish and the Dutch during the Revolt of the Netherlands. Indeed, the Revolt witnessed something of a frenzy of fortress building, so that by the end of the century few towns of any size in the Netherlands were without their defences' (*Ibidem*, p. 36).

eral towns proceded to the destruction of the monasteries outside their walls when they heard that van Rossum was coming their way. In 1542, when the defenders of Antwerp heard that van Rossum and his army were marching towards their town, they burned down the church of St Willibrord, the Carthusian monastery, the monastery of Ternonnen and the beguinage of Sion near the walls as a precaution.[55] In 1543 the monastery of the Regular Nuns just outside Helmond was pre-emptively demolished by the town's garrison.[56] Van Rossum's 'fame' – or rather 'infamy' – was so widespread, that the mere rumor of his coming could cause buildings to be demolished. This is apparently precisely what happened in Kampen in 1543. The hospital of St Catherine and Mary Magdalen was burned to the ground, but Van Rossum never came.[57]

During the seventies and eighties of the sixteenth century, many Calvinist town governments ordered monasteries to be destroyed for strategic reasons. A very good example is Mechelen. In this town, rich in ecclesiastical buildings, the ones situated outside of the city wall suffered more that their share of destruction. Alternately in Spanish and 'Staatse' (i.e. of the Dutch 'States') control, the town experienced two major 'waves' of pre-emptive destruction, corresponding to two military emergencies. The first wave, in 1572, was a reaction to the coming of the Duke of Alva and his army. By command of the military governor, Bernard of Merode, the monasteries of Thabor, Bethany, Blijdenberg and the beguinage – situated east of the town – were partly destroyed, the chapels of St Lambert and St Nicholas completely. The second 'razing' of the area outside the city walls, ordered by the military governor Pontus de Noyelles, was in preparation of the coming of the Spanish armies of Don Juan in 1578. Even more buildings were destroyed: the monastery of Thabor (again), the beguinage (again), the monasteries of Muizen and Terzieken, the monastery of Hanswijk and its church, the church of Nekkerspoel, and the church of St Nicholas. The monastery of Blijden-

---

[55] Prims, *Geschiedenis*, vol. 7: 3, pp. 210, 218 and 246; Goetschalckx, *Geschiedenis*, pp. 227-228. After the buildings of the Carthusian monastery had been cleared, they were torched. The church, the chapter hall and all large buildings were destroyed; only the chapel of St Catherine outside of the monastery, the horse mill and a number of isolated cells survived.

[56] Schoengen, *Monasticon Batavum*, vol. 2, p. 90. Other examples: Zoutleeuw: in 1543, because of the rumoured threat of war, the church of the beguinage – situated outside, but close to the town walls – was destroyed, and there was a plan to demolish the buildings of the monastery of the Scholars (*Scholieren*) which had been left standing in 1507 (Bets, *Zout-Leeuw*, vol. 2, pp. 173 and 194).

[57] Don, 'Kerkelijk leven', p. 238.

berg was only saved from further destruction by the fact that the wind that day blew towards Mechelen, and burning the monastery would have endangered the town.[58]

These Calvinist authorities probably had less qualms about destroying a Catholic monastery than their Catholic predecessors. Indeed, during the seventies and eighties of the sixteenth century, many monasteries and convents in the Low Countries were abolished, and their inhabitants turned out, or given a pension. However, it would probably be wrong to consider the argument of the Protestant authorities that it was a military necessity for these monasteries to disappear merely as a convenient specious argument that would enable them to carry through some ulterior, anti-Catholic agenda (as some authors do[59]). Indeed, Catholic authorities before had put the safety of the town before that of individual monasteries. In 1578, in the same year that the Mechelen monasteries were destroyed out of fear for Don Juan, that same Don Juan fortified the town of Bruges, and in order to clear his field of fire from the city walls the church of St Catherine, the monasteries of the Annuntiates and the Carthusians, and the leper house of St Mary Magdalen were demolished.[60]

---

[58] Schoeffer, *Historische aanteekeningen*, vol. 1, pp. 150, 179, 241, 245, 283; vol. 2, pp. 125, 127, 325, 346, 349, 368, 380; Installe, 'Verwoesting', pp. 161-162 and 173; Van Autenboer, 'Mechelen'. A result of the war and the consecutive destruction of the religious institutions outside the town walls was that Mechelen was reduced to the area within its walls, and that after the reconstruction of most of the demolished monasteries within the town walls, there was a distinct predominance of the clerical population in the town (*Ibidem*, p. 173). Some other examples of religious buildings being destroyed by command of Protestant governments: Courtrai: in 1578, the Groeninghe Abbey had to go, because it was situated too closely to the town walls; the same was true for the leper house and its chapel (Maddens, 'De Nieuwe Tijd', pp. 280 and 318; De Potter, *Kortrijk*, vol. 3, pp. 370-371); Ghent: in 1578, the monastery of the Franciscan Nuns had to make place for an extension of the town's fortifications (Roggen, *De Clarissenorde*, p. 60); Gouda: the town started to demolish the *Regulierenklooster* to make the construction of a fortification possible, but in 1576, after the Pacification of Ghent, the plans for additional fortifications were postponed and further demolition was deferred; what had been left standing was torn down only in 1580 (B. van den Berg & H.J. Sprokholt, 'Begrensd door muren en wallen', in: P.H.A.M. Abels e.a. (eds.), *Duizend jaar Gouda. Een stadsgeschiedenis*, Historische Vereniging Die Goude, Dertigste verzameling bijdragen (Hilversum, 2002), pp. 275-295, 276-277; Kampen: 1572: the hospital of St Catherine and its chapel, outside the Venepoort, were torn down to prevent that the Spanish enemy would find shelter there (Van Mierlo, 'Ontwikkeling', p. 41).

[59] For instance: Schoeffer, *Historische aanteekeningen*, vol. 1, pp. 150, 179, 245 (he calls it a 'pretense'); Installe, 'Verwoesting', p. 161 ('pretense').

[60] Van Houtte, *De geschiedenis van Brugge*, pp. 358 and 368. Another example of a religious building destroyed by order of a Catholic government: Breda: in 1574, the leper house and its chapel were destroyed for military reasons (Placidus, 'Geschiedenis', p. 166).

In each case, military considerations seem to have prevailed in times of war. Even that staunch defender of the Catholic faith, the Emperor Charles V, ordered the abbey of St Bavon in Ghent to be destroyed to make room for the 'Spanish Castle' (1540),[61] and he had the monastery of St Catherine near Utrecht turned into the castle 'Vredenburg'(1529).[62]

What precedes considered religious buildings in times of war as liabilities, at best useless to the defenders of a town, at worst dangerous. As we have indicated before, an enemy planning to take a certain town would have a very different opinion of these buildings outside the walls. To him, they were a source of food, possibly other kinds of loot (horses, ...), accommodation and – above all – shelter. Indeed, there are many examples of religious buildings being used as such. The nearby Carthusian monastery was used as a fortification during several sieges of Amsterdam in the sixties and seventies of the sixteenth century. In 1542, the church of St Willibrord near Antwerp served a similar purpose for the Guelders soldiers. The monastery of the Franciscans near Leeuwarden functioned in 1498 as a base for Duke Albert of Saxony; that same duke had nine years earlier used the monastery of Danenbroek while laying siege to the town of Tienen. In 1527 even the Bishop of Utrecht, denied entrance into his own cathedral town, laid siege on Utrecht and used the monastery of Vredendaal as a fortification and headquarters.[63] The Benedictine abbey of St Lawrence, just outside the St Martin's Gate at Liège, was often during the fifteenth, sixteenth and seventeenth centuries involved in armed conflicts; because of its vicinity to the town and its fortified structure, it was often at stake in the struggles between defenders and attackers.[64]

---

[61] M. Boone, "Civitas mori potest si authoritate superioris damnetur': politieke motieven voor het bewust verwoesten van steden (14de – 16de eeuw)', in: *Destruction et reconstruction de villes*, pp. 339-368, 362 and 364. The community of Benedictine monks was transformed into a secular chapter, and moved to the church of St John, which then was renamed the church of St Bavon. The abbey and part of the abbey village were turned into a fortification with bastions according to Italian models. Already in 1469, Charles the Bold had entertained the idea of building a castle on the site of the abbey of St Bavon.

[62] We once more see the domino-effect we have mentioned before: in order to build the citadel, the Knights of the Order of Saint John had to vacate the monastery of St Catherine; they moved to the monastery of the Carmelites, who, in their turn, were transferred to the parish church of St Nicholas, where they reestablished their monastery (Schoengen, *Monasticon Batavum*, vol. 3, p. 124).

[63] Van der Does, *Maarten*, pp. 46-48.

[64] Gaier, 'Le destin', p. 219. Other examples: Liège: in 1568, William of Orange stayed in the abbey of St Lawrence near Liège when his army tried to cross the Liège bridges (*Ibidem*, p. 222).

Sometimes, the strategic position of the building was of greater importance than the shelter it could offer. In 1466, during the siege of Dinant by Charles the Bold, the duke had the Franciscan monastery outside the Gate of St Anne partly destroyed in order to be able to position his artillery at that location.[65]

Apart from burning them down, there was still another way to prevent that the enemy would avail himself of these strategically-important buildings: the town itself could take them, as a precaution. This is exactly what happened in Antwerp: in 1435, in order to prevent that the Duke of Burgundy, Philip the Good, would use the abbey of St Michael – then already incorporated within the town walls – as a bastion, the town itself occupied the abbey.

Furthermore, throughout the centuries, churches and monasteries were used by the terrified inhabitants of hamlets, villages, towns and cities as a place of refuge, though not always successfully so. More than once, the sanctity of the building did not protect it from being ransacked or destroyed. When sixteenth-century Dinant was taken by the troops of Francis of Cleve, his mercenaries bashed in the doors of the church of Our Lady, where the population had taken refuge, and the building was burned to the ground.[66]

Peace Once More

In the foregoing has been shown that religious buildings could have important functions both in peacetime and in times of war. However, their presence could also be instrumental in the bringing about of the much desired peace. Indeed, monasteries in particular were ideally suited for peace negotiations: large rooms – such as refectories – and guest quarters were usually readily available, they could be considered as both 'neutral' and 'sacred' territory, and the authority and popularity of some religious orders or individuals might make these suitable mediators.[67] Many examples of truces and peaces being concluded in monasteries can be found in the literature, though urban histories tend to mention only that

---

[65] J. Baetens, 'Minderbroederskloosters in de Zuidelijke Nederlanden. Kloosterlexicon. 20. Dinant', *Franciscana*, 37 (1982), pp. 41-45, 43.

[66] C. Baes, 'La guerre au XVIe siècle: un vecteur de destruction', in: *Destruction et reconstruction*, pp. 185-206, 196. Many other examples can be found, for instance: Boxtel: in 1543, when van Rossum came to the area, the population hid its possessions in the parish church, but the soldiers entered and carried everything away (Van der Does, *Maarten*, p. 87). See also Nolet & Boeren, *Kerkelijke instellingen*, pp. 102-103.

[67] Bakker, *Bedelorden*, p. 81; Van Uytven, 'Wereldlijke overheid', pp. 186-187.

a peace was concluded, not where. For instance, monasteries near Groningen – amongst which were the Dominican monastery of Winsum and the convent of Tertiaries of Mary ten Hoorn – served as venues for negotiations;[68] the peace between the revolting craft guilds of Louvain and Duke Wenceslas of Brabant was concluded in the monastery of Terbank in 1380;[69] the so-called *Paix des Mineurs* of 1460 was named after the monastery of the Friars Minor in Liège where it was concluded,[70] *etcetera*.

After the fighting had stopped and peace had been concluded, the town churches became centres of diverse activities. Masses were said or sung to thank God for the end of violence, or, after revolts, masses were paid for by the defeated as a way of expiation. But churches were also ideal places to show to all and sundry, winners and losers, that God had stood by the victorious party. In 1426 after the town of Hoorn had put to flight the Countess Jacqueline of Bavaria and her supporters – amongst whom was the town of Alkmaar – the captured banner of Alkmaar was put on display in the Great Church of Hoorn, as a sign of victory.[71] After Charles the Bold had conquered Liège in 1468, his personal standard was hung in the nave.[72] Another good example of this kind of 'bragging' behaviour is to be found in Courtrai, in the beginning of the fourteenth century. The Battle of the Spurs, indeed, was named after the golden spurs which were collected from dead Frenchmen on the battlefield. They were hung in the vault of the Church of Our Lady in Courtrai, from whence they were removed by the French in 1382, after their victory in the Battle of Westrozebeke.[73]

Sometimes, this wish to demonstrate God's approval was already present even during the hostilities. In 1468, Liège had purposely been

---

[68] Bakker, *Bedelorden*, pp. 52 and 153 (1514: Ten Hoorn was the venue for negotiations between the town of Groningen and representatives of the emperor).

69 Henne & Wauters, *Histoire*, vol. 1, p. 138.

[70] A. Lallemand, *La lutte des états de Liège contre la Maison de Bourgogne (1390-1492)* (Brussels, 1910), p. 81.

[71] P. Koster, *Hoorn in de Middeleeuwen. De economische ontwikkelingsgang van een Westfriesche stad* (Amsterdam, 1929), p. 21; F. De Potter, *Geschiedenis van Jacoba van Beieren (1401-1436)*, Mémoires couronnés et autres mémoires publiés par l'Académie royale des sciences, des lettres et des beaux-arts de Belgique. Collection in -8°, vol. 31, 6 (Brussels, 1881), p. 146.

[72] H. Van Der Velden, *The Donor's Image. Gerard Loyet and the Votive Portraits of Charles the Bold*, Burgundica, vol. 2 (Turnhout, 2000), pp. 93 and 96.

[73] This is, at least, what is found in many studies. Some, however, claim that it is a myth (see, for instance, P. Despriet, *Kortrijk 1302. Keerpunt in de Frans-Vlaamse oorlog (1297-1305)* (Courtrai, 2002), p. 152).

destroyed by Charles the Bold, Duke of Burgundy. However, many ecclesiastical buildings had been spared. These buildings became the centre around which Liège was rebuilt, while the town hall and the 'perron', symbol of the town's liberties, returned only later in the town's history.[74] Charles the Bold not only donated an important relic of St Hubert to the cathedral, he also had himself portrayed with St George, a clear reference to the divine nature of his authority.[75] In this way, the religious buildings in town were used to emphasize the God-given origin of the victor's power, and to make this power more visible.[76]

Conclusion

As we have seen in the foregoing, the churches and monasteries in or near towns had little chance to escape the world of violence that so often threatened the late medieval towns. As an integral part of the urban community, they were either involved in the communal effort to protect the town and its inhabitants, or they suffered the consequences of that desire, or of the war itself.

In relatively peaceful times, an important role in the town's defensive system was reserved for the church tower, which often doubled as the town's belfry. Apart from that, it was usually the presence of large rooms or spaces for storage or construction that determined the town's use of religious buildings for military purposes.

It was mainly in times of war that the 'common good' of the entire town was weighed against that of individual monasteries and churches, in particular those situated outside the town walls. In case of acute danger, the common good almost invariably won, and dangerously-situated religious buildings were swiftly destroyed as a precaution. We assume that the inhabitants of these institutions did not always accept the necessity of that decision, but only few objections have found their way into the secondary literature on that subject. More objections are found, however, when the absence of immediate danger allowed for discussion and negotiation. In such case, town governments could occasionally be swayed to wait with the destruction until it became really absolutely essential to the safety of the town. Our data show an increase in the use of this technique of the 'scorched earth' in the sixteenth century, but in order to find out why this is so, further detailed research would have to

---

[74] See also: Van Der Velden, *The Donor's Image*, p. 97.
[75] *Ibidem*, 81 *et passim*.
[76] Boone, 'Civitas', pp. 366-367.

be done. The development was stimulated by changes in military strategics, armament and architecture.

A role more fitting for a religious building was that of a negotiation space, a place where treaties were brokered and peace was concluded. Occasionally, an ecclesiastical building was used by the victor to proclaim his victory, and acclaim the divine inspiration that led him to it.

K.U.Leuven Campus Kortrijk

Jan KUYS

WELTLICHE FUNKTIONEN SPÄTMITTELALTERLICHER PFARRKIRCHEN IN DEN NÖRDLICHEN NIEDERLANDEN

Als Bischof Hartbert von Utrecht (1139-1150) nach seiner Rückkehr von einem Romzug den Einwohnern von Groningen, die sich während seiner Abwesenheit in einer Schwurgenossenschaft gegen ihn zusammengeschlossen hatten, seinen Willen wieder auferlegen wollte, musste er militärisch eingreifen. Als Reaktion darauf verschanzten sich die Einwohner in der Groninger Walpurgiskirche, so dass der Bischof sie mit Hilfe von Belagerungswerkzeugen von dort vertreiben musste. Der Verfasser der um 1232/1233 entstandenen anonymen Chronik *Quedam Narracio de Groninghe, de Thrente, de Covordia et de diversis aliis sub diversis episcopis Traiectensibus* schreibt empört, dass die Groninger das Haus Gottes zu einem Haus des Krieges gemacht hätten.[1] Bei seiner Darstellung, wie die Angehörigen des Utrechter Bischofs selbst später dieselbe Kirche als Wehranlage benutzten, zeigt er keine Empörung. Egbert, der Präfekt des Bischofs in der Stadt Groningen, war im Jahr 1227 in einem Streit mit dem Burggrafen von Koevorden verwickelt, wurde aus seiner Stadt vertrieben und musste nach Friesland fliehen. Bald darauf kehrte er mit friesischen Anhängern zurück und brachte die Stadt wieder in seinen Besitz. Seine friesische Anhängerschaft plünderte zunächst die Stadt und legte sie anschließend in Schutt und Asche. Egbert baute daraufhin die Sankt-Walpurgiskirche zu einer Wehranlage um, mit der er sich erfolgreich gegen neue Angriffe seiner Gegner wehren konnte. Später wurde die Kirche von bischöflichen Kriegsleuten noch als Gefängnis benutzt.[2] Auch im Spätmittelalter wurden Kirchen, vor allem auf dem

---

[1] H. van Rij (Hg. und Übers.), *Quedam narracio de Groninghe, de Thrente, de Covordia et de diversis aliis sub diversis episcopis Traiectensibus / Een verhaal over Groningen, Drente, Coevorden en allerlei andere zaken onder verschillende Utrechtse bisschoppen* (Hilversum, 1989), S. 4: '... ipsum oppidum potenter intravit et illos, qui armatu manu se de ecclesia beate Walburgis defendebant, per machinas, sicut hodie in muris apparet, inpugnavit et eos, qui de ecclesia domum belli fecerant, captivans omnes cives iurare compulit, ...'
[2] Ders., *Quedam narracio*, S. 44: 'ecclesiam beate Walburgis in modum castri munit'; S. 58: 'captivos vero in durissimis vinculis usque ad adventum sui novi episcopi in ecclesia beate Walburgis servaverunt'.

Lande, gelegentlich als Wehranlage oder als letzter Zufluchtsort von Kriegsleuten benutzt.[3]

Formen profaner Benutzung einer Kirche, wie sie hier beschrieben sind, blieben in den Niederlanden eine Ausnahme. Kirchen fungierten jedoch in Notfällen als letzter Zufluchtsort für diejenigen, die von Feinden, aber auch zum Beispiel vom Hochwasser bedroht waren. Nicht wegen ihres sakralen Charakters suchte man in Notfällen ihren Schutz, sondern wegen ihrer Bauart. Sie waren lange Zeit der einzige Steinbau in einer Ortschaft. Ihr Turm konnte als Wehrturm dienen und stand üblicherweise in der niederländischen Polderlandschaft am höchsten Punkt des Dorfes, so dass sich Menschen und Vieh dorthin retten konnten.

Solche Ereignisse waren allerdings Ausnahmefälle, die ich in diesem Vortrag beiseite lassen will. Ich will mich hier mit der alltäglichen Nutzung von Kirchen für eine Reihe von weltlichen Funktionen befassen. Es handelt sich hierbei um Funktionen, die zumeist so alltäglich sind, dass sie in den Quellen oft kaum Spuren hinterlassen haben, Funktionen, die durch ihren alltäglichen Charakter kaum aufgefallen sind, trotzdem aber unser Erstaunen wecken können, weil sie uns zeigen, wie sehr sich kirchliche und weltliche Funktionen der Kirche vermischt haben. Wir sind zu schnell dazu geneigt, zu vergessen, dass die Scheidung zwischen Staat und Kirche im Mittelalter noch nicht so selbstverständlich war wie heute. Ein wichtiger Grund für die weltliche Benutzung der Kirchen liegt darin, dass die Kirchenpflegschaft sich in den Händen von Laien befand und dass die Kirchenvögte meist von der weltlichen Obrigkeit angestellt und kontrolliert wurden. In den Städten wurde zudem der Bau der Pfarrkirche meist durch die Stadt angeregt, betreut und finanziert. In den Quellen werden vom Stadtrat eingestellte Kirchenvögte in den nördlichen Niederlanden ab dem 14. Jahrhundert häufig erwähnt.[4] Die enge Verbundenheit zwischen Stadtverwaltung und der Verwaltung des Kirchspiels hat dazu geführt, dass die Städte ihren Pfarrkirchen problemlos und dauerhaft weltliche Funktionen auferlegen konnten. Die wichtigsten dieser

---

[3] Beispiele in J. Kuys, *De ambtman in het kwartier van Nijmegen (ca.1250-1543)* (Nimwegen, 1987), S. 276; A. Janse, *De sprong van Jan van Schaffelaar. Oorlog en partijstrijd in de late Middeleeuwen* (Hilversum 2003), S. 58-61.

[4] I.H. van Eeghen, 'De geestelijke en wereldijke functionarissen verbonden aan de Oude of S. Nicolaaskerk te Amsterdam (tot 1578)', *Nederlands Archief voor Kerkgeschiedenis*, neue Folge 37 (1949-1950), S. 65-109, 76-80; A.T. Schuitema Meijer, *De kerkgebouwen en andere kerkelijke goederen in de stad Groningen. Historisch-juridisch onderzoek* (Groningen, 1950), S. 6-9; J. van der Kluit, 'Wat deden de kerkmeesters eigenlijk?', in: M. Groothedde u.a. (Hgg.), *De Sint-Walburgiskerk in Zutphen. Momenten uit de geschiedenis van een middeleeuwse kerk* (Zutphen, 1999), S. 217-228, 217.

weltlichen Funktionen, vor allem im städtischen Kontext, beabsichtige ich im Folgenden an Hand einiger Beispiele darzulegen.

Sicherung der Stadtprivilegien und Stadtsiegel

Für eine mittelalterliche Stadt waren, wie für alle mittelalterlichen Institutionen, die Originalurkunden ihrer Privilegien so wertvoll wie ihre Freiheiten selbst, denn diese Urkunden bildeten die formale Grundlage jeglicher städtischen Freiheit. Städtische Freiheit ohne den Besitz dieser Urkunden war kaum vorstellbar. Deshalb wurden sie wie ein kostbarer Schatz bewahrt. Was lag mehr auf der Hand als diesen Schatz in der Stadtkirche zu bewahren, die für lange Zeit das einzige steinerne Gebäude der Stadt war? Der Ursprung dieser Gewohnheit läßt sich in den Städten nicht genau feststellen; vermutlich hat aber die Verwaltung mancher jungen Stadt schon bald nach dem Empfang des ersten Privilegs, dem Beispiel älterer meist kirchlicher Körperschaften folgend, ihre Urkunden dem sicheren Raum einer Kirche anvertraut. Da die meisten Städte erst im Laufe des 14. Jahrhunderts ein Rathaus erhielten, gab es eigentlich auch keine Alternative zur Kirche als Aufbewahrungsort.

Die Nimwegener Stadtrechnung des Jahres 1422/23 führt eine Ausgabe für 'een schreyne dair men onse privilegien in leggen sall, in der stat kyst' auf. Die Aufbewahrung dieser Kiste in einer Sakristei der Stadtkirche ist für 1425/26 belegt. Die Nimwegener Stadtkiste diente nicht nur der Bewahrung von Privilegien, sie wurde auch zur Aufbewahrung des Stadtsiegels und gelegentlich als Geldkiste genutzt. Verschlossen wurde die Kiste mit drei Schlüsseln, von denen einer beim Rat blieb und die zwei anderen Vertretern der Gilden zuerteilt wurden. Die Kirche war allerdings nicht immer ein so sicherer Aufbewahrungsort, wie man es sich für Stadtprivilegien gewünscht hätte. Als 1429 der Kirchturm niederbrannte, retteten vier Männer die Kiste aus der Kirche. Die Zahl von vier Trägern ist ein Indiz für den Umfang und das Gewicht der Stadtkiste. Weil das Feuer nur den Turm zerstörte und die Kirche selbst bewahrt blieb, ist die Kiste vermutlich schon bald an ihren alten Standort zurückgekehrt. Der Turmbrand war übrigens eine indirekte Folge einer anderen städtischen Funktion der Kirche; er war durch Fahrlässigkeit städtischer Wächter entstanden.[5]

In der ersten Hälfte des 16. Jahrhunderts verfügte die Stadt neben der Kiste in der Kirche auch über eine Kiste im Rathaus. 1566 wurde zur

---

[5] Willem van Berchen, *De nobili principatu Gelrie et eius origine*, L.A.J.W. Sloet van de Beele (Hg.) (Den Haag, 1870), S. 69: 'Que quidem turris, [...] neglectu vigilum, ex eadem civitate custodientium, [...] totaliter extitit concremata'.

Aufbewahrung der Stadtprivilegien in der neuen Kapelle des Heiligen Grabs am Nordportal der Nimwegener Stadtkirche ein kleiner Raum abgetrennt, in dem ein Schrank mit Schubladen (*Blok*) zur Bewahrung der Urkunden aufgestellt wurde. Der Raum wurde mit einer schweren Holztür abgeschlossen. Dieser *Blok* hat bis zum Jahre 1849 in der Kirche gestanden und seine Funktion beibehalten.[6]

Ähnlich wie in Nimwegen bewahrte die Stadt Zutphen ihre Privilegien ebenfalls in der Sakristei (*gerfkammer*) der Pfarrkirche. Diese Praxis ist hier 1419 erstmals urkundlich belegt, kann aber erheblich älter sein. Das älteste Zutphener Stadtprivileg wurde im Jahre 1190 ausgefertigt, das erste Rathaus wird erst 1339 erwähnt. Auch hier wurde das Archiv einmal ernsthaft bedroht, als 1446 der Turm der Pfarrkiche abbrannte. Zum Glück konnte auch hier die *statkyste* noch rechtzeitig aus der Kirche gerettet und im Haus eines Schöffen sichergestellt werden. Am nächsten Tag wurde die Kiste dann vorläufig ins Rathaus gebracht. Später wurde sie allerdings wieder in der Sakristei abgestellt, bis sie in der Reformationszeit endgültig ins Rathaus gelangte.[7]

Die Stadt Amsterdam lagerte ihre Privilegien in der ältesten der zwei Pfarrkirchen, der *Oude Kerk*, in einem Raum, der ursprünglich als *het secreet* (übersetzt: geheime Stelle) bezeichnet wurde, im 19. Jahrhundert den Namen *IJzeren kapel* (Eiserne Kapelle) erhielt, den sie der eisernen Tür verdankt, mit der sie abgeschlossen wurde. Die Eiserne Kapelle war ein kleiner Raum über den Gewölben einer Kapelle (der sogenannten *Librije*). Die eiserne Zugangstür befand sich in der Wand einer höheren benachbarten Kapelle in etwa fünf Metern Höhe, so dass sie nur über eine Leiter erreichbar war. Der Raum ist 1498 erstmals als Lagerraum für die Privilegien belegt und ist höchstwahrscheinlich nach 1482 erbaut worden. Der dort abgestellte Schrank entstand in den Jahren 1462-1467 und hat vorher an einer anderen Stelle in der Kirche gestanden. Wahrscheinlich ist er dort eingemauert gewesen. Vermutet wird, dass die Stadt seit ihrer Entstehung (Ende 13. Jahrhunderts) die alte Kirche zur Aufbewahrung der Privilegien benutzt hat, zumal sie damals noch lange über kein Rathaus verfügten sollte. Der Urkundenschrank wurde 1892 samt seinem Inhalt ins Stadtarchiv überführt.[8]

---

[6] G.A.P.M. Willemsen, 'De bewaarplaats van de privileges', in: *Het Stadhuis van Nijmegen* (Nimwegen, 1982), S. 98-100.

[7] M.M. Doornink-Hoogenraad, 'Uit de historie van Zutfens archief en bibliotheek', *Nederlands Archievenblad*, 56 (1951/1952), S. 15-27.

[8] W.F.H. Oldewelt, 'De charterkast uit de IJzeren Kapel in de Oude Kerk', *Jaarboek Amstelodamum*, 29 (1932), S. 1-7; B. Bijtelaar, 'Het complex smidskapel, zuiderportaal, librije en ijzeren kapel van de Oude Kerk', *Jaarboek Amstelodamum*, 60 (1968), S. 15-52;

Viele andere Städte verwahrten ihre Privilegien in einer Kirche. In Rotterdam wurden die Privilegien um 1500 in der Pfarrkirche gelagert, in Haarlem waren die Privilegien in einem Raum über einer Kapelle an der Südseite der Stadtkirche untergebracht. Zu Leiden beherbergte der Turm der Petrikirche die Stadturkunden, aber nach dem Einsturz des Turms im Jahr 1512 wurden sie dauerhaft zum Rathaus überführt.[9] Für Maastricht wird 1513 erwähnt, dass die Stadtkiste mit den Stadtprivilegien sich in einem Turm der Kirche des Liebfrauenkapitels befand. Dort wurden die Privilegien zusammen mit den Urkunden und Akten des Liebfrauenkapitels aufbewahrt, bis sie vermutlich im Jahr 1665 ins neue Rathaus überführt wurden.[10]

Ich könnte noch weitere Beispiele aus anderen niederländischen Städten anführen, die ihre Privilegien in der Pfarrkirche bewahrten. Es war allerdings nicht so, dass jeder Stadtrat seine Originalurkunden immer und von Anfang an in einer Kirche aufbewahren ließ. In 's-Hertogenbosch wurde der Schrein mit den Stadtprivilegien und Stadtsiegeln, dort *stadscomme* genannt, erst 1399 in die Pfarrkirche überführt und dort in der Liebfrauenkapelle neben dem Westturm eingemauert, obwohl die Stadt bereits 1185 ihr erstes Privileg erhalten hatte.[11] Die Groninger Stadtkiste hatte, so lässt sich um 1541/1542 feststellen, keinen festen Bewahrplatz, sondern wurde abwechselnd in einer der Wohnungen der vier Bürgermeister aufbewahrt. Die Kiste wurde auf Kosten der Stadt vom einen zum anderen Haus transportiert, wahrscheinlich kurz nach jedem Ratswechsel, wobei derjenige Bürgermeister, der mit der Aufbewahrung beauftragt wurde, die Kiste wahrscheinlich während seiner zweijährigen Amtszeit hindurch zu Hause aufzubewahren hatte. 1559 gelangte die Stadtkiste dann endgültig ins Ratszimmer im Rathaus. Es ist leider nicht zu ermitteln, seit wann die Groninger Stadtkiste in den Privathäusern der

---

H. Janse, *De Oude Kerk te Amsterdam. Bouwgeschiedenis en restauratie* (Zeist / Zwolle, 2004), S. 116-118.

[9] H. ten Boom, 'De eerste secretarissen van Rotterdam. Gegevens over ambt, werkzaamheden en personen tot circa 1530', *Rotterdams Jaarboekje*, 8. Folge, 7 (1979), S. 151-174, 156; F. Allan, *Geschiedenis en beschrijving van Haarlem, van de vroegste tijden tot op onze dagen*, 4 Teile (Haarlem, 1874-1883), Teil 3, S. 421; J.C. Overvoorde & J.W. Verburgt, *Archief der Secretarie van de stad Leiden 1253-1575. Inventaris en regesten* (Leiden, 1937), S.XXI-XXIII.

[10] M.L. de Kreek, *De kerkschat van het Onze-Lieve-Vrouwekapittel te Maastricht* (Utrecht, 1994), S. 75-78, 81.

[11] R. van de Laar, 'De stadscomme in de Sint Janskerk', in: *Vriendenboek stadsarchivaris Kuyer. Aangeboden aan drs. P.Th.J. Kuyer, archivaris van 's-Hertogenbosch bij zijn pensionering* ('s-Hertogenbosch, 1980), S. 137-154; C. Peeters, *De Sint Janskathedraal te 's-Hertogenbosch* (Den Haag, 1985), S. 212, 416.

Bürgermeister aufbewahrt wurde. Die ältesten Originalurkunden im Groninger Stadtarchiv entstammen der zweiten Hälfte des 13. Jahrhunderts. Das Stadtsiegel, das sich am Ende des 14. Jahrhunderts sicher in der Stadtkiste befand, existierte vermutlich bereits 1245. Deshalb könnte die Groninger Stadtkiste der Mitte des 13. Jahrhunderts entstammen. Ihr Aufbewahrungsort vor 1541/1542 bleibt allerdings undeutlich, genauso wie die Gründe für ihre Aufbewahrung in den Bürgermeisterhäusern.[12]

Auch auf dem Lande dienten die Kirchen zur sicheren Aufbewahrung von Archivalien. Obwohl die archivarische Überlieferung hier im Vergleich mit den Städten geringer ist, liefern vereinzelte Belegstellen den Eindruck, dass dies eine durchaus übliche Funktion vieler Dorfkirchen war. In Norg, in der Region Drenthe, befand sich in der Dorfkirche eine *carspelkiste* (Kirchspielkiste), in der die Kirchenmeister und die Kirchspielgemeinschaft ihre Urkunden bewahrten.[13] In Ortschaften, wo regelmäßig ein Gericht tagte, konnte das Gerichtsprotokoll und das weitere Gerichtsarchiv in der Pfarrkirche deponiert werden. Das Landrecht des *Rijk* von Nimwegen des Jahres 1532 verordnete, dass an beiden Gerichtsorten dieses Amtes das Gerichtsprotokoll in einer verschlossenen Kiste in der jeweiligen Dorfskirche sicher bewahrt werden musste. Die drei Schlüssel jeder Kiste sollten dem Gerichtsschreiber und zwei Gerichtsleuten aus der Ritterschaft übergeben werden.[14]

Der Kreis derjenigen, die ihre Urkunden in der Archivkiste in einer Dorfkirche aufbewahrten, konnte sehr vielfältig sein: der Pfarrer, die Kirchenmeister, die Dorfgemeinschaft bzw. Markengenossenschaften oder Gerichtsleute. Ob sie alle ihre Unterlagen derselben Kiste anvertrauten, ist allerdings unklar. Hier sei darauf hingewiesen, dass auch in der Stadt verschiedene Körperschaften die Pfarrkirche als Bewahrraum ihrer Archivalien benutzen konnten. An erster Stelle ist hierbei an die Gilden und Bruderschaften zu denken, wobei Letztere allerdings nicht unbedingt als weltliche Organisation bezeichnet werden können.

In den nördlichen Niederlanden hat eine besondere Art Körperschaft ebenso wie die Städte über eigene Privilegien und weitere Archivalien verfügt, nämlich die Deichverbände, die ab dem 13. Jahrhundert in den

---

[12] A.T. Schuitema Meijer, unter Mitarbeit von E. van Dijk & W.K. van der Veen, *Historie van het archief der stad Groningen* (Groningen, 1977), S. 7-9.

[13] F.J. Bakker, 'De kerk in Drenthe vóór de Reformatie', in: M.A.W. Gerding u.a. (Hgg.), *'In alle onwetenschap, bijsterije unde wildicheyt'. De reformatie in Drenthe in de zestiende en zeventiende eeuw* (Delft, 1998), S. 15-52, 26.

[14] H. van Heiningen, *Tussen Maas en Waal. 650 jaar geschiedenis van mensen en water* (Zutphen, 1972), S. 463-464.

Küstenregionen und in den Flussniederungen entstanden sind. Noch weniger als die neu gegründeten Städte verfügten sie über einen eigenen ständigen Verwaltungssitz. Es ist möglich, dass einzelne Deichgenossen oder Heimräte, soweit sie adlige Herren und Großgrundbesitzer waren und über ein steinernes Haus verfügten, die Privilegien, die übrigens meist in mehreren Originalen ausgefertigt wurden, zu Hause bewahrt haben.[15] Wenn sich unter den Deichgenossen Abteien befanden, dienten wahrscheinlich die jeweiligen Abteikirchen als Aufbewahrungsort. In den meisten Fällen haben die Deichverbände ihre Privilegienkisten allerdings wohl in Pfarrkirchen aufbewahrt. Dass die Lagerung in einer 'fremden' Stadtkirche nicht ganz ungefährlich war, weil so z. B. die Verfügungsgewalt über die eigenen Archivalien beeinträchtigt werden konnte, zeigt das Beispiel der Hoogheemraadschap Delfland aus der Mitte des 15. Jahrhunderts. Die Heimräte von Delfland hatten ihre Privilegien in einer Kiste in der Alten Kirche zu Delft gelagert 'ou leursdiz previlege, lettres et commissions gisoient en ung coffre que aucuns leurs predecesseurs heemrades y avoient fait mectre et apporter en temps passé pour les dangiers du feu et des guerres, qui lors estoient ou pais'.[16] Anlässlich eines Grenzkonfliktes mit dem Deichverband von Schieland wollten die Delflander Heimräte ihre Privilegien nachsehen und ihren Kollegen von Schieland vorlegen. Die Nachbarn von Schieland gaben sich nämlich nicht mit Abschriften zufrieden und forderten einen Blick in die Originalurkunden. Der Rat der Stadt Delft verweigerte aber den Delflander Heimräten den Zugang zur Kirche und damit zu ihrer Archivkiste. Als die Heimräte die Stadt vor ihr Gericht riefen und verurteilten (das Hoogheemraadschap hatte wie andere Großdeichverbände die hohe Gerichtsbarkeit inne), appellierte Delft an den Landesherrn Philip von Burgund und seinen Großen Rat. Dessen Urteil vom 6. Mai 1453 hob u. a. das Urteil der Heimräte auf. Es erkannte ihnen zwar das Recht zu, ihre Privilegien zu konsultieren und kopieren zu lassen, allerdings nicht ohne die Stadtschöffen von Delft dazu einzuladen. Die Hoogheemraadschap erhielt einen Schlüssel, ihr wurde jedoch untersagt, das 'Köfferchen' mit ihren Privilegien aus der Kirche zu

---

[15] Bei dem Deichverband (*hoogheemraadschap*) Rijnland wurde die Privilegienkiste bis ins 16. Jahrhundert traditionell vom ältesten Heimrat in seiner Privatwohunug in der Stadt Leiden verwahrt. Siehe S.J. Fockema Andreae, *De oude archieven van het hoogheemraadschap van Rijnland 1255-1857* (Leiden, 1933), S. 1-2, 8.

[16] S.J. Fockema Andreae (Hg.), *Rechtsbronnen van de vier hoofdwaterschappen van het vasteland van Zuid-Holland (Rijnland; Delfland; Schieland; Woerden)* (Utrecht, 1951), S. 69.

entfernen. Dadurch wurde die freie Verfügungsgewalt über das eigene Archiv erheblich eingeschränkt.[17]

Maß und Gewicht

Zur Sicherung der guten Ordnung des Handels und zum Schutz der Interessen seiner Bürger übte der Stadtrat Aufsicht über das Maß- und Gewichtswesen aus. Damit jeder Einwohner oder Fremde die lokalen Maße und Gewichte nachprüfen konnte, wurden an öffentlichen Einrichtungen Muster von Hohlmaßen und Längenmaßen angebracht. Bei diesen öffentlichen Einrichtungen konnte es sich um das Rathaus, das Waagengebäude, das Gewandhaus oder die Kirche handeln. Leider gehören die öffentlichen Maße zu den Gegenständen, die ob ihrer Alltäglichkeit schlecht dokumentiert sind. Eine der wenigen, allerdings auch erfreulich frühen Belegstellen ist eine Urkunde der Lütticher Schöffen zu Maastricht des Jahres 1243. Sie bestimmt hinsichtlich des Maß- und Gewichtswesens des Lütticher Bischofs zu Maastricht: 'Item mensura annone, mensura vini, mensura pannorum et virga de qua mensuratur terra, sunt apud sanctam Mariam in Traiecto' ('Das Kornmaß, das Weinmaß, die Elle und die Rute, mit der das Land vermessen wird, befinden sich in der Liebfrauenkirche zu Maastricht'). Diese Bestimmung wird in der ältesten Maastrichter Verfassungsurkunde, der so genannten *Alde Caert* von 1284, wiederholt. Im Kirchenschatz der Kirche befindet sich heute noch ein Hohlmaß der Stadt aus dem Jahre 1589. Von der Elle ist bekannt, dass sie bis zum Jahre 1777 an einer Kette im Kirchenportal gehangen hat. Ebenso wurden die Normalgewichte in einer Kiste im Archivraum der Kirche bewahrt.[18] Im Moment ist mir keine andere Kirche in den Niederlanden bekannt, die gleich der Liebfrauenkirche von Maastricht diese durchaus weltliche Funktion einnahm. Ob sie allerdings tatsächlich so einzigartig war, bedarf noch der Überprüfung.

Die Kirche als Verwaltungs- und Informationszentrum

Es gibt keinen zentraleren Ort für eine mittelalterliche Gemeinschaft als die Pfarrkirche. Kein Gläubiger konnte sich ihr längerfristig entziehen. Aufgrund des Pfarrzwangs gab es nur beschränkte Möglichkeiten zur

---

[17] Th.F.J.A. Dolk, *Geschiedenis van het hoogheemraadschap Delfland* (Den Haag, 1939), S. 38-42.
[18] De Kreek, *De kerkschat*, S. 79-80.

Erfüllung der Sonntagpflicht außerhalb der eigenen Pfarrkirche, also zum Beispiel in einer Klosterkirche oder einer Kapelle, und solche Ausnahmen galten nicht an Festtagen. Der kirchlichen Funktion der Pfarrkirche war es zu verdanken, dass sie auch im weltlichen Bereich zum Zentrum wurde für die Verbreitung von Klatsch, Nachrichten, Aufrufen und verschiedensten öffentlichen Bekanntmachungen der Obrigkeiten. Daneben diente die Kirche als Treffpunkt für verschiedenste Aktivitäten. Der Turm mit seinen Glocken war dabei ein wichtiges Hilfsmittel, um die Umgebung zu informieren, die Bevölkerung zu warnen oder zu mobilisieren. Trotz mangelnder Belege scheint es mir nicht zu gewagt, zu unterstellen, dass die Pfarrkirchen diese größtenteils außerkirchlichen Funktionen von Anfang an ausgeübt haben. Nachgewiesen sind sie erst seit dem 13. Jahrhundert und hauptsächlich im offiziellen Bereich, d. h. dem der kirchlichen und weltlichen Obrigkeiten.

In einem Schiedsspruch zwischen den Grafen von Flandern und Holland wurde 1290 u. a. festgelegt, dass in der strittigen Grafschaft Seeland westlich der Scheldt 67 Geschworene angestellt werden sollten, die noch bestehende Streitfälle untersuchen und beilegen sollten. Die Sitzungstage dieser Geschworenen wurden jede Woche frühestens am Mittwoch abgehalten und mussten am vorhergehenden Sonntag in der Kirche angekündigt werden. Der französische Text dieses Schiedsspruchs liefert eine knappe Beschreibung, wie solche Sitzungstage abzulaufen hatten und dass sie in der Kirche angekündigt werden sollten. Er gibt allerdings nicht an, auf welche Weise diese Ankündigung zu erfolgen hat.[19]

Spätere mittelniederländische Quellen sprechen in ähnlichen Zusammenhängen von *kerkgebod* oder *kerkenspraak*, ohne einen inhaltlichen Unterschied zu machen. Der Begriff *kerkenspraak* war vor allem im Osten der Niederlande üblich. Unter Kerkgebod *kerkenspraak* verstand man, oder eine Bekanntmachung eines Beschlusses oder einer Verordnung, eine Ansage, eine Aufkündigung, ein Gebot oder ein Verbot. Ein *kerkenspraak* konnte mündlich, schriftlich oder auf beide Weisen verkündigt werden.

Der *kerkenspraak* entwickelte sich bald zu einem notwendigen Schritt formeller Prozeduren weltlicher Obrigkeiten. Im Deichrecht des Landes von Vollenhove aus den Jahren 1354-1363 wird vorgeschrieben, dass die Versammlung der Deichgenossen erst nach zwei Ankündigungen mittels

---

[19] J.G. Kruisheer (Hg.), *Oorkondenboek van Holland en Zeeland tot 1299*, Teil 4 (Assen, 1997), Nr. 2490, S. 851: 'et convient que li jors de plait soit anonchiés auant es eglises par un dimanche atenir le jour de plait au mercredi siwant aprés v puis celui mercredi a vn autre jor certain en cele meisme semaine'.

eines *kerkenspraak* gültige Mehrheitsbeschlüsse fassen kann. Zur Feststellung, dass Deichgenossen ihr Deichstück nicht oder nicht ordnungsgemäß unterhalten haben, mussten sie in zwei *kerkenspraken* zur Wiederherstellung ihres Versäumnisses aufgerufen worden sein. Wenn sie nicht reagierten, hatten die Heimräte das Recht, die einschlägigen Deichstücke gegen Bezahlung instandsetzen zu lassen und sich den Kostenaufwand über die Güter der Nachlässigen zurückzuholen.[20] Auf für die Jahresabrechnung diverser Körperschaften (Gilden, Bruderschaften, Deichgenossenschaften) konnte eine Ankündigung durch *kerkenspraak* verlangt werden, um so die Anwesenheit aller Interessierten bei der Präsentation der Jahresabrechnung sicherzustellen.

Auch in der Stadt- und Dorfverwaltung konnte der *kerkenspraak* als Mittel in Prozeduren gegen nachlässige Einwohner, aber auch in Gerichtsverfahren dienen. Der *kerkenspaak* war auf jeden Fall als Mittel zur Bekanntmachung, aber auch zur einschärfenden Wiederholung von Gesetzen vorgeschrieben. Stadtrat und landsherrliche Behörden benutzten ihn zum Aufbieten der Steuerpflichtigen zur Steuererklärung oder zur Umlage einer Kopfsteuer[21], aber auch zum Auffordern des Landesaufgebots zur Musterung der Waffenausrüstung der Wehrpflichtigen.

Um 1500 wurde sicherlich nicht mehr alles nur noch während oder nach der Hochmesse am Sonntag verlesen. Manches wurde vermutlich damals an der Kirchenmauer angeschlagen und war damit jedem Lesenden zugänglich, der damit den Vorteil hatte, nicht bis zum Sonntag warten zu müssen und zudem die Möglichkeit hatte, alles nach der sonntäglichen Verkündigung in der Kirche auch noch einmal nachlesen zu können.

Stadtglocken und mechanische Uhren

Die Kirchenglocke spielte in der mittelalterlichen Gesellschaft sowohl eine kirchliche als auch eine weltliche Rolle. Wenn die Glocke für die Frühmesse läutete, war das zugleich das Signal für die Öffnung der Stadttore und für den Beginn des Arbeitstages. Abends kündigte sie das Ende des Arbeitstages an.[22] Ihr Hörbereich bestimmte symbolisch die Grenzen

---

[20] A.A. Beekman, *Het dijk- en waterschapsrecht in Nederland vóór 1795*, Teil 2 (Den Haag, 1907), S. 937.

[21] R.J. Fruin (Hg.), *Informacie up den staet faculteyt ende gelegentheyt van de steden ende dorpen van Hollant ende Vrieslant om daernae te reguleren de nyeuwe schiltaele gedaen in den jaere MDXIV* (Leiden, 1866), S. 88.

[22] In Delft existierte sogar eine spezielle 'Arbeitsglocke' (*werkklok*). Siehe L.J. Meilink-Hoedemaker, *Luidklokken en speelklokken in Delft. Een cultuur-historische studie over een Nederlands erfgoed* (Utrecht, 1985), S. 16.

der Stadtfreiheit. Im Falle städtischer Revolten war der Besitz der Glocken von großer taktischer Bedeutung. Deshalb versuchten die Aufständischen immer so schnell wie möglich die Stadtglocken in ihre Gewalt zu bringen. Glocken riefen die Gläubigen zum Gottesdienst auf; sie riefen sie aber auch zur Kirche oder an einen anderen Ort, um Gefahren abzuwehren. Gefahren konnten von vielerlei Art sein: feindliche Truppen, Plünderer, Brand, Hochwasser. Städte verfügten über eine Brandglocke (*vuerklock*) zur Alarmierung der Einwohnerschaft, die beim Läuten dieser Glocke mit ihren Eimern an die Unheilsstelle erscheinen musste. Brandglocken werden in einigen Stadtrechnungen aus der zweiten Hälfte des 14. Jahrhunderts erwähnt.[23] Zu Deventer wird ab 1357 zudem eine 'Nachbarglocke' (*buerklock*) erwähnt. Es handelt sich hierbei buchstäblich um die Glocke der Nachbarschaft, d. h. die Bürgerglocke, die von der städtischen Obrigkeit benutzt wurde. Sie rief die Bürgergemeinde zur Versammlung oder zur Verteidigung der Stadt auf.[24] In Dordrecht wurden die Bürger durch eine Glocke der Pfarrkirche zur Zahlung ihrer Kopfsteuer aufgefordert.[25] Meistenfalls hingen die Glocken der Stadt im Turm der Hauptkirche, dessen Bau im Auftrag und auf Kosten der Stadt zustande gekommen war.

Eine technische Innovation war im 14. Jahrhundert die Einführung der mechanischen Uhr, wobei eine Glocke die Stunden schlug. Die neue Technik hatte sich um 1370-1380 über fast alle größeren europäischen Städte verbreitet. Die Städte ließen zum öffentlichen Nutzen eine Uhr in einen Turm, meist den Turm der Hauptkirche, einbauen. In Großstädten folgten bald weitere öffentliche Uhren. Unter den Stadtdienern werden seitdem Uhrwächter aufgeführt, soweit nicht der Küster mit der Wartung der Uhr beauftragt war.[26] Öffentliche Uhren werden in niederländischen

---

[23] C.M. Hogenstijn, *De torenmuziek van Deventer. Een geschiedenis van torens, uurwerken, lui- en speelklokken van de Grote of Lebuïnuskerk te Deventer* (Deventer, 1983), S. 38; W.J. Alberts (Hg.), *De stadsrekeningen van Arnhem*, Teil 2 (Groningen, 1969), S. 53, 89.
[24] Hogenstijn, *De torenmuziek*, S. 41.
[25] Th.W. Jensma & A. Molendijk, *De Grote of Onze Lieve Vrouwekerk van Dordrecht. Koor en Kapittel* (Dordrecht, 1983), Quellenanhang, S. 163: 'Alsoe in 't openbaer mitter klocke gecondicht is geweest ende een ygelyck gewaerscuwet dat hij siin hooftgelt betalen soude binnen zekeren tijden' (1474).
[26] Hogenstijn, *De Torenmuziek*, S. 49; G. Dohrn-van Rossum & R. Westheider, 'Die Einführung der öffentlichen Uhren und der Übergang zur modernen Stundenrechnung in den spätmittelalterlichen Städten Niedersachsens', in: C. Meckseper (Hg.), *Stadt im Wandel. Kunst und Kultur des Bürgertums in Norddeutschland 1150-1650*, Teil 4 (Stuttgart / Bad Cannstatt, 1985), S. 317-331, 324-325; G. Dohrn-van Rossum, *Die Geschichte der Stunde. Uhren und moderne Zeitordnung* (München, 1992), S. 150-163, auf S. 362, Anm. 90 Daten zur Verbreitung der öffentlichen Uhren. Eine englische Übersetzung dieses

Städten seit 1369 erwähnt. Sie befanden sich ebenfalls meist im Turm der Hauptkirche. Über die Verbreitung der mechanischen Uhr in Kleinstädten und Dörfern fehlen Angaben.[27]

Kirchentürme bieten eine gute Aussicht über die weite Umgebung. Deshalb waren jedenfalls auf dem höchsten Kirchturm, und gegebenenfalls auf weiteren Türmen in der Stadt, städtische Wächter anzutreffen. Auch über diesen Weg diente der Kirchturm den weltlichen Interessen, der Abwehr feindlicher Angriffe und der Feuerwache.[28] Im Turm der Petrikirche zu Leiden wurde 1426 für die städtischen Wächter eine Wartestube gebaut; ein Mast mit einem Korb diente den Wächtern als Alarmzeichen im Falle drohender Gefahr.[29] Die Nimweger Turmwächter waren im Jahr 1428 selbst nicht allzu vorsichtig beim Kochen oder bei der Heizung ihrer Wachstube, so dass der Turm der Pfarrkirche abbrannte.[30]

Die Ratskapelle

Bei der so genannten Ratskapelle handelt es sich um einen Zweifelsfall. Diente sie vor allem dem Gottesdienst oder war sie an erster Stelle eine weltliche Anstalt? Als eigenständige kirchliche Einrichtung ist sie für die Niederlande kaum erforscht worden. Ihre Verbreitung über die mittelalterlichen Städte Deutschlands ist nur teilweise geklärt.[31] In der

---

Buches erschien unter dem Titel *History of the Hour. Clocks and Modern Temporal Orders* (Chicago, 1996).

[27] Utrecht 1369 (S. Muller (Hg.), *De middeleeuwsche rechtsbronnen der stad Utrecht*, Teil 1 (Den Haag, 1883), S. 89), Deventer 1370 (Hogenstijn, *De torenmuziek*, S. 42, 49), Zutphen 1383 (R. Wartena (Hg.), *De stadsrekeningen van Zutphen 1364-1445/46*, Teil 1 (Zutphen, 1977), S. 30), Arnheim 1384 (Alberts (Hg.), *De stadsrekeningen van Arnhem*, Teil 2, S. 97).

[28] Städtische Turmwächter werden z. B. um die Mitte des 14. Jahrhunderts zu Deventer erwähnt (Hogenstijn, *De torenmuziek*, S. 50) und 1378/79 zu Zutphen (Wartena, *De stadsrekeningen van Zutphen*, Teil 1, S. 12).

[29] B. van den Berg, *De Pieterskerk in Leiden* (Utrecht, 1992), S. 10, nach A. Meerkamp van Embden (Hg.), *Stadsrekeningen van Leiden (1390-1434)*, Teil 2 (Amsterdam, 1914), S. 107: 'Den cost van den huusgen up sinte Pieterstoorn'.

[30] Vgl. oben Anmerkung 5.

[31] Zur Ratskapelle: H. Maurer, 'Die Ratskapelle. Beobachtungen am Beispiel von St. Lorenz in Konstanz', in: *Festschrift für Hermann Heimpel zum 70. Geburtstag am 19. September 1971*, Teil 2 (Göttingen, 1972), S. 225-236, unveränderter Nachdruck in: M. Warnke (Hg.), *Politische Architektur in Europa vom Mittelalter bis heute* (Köln, 1984), S. 296-309; U. Heckert, 'Die Ratskapelle als Zentrum bürgerlicher Herrschaft und Frömmigkeit. Struktur, Ikonographie und Funktion', *Blätter für deutsche Landesgeschichte*, 129 (1993), S. 139-164; Ders., *Die Ratskapelle als religiöses und politisches Zentrum der Ratsherrschaft in deutschen Städten des späten Mittelalters* (Bielefeld, 1997).

niederländischen Literatur zur Städtegeschichte wird sie nicht genannt und ist deshalb als Sondertypus der Kapelle nicht bekannt. Trotzdem kann sie auch in einigen niederländischen Städten nachgewiesen werden. Als wichtige Merkmale einer Ratskapelle gelten, dass der Rat die Kirchenpflegschaft innehatte, einen eigenen Kaplan (*stattkaplan*) anstellte, vor Beginn seiner Sitzungen dort die Messe hörte, dass die Kapelle eine Ratsglocke hatte oder dass offizielle Bekanntmachungen an den Türen oder an der Mauer der Ratskapelle angeschlagen wurden. Nicht jede Ratskapelle hatte alle diese Funktionen. Eine Kapelle war auf jeden Fall keine Ratskapelle, wenn der Stadtrat nur das Kollationsrecht an derer Altären besaß. Äußerlich waren sie verschieden: Sie konnten im Rathaus eingebaut sein, an einer Kirche angebaut sein oder ein selbständiges Gebäude darstellen. Durchschlagend war ihre Funktion: die vorrangige oder ausschließliche Benutzung durch den Rat. Im deutschsprachigen Gebiet werden Ratskapellen, wenn auch noch spärlich, um 1300 zum ersten Mal erwähnt, treten dann aber ab der Mitte des 14. Jahrhunderts häufig in Erscheinung.[32]

Das älteste niederländische Beispiel einer Ratskapelle findet man in Utrecht, wo man um 1391 damit begann, sie an die Pfarrkirche (*Buurkerk*) anzubauen, ohne dass der Bau vollendet wurde. Später wurde in den Jahren 1437-1450 an der Nordseite des Turms tatsächlich eine Ratskapelle erbaut.[33] Für die heutigen Niederlanden ist meines Wissens nur die Ratskapelle der Stadt Kampen relativ gut erforscht worden. Um 1462 vom Rat gegründet, erscheint sie auch als 'Jerusalemkapelle' in den Quellen, weil sie zugleich Sitz einer bescheidenen Jerusalembruderschaft war, die vom Rat erheblich gefördert wurde. Im selben Jahr wurde vom Rat ein Ratskaplan oder Schöffenkaplan zur Bedienung dieser Jerusalemkapelle angestellt, der von der Stadt ein jährliches Gehalt empfing. Im 16. Jahrhundert wurde sie überwiegend als 'Schöffenkapelle' (*schepenkapel, capella senatorum, capella scabinorum*) beschrieben. Städtische Verordnungen wurden hier angeschlagen. Sie befand sich in einem Ausbau am Chor der Hauptkirche, der nach der Reformation abgeschossen, zu einem Lagerraum degradiert wurde und später abgerissen worden ist. Merkwürdig ist im Hinblick auf Kampen, dass in den Jahren 1540 und 1552 von einer

---

[32] Heckert, *Die Ratskapelle*, S. 14-16.
[33] Th. Haakma Wagenaar, *De bouwgeschiedenis van de Buurkerk te Utrecht. Proeve eener historische voorbereiding van de restauratie van een middeleeuwsch monument* (Utrecht, 1936), S. 132, 148, 151, 171-172, 183, 203, 216, 222, 225, 226; W.H. Vroom, *De financiering van de kathedraalbouw in de middeleeuwen, in het bijzonder van de dom van Utrecht* (Maarssen, 1981), S. 345.

Schöffenkapelle im Rathaus die Rede ist. Weil es keine Angaben dafür gibt, dass an dieser Kapelle ein Altar oder eine Pfründe verbunden war, kann es kaum mehr als eine kleine Betkapelle gewesen sein.[34] An der Lebuinuskirche zu Deventer wurde 1494-1499 eine Kapelle mit dem Namen *Raadskapel* oder *Magistraatskapel* angebaut. Alle Spuren ihrer früheren Funktion sind längst verschwunden, vermutlich seit der Reformation, als man sie in eine Werkstatt der Kirchenfabrik umwandelte. Nach der letzten Restaurierung ist nur ein leerer Raum übrig geblieben, für den allerdings der ursprüngliche Name beibehalten worden ist.[35] Eine ähnliche Situation besteht zu Arnheim: Auch hier lässt sich in der Pfarrkirche ein Raum neben der Südseite des Westturms nachweisen, der noch heutzutage den Namen von 'Raadskapel' trägt. Aus bauhistorischen Gründen wird diese Kapelle auf das dritte Viertel des 15. Jahrhunderts datiert, schriftlich ist sie allerdings bis heute nicht dokumentiert worden.[36]

Ebenso wie in Deutschland sind die Fragen nach Alter, Herkunft, Verbreitung und Typologie der Ratskapelle auch in den Niederlanden noch weitgehend unerforscht.[37]

Notariat

Unzählige Notariatsurkunden sind in einer Kirche oder Kapelle aufgesetzt worden. Parteien und Zeugen erschienen vor einem Notar in der Sakristei, vor einem Altar oder sogar im Chor.[38] In der Stadt 's-Hertogenbosch wurden im Spätmittelalter 17,8 % der Notariatsurkunden in der Hauptkirche und insgesamt 22 % in einer Kirche, Kapelle oder auf dem Friedhof ausgestellt. Ein Notar, der zugleich stellvertretender Pfarrer war, setzte sich sogar mit einem Angehörigen seiner Pfarrei in den Beichtstuhl, um dort sein Testament aufzunehmen. Nur ein Teil der Akten bezog

---

[34] R.J. Kolman, 'De pelgrims van Jeruzalem te Kampen (ca. 1450-1580)', *Kamper Almanak* (1987/1988), S. 155-214, 178-186.

[35] D.J. de Vries, 'De bouwgeschiedenis van de Lebuinus tussen circa 1450 en de reformatie', in: A.J.J. Mekking (Hg.), *De Grote of Lebuinuskerk te Deventer. De 'Dom' van het Oversticht veelzijdig bekeken* (Zutphen, 1992), S. 71-101, 88.

[36] A.G. Schulte, *De Grote of Eusebiuskerk in Arnhem. IJkpunt van de stad* (Utrecht, 1994), S. 63, 210.

[37] Maurer, 'Die Ratskapelle', S. 235-236; Heckert, 'Die Ratskapelle', S. 9-10.

[38] Beispiele: A.Fl. Gehlen, *Het notariaat in het tweeherig Maastricht. Een rechtshistorische schets van de inrichting en practijk van het Maastrichtse notariaat vanaf zijn opkomst tot aan het einde van de tweeherigheid over de stad (1292-1794)* (Assen, 1981), S. 66, Anm. 146; C. van Heel, *Drie middeleeuwse notariële protocollen uit Zaltbommel, Zutphen en 's-Heerenberg* (Arnheim, 1982), S. 14-59.

sich auf das Gotteshaus, wo sie aufgenommen wurde.[39] Der Inhalt der Akte bestimmte also nicht den Ort der Ausfertigung. Für den Brauch, die Akten in einer Kirche oder Kapelle auszufertigen, gibt es neben der Ortsbezogenheit auch noch andere Gründe. Notare arbeiteten sowieso selten in ihrem eigenen Haus oder verfügten dort über eine Schreibstube. Sie übten ihr Amt grundsätzlich in der Öffentlichkeit aus, wobei die Kirche als öffentlicher Raum auf der Hand lag. Außerdem hatten sie als Geistliche oft eine amtliche Beziehung zu einer Kirche, so dass es auf der Hand lag, dass sie dort ihr Amt ausübten. Notfalls konnte man in einer Kirche auch unter den anwesenden Geistlichen schnell und bequem Zeugen anwerben.

Kirchenbibliotheken

Eine relativ späte Entwicklung ist die Einrichtung einer Stadtbibliothek in einer Kirche. Dass Bücher zum Inventar einer Kirche gehörten und die Büchersammlung zu einer Bibliothek anwachsen konnte, ist bekannt. Zuerst und vor allem gab es in einer Kirche die liturgischen Bücher, die dem Gottesdienst dienten und meist in der Sakristei aufbewahrt wurden. Daneben konnten weitere nichtliturgische Bücher den Priestern zur Verfügung stehen: die Bibel, Bibelkommentare, Homiliare, Schriften der Kirchenväter, Heiligenleben, juristische Literatur und Nachschlagwerke. In den größeren Stadtkirchen, die über eine erhebliche Büchersammlung verfügten, ist seit dem 15. Jahrhundert manchmal eine so genannte *Librije* nachweisbar, eine Bibliothek in einem separaten Raum, die sich oft in der Nähe der Sakristei, häufig über ihr befand. Interessant wird es, wenn nachzuweisen ist, dass eine solche *Librije* nicht nur von Geistlichen, sondern auch von Laien benutzt werden konnte. Die Kirchenbibliothek wurde damit zu einer öffentlichen Leihbibliothek. Dew frühesten Beleg einer solchen öffentlichen Bibliothek fand ich zu Delft, wo eine Liste aus dem Jahre 1436 60 'Mitglieder' der Bibliothek in der Alten Kirche auflistet. Es handelt sich um männliche Bürger von Delft, Patrizier wie Handwerksleute, die gegen Zahlung einen Schlüssel empfangen hatten. Die Sammlung war jedoch mit drei Büchern (*duytschen boken*) sehr beschränkt.[40] Für zwei Stadtkirchen gibt es Belege dafür, dass es dort seit

---

[39] A.H.P. van den Bichelaer, *Het notariaat in stad en Meijerij van 's-Hertogenbosch tijdens de late midddeleeuwen (1306-1531). Een prosopografisch, diplomatisch en rechtshistorisch onderzoek* (Amsterdam, 1998), S. 467-468.
[40] D.P. Oosterbaan, *De Oude Kerk te Delft gedurende de Middeleeuwen* (Den Haag, 1973), S. 87.

dem zweiten Viertel des 15. Jahrhunderts eigenständige Bibliothekräume oder mindestens nichtliturgische Kirchenbibliotheken gegeben hat. Auch für verschiedene Pfarrkirchen sind nichtliturgische Kirchenbibliotheken seit der zweiten Hälfte des 15. Jahrhunderts nachgewiesen.[41] Die öffentliche Funktion der meisten Kirchenbibliotheken ist aber, mit Ausnahme von Delft, erst im 16. Jahrhundert nachweisbar. Vermutlich wurden damals die Dozenten und Schüler der Lateinschule zu häufigen Benutzern der örtlichen Kirchenbibliothek. Wenn die Stadtregierung von Hoorn 1535 den Bau einer neuen Sakristei mit einem Obergeschoss für die *Librije* in Auftrag gibt und finanziert, lässt dies den Schluss zu, dass diese *Librije* einer Stadtbibliothek gleichzusetzen ist. In Dordrecht stand die Stadtbibliothek (*der stede library*) 1559 unter der Aufsicht des Rektors der Lateinschule. Wahrscheinlich ist sie identisch mit der Bibliothek der Hauptkirche (*librarie van de Grote kerk*), für die im Jahr 1571 auf Rechnung der Stadt ein Aufsichtsbeamter angestellt wurde.[42]

Weltberühmt ist die *Librije* der Sankt Walpurgiskirche zu Zutphen – allerdings mehr als Gebäude als wegen ihrer Büchersammlung. Der Besucher, der in diesen überwölbten an der südlichen Seite des Chors angebauten Raum mit seinen langen Pulten und den darauf an Ketten

---

[41] Haarlem: 1428 (W.C.M. Wüstefeld, *De boeken van de Grote of Sint Bavokerk. Een bijdrage tot de geschiedenis van het middeleeuwse boek in Haarlem* (Hilversum, 1989), S. 12), Delft: 1434 (Oosterbaan, *De Oude Kerk*, S. 87); Utrecht: 1448/49 (K.O. Meinsma, *Middeleeuwsche bibliotheken* (Amsterdam, 1902), S. 96-97); Appingedam: 1462 (J.M.M. Hermans, *Boeken in Groningen voor 1600. Studies rond de librije van de Sint-Maarten* (Groningen, 1987), S. 153, 350 Anm. 4); Groningen, Sankt Martini: vermutlich um 1470 (Hermans, *Boeken in Groningen*, S. 155); Kampen: 1480 (C.N. Fehrmann, 'De bouwgeschiedenis van de Sint-Nicolaas- of Bovenkerk te Kampen naar de archivalische gegevens', *Bulletin van de Koninklijke Nederlandse Oudheidkundige Bond*, 71 (1972), S. 65-71, 70; Kolman, 'De pelgrims', S. 181); Gouda: 1487 (W.A. Zuijderhoudt-Hulst, *Geschiedenis van de Goudse librije gedurende het verblijf in de St. Janskerk* (Meppel, 1976), S. 18); Zutphen: um 1500 (W. van Dongen, 'Boekbanden uit de Librije te Zutphen', in: A.J. Geurts (Hg.), *Middeleeuwsche boeken en teksten uit Oost-Nederland* (Nimwegen / Grave, 1984), S. 137-212, 137-138; A.J. Geurts, 'Boekenbezit in Zutphen vóór 1600. Een eerste verkenning', in: E. Cockx-Indestege & F. Hendrickx (Hgg.), *Miscellanea Neerlandica. Opstellen voor dr. Jan Deschamps ter gelegenheid van zijn zeventigste verjaardag*, Teil 3 (Löwen, 1987), S. 31-50, 33-37); Hoorn: vor 1533 (R.P. Zijp, *De Librije van Enkhuizen* (Enkhuizen, 1991), S. 10); Tiel: 1554 (J. Kuys u.a. (Übers.), *De Tielse kroniek. Een geschiedenis van de Lage Landen van de Volksverhuizingen tot het midden van de vijftiende eeuw, met een vervolg over de jaren 1552-1566* (Amsterdam, 1983), S. LXI, 176-177); Alkmaar: sehr wahrscheinlich vor 1570 (G.I. Plenckers-Keyser & C. Streefkerk, 'De librije van Alkmaar', in: *Glans en glorie van de Grote kerk. Het interieur van de Alkmaarse Sint Laurens* (Hilversum, 1996), S. 263-274); Edam: vor 1576 (*Boeken uit de Librije van Edam* (Den Haag, 1984), S. 7, 10).

[42] J.L. van Dalen, *De Groote Kerk (Onze Lieve Vrouwenkerk) te Dordrecht* (Dordrecht, 1927), S. 76.

gefesselten Büchern eintritt, wähnt sich im Mittelalter. 'Wähnt sich', denn der Bau dieser Bibliothek wurde erst 1561 in Angriff genommen und wurde 1564 beendet. Über die Geschichte der früheren Bibliothek dieser kombinierten Stift- und Pfarrkirche sind fast keine Angaben vorhanden. Sie war im Vergleich mit der späteren *Librije* beschränkten Umfangs und war um 1500 in einem kleinen Raum über dem Kapitelhaus untergebracht worden. Seit der Eröffnung der neuen *Librije* 1564 wurde dieser Raum als die *Olde Librije* angedeutet und von den Kirchenvögten als Archivraum benutzt. Obwohl ein Zutphener Bürgermeister dieser älteren Stiftsbibliothek seine Bücher vermacht hat, als die *Librije* von 1564 noch nicht existierte, gibt es keine expliziten Hinweise dafür, dass die damalige Stadt diese Kirchenbibliothek unterstützt hat oder dass sie den Zutphener Bürgern zugänglich war. Die Büchersammlung der *Librije* von 1564 ist, wie gesagt, weniger eindrucksvoll als ihr Bau. Sie enthält lediglich 22 Handschriften und in ihrer Mehrzahl Inkunabeln und Postinkunabeln, die zum größten Teil erst nach 1564 beschafft worden sind. Interessant ist allerdings die Tatsache, dass die *Librije* als Kirchen- und Stadtbibliothek auch mit der Zielsetzung konzipiert war, zur Bekämpfung reformatorischer Auffassungen zu dienen. Für die Leser ließ man von einem Schmied mehr als 60 Schlüssel anfertigen. Anfangs besaß die *Librije* etwa 20 Handschriften und mehr als 60 gedruckte Bücher; die Sammlung wurde dann aber von den Kirchenmeistern bald ausgebreitet.[43]

Die Quellenlage ermöglicht es kaum, die Kirchenbibliothek von der öffentlichen Stadtbibliothek zu unterscheiden, um so mehr weil es den Anschein hat, dass mehrere in einer Kirche eingerichtete Bibliotheken beide Funktionen erfüllt haben. Häufig scheint die städtische Lateinschule dabei ein wichtiges Bindeglied zwischen Bürgerschaft und Kirchenbibliothek gewesen zu sein.

Schlussbemerkung

Die spätmittelalterliche Pfarrkirche musste bzw. konnte sehr verschiedene weltliche Funktionen erfüllen. Hierbei ist allerdings zu bemerken, dass nicht jede Pfarrkirche alle hier beschriebenen Funktionen tatsächlich ausführte. Ihre tatsächliche Rolle für das weltliche Leben hing vor allem von den lokalen Bedürfnissen ab. Wo es kein Rathaus oder ähnliche öffentliche Einrichtungen gab, konnte die Pfarrkirche zum Mittelpunkt der Stadtverwaltung werden. Auch in den Städten, die später über ein

---

[43] Meinsma, *Middeleeuwsche bibliotheken*, S. 198-229.

Rathaus verfügten, blieb die Pfarrkirche in vielerlei Hinsicht eine Nebenstelle des Rathauses. Sie diente als Archivraum, Anschlagsäule für öffentliche Bekanntmachungen, Wachtposten zur Feuerwache und zum frühzeitigen Erkennen feindlicher Angriffe. Die Pfarrkirche diente ebenfalls als 'Kommunikationszentrum' *avant la lettre* durch den Brauch der Kirchensprachen, das Anschlagen schriftlicher Bekanntmachungen und Berichte und durch die Anwesenheit von Bürgerglocken und der mechanischen Uhr. Die 'kommunikative' Funktion einiger städtischer Pfarrkirchen wurde in der frühen Neuzeit noch dadurch erweitert, dass die Kirchenbibliothek dem Publikum eröffnet wurde. Nur selten diente sie als Versammlungsraum des Stadtrats oder zur Schöffenwahl. Zwar ist bekannt, dass zu Dordrecht sich die Schöffen 1437 in der Sakristei der Hauptkirche versammelten, wobei es allerdings undeutlich ist, ob es sich hierbei um eine Gewohnheit handelte.[44] Zu Nimwegen versammelte sich die Stadtgemeinschaft 1361 noch in der Hauptkirche, wenn sie der Stadtrat über dringliche oder wichtige Angelegenheiten zu befragen wünschte, später ist diese Praxis allerdings nicht mehr belegt. Angenommen wird, dass die Gilden die Rolle des *vulgiloquium* übernommen haben.[45]

Nicht jede Stadt- oder Dorfverwaltung hat die Kirche unbedingt und ausschließlich als Aufbewahrungsort für ihre Archive benutzt. Wenn Archive in einer Kirche aufbewahrt wurden, beschränkte man sich auf die Originalurkunden der wichtigsten Privilegien, denen manchmal die Stadtsiegel hinzugefügt wurden. Andere Archivstücke wurden meist im Rathaus aufbewahrt. Nicht nur die Stadtverwaltung konnte ihre Archive in der Pfarrkirche lagern; auch die Deichverbände kommen als mögliche obrigkeitliche Benützer in Frage. Die Aufbewahrung von Normalmaßen und Normalgewichten in der Maastrichter Liebfrauenkirche scheint ein Sonderfall gewesen zu sein.

Einige städtische Pfarrkirchen beherbergten eine Ratskapelle, die vor allem den weltlichen Interessen des Stadtrats, nicht aber denen der ganzen Bürgerschaft oder Bevölkerung diente. Sie kann, falls sie an einer Kirche angebaut war, als Ausdruck einer weiteren weltlichen Funktion einer Kirche bezeichnet werden. Das Phänomen der Ratskapelle ist in der niederländischen Forschung relativ unbekannt geblieben und ist noch weiter zu erforschen.

Von einer militärischen Funktion der Pfarrkirchen war nur vereinzelt, aber schon relativ früh die Rede. Auf dem Lande übten die Dorfkirchen

---

[44] Van Dalen, *De Groote Kerk*, S. 246.
[45] *Het Stadhuis van Nijmegen*, S. 10, Anm. 72: 'ante summum altare in communi vulgiloquio magistrorum civium, scabinorum, consulum et totius communitatis Novimagensi maiore campana propter hoc tribus vicibus pulsata'; F. Gorissen, *Stedeatlas van Nijmegen* (Arnheim, 1956), S. 95.

gelegentlich die Funktion einer Wehranlage aus. In den ummauerten Ortschaften blieb den Kirchen diese schmähliche Rolle im Spätmittelalter erspart. Die einzige, nicht ausschließlich militärische Funktion, die sich fast überall, in Städten und Dörfern, nachweisen lässt, ist die Benutzung des Kirchturms als Wachtposten und Turm, in dem die Alarmglocken hingen.

Notare haben ihren Beruf häufig in einer Kirche ausgeübt; sie sind im Spätmittelalter noch als geistliche Funktionäre zu bezeichnen, und ihre Aktivitäten befanden sich oft im Grenzbereich vom Weltlichen und Geistlichen. Rechtsprechung in der Kirche ist eine Ausnahme geblieben.

Grenzfälle hat es, wie beim Notariat, immer gegeben. Was soll man halten von Austeilungen an die Armen, die, meist periodisch an festen Terminen, in den Kirchen stattfanden? Die Hauptkirche zu Haarlem beherbergt noch heutzutage eine Brotbank aus dem letzten Viertel des 15. Jahrhunderts. Hierbei handelt es sich um eine Art Ladentisch, an dem den Armen der Stadt Brot und andere Nährungsmittel übergeben wurden.[46] Zweifellos haben Armenmeister auch an anderen Orten ihre Spenden in der Pfarrkirche verteilt. Ist aber diesbezüglich in der spätmittelalterlichen Stadt noch von einer rein kirchlichen Funktion die Rede? Wurden hier kirchliche oder weltliche Aufgaben von kirchlichen oder weltlichen Funktionären erfüllt? Dies ist eine Frage, die sich die weltlichen und kirchlichen Behörden bzw. die einfachen Gläubigen des Mittelalters wohl nie gestellt haben. Für sie gab es noch keine Trennung zwischen Staat und Kirche. Auch ist darauf hinzuweisen, dass der Kirchenbau meist von der weltlichen Obrigkeit finanziert und betreut wurde, wodurch die Pfarrkirche faktisch ein weltliches Gebäude war. Dass ihr, neben der kirchlichen, auch einige weltliche Funktionen auferlegt wurden, kann aus der Sicht des Baus eigentlich nicht erstaunen.

Was jedoch bei dem allem aus heutiger Sicht so auffällig bleibt, ist die Selbstverständlichkeit aller dieser weltlichen Aktivitäten in einer kirchlichen Umgebung. Dieser Umstand erschwert die historische Forschung zu den weltlichen Funktionen von Pfarrkirchen, weil sie in den Quellen oft nur beiläufig erwähnt werden. Abermals zeigt diese Tatsache, dass in einer spätmittelalterlichen Pfarrkirche eine körperliche Trennung von Kirche und Welt noch nicht vorstellbar war.[47]

Radboud Universiteit Nijmegen

---

[46] *De Bavo te boek bij het gereedkomen van de restauratie van de Grote of St.-Bavo kerk te Haarlem* (Haarlem, 1985), S. 128-130.

[47] Für die Überprüfung des deutschen Textes bedanke ich mich bei meinem Kollegen Dr. Albrecht Diem.

Jacoba van LEEUWEN

PRAISE THE LORD FOR THIS PEACE!
THE CONTRIBUTION OF RELIGIOUS INSTITUTIONS TO THE CEREMONIAL PEACE-PROCLAMATIONS IN LATE MEDIEVAL FLANDERS (1450-1550)

Recently, medievalists have given attention to the communication of power. The emphasis in this research is not on power but on the representation, the performance or the staging of power.[1] The rise of the State at the end of the Middle Ages has made the analysis of the symbolic communication of rulers seem particularly important. Besides political strategies, various ceremonies were employed to further State formation, such as the elaboration of festive Joyous Entries and the ruler's participation in town spectacles like tournaments and banquets. After a conflict, rituals of reconciliation and submission were performed to demonstrate the ruler's triumph.[2]

Another event that was staged to promote the Central State was the ceremonial proclamation of peace-treaties in every town of the realm. Historical research has so far not paid much attention to this ceremony.

---

[1] P. Buc, *The Dangers of Ritual. Between Early Medieval Texts and Social Scientific Theory* (Princeton, 2002); H.-W. Goetz, *Moderne Mediävistik. Stand und Perspektiven der Mittelalterforschung* (Darmstadt, 1999), pp. 212-216; Althoff & L. Siep, 'Symbolische Kommunikation und gesellschaftliche Wertesysteme vom Mittelalter bis zur französischen Revolution. Der neue Münsterer Sonderforschungsbereich 496', *Frühmittelalterliche Studien*, 34 (2000), pp. 413-446.

[2] On such rituals in medieval Flanders, see: E. Lecuppre-Desjardin, *La ville des cérémonies: recherche sur l'espace public dans les villes des anciens Pays-Bas bourguignons (XIVe-XVe s.)* (Paris, 2004); J.D. Hurlbut, *Vive Bourgongne est nostre cry: Ceremonial Entries of Philippe the Good and Charles the Bold (1419-1477)*, Burgundica (Turnhout, 2001); W.P. Blockmans & A. Janse (eds.), *Showing Status. Representation of Social Positions in the Late Middle Ages*, Medieval Texts and Cultures of Northern Europe, vol. 2 (Turnhout, 1999); P. Arnade, *Realms of Ritual. Burgundian Ceremony and Civic Life in Late Medieval Ghent* (Ithaca / London, 1996); A. Brown, 'Civic Ritual: Bruges and the Counts of Flanders in the Later Middle Ages', *The English Historical Review*, 112 (1997), pp. 277-299; E. van den Neste, *Tournois, joutes, pas d'armes dans les villes de Flandre à la fin du Moyen Age (1300-1486)*, Mémoires et documents de l'Ecole des chartes, vol. 47 (Paris, 1996); M. Boone, 'Urban Space and Political Conflict in Late Medieval Flanders', in: M. Howell, P. Arnade & W. Simons (eds.), *Proceedings of the Conference Fertile Space: The City in Northern Europe 1100-1650. Darmouth College, Hanover (N.H. USA) 15-16 May, 1999*, Journal of Interdisciplinary History, 32 (2002), pp. 621-640.

Some authors have mentioned the peace celebrations in a general overview on civic festivities,[3] while others have published short contributions about just one proclamation.[4] However, a more profound study of the elaboration, symbolic implications and evolution of these ceremonies is lacking.

In fact, these proclamations represented a very particular situation in which symbolic communication took place, since the inhabitants of the town could not witness the statutory act that was celebrated, as in a Joyous Entry. In the ceremony the town had to be informed about an event that had taken place elsewhere and earlier. Since this celebration was often imposed by the central government, it was not likely that the subjects would express their support spontaneously.[5] Thus, the municipality had to do its utmost to convince the inhabitants of the importance of the treaty and to demonstrate its legitimacy. In order to strengthen the town's identification with the peace the municipality employed various means. Mostly, political communication-strategies were involved; however, sacral symbols also played an important role.

This essay seeks to explore which sacral traditions were appropriated in the solemn peace-proclamations. It analyses how religious institutions collaborated and in which stages of the ceremony they were asked to contribute. Moreover, it analyses how this appropriation of sacral means was motivated and whether the meaning of the symbols which were employed was changed in this process. It may be that the transfer from one context

---

[3] A.K.L. Thijs, 'Private en openbare feesten: communicatie, educatie en omgaan met macht (Vlaanderen en Brabant, 16de-midden 19de eeuw)', *Volkskunde*, 101 (2000), pp. 139-140; B. Ramakers, *Spelen en figuren: toneelkunst en processiecultuur in Oudenaarde tussen Middeleeuwen en Moderne Tijd* (Amsterdam, 1996), pp. 143-151; H. Soly, 'Plechtige intochten in de steden van de Zuidelijke Nederlanden tijdens de overgang van Middeleeuwen naar Nieuwe Tijd: Communicatie, propaganda, spektakel', *Tijdschrift voor Geschiedenis*, 97 (1984), p. 342; B. Ouvry, 'Officieel ceremonieel te Oudenaarde, 1450-1600', *Handelingen van de Geschied- en Oudheidkundige Kring van Oudenaarde van zijn Kastelnij en van den Lande tusschen Marcke en Ronne*, 22 (1985), pp. 38-45; W. Hüsken, 'Kroniek van het toneel in Brugge (1468-1556)', *Verslagen en mededeelingen van de Koninklijke Vlaamse Academie voor Nederlandse Taal- en Letterkunde* (1992), pp. 18-252; Idem, 'Politics and Drama: The City of Bruges as Organizer of Drama Festivals', in: A.E. Knight (ed.), *The Stage as Mirror. Civic Theatre in Late Medieval Europe* (Cambridge, 1997), pp. 164-187; A.-L. Van Bruaene, *Om beters wille. Rederijkerskamers en de stedelijke cultuur in de Zuidelijke Nederlanden (1400-1650)* (Ghent: unpublished PhD University of Ghent, 2003).

[4] A. Viaene, 'Bij een driehonderdste verjaring. Het grote vredefeest van 1660 te Brugge', *Biekorf*, 61 (1960), pp. 161-166; A. Dewitte, 'Solemniteyten ende ceremonien van blytscap over den pays met Vranckerycke. Brugge, 7 juni 1598', *Biekorf*, 80 (1980), p. 122.

[5] Thijs, 'Private en openbare feesten'; W. Blockmans & E. Donckers, 'Self-Representation of Court and City in Flanders and Brabant in the Fifteenth and Early Sixteenth Centuries', in: W. Blockmans & A. Janse (eds.), *Showing Status*, pp. 81-111.

into another added new layers of meaning to the tradition that was appropriated.⁶

In what follows we will first sketch a short outline of Flemish history between 1450 and 1550. Then, we will analyse the various components of the ceremonial peace-proclamations. Thirdly, we will explore how religious institutions participated in these ceremonies. And finally we will try to explain why these institutions were asked to contribute to the ceremony and what motivated the appropriation of sacral symbols.

The Proclamation of Peace-Treaties in Flanders 1450-1550

From 1384 onwards the county of Flanders was ruled by the Burgundian dukes. These rulers wished to create a centralized state, much to the detriment of the wealthy Flemish towns that defended their autonomy with great intensity. In 1449 a serious conflict broke out between Ghent and the Burgundian duke Philip the Bold. When this war ended in 1453, the duke imposed the 'Treaty of Gavere' on Ghent and deprived the town of many privileges. This treaty was to be proclaimed in the small towns to demonstrate the duke's victory over the rebellious city of Ghent.⁷ Some fifteen years later Charles the Bold succeeded his father, who had recently passed away. In 1468 he concluded peace with the French king. This 'Treaty of Péronne' had to be celebrated in all towns of the realm in order to underline the power of the duke.⁸

In April 1482 Mary, Duchess of Burgundy, the daughter of Charles the Bold, died unexpectedly. This instantly created a political vacuum in Flanders. The heir, Philip the Fair, was a minor and could therefore not immediately succeed. His father, Maximilian of Austria, wanted to reign as his guardian and regent, but the county of Flanders put up much resistance. Moreover, the French king Louis XI threatened to invade Flanders. The 'Treaty of Arras' concluded on 23 December 1482 between Maximilian and the French king was very much in favour of the Flemish towns

---

⁶ G. Althoff, 'Die Kultur der Zeichen und Symbole', *Frühmittelalterliche Studien*, 36 (2002), pp. 1-19; V. Plesch & K. Asley, 'The Cultural Processes of Appropriation', *Journal of Medieval and Early Modern Studies*, 5 (2002), pp. 1-15.

⁷ J. Haemers, *De Gentse opstand (1449-1453). De strijd tussen rivaliserende netwerken om het stedelijke kapitaal*, Standen en Landen, vol. 105 (Kortrijk-Heule, 2004); M. Boone, *Gent en de Bourgondische hertogen ca. 1384 – ca. 1453 Een sociaal-politieke studie van een staatsvormingsproces*, Verhandelingen van de Koninklijke Academie voor Wetenschappen, Letteren en Schone Kunsten van België – Klasse der Letteren, vol. 133 (Brussels, 1990).

⁸ R. Vaughan, *Charles the Bold. The Last Valois Duke of Burgundy* (London, 1973).

since it confirmed all their privileges. On 5 June 1483 the succession was finally arranged: a regent would rule the county of Flanders on behalf of Philip the Fair. However, Maximilian did not acknowledge his defeat so easily: from 1484 onwards he waged war against the Flemish towns and in July 1485 he overthrew the regency. The 'Treaty of Sluis' (28 June 1485) punished the towns drastically for their defiance and installed Maximilian as the regent for his son. His triumph was short-lived, since in November 1487 a new revolt broke out in Ghent. The French King Charles VIII resolved to support the Flemish rebels and demanded that they should proclaim the 'Treaty of Arras' (1482) in every town of the county. On 5 February 1488 Maximilian was imprisoned in Bruges. He was only released on 16 May after confirming the 'Treaty of Bruges'. Soon afterwards the war started all over again. At first, the French King Charles VIII still supported the Flemish towns, but on 22 July 1489 he issued the 'Treaty of Frankfurt' with Maximilian and in December 1489 the two rulers concluded the 'Peace of Montil-lez-Tours'. This last text was proclaimed in all Flemish towns. On 29 November 1490 Bruges was subdued with the 'Peace of Damme', and on 29 July 1492 Ghent was finally defeated with the 'Peace of Cadzand', a text that was proclaimed in the other Flemish towns as well. In May 1493 the 'Peace of Senlis' ended the war with France. This treaty was celebrated throughout the entire county.[9]

When Philip the Fair came to power in 1494, tensions with the French king were still strong, since this ruler was the sovereign of Flanders. Only in October 1501, with the 'Treaty of Trente' were both rulers reconciled and in 1508 the 'Peace of Cambrai' united them again. In 1513 the French and the English king concluded a peace that also had its effects on the Low Countries, since it reopened trade with these realms, thus the text was proclaimed in the Flemish towns as well. Two years later, in 1515 Charles V was installed as the ruler. He first tried to make an approach to France, but from 1521 onwards war with this kingdom was inevitable. In 1525 the French King Francis I was imprisoned and forced to sign the

---

[9] W.P. Blockmans, 'Autocratie ou polyarchie? La lutte pour le pouvoir politique en Flandre de 1482 à 1492, d'après des documents inédits', *Bulletin de la Commission royale d'histoire*, 140 (1974), pp. 257-368; Idem, 'La position du comté de Flandre dans le royaume à la fin du XVe siècle', in: B. Chevalier & P. Contamine (ed.), *La France de la fin du XVe siècle; renouveau et apogée. Economie – Pouvoirs – Arts – Culture et conscience nationales. (Tours. Centre d'Etudes Supérieures de la Renaissance 3-6 octobre 1983)*, Centre National des Recherches Scientifiques (Paris, 1985), pp. 71-89; R. Van Uytven, 'Crisis als cesuur 1482-1494', in: *Algemene geschiedenis der Nederlanden*, 5 (1980), pp. 420-435.

'Peace of Madrid' in January 1526 in which he resigned his position as sovereign lord of Flanders. However, when he was released, the war started all over again, until the 'Peace of Cambrai', or 'Ladies' Peace' (6 August 1529), confirmed the renunciation of the French claims on Flanders. Therefore, this treaty had to be proclaimed in the entire realm. In the following years Charles V and Francis I mainly fought over Milan, and the two treaties that were concluded about this duchy were also published in Flemish towns: the 'Peace of Nice'(1538) and the 'Peace of Crépy' (1544).[10]

From 1450 onwards, but especially after 1482, a great number of peace-treaties were issued in Flanders. These treaties concerned both peace-agreements between the ruler and a particular town, and those concluded between two rulers, one of which usually was the French king. It was often stipulated that the towns of Flanders had to confirm the text or that the treaty had to be proclaimed there. Moreover, the ruler issued special orders for the publication of a certain treaty in which he often described how the proclamation had to be performed.[11] During a rebellion the towns could also decide to have a text published, as was the case with the 'Treaty of Arras' (1482) in 1488. But how were these publications staged and celebrated?

Peace-Treaties as Symbolic Objects: The Solemn Proclamation Ceremony

In the past, rituals and written documents were often considered as two opposites. Either a matter was dealt with in writing or a ritual was performed. Recently, it has been argued that in the Middle Ages written and symbolic communication were often combined. Charters and privileges were issued, read and destroyed in a ritual setting. During official proclamations sounds, colours and gestures completed the written word and legitimized its importance. Moreover, the documents themselves often functioned as symbolic objects, as visual signs of power.[12] The solemn

---

[10] W.P. Blockmans & J. Van Herwaarden, 'De Nederlanden van 1493 tot 1555: binnenlandse en buitenlandse politiek', in: *Algemene geschiedenis der Nederlanden*, vol. 5 (1980), pp. 443-492; W.P. Blockmans, *Keizer Karel V: de utopie van het keizerschap* (Louvain, 2000).

[11] E.g. E. Gailliard, 'De processiën generaal en de 'hallegeboden' te Brugge', *Verslagen en mededeelingen der Koninklijke Vlaamse Academie voor Taal- en Letterkunde* (1912), p. 1162; L. Pée, 'Vande processien ende ommeganghen'. Peiling naar de religieuze en profane elementen in de Dendermondse ommegangen', *Gedenkschriften van de Oudheidkundige kring van het Land van Dendermonde IV*, 18 (1999), p. 21.

[12] M. Clanchy, *From Memory to Written Record* (Oxford, 1979), pp. 205-206; K. Heidecker, 'Introduction', in: K. Heidecker (ed.), *Charters and the Use of the Written*

proclamation of peace-treaties in medieval Flanders illustrates this very well. Usually, this ceremony consisted of two elements: the proclamation organized by the municipality and the obligatory affirmation of support by the inhabitants of the town.

As stated, the audience could not witness the statutory act of the peace-making itself. The municipality of the town, however, could dispose of an important symbol of this political agreement: a copy of the text, with the seals of the parties involved. During the proclamation, this document was shown to the town's inhabitants in a ceremonial setting. Usually, the bailiff of the town had to proclaim the text; however in some instances, the publication was performed by a herald or a high official from the ruler.[13] When the original document was not formulated in the town's mother tongue, a translation of the treaty was read afterwards, so that all subjects would understand its contents. Official witnesses were to be seen surrounding the document. First of all the members of the town's municipality had to publicly support the text. Moreover, representatives of the parties involved could be present, thus re-staging the event of the peace.[14] Both groups of official witnesses had to grant the document credibility and legitimacy. These proclamations were staged in an impressive architectural setting. Important political buildings, like the town hall or the belfry were used for this purpose. These settings communicated the power

---

Word in Medieval Society, Utrecht Studies in Medieval Literacy (Utrecht, 1999), pp. 11-12; J. Rauschert, 'Gelöchert und befleckt. Inszenierung und Gebrauch städtischer Rechtstexte und spätmittelalterliche Öffentlichkeit', in: *Text als Realie. Internationaler Kongress Krems an der Donau 3. bis 6. Oktober 2000*, Österreichische Akademie der Wissenschaften. Philosophisch-historische Klasse. Sitzungsberichte, vol. 704. Veröffentlichungen des Instituts für Realienkunde des Mittelalters und der frühen Neuzeit, vol. 18 (Vienna, 2003), pp. 163-181; J. van Leeuwen, 'Rebels, Texts and Triumph. The Use of Written Documents during the Revolt of 1477 in Bruges', in: M. Mostert & P. Schulte (eds.), *Trust in Writing. Papers from the Fifth Utrecht Symposium on Medieval Literacy, Organized by the Pionier Project Verschriftelijking in Collaboration with the Historisches Seminar der Universität zu Köln, Utrecht, 28-29 November 2002*, Utrecht Studies in Medieval Literacy (Turnhout, 2005).

[13] E.g. in 1485 the chancellor of Brabant proclaimed a peace-treaty in Bruges: Nicolaes Despars, *Cronijcke van den lande ende graefscepe van Vlaenderen van de jaeren 405 tot 1492*, J. De Jonghe (ed.), 4 vols. (Bruges, 1837-1840), vol. 4, p. 262. A herald of the English king was in Bruges to proclaim a treaty in 1489: *Het boeck van al 't gene datter geschiedt is binnen Brugghe sichtent jaer 1477, 14 februarii tot 1491*, C. Carton (ed.), Maetschappy der Vlaemsche bibliophilen, Third series, vol. 2 (Ghent, 1859), pp. 269-270 and a herald of the French king travelled through Flanders in 1488 to proclaim the 'Treaty of Arras' from 1482: Filips Wielant, *Les antiquités de Flandre de Philippe Wielant*, J.J. De Smet (ed.), Commission royale d'Histoire, First series in -4°. Corpus chronicorum Flandriae, vol. 4 (Brussels, 1865), p. 331.

[14] E.g. in Bruges, on 5 December 1489, representatives of the French king were present during the proclamation of the 'Peace of Tours': Despars, *Chronijke*, vol. 4, p. 445.

of the town and were often decorated especially for the event. Tapestries, torches and candles were used to focus the visual attention of the audience on the proclamation. Auditive means were also employed to emphasize the solemnity of the event. The sounding of trumpets and the pealing of bells announced that a proclamation would take place.[15] Sometimes, coins were distributed amongst the audience, so that the spectators would remember the event afterwards.[16] The proclamation was an important event, since it made the peace-treaties binding in a political sense, for the rulers as well as for the subjects.[17]

The second element of the ceremony was the imposed affirmation of support from the inhabitants.[18] Usually, one or more days after the proclamation, general processions and masses were organized to praise God for the peace that had been established. In some years, the citizens were also incited to participate more actively in symbolic competitions. After dark, a bonfire competition transformed the town into a festive space.[19] The spectators could watch this spectacular illumination, while enjoying the free wine and beer offered by the municipality. Moreover, theatre companies competed on the central market square and entertained the inhabitants with farces and allegorical plays celebrating the peace. Often, the municipality rewarded a prize to the best performance. As a result of these additional festivities, the ceremonial peace-proclamation was prolonged with several hours or even several days and all the subjects were incited to participate in the festive atmosphere.

The Contribution of Religious Institutions to the Peace-Celebrations

The Statutory Act of the Proclamation

Peace-celebrations in medieval Flemish towns involved the use of a document as a symbolic object. The subjects were gathered on a central location to hear the contents of the peace. In this process the charter was shown to them in a splendid setting, and official witnesses publicly supported the text.

---

[15] E.g. in Bruges, on 6 December 1489: *Boeck*, pp. 317-321.
[16] Mentioned in Bruges in 1488: Despars, *Chronijke*, vol. 4, p. 262; *Boeck*, pp. 222-225.
[17] Blockmans & Donckers, 'Self-Representation', p. 87.
[18] *Ibidem*, p. 88.
[19] E.g. on several occasions in Tielt: A.L. De Vlaminck, *Jaerboeken der aloude kamer van rhetorika, het roosjen, onder kenspreuk: ghebloeyt int wilde, te Thielt* (Ghent, 1862), pp. 48-49 and 53.

Usually, religious institutions were not so much involved in these political aspects of the peace-festivities. During the official proclamation the local clergy were not present as official witnesses surrounding the document. Indeed, they were not urged to express their support of the text during the solemn proclamation. In Bruges in 1489 the Bishop of Paris and the Abbot of Saint Denis attended the publication of the 'Treaty of Montil-lez-Tours' as ambassadors of the French king.[20] Thus, their assistance served to visualize one of the parties involved and was not intended to grant the ceremony a sacral dimension.

In the medieval town, churches often functioned as communication centres where important news was announced and gossip was spread. Public regulations were often proclaimed or posted in the parish church. However, in most cases the proclamation of a peace-treaty was situated in a civic setting, like the town hall, the belfry or another building that was commonly used for official proclamations. These politically important locations were richly decorated with symbols of the power of the urban and 'national' authorities; they were authoritative spaces that could only be used by competent persons.[21] The peace-treaty was shown in this framework to enhance its legitimacy and credibility. Therefore, the symbolic impact of these buildings cannot be underestimated. The only exceptions to this rule can be found in late medieval Ghent. In 1482 the 'Treaty of Arras' was concluded on 23 December and the news reached Ghent on Christmas Eve. Therefore, the town's aldermen decided to have the text proclaimed in every church during the Christmas service. This measure seems to have been mainly inspired by practical purposes, since it was a means to reach the entire population on this festive night. The next day, the text was officially published at the town hall.[22] In 1492 a mass

---

[20] Bruges, 5 December 1489: Despars, *Chronijke*, vol. 4, p. 45; *Boeck*, p. 317; Gilliodts-Van Severen, *Inventaire des archives de la ville de Bruges. section première, inventaire des chartres*. 9 vols., Archives de la ville de Bruges (Bruges, 1878-1885), vol. 6, p. 336.

[21] About Flemish town halls and belfries: R. Van Uytven, 'Flämische Belfriede und südniederländische städtische Bauwerke im Mittelalter: Symbol und Mythos', in: A. Haverkamp & E. Müller-Luckner (eds.) *Information, Kommunikation und Selbstdarstellung in mittelalterlichen Gemeinden* (Munich, 1998), pp. 125-159; P. Stabel, 'The Market-Place and Civic Identity in Late Medieval Flanders', in: M. Boone & P. Stabel (eds.), *Shaping Urban Identity in Late Medieval Europe – L'apparition d'une identité urbaine dans l'Europe du bas moyen âge,* Studies in Urban Social, Economic and Political History of the Medieval and Early Modern Low Countries, vol. 11 (Louvain / Apeldoorn, 2000), pp. 43-64.

[22] *Dagboek van Gent van 1447 tot 1470 met een vervolg van 1477 tot 1515*, V. Fris (ed.), Maatschappy der Vlaamsche Bibliophilen, Fourth series, vol. 12, 2 vols. (Ghent, 1901-1904), vol. 2, p. 258.

was organized in the church of St Nicolas, and according to a Ghent chronicler the 'Treaty of Cadzand' was published there before the departure of the procession celebrating this event.[23] Possibly, this was an additional proclamation too, since on other occasions peace-treaties were published from a window of the town hall or from the *Tooghuis*, the public bay window on the Vrijdagmarkt.[24] A supplementary publication at a sacral space was probably staged to confirm the importance of the document and to reach as many people as possible.

The accounts of many Flemish towns demonstrate that local churches were paid to ring their bells to celebrate the peace. Instead of the communal bell of the town, the big bell of the local parish was rung 'in praise of God and the peace'.[25] In Furnes, the time bell was rung, while in Grammont, all the bells of the local parish were rung.[26] It is not always very clear when this took place: was the bell also rung during the proclamation of the text? Town accounts from sixteenth-century Audenarde suggest so, since they state that the bell was rung on the day of the proclamation as well as during the procession.[27] Thus, the sound of the church bells might have called upon the inhabitants to witness the publication. However, the chiming of the church bells is more likely to be explained as a means to involve the entire population of the town so that these subjects would affirm their support. Often, not only the main parish was asked to ring its bells, but other churches, chapels and monasteries in the town had to contribute as well. When the 'Peace of Péronne' was proclaimed in Ghent in 1468 the bells of the four main parish churches, the comital collegiate church, and the parish churches of the main abbeys were rung.[28] In Bruges in 1491 it is explicitly mentioned that the seven

---

[23] *Dagboek*, vol. 2, p. 271.

[24] E.g. in 1489 on the *Vrijdagmarkt* (Friday Market): *Dagboek*, vol. 2, p. 266. About the *Tooghuis*, see: Arnade, *Realms of Ritual*, pp. 47-48.

[25] Several examples can be found in: A. Viaene, 'Luiden en beiaarden met kerkklokken in oud-Vlaanderen', *Biekorf*, 69 (1968), pp. 65-75. In Tielt, bell-ringers were paid for the proclamation of peace-treaties in 1508 and 1529: F. Hollevoet, *Stadsrekeningen Tielt: 1500-1610*, Historische bronnen – De roede van Thielt (Tielt, 2000), p. 47 and 75; Furnes, 1453: F. De Potter, F. Ronse & P. Borre, *Geschiedenis der stad en kastelnij van Veurne*. 2 vols. (Ghent, 1873-1875), vol. 1, p. 176.

[26] Furnes: De Potter, Ronse & Borre, *Geschiedenis*, p. 176; Grammont: V. Fris, *Uittreksels uit de stadsrekeningen van Geeraardsbergen van 1475 tot 1658* (Ghent, 1912), p. 50.

[27] L. Van Lerberghe & J. Ronsse, *Audenaerdsche Mengelingen*, vol. 6 (Audenarde, 1854), p. 296.

[28] 'Item ghegheven ten beveelne van scepenen den beyaerders van den keerken binnen Ghend ter causen van dat zij beyaerdden bi laste van scepenen vorn. omme de vors. blijde tijdinghe vanden paeyse tusschen den coninc ende onsen harden gheduchten heere ende prinche te wetene van den kerken van st Jans, van st Michiels, sente Niclaus ende van sente

parish churches and the four mendicant orders rang their bells all day through and even until midnight.[29] One year earlier, in 1490, the bells of all the churches were rung until ten p.m.[30] The auditive setting of the peace-proclamation thus lasted longer than the actual publication and this prolonged the festive atmosphere. This very strong sound was used to mark the ritual time of the event since it clearly excluded the peace-proclamation from everyday life. Thus, each inhabitant of the town was almost automatically involved.

The Affirmation of Support

A second series of symbolic events that took place in the context of a peace-proclamation can be labelled as means to encourage the inhabitants of the town to express their support. During or shortly after the proclamation of the peace the town's municipality announced further activities. They invited the citizens to join a procession and awarded prizes for bonfires and theatre competitions. These festivities usually took place one or more days after the actual proclamation, thus prolonging the event.

In several towns, a Holy Mass was celebrated in order to praise the Lord for the peace that had been achieved. Such services seem to have been quite solemn. In 1453 the accounts of Damme mention that the choir sang and that the organ played to celebrate the 'Treaty of Gavere'. During a mass in Audenarde in 1544 singers of the local parish as well as singers employed by a local noble family performed.[31] On 7 April 1489 a treaty between England and Flanders was proclaimed from the belfry of Bruges. After this publication all the official witnesses of the event formed a *cortège* and went to St Donatian's church, where a *Te deum* was sung.[32] In other towns, we find evidence that the inhabitants were

---

Jacops met sente Verhilden elken 12 g die van shelichs kerst, van st Pieters ende Eckerghem elken 8 g den vors 18^{en} dach van octobre anno 68': Ghent, Municipal Archives, Town Accounts, 400: 22, fol. 81 r°. In January 1483, the bells of the main churches in town were chimed as well: 'Item betaelt ten bevele van scepenen den beyaerders van den prochiekercken ende andre kercke van deser stede over haerlider moite ende aerbeit int luden doe de tydinghe commen was van den payse van Vranckrijcke': Ghent, Municipal Archives, Town Accounts, 400: 28, fol. 136 r°.

[29] *Boeck*, p. 418.
[30] *Ibidem*, p. 408.
[31] Damme, 1453: E. Vander Straeten, *Le théatre villageois en Flandre. Histoire, littérature, religion politique, moeurs*, 2 vols. (Brussels, 1881), p. 33; Audenarde, 1544: L. Van Lerberghe & J. Ronsse, *Audenaerdsche Mengelingen*, vol. 6, p. 295.
[32] *Boeck*, p. 270.

also asked to attend mass. In sixteenth-century Audenarde a prize was awarded for the guild that would enter mass in the most festive way, representing the patron saints of their community accompanied by virgins and angels.[33] During these services sermons were preached to praise God for the peace. In Ghent in 1482 the sermons during the celebrations of Christmas Eve explicitly mentioned the recently achieved Peace of Arras.[34] Moreover, the town accounts demonstrate that the municipality could also pay for sermons to be delivered in the town or in the procession. In smaller towns, often just one preacher was paid,[35] while in Bruges and Ypres two or even four friars were rewarded for writing and preaching sermons, mainly during the procession.[36]

As stated above, the municipalities often awarded prizes for the most impressive bonfire or the best play that was performed during the peace-celebrations. By organizing these spectacles, the municipality wished to expand the festivities. Moreover, they wished to urge the inhabitants of the different neighbourhoods to participate. Religious institutions usually did not enter these competitions; however, the theatre plays and fires could be staged at their doorstep. Only in Furnes, in 1453, it is mentioned that the *scholaster* and the pupils of the St Walburga chapter built a stage and performed comic plays during the celebration of the peace.[37] After the proclamation of the 'Treaty of Senlis' in 1493 the municipality of Wervicq rewarded a prize for the best play that was performed during the celebrations. The first prize was a statue of St Medard, the patron of the local parish. Rhetoricians from several Flemish towns competed and they were asked to hand in their texts beforehand. Three monks, a Dominican, a Carthusian and an Augustinian, were invited to judge the competition.[38] In Bruges, we sometimes find that religious buildings were illuminated at night. In 1491 the seven parish churches, the convents of the four

---

[33] Ouvry, 'Officieel ceremonieel', p. 40.
[34] *Dagboek*, vol. 2, p. 258.
[35] Damme 1453: Vander Straeten, *Le théatre villageois*, p. 33.
[36] Ypres 1453: 'Den eersten dach in ougst den predicanten die predecten over den pays in de generaele processie': Brussels, General Archives, Chamber of Accounts, 38677, fol. 33 v°; 1488: 'den 18sten dach van der voors. maend den predicanten van den frere-mineuren ter processie generale viere cannen wijns': Brussels, General Archives, Chamber of Accounts, 38712, fol. 73 v°. Bruges 1483: two sermons: Gilliodts-Van Severen, *Inventaire*, vol. 6, p. 336; 1489: four sermons: *Ibidem*, pp. 335-336; 1488: two sermons: 'Item betaelt 8 in decembre meesters Pieter Muelere ende Joos van Assele ter causen van twee sermoenen bij hemlieden ghedaen in eenre processie generael ghedreghen tsinte Donaes ter blijscepe van den payse': Bruges, Municipal Archives, *Town Accounts*, 1490-1491, fol. 62 v°.
[37] De Potter, Ronse & Borre, *Geschiedenis*, p. 176.
[38] Van Bruaene, *Om beters wille*.

mendicant orders and all the other chapels and churches that rang their bells were also illuminated by torches.[39] Two years earlier, a large bonfire was lit in front of the church of St Walburga, which was decorated with a red cloth. Apparently, this illumination was not a religious initiative, but was part of a larger illumination of the district in which this church was situated. In earlier years, large bonfire festivities in specific districts were organized as well, but then no visual stress was laid on a religious building.[40] The illumination of the town by night was a very powerful means to underline the exceptional nature of the event. Since massive illumination was quite expensive, this was reserved for very special occasions. In fact, candles and torches referred to liturgical symbolism and were employed by rulers to underline the divine approval of their power.[41] Thus, the public illumination of the town might have had some sacral dimensions as well.

In the context of peace-celebrations, the town's aldermen could decide to organize a banquet. Usually, the municipality invited the bailiff and the local elite to a glass of wine, some sweets or a meal. When a herald of the ruler or other ambassadors were present, they were invited to an impressive banquet in the town hall. The town governors often entertained them with plays and fools and sent them sweets or precious gifts in order to promote good relations between the town and the higher authorities.[42] In some smaller towns, it is mentioned that religious authorities attended these festivities as well. In sixteenth-century Thielt, for example, the municipality invited the clergymen of the town to a meal. Together they watched the bonfires and the plays that were performed.[43] In Grammont, the municipality invited the prior and the provost of the local Benedictine convent to pledge themselves to the peace.[44] In Bruges, the aldermen did not invite the clergy to the banquet, but they donated casks of wine to all the monasteries in the town and its vicinity. The town accounts formulate the motivation behind this gift in terms of a form of charity in order to praise God for the

---

[39] *Boeck*, p. 418.
[40] *Ibidem*, p. 321.
[41] E. Lecuppre-Desjardin, 'Les lumières de la ville: recherche sur l'utilisation de la lumière dans les cérémonies bourguignonnes (XIVe-XVe siècles)', *Revue historique*, 301 (1999), pp. 23-43.
[42] E.g. in Bruges in 1483, representatives of the French king received falcons: Gilliodts-Van Severen, *Inventaire*, vol. 6, p. 231.
[43] 1507: Hollevoet, *Stadsrekeningen*, p. 60 and A.L. De Vlaminck, *Jaerboeken*, p. 60.
[44] Fris, *Uittreksels*, p. 50.
[45] 1489: 'Betaelt van den coope van eene pype wyns ... de welke ter eeren van Gode ende den blyden payse ghedeelt ende ghegheven was den cloosteren ende oordenen van

peace.⁴⁵ The same motivation was given for the custom of distributing bread, meat and wine amongst the town's poor in the context of peace-celebrations, as was the case in fifteenth-century Damme and sixteenth-century Kaprijke.⁴⁶

In all the towns we studied, a general procession was organized during the celebration of the peace. This procession was not a spontaneous initiative of the religious institutions, but imposed by the municipality or the count. The ruler often cited three reasons for this. First, the procession had to express the gratitude for the peace that was established; secondly, the town had to pray that the treaty would be observed in the future; and thirdly, the subjects were asked to plead that the ruler would stay in good health. Often, the municipality added a fourth intention and stated that the procession should also pray that the town would be free of disease and hunger.⁴⁷

Usually, these processions were ordered to start before noon and in some cases they did not leave the religious building. In Bruges in 1514, the procession stayed in St Donatian's church.⁴⁸ And in 1538 the aldermen of Audenarde organized a procession in the convent of the Franciscans.⁴⁹ However, in the majority of the ceremonies, the procession was conducted through the main streets of the town. The participants had to assemble in front of a parish church, like St Donatian's in Bruges. In Ypres, however, the procession started at the Dominicans.⁵⁰

---

dezer stede omme gods wille' (Gilliodts-Van Severen, *Inventaire*, vol. 6, p. 336); 1493: 'betaelt van den coope van een vate wyns twelke ter eeren van den almoghenenden god ende den blyden payse ghesonden ende ghepresenteirt was alle den cloostren buuten ende rondomme deser stede' (*Ibidem*, p. 367).

⁴⁶ Damme 1453: Vander Straeten, *Le théatre villageois*, p. 33; Kaprijke: G. Van Keirsbilck, 'Letterkundig leven te Kaprijke in de vijftiende en zestiende eeuw', *Koninklijke soevereine hoofdkamer van retorica 'De Fonteine' te Gent. Jaarboek 1964-1965 (Second series, vols. 6-7)*, p. 17.

⁴⁷ Bruges: Gailliard, 'De processiën generaal', pp. 1163-1168 and 1186-1189; Hüsken, 'Kroniek', p. 244; Ypres: I.L.A. Diegerick, 'Correspondance des magistrats d'Ypres, députés à Gand et à Bruges, pendant les troubles de Flandre sous Maximilien, duc d'Autriche, roi des romains etc.', *Annales de la Société d'émulation pour l'étude de l'histoire et des antiquités de la Flandre*, 13 (1851), pp. 47-170; 14 (1856), pp. 3-142 and 311-393: annex 1, Comments: Brown, 'Civic ritual', p. 293.

⁴⁸ Gailliard, 'De processiën generaal', p. 1164.

⁴⁹ L. Van Lerberghe & J. Ronsse, *Audenaerdsche Mengelingen*, vol. 1 (Audenarde, 1845), p. 39.

⁵⁰ Ypres 1488: Diegerick, 'Correspondance', annex 1; 'in de processie ... ten cloostre van den jacopijnen ghehouden te ... weerdchede van den paeyse': Brussels, General Archives, Chamber of Accounts, 38712, fol. 99 v°.

In Ghent, the procession usually linked two of the main parish churches of the town and often passed the belfry and the town hall.[51] For six processions in Bruges we are able to reconstruct the route that was chosen. These processions always started and ended in the collegiate church of St Donatian. They encompassed a very small area compared with the annual procession of the Holy Blood which followed the fourteenth-century town walls, thus including the whole town. General processions on the occasion of peace-proclamations, on the contrary, barely left the twelfth-century walls of Bruges.[52] Twice, a very small circuit was followed that just included the Castle Square (*Burgplein*) and the market place.[53] The main political buildings, such as the town hall and the belfry, were situated in this area. The collegiate church of St Donatian, which played an important role in the peace-ceremonies, was also situated there. In 1483, 1488 and 1490 a slightly longer circuit was followed, which passed the Franciscan convent.[54] In 1526, however, the procession followed a different route, taking in the trade centre of the town.[55] Usually, the municipality of Bruges ordered that the houses along the route should be decorated with tapestries, statues and flowers.[56] Thus, the political (and commercial) heart of the town was transformed into a festive, ritual space that was blessed during the procession. On all of these occasions, strong political symbols like the belfry, the town hall and the comital collegiate church were included into the route. Like this, emphasis was put on the political importance of the treaty that was being celebrated. Religious blessing and political space reinforced each other and thus legitimized the peace that was concluded.

In the general processions of Audenarde and Termonde, the Blessed Sacrament was paraded.[57] In Thielt, the relics of St Peter were shown, the

---

[51] E.g. in 1488 the inhabitants had to assemble in St Nicholas' church and Mass was sung in St John's: 'Item betaelt Roelant Ghijs trompet van dat hij gheboot dat men draghen zoude generale processie dan of de verghaderinghe werdt tSente Niclaeus ende men zal den dienst doen tsent Jans. Actum 21 mey 88': Ghent, Municipal Archives, Town Accounts, 400: 29, fol. 364 r°. In 1492, the procession departed from St James' church and Mass was sung in St Michael's: *Dagboek*, vol. 2, p. 271.

[52] Brown, 'Civic Ritual', p. 289.

[53] On 7 April 1489 and 6 December 1489: *Boeck*, p. 289 and 317-321.

[54] *Ibidem*, pp. 48-49, 223 and 408.

[55] Gailliard, 'De processiën generaal', pp. 1188-1189.

[56] Bruges 1526: Gailliard, 'De processiën generaal', pp. 1121, 1189; Audenarde: Ramakers, *Spelen en figuren*, p. 145; Ypres: Diegerick, 'Correspondance', annex 1.

[57] Audenarde: Van Lerberghe & Ronsse, *Audenaerdsche Mengelingen*, vol. 1, p. 39; Ramakers, *Spelen en figuren*, p. 145; D.J. Van Der Meersch, 'Kronijk der rederijkamers van Audenaerde', *Belgisch Museum*, 7 (1843), p. 200; Termonde: Pée, 'Vande processien', p. 18.

patron of the town's parish.[58] In Bruges, various relics were carried. In January 1483, the remains of the SS Donatian, Boniface and Eloi were carried in the procession.[59] These relics belonged to the two original parish churches in the town of Bruges, Our Lady's Church and the church of St Saviour and to the chapter of the Bruges castle. By carrying these relics, Bruges' most important parishes – and thus the entire town population – were represented in the procession. In 1489 and 1490, only the relic of St Donatian was paraded.[60] This relic strongly referred to comital power, since the count had donated these relics to the collegiate church he had founded.[61] Only once, the Holy Blood was shown. In May 1488, the Emperor Maximilian and the Three Members of Flanders finally reached peace after three months of rebellion. This treaty was signed in Bruges on 16 May during a solemn ceremony. One day later, the text was proclaimed from the town hall and on 18 May the relic of the Holy Blood was carried through town.[62] Brown has argued that this relic in particular was associated with civic pride and the defence of the town's privileges.[63] Its use in 1488 is therefore no surprise, since the peace achieved in that year recorded the town's victory over the Emperor Maximilian.

Usually, only the local clergy participated in the procession, but the accounts from medieval Furnes mention that the religious members of the collegiate church of St Peter of Lo joined the parade. The same account indicates that it was not just the local aldermen and councillors of Furnes who were involved, as was the case in other towns, but representatives from Nieuport as well.[64] In other towns, the local bench of aldermen, the mayor and the bailiff usually participated in the *cortège* and members of the town's guilds were asked to join.[65] The representatives of the parties that had concluded the peace could also take part in the procession, but this rarely happened. In many towns, singers and

---

[58] Hollevoet, *Stadsrekeningen*, p. 47.
[59] *Boeck*, p. 48-49; Gilliodts-Van Severen, *Inventaire*, vol. 6, p. 231.
[60] *Boeck*, pp. 318-319; Anthonis De Roovere, *Excellente cronijcke van Vlaenderen*, W. Vorsterman (ed.) (Antwerp, 1531) (Antwerp, Municipal Library, KW. 7475), fol. 270 r°; Gilliodts-Van Severen, *Inventaire*, vol. 6, p. 231
[61] Brown, 'Civic ritual', pp. 289-290.
[62] Anthonis De Roovere, *Excellente cronijcke*, fol. 257 v°; *Boeck*, p. 225; Diegerick, 'Correspondance', p. 221.
[63] Brown, 'Civic Ritual', pp. 292-293; Boone, 'Urban Space', p. 632.
[64] In 1492: De Potter & Borre, *Geschiedenis der rederijkerskamer*, pp. 19-20.
[65] E.g. in Audenarde: Ramakers, *Spelen en figuren*, p. 145; Termonde: Pée, 'Vande processien', pp. 18-19.

musicians joined the parade[66] and poor men were paid to carry the torches that flanked the relics.[67] During the processions the *cortège* sometimes paused, and during these intermissions the relics were placed on an altar and all the participants kneeled and worshipped God.[68]

The municipality often emphasized that all inhabitants were obliged to participate. In Ypres for example, it was explicitly ordered that all the taverns in the town had to be closed during the procession.[69] Moreover, the subjects were encouraged to participate more actively. In some towns competitions were organized for mystery plays and *tableaux vivants* in the context of the procession. Mostly, these plays were performed in the parade itself, e.g. in Roulers,[70] Audenarde,[71] Kaprijke,[72] Furnes[73] and possibly Bruges.[74] In fifteenth-century Ypres, silent figures (*stomme figueren*) or *tableaux vivants* had to be performed on the corners of the streets where the procession would pass.[75] It is not always clear which plays were performed. In Ypres, it was stipulated that *personnages* should be shown, either referring explicitly to the peace or just beautiful ones. The guilds and companies that wished to compete had to present themselves in the town hall. There, lots would be drawn to distribute the locations where they had to play.[76] In the Furnes procession on the occasion of the Peace of Senlis (1493), plays were performed as well. According to the town's accounts various 'misterien uuten Bijbele' (mysteries from the Bible) were performed by neighbourhood festive groups. Rhetoricians from the neighbouring town of Nieuport completed the parade with 'historien accorderende den payse' (plays referring to the peace). A local

---

[66] E.g. in Termonde: Pée, 'Vande processien', pp. 18-19; Bruges 1529: Hüsken, 'Politics and Drama', p. 179.

[67] Bruges in 1483 and 1488: Gilliodts-Van Severen, *Inventaire*, vol. 6, p. 231 and 336.

[68] Bruges on 18 May 1488: *Boeck*, p. 225.

[69] The same goes for Audenarde: Ramakers, *Spelen en figuren*, p. 144; Bruges: Gailliard, 'De processiën generaal', p. 1124.

[70] 1538: De Potter, *Schets eener geschiedenis van de stad Roeselare* (Roulers, 1875), p. 129.

[71] Ramakers, *Spelen en figuren*, p. 144; Ouvry, 'Officieel ceremonieel', pp. 41-42.

[72] Van Keirsbilck, 'Letterkundig leven', p. 17.

[73] 1492 and 1493: F. De Potter & P. Borre, *Geschiedenis der rederijkerskamer van Veurne onder kenspreuk: arm in de beurs en van zinnen jong* (Ghent, 1870), pp. 19-20.

[74] Diegerick, 'Correspondance', p. 221.

[75] *Ibidem*, annex 1.

[76] 'de schoonste ende zierlicxte figuren oft personaigen naest metter payse accorderemde ende comparerende': Diegerick, 'Correspondance', annex 1; 'Den title ende gheselscepe vanden groenaerds van ... de scoonste ende chierlicxste stomme figuren ghetoocht thebbene ghelijckende den zelven paeyse voor den upperprijs': Brussels, General Archives, Chamber of Accounts, 38712, fol. 99 v°-100 r°.

priest was paid to supervise these performances.[77] In Audenarde, the rhetoricians composed ballads and refrains for the procession. The surviving texts from 1544 demonstrate that the *tableaux vivants* from the yearly *Corpus Christi* procession were reused in the peace-celebrations.[78]

We can conclude that in most cases the main parish church of the town was involved in the organization of peace-ceremonies. It was often a collegiate church, like in Bruges, Termonde and Furnes. To a lesser extent, the mendicant orders also contributed to the festivities. The other monasteries, churches and chapels could be invited to ring their bells and to have their members join the procession. In the smaller towns, the clergy was also asked to join banquets and theatre-competitions: here, the ties between the political and religious elite seem to have been tighter.

The religious institutions mainly contributed to the second element of the ceremony: the obligatory affirmation of support. Often, their participation was clearly isolated from the political and 'profane' celebrations, as a kind of sacral in-between. The processions and masses were usually organized one or two days after the proclamation, before noon, while bonfire and theatre competitions were organized after dark. However, this separation between religious and profane components was not always strictly adhered to. In 1489, the general procession in Bruges started before the proclamation. When the procession reached the belfry, the relics of St Donatian were rested on an altar, richly adorned with a golden cloth, candles and censers. During this intermission, the peace-treaty was proclaimed in a solemn ceremony, and then the procession continued.[79]

The Appropriation of Sacral Traditions

Recent research has demonstrated that medieval rituals were not irrational routines, but functioned as political instruments applied intentionally to achieve a certain effect. On the one hand, recognizability and repeatability were of major importance. Therefore, the organizer appropriated traditions and customs. On the other hand, he adapted these symbols to the specific context in which they were to be used. Thus, new layers of meaning could be attached to an existing symbol. It was of the utmost importance that the limits of recognizability were not crossed: whenever the balance between tradition and innovation was disturbed,

---

[77] Furnes: De Potter & Borre, *Geschiedenis*, pp. 19-20.
[78] Ouvry, 'Officieel ceremonieel', pp. 41-42; Ramakers, *Spelen en figuren*, p. 151.
[79] *Boeck*, pp. 318-319.

the ritual lost its strength and the legitimacy of the event was seriously questioned.[80]

As we have argued, the peace-ceremonies had a very particular character, since they celebrated something which had taken place elsewhere and earlier. Since the town population could not witness the statutory act of peace-making itself, it was difficult to propagate this treaty. Therefore, the count and the municipality developed a ceremony that would strengthen the town's identification with the peace and involve the inhabitants emotionally in the event.[81] Various traditions were appropriated to enhance the recognizability of the ceremony. Principally, profane festive traditions were employed, mostly inspired by the elaboration of Joyous Entries. During these spectacular feasts, the town was decorated and the local musicians created a joyful atmosphere. In the evening, the municipality organized bonfire and theatre competitions, as was also the case during several peace-celebrations.[82] Moreover, these solemn proclamations were staged in meaningful political spaces, such as the belfry and the town hall, and bore references to other official publications of regulations and banishments from the town's bay window.[83]

Besides these profane traditions, sacral symbols were also appropriated. The contribution of religious institutions was thus not the spontaneous initiative of these churches and convents, but imposed by political power. These religious interventions had to demonstrate divine support for the peace; however, various other reasons stand out to explain why the political authorities employed sacral traditions during the ceremonial peace-proclamations.

First of all, the religious services were rooted in a much older tradition and would thus be recognized by the inhabitants of the town. The ringing of church bells was a very significant means to create a solemn atmosphere. Initially, these bells invited the worshippers to Holy Mass, and thus they referred to divine grace. In the medieval town, they were chimed for many solemn events, like the birth, marriage and death of a ruler, or a military victory. During Joyous Entries, the bells of all the churches,

---

[80] G. Althoff, 'Zur Bedeutung symbolischer Kommunikation für das Verständnis des Mittelalters', *Frühmittelalterliche Studien*, 31 (1997), pp. 370-389; Buc, *The Dangers of Ritual*; G. Koziol, *Begging Pardon and Favor. Ritual and Political Order in Early Medieval France* (London, 1992), p. 296.

[81] Blockmans & Donckers, 'Self-Representation'.

[82] Lecuppre-Desjardin, *La ville*; Arnade, *Realms of Ritual*, pp. 135-142; Hurlbut, *Vive Bourgongne*; Hüsken, 'Politics and Drama'.

[83] Van Uytven, 'Flämische Belfriede', p. 154; Stabel, 'The Market-Place', p. 54; Boone, 'Urban Space', p. 63.

convents and chapels were rung as well.[84] For the same events sermons, masses and general processions were organized.[85] Thus, these sacral traditions were recognized as a festive means of marking the ceremonial time of the event, just as much as the bonfires and the theatre competitions. All these festive events had to exclude the peace-ceremony from everyday life and make it a truly exceptional event.

Secondly, the religious traditions that were appropriated during the peace-celebrations bore strong references to political power. Since political authorities often employed them to propagate their status, new layers of meaning were added to the original sacral core. Municipal authorities quite soon appropriated church bells as a very practical means of communication. Originally, these bells were rung in case of danger or storm and to announce the proclamation of exiles and other regulations. In these instances, the church bells also symbolized the power of the municipality and the communication between the government and the subjects. Only later, town bells were installed in the belfries to serve all these goals, but until the Late Middle Ages several political signals were still communicated with church bells. Thus, in the medieval town the church bells also bore a strong political connotation.[86]

From the fourteenth century onwards, local municipalities became extremely interested in the sacral foundation of their power. In this period, aldermen's chapels were founded to provide the governors with divine inspiration.[87] On festive occasions, like the installation of a new bench of aldermen, masses were organized in the town's main parish church.[88] Moreover, the municipality participated in the yearly processions and organized masses, sermons and general processions in times of crisis.[89]

---

[84] Viaene, 'Luiden en beiaarden'; J.D. Hurlbut, 'Noise in Burgundian Ceremonial Entries', in: C. Davidson, *Material Culture & Medieval Drama*, Early Drama, Art, and Music Monograph Series, vol. 25 (Kalamazoo, 1999), pp. 128-129.

[85] Brown, 'Civic Ritual', pp. 289-90; Gailliard, 'De processien generaal'; Pée, 'Vande processien'; Ouvry, 'Officieel ceremonieel'; Ramakers, *Spelen en figuren*, pp. 143-144.

[86] A. Lehr, *Van paardebel tot speelklok. De geschiedenis van de klokgietkunst in de Lage Landen*, Cultuurgeschiedenis der Lage Landen, vol. 7 (Zaltbommel, 1981), p. 119; A. Haverkamp, "... an die große Glocke hängen'. Über Öffentlichkeit im Mittelalter', *Jahrbuch des Historischen Kollegs*, 16 (1995), p. 72; G. Dohrn-van Rossum, *Die Geschichte der Stunde. Uhren und Moderne Zeitordnung* (Munich, 1992).

[87] U. Heckert, *Die Ratskapelle als religiöses und politisches Zentrum der Ratsherrschaft in den deutschen Städten des späten Mittelalters* (Bielefeld, 1997).

[88] J. van Leeuwen, 'Geluid, muziek en entertainment. Het gebruik van auditieve communicatiemiddelen tijdens het ritueel van de wetsvernieuwing in Gent, Brugge en Ieper (1379-1493)', *Revue belge de philologie et histoire, in press*.

[89] Brown, 'Civic ritual', p. 289; Gailliard, 'De processien generaal', p. 1095; Blockmans & Donckers, 'Self-Representation', p. 84.

From the second half of the fifteenth century onwards, the Burgundian rulers appropriated these traditions for the propaganda of their centralized power. In 1475, Charles the Bold had learned that the French king had organized processions and sermons in which the reputation of Burgundian duke was seriously blackened. Therefore, he urged the Flemish towns to organize a procession and ordered that excellent preachers would be secretly instructed to give the duke high praise and to refer to all the sacrifices he had made for his people.[90] As such, general processions, masses and sermons were clearly employed as means of propaganda for Burgundian power. In the second half of the fifteenth century, the number of processions, masses and sermons for a political purpose increased significantly. These manifestations were closely associated with the duke's needs and ambitions.[91]

It was not just religious traditions that were made to carry references to authorities: religious spaces and objects could also acquire associations with political power. As we have demonstrated, the relics that were paraded during general processions could have referred to the power of the count, or be closely connected with civic pride.[92] Comital chapters in general, and St Donatian's in Bruges in particular, must have generated political associations. The route of the processions in Bruges and possibly in Ghent too clearly outlined the political space in these towns, with references to comital and communal power, and in the sixteenth century to commercial power.

Sacral traditions, spaces and objects were often employed because they suggested the divine approval of comital and civic power. Because of this frequent use, new layers of meaning were added to these religious means, so that they acquired strong associations with authorities and were possibly partly perceived as political symbols. Thus, the sacral traditions could also have enforced the political legitimacy of the peace-treaty. However, this authority was much more strongly propagated by the other media that were employed, like the use of significant political spaces and the presence of official representatives of the town, the count and the parties involved.

In the ceremonial peace-proclamations, the peace-treaty played a central role as a symbolic object. This document was shown and read out loud, possibly accompanied by the sound of pealing church bells. However, the majority of the religious interventions studied here were performed in a second phase of the ceremony. After the proclamation itself, the municipality could announce further celebrations. Then, the

---

[90] Gailliard, 'De processien generaal', p. 1100.
[91] Brown, 'Civic Ritual', p. 289; Blockmans & Donckers, 'Self-Representation', p. 84.
[92] Brown, 'Civic Ritual', pp. 289-293.

more secular elements of the ceremony were interrupted by an interval which was more sacred in nature, since masses, processions and sermons were to take place before noon. In the evening, bonfires and theatre competitions concluded the festivities. By organizing these additional events, the municipality prolonged the ceremony with at least several hours and in some cases a few days. Gradually, the peace-celebrations expanded from one day in the 1450s to more than a week in the seventeenth century.[93] In particular the number of general processions was augmented, since from the end of the fifteenth century onwards it was ordered that these processions had to go out on two or more consecutive days or even that they had to be repeated during several weeks.[94] In this way, the joyous event reverberated and resounded during a longer period of time. During the masses and in the sermons explicit references were made to the peace, preachers probably summarized the contents of the treaty and explained its importance for the town.[95] Moreover, in the procession, *tableaux vivants* could visually represent the peace. Therefore, the religious interventions might have served as a didactic tool to allow the event to be memorized. One or more days after its proclamation, the contents of the treaty were repeated and the subjects were thus reminded that something important had happened. This reiteration clearly had a mnemonic impact, since it helped the inhabitants to remember at least the parties involved and possibly some of the contents of the peace too. Of course, this goal was also achieved by the theatre competitions where it was sometimes explicitly ordered that the plays and farces should refer to the peace.[96]

---

[93] Bruges 1483: four days: *Boeck*, pp. 47-51; 1526: three days: Gailliard, 'De processien generaal', p. 1187. The celebrations organized after the publication of the 'Peace of Munster' (1648) started on 18 March and additional festivities were organized until 4 April: Viaene, 'Bij een drie honderdste verjaring'. However, in 1598, the celebration of the 'Peace of Vervins' took place during just one day: Dewitte, 'Solemniteyten', p. 122.

[94] E.g. in Furnes in 1493, three consecutive days: De Potter & Borre, *Geschiedenis*, p. 20. In Bruges, it was ordered in 1516 that a procession was to be organized every week until further instructions were given: Gailliard, 'De processien generaal', p. 1168. In the seventeenth century, the procession could be left out: Viaene, 'Bij een drie honderdste verjaring', p. 162. The theatre competitions could also be spread over several weeks, e.g. in Bruges after the proclamation of the 'Peace of Senlis' on 4 July, it was ordered that plays should be performed every Sunday until 1 September: Hüsken, 'Politics and Drama', p. 181; Gilliodts-Van Severen, *Inventaire*, vol. 6, p. 367.

[95] This is explicitly mentioned in the town accounts of Ypres in 1453: 'Den eersten dach in ougst den predicanten die predecten over den pays in de generaele processie': Brussels, General Archives, Chamber of Accounts, 38677, fol. 33 v°.

[96] Hüsken, 'Politics and Drama', pp. 172-175; Idem, 'Kroniek', pp. 236-251; Ramakers, *Spelen en figuren*, pp. 150-152.

The main goal of the ceremonial peace-proclamations was to make sure that the town's population felt emotionally involved. As we have emphasized earlier, the peace-celebrations were the initiative of the ruler and the municipality, and it was not likely that the subjects would express their support spontaneously. Therefore, they were encouraged to participate. First of all, the inhabitants were expected to function as the audience for the proclamation. The chiming of church bells might have called upon the subjects to witness the publication. However, the inhabitants were also expected to participate more actively in the celebrations and express their solemn consensus. The municipality, for instance, obliged them to watch the general processions and even attend the masses. Sometimes prizes were rewarded for performances in the *cortège* or at the corners of the streets where the parade should pass. Such symbolic competitions fulfilled a very important role in the celebrations. The various social groups in the town were visible, but their internal differences were conducted in the service of the state power. Thus, an ideal image of a harmonious community was shown. By appealing to the pride of each segment, a peaceful competition had to heighten the sense of unity in the town.[97]

Indeed, during the peace-ceremonies the social order in the town had to be demonstrated. The sacred segments of the town were, for example, represented in the chiming of the bells and in the relics that were paraded. Traditionally, processions demonstrated the social hierarchy and harmony in the urban community. In the yearly processions this social coherence was demonstrated in a festive way. During the peace-ceremony, it was communicated on a smaller scale, but the various guilds and segments were still invited to join the parade. Moreover, the procession could also be used to symbolize the restoration of peace and order in town. In 1490, after years of rebellion, Bruges finally concluded peace with the Emperor Maximilian. Two days after the proclamation, a general procession was organized. In the parade, the relics of St Donatian were shown. The procession started in St Donatian's church and reached the marketplace. There, in front of the belfry, it met the guilds and crafts of the town. The members of these social segments had been lining the streets for eleven days demanding peace. No banners were on display, but the patricians

---

[97] This is, of course, also true for the theatre and bonfire competitions in the towns: Van Bruaene, *Om beters wille*; Arnade, *Realms of Ritual*, pp. 138 and 142; Blockmans & Donckers, 'Self-Representation', pp. 90-91; E. Lecuppre-Desjardin, 'Un modèle de scénographie urbaine: l'exemple des Pays-Bas bourguignons au XVe siècle', *Revue du Nord*, 81 (1999), p. 685.

carried the flag of the Count of Flanders. When the procession reached this assembly, this flag was lifted and carried along in the procession, all the guilds and crafts then followed the parade into the Donatian's church.[98] Thus came a symbolic end to the occupation of the market place and was the peace in town restored.

During ceremonial peace proclamations, sacral traditions were appropriated because they suggested divine support of the achieved peace. Moreover, other layers of meaning were added to this sacral core. Processions, masses and the chiming of church bells were recognizable as festive means and had acquired strong associations with political power. These traditions could serve as didactic tools to memorize the peace and were employed to symbolize social harmony and communal consensus. Many of these functions cannot be linked exclusively to the religious traditions, but these interventions must be understood within the larger framework of the peace-ceremonies as a whole.

Conclusion

Between 1450 and 1550, Flanders became part of a larger central state. The Burgundian dukes and the Habsburg emperors employed the proclamation of peace-treaties as a means to propagate their power. On the other hand, rebellious towns could also proclaim peace-treaties on their behalf. These peace-celebrations offer a very particular communicative situation, since the inhabitants of the town did not witness the actual peace-making itself, but were informed about an event that had taken place elsewhere and earlier. Thus, the municipality had to do its utmost to convince the subjects of the importance of the treaty and to demonstrate its legitimacy. In this contribution, we have analyzed how religious institutions contributed to these festivities and which sacral traditions were appropriated for this purpose.

In most cases, the peace-ceremony consisted of two elements: the proclamation of the treaty and the obligatory affirmation of support from the inhabitants of the town. Religious events, like masses, processions and sermons, which were conducted on these occasions, often functioned as a kind of sacred interval that was preceded and followed by political events. Religious space was only seldom used for the proclamation and religious institutions were usually not involved in the bonfire and theatre competitions which were organized by the municipality.

---

[98] *Boeck*, pp. 408-409.

However, this does not imply that the religious elements just communicated the divine support of the peace. On the contrary, additional layers of meaning were added to the sacral core of the tradition. Processions, relics, masses and sermons were recognized as festive means marking the ceremonial time of the event. Moreover, these traditions had acquired associations with political power and were employed to demonstrate the (restored) social order. Finally, they functioned as a didactic tool to reinforce the process of memorizing the peace.

These additional layers of meaning explain why a sacral tradition was appropriated, but they cannot be linked exclusively to the religious events used on these occasions. The use of profane spaces, the sound of communal bells and trumpets, the participation of authorities and the organization of various competitions were employed for the same purposes. Thus, we cannot truly separate the religious services from the political context. Their meaning and use were integrated in an elaborate communication-strategy which was applied to stress the importance of the peace.[99]

Katholieke Universiteit Leuven

---

[99] I would like to thank dr. Andrew Brown and dr. Sheila Sweetinburgh for their help in correcting the English text. In am also greatly obliged to the Bijzonder Onderzoeksfonds of the K.U.Leuven for giving me the opportunity to write this essay.

Brigitte DEKEYZER

FOR ETERNAL GLORY AND REMEMBRANCE: ON THE REPRESENTATION OF PATRONS IN LATE MEDIEVAL PANEL PAINTINGS IN THE SOUTHERN LOW COUNTRIES

'In the great works of art of the fifteenth century, notably in the altarpieces and tombs, the nature of the subject was far more important than the question of beauty. Beauty was required because the subject was sacred or because the work was destined for some august purpose. This purpose is always of a more or less practical sort. The triptych served to intensify worship at the great festivals and to preserve the memory of the pious donors. The altar-piece of the Lamb by the brothers Van Eyck was opened at high festivals only'.[1] Joos Vijd and Elisabeth Borluut are portrayed kneeling on the outer panels of the *Adoration of the Lamb* by Van Eyck (Ghent, St Bavo's Cathedral), in the hope of indeed eventually being assumed into the heavenly realm revealed by the inner panels of the polyptych. On the one hand, the portraits express the religious expectations and the patrons' concern for their salvation – in one sense, they hope in this way to purchase their soul's repose – while on the other, these are status symbols and commemorative representations through which the worldly figures will remain visible as family members for their descendants.

A nice example of such multiple intentions is offered by the *Madonna with Canon Van der Paele* by Jan van Eyck (Bruges, Groeningemuseum).[2] On the one hand, the patron attempts, through the work of art, to assure his salvation and his memory, while on the other, he establishes his prestige in relation to the chapter of which he was a member. In 1434,

---

[1] See J. Huizinga, *The Waning of the Middle Ages: a Study of the Forms of Life, Thought and Art in France and the Netherlands in the XIVth and XVth Centuries*, F. Hopman (transl.) (London, 1972), p. 234.

[2] W.H.J. Weale, 'Inventaires du trésor de la collégiale de Saint Donatien à Bruges, 1347-1539', *Le Beffroi*, 2 (1864-65), pp. 9-30, 104-138, esp. pp. 28-29, no. 31; A. Janssens de Bisthoven, *Stedelijk Museum voor Schone Kunsten (Groeningemuseum) Bruges, vol. 1: De Vlaamse Primitieven*, Corpus van de vijftiende-eeuwse schilderkunst in de Zuidelijke Nederlanden, vol. 1, 2nd rev. ed., (Brussels, 1981²), pp. 194-233; M.P.J. Martens, 'Het onderzoek naar de opdrachtgevers', in: B. Ridderbos & H. Van Veen (eds.), *'Om iets te weten van oude meesters'. De Vlaamse Primitieven – herontdekking, waardering en onderzoek* (Heerlen, 1995), pp. 349-393, esp. pp. 378-381.

Joris van der Paele instituted the first chaplaincy at the altar of St Peter and St Paul in the southern aisle of the church of St Donatian in Bruges. The foundation consisted of three weekly masses, the sprinkling of the patron's tomb with holy water and the reading of the *Miserere Mei* and the *De profundis* after every mass. In 1440, he provided additional funds for the celebration of an annual Requiem Mass. Three years later, he instituted a second chaplaincy entailing four additional masses. He also donated a great number of precious items to the chapel for the celebration of all these masses. In this way, Van der Paele ensured that a mass for his salvation would be read daily and that his tombstone would be sprinkled with holy water. The crowning achievement of all these institutions was the commissioning of the painting by Jan van Eyck. This would also establish Van der Paele as a pious patron in the eyes of his descendants and the portrait would preserve his memory. As Maximiliaan Maartens points out, 'it is true that by investing in foundations the interests of the chapter were well served, but he himself also profited from this: the chaplains would pray for his soul in perpetuity. Moreover, he would be commemorated, not leastwise through the presence of his portrait in the painting. All of this reveals the foundation as a carefully considered and rationally planned investment'.[3] A similar 'ambition' is evident in the act of institution of the *Last Judgement* (Beaune, *Hôtel-Dieu*) (between 1443 and 1451) by Rogier van der Weyden, in which the patron, chancellor Rolin, explicitly declares himself to be acting in the interest of his salvation, 'in the hope of making the felicitous transaction whereby my worldly goods, received through God's goodness, are exchanged for heavenly riches, thus making the ephemeral permanent'.[4]

The aim of this article is not to reveal in more detail the multiple functions of commemorative works intended for religious and thus public spaces, but rather to explore whether, how and why the representation of the patron in works of art commissioned by secular patrons (high officials, the affluent bourgeoisie and members of confraternities) evolved in the course of the fifteenth century. In the selection of the works, I have taken as my point of departure the categories of commemorative works distinguished by Truus van Buren – in turn a reworking of Otto Oexle's article *Memoria und Memo-*

[3] Martens, 'Het onderzoek', p. 381.
[4] S.N. Blum, *Early Netherlandish Triptychs: A Study on Patronage* (Berkeley (L. A.), 1969), p. 136. See in this context also Ph. Ariès, *L'homme devant la mort* (Paris, 1977), pp. 271-275; Ph. Lorentz, 'Le chancelier Rolin et Rogier van der Weyden', in: *La bonne étoile des Rolin. Mécénat et efflorescence artistique dans la Bourgogne du XVe siècle*, exh. cat. (Autun, 1994), pp. 43-47.

riabild – in her book *Leven na de dood. Gedenken in de late Middeleeuwen*:[5] (1) 'epitaphs', in which the commemoration of the deceased is central and in which the attention to the salvation of the soul takes precedence; (2) 'family works', in which a married couple, an immediate family or a more extended family is represented in order to emphasize the insolubility of the family ties transcending death itself; (3) 'confraternity-' and 'guild-works', which are found above or next to the altars of the corporations and which, among other things, are intended to ensure the salvation of members of such organisations; (4) 'institution-' and 'donation-works', intended to commemorate an institution or a donation. The fifth group, the 'successors' series', made up of portraits of officials from secular and ecclesiastical institutions who succeeded one another over time, falls outside this categorization, as they are less important for the purposes of the present article (this is essentially a series of paintings and not of independent altarpieces portraying patrons). I shall present the different commemorative works according to their type and look for the presence of an evolution in the representation of the patrons. Naturally, considering the theme of the congress, the choice of works has so far as possible been limited to those intended for churches and for which the identity of the secular patron(s) is known. As a result of this categorization, the number of examples is extremely limited, since there are very few works for which both the secular patron and the intended location is known with certainty.

A second section investigates the iconographic basis for the representation of the secular patron in fifteenth-century panel paintings. This may be found in the older art of book illumination.

I. The Place and Meaning of the Representation of Patrons in South Netherlandish Altarpieces

Type 1: Patrons on the Outer Panels

In the *Triptych of the Last Judgement* by Hans Memling, now preserved in Gdansk in the Muzeum Narodowe (Ill. 1), the patrons are

---

[5] T. van Bueren, *Leven na de dood. Gedenken in de late Middeleeuwen*, exh. cat. (Utrecht, Museum Catharijneconvent) (Turnhout, 1999), pp. 13-14; O.G. Oexle, 'Memoria und Memorialbild', in: K. Schmidt & J. Wollasch (eds.), *Memoria. Der geschichtliche Zeugniswert des liturgischen Gedenkens im Mittelalter*, Münstersche Mittelalter-Schriften, vol. 48 (Munich, 1984), pp. 384-440. See also the critique of this view in P. Trio, 'De dood herleeft. Nieuw onderzoek naar memorievieringen en memorietafels in de late Middeleeuwen ten noorden van de Grote rivieren', *Signum. Tijdschrift van de contactgroep voor sociaal-economische en institutioneel-juridische geschiedenis van geestelijke en kerkelijke instellingen in de Nederlanden in de Middeleeuwen*, 15 (2003), pp. 66-75.

depicted on the outer panels of the triptych.[6] The Florentine Angelo di Jacopo Tani (1415-1492) and his wife Caterina di Francesco Tanangli (1446-1492), kneel praying in front of a niche, in which are depicted respectively the Madonna with Child and St Michael. The patrons' coats of arms hang from the polygonal niche socle. When the triptych is opened, a large representation of the Last Judgement is revealed, with Christ in blood-red vestments dispensing his blessing, surrounded by the intercessors Mary, John the Baptist and the Apostles. Under this appears St Michael in a rigorous vertical composition. He weighs the souls, while angels and devils separate the good from the bad. On the left-hand panel, the blessed are led by St Peter to the gates of heaven, while on the right-hand panel devils cast the evil-doers into damnation.

The exceptionally large triptych (the central panel measures 221 x 161 cm), commissioned by Angelo Tani in 1467, was originally intended for the chapel of St Michael in the church of Badia Fiesolana near Florence, but never arrived at its destination. The pirate Paul Benecke, working for the German Hanseatic League made off with the work close to the Flemish coast at the Zwin, taking it to Gdansk to be placed on the altar of the Guild of St George in the church of Our Lady.

Situated on the outer panels, the patrons are separated from the blessed world shown on the left-hand side of the opened altarpiece. They are not yet part of the realm of the blessed, but through the Virgin and Child together with St Michael they express their hope of eventually being taken up into the sweet hereafter. Angelo directs his gaze clearly towards St Michael, while Caterina looks at the mother and child. The link between the patron and the heavenly sphere for which he yearns is thus not direct, but referential. Separated spatially and visually from paradise, they nonetheless express their desire to dwell in that better world someday.

In the older *Adoration of the Lamb* (Ghent Altarpiece) by Jan van Eyck, intended for the church of St John (the present St Bavo's Cathedral in Ghent) and dated 1432-1435, the procedure is exactly the same. Here too, the patrons, Joos Vijd and Elisabeth Borluut, are shown on the outer panels and are not yet participants in the blessed scene revealed when the panels are opened.[7] And yet there is more going on here than

---

[6] D. De Vos, *Hans Memling, het volledige oeuvre* (Antwerp, 1994), pp. 82-89 (with references to the literature).

[7] R. Van Elslande, 'De geschiedenis van de Vijt-Borluutfundatie en het Lam Gods', *Ghendtsche Tydinghen*, 14, 6 (1984), pp. 342-348; A. Rooch, *Stifterbilder in Flandern und Brabant, Stadtbürgerliche Selbstdarstellung in der sakralen Malerei des 15. Jahrhunderts*, Kunst, Geschichte und Theorie, vol. 9 (Essen, 1988), *passim*.

in the work by Hans Memling, for the Annunciation taking place just above the heads of Joos Vijd and Elisabeth Borluut leaves the future in little doubt: just as the prophets and sibyls that appear in the lunettes above predict the coming of a divine child, so the Annunciation to Mary looks forward to redemption. The two Johns appearing between the patrons function as intercessors. Compared with the *Triptich of the Last Judgement* by Hans Memling (Ill. 1), the link between the outside and inside of the work is more explicit, thus the guarantee of eventual admission into heaven that much greater.

Type 2: Patrons on the Inner, Side Panels

On most altarpieces, however, the patrons are not depicted on the outer panels, but on the inner ones. The way in which they are connected to the central scene differs from panel to panel. The oldest type separates the patron from the realm of the blessed and thus makes a clear distinction between the sacred and secular worlds. An excellent example of this is the *Abegg Triptych* (Riggisberg, Abegg-Stiftung) of 1438-1440, ascribed by some scholars to Rogier van der Weyden (Ill. 2).[8] The patron, very likely the Italian Oberto de Villa, a court official to the Duke of Savoy and a member of the French *orde du Camail* or *du Porc-épic* (note his necklace), is kneeling in an open portico and gazes in devotion at the central scene unfolding before his eyes: the crucifixion of Christ, with the emotional onlookers around him. The panel was probably originally intended for the church of St George in Chieri, which had been completely rebuilt at the expense of the De Villa family. The system of separation used by the artist, where the patron is, as it were, pushed to one side, following the sacred events from a doorway, likely makes its first appearance in a work by Robert Campin, the *Mérode Triptych*, painted around 1422 (New York, The Metropolitan Museum of Art, The Cloisters Collection) (Ill. 3) and in the *Werl panels* of 1438 (Madrid, Museo del Prado), alternatively ascribed to Robert Campin and Rogier van der Weyden. In both works, an open door offers a view of the sacred scene and the patrons are thus brought together on one panel.

In some cases – and these become more common and more widely spread as time goes on – the patrons (if a married couple), often accompanied by their patron saints, are portrayed on both the right- and left-hand panels. This is, for example, the case in the *Triptych of the Dukes*

---

[8] D. De Vos, *Rogier Van der Weyden* (Antwerp, 199), pp. 210-216 (with references to the literature).

of Bourbon (Moulins, Cathedral), painted at the end of the fifteenth century by the Master of Moulins (Ill. 4), with as its model Van der Goes' *Bonkil Altarpiece* (Edinburgh, National Gallery of Scotland).[9] Pierre II of Bourbon and his wife, Anne de France, are shown kneeling on the left and right panels respectively. There is no visual connection with the central scene in which the Madonna with Child appears. The same is true, but less obvious, in the *Portinari Triptych* by Hugo van der Goes (Florence, Galleria degli Uffizi), commissioned by Tommaso Portinari, a representative of the Medici bank in Bruges, and intended for the hospital of Santa Maria Nuova in Florence.[10] On 28 May 1483, the painting arrived in the city and was placed on the high altar of the church of St Giles, which was connected to the hospital. A similar example is the *Moreel Triptych* (Bruges, Groeningemuseum) of 1484 by Hans Memling, painted on a commission for Willem Moreel and intended for the altar of St Maurus and St Giles in St James' church in Bruges (the deed of foundation still exists!).[11] Although the altarpiece does form a visual unity, the transition between the landscapes on the middle panel and on the side panels is not seamless. For example, the little path running behind St William of Malewal, patron saint of the work's commissioner, breaks off at the frame of the left-hand panel and does not appear again on the middle panel.

In other, later compositions, the separation between the patrons and the central scene is abandoned altogether, by allowing the landscape or the row of houses of the central panel to continue from the central panel onto the side panels. The *Baptism of Christ* (Bruges, Groeningemuseum) of 1502-1508 by Gerard David is very interesting in this regard, since by continuing the landscape, the middle and side panels are intimately linked to one another (Ill. 5).[12] David 'achieved continuity among all the three panels by bridging the frame with two small figures pointing from the left wing toward the centre and an arrangement of trees at the right that extends into the central panel. The separation of the wings from the central panel appears to be only an artificial one'.[13] There is a strong visual

---

[9] Ph. Lorentz & A. Regond (eds.), *Jean Hey: le Maitre de Moulins*, exh. cat. (Moulins, 1990); E. Dhanens, *Hugo van der Goes* (Antwerp, 1998), p. 323.

[10] Dhanens, *Hugo van der Goes*, pp. 250-301 (with references to the literature).

[11] De Vos, *Hans Memling*, pp. 238-244, nr. 63 (with references to the literature).

[12] Janssens de Bisthoven, *Stedelijk Museum*, pp. 130-162; H. Van Miegroet, *Gerard David* (Antwerp, 1989), pp. 293-295, cat. nr. 23; M.W. Ainsworth, *Gerard David, Purity of Vision in an Age of Transition* (Amsterdam / New York, 1998), pp. 222-234.

[13] Ainsworth, *Gerard David*, 226.

unity and the spatial separation between the side panels and the middle panel is no longer in evidence. The commissioner, Jan de Trompes, with his son and the patron saint on the left and his wife, Elisabeth van der Meersch, with their four daughters and patron saint on the right, both appear physically present. In this way, the two 'events' (the Baptism and the patrons praying), which of course take place in completely different historical contexts, are temporally linked.[14]

Type 3: Patrons on the Central Inner Panel

a. The 'explicit' portrait[15]

From this point, it is a small step in technical terms to altarpieces in which the patrons are represented on the middle panel.[16] And yet they do not often appear in the central scene – the result of an 'increased respect' for the religious content.[17] The *Triptych with the Crucifixion* (Vienna, Kunsthistorisches Museum) of 1443-1445 by Rogier van der Weyden is one of the exceptions (Ill. 6).[18] Instead of observing the events from the side panels, the patrons kneel at the foot of the cross – the unidentified patron even clearly gazing up at the crucified Christ. There is no difference in scale or in physical stature between the patrons, Christ, Mary and John, and the figures seem to be situated in the same space. And yet, despite their proximity, there is something of a mental and thus visual barrier built in, since the patrons have taken up a position in a crevice in the rocky terrain and are thus in a sense separated from the cross. Didier Martens is thus on the mark when he notes that 'placé dans l'image à une certaine distance des acteurs du drame sacré, il en est, en outre, fréquemment séparé par l'un ou l'autre dispositif formel faisant fonction de bar-

---

[14] The altarpiece was given by the Jan de Trompes family to the Broederschap van de Gezworen Klerken van de Vierschaar in 1520 and placed in their chapel (St Lawrence) in the church of St Basil in Bruges.

[15] The terminology used by Didier Martens: 'Portrait explicite et portrait implicite à la fin du Moyen Âge: l'exemple du Maître de la Légende de sainte Catherine (alias Piérot de le Pasture)', *Jaarboek van het Koninklijk Museum voor Schone Kunsten Antwerpen* (1998), pp. 9-67.

[16] Explicit portraits of patrons placed in the centre of the composition do not occur often in South Netherlandish panel painting. Moreover, the patrons are seldom identified and the intention can no longer be determined. This is also the case for the examples cited.

[17] M. Davies, *Rogier van der Weyden. An Essay, with a Critical Catalogue of Paintings Assigned to Him and to Robert Campin* (Bristol / Venice, 1972), p. 241.

[18] De Vos, *Rogier Van der Weyden*, pp. 234-237, nr. 13 (with references to the literature).

rière symbolique: muret, fossé, prie-Dieu, ébrasement d'une porte ou d'une fenêtre, montants de l'encadrement dans un triptyque ...'[19] The same is true of the *Pietà* (Madrid, Museo del Prado), also by an artist from the entourage of Rogier van der Weyden, in which the patron observes the events from behind a rock.[20] The panel painter Dirk Bouts also makes use of this technique. In his *Ecce Agnus Dei* (Munich, Bayerische Staatsgemäldesammlungen, Alte Pinakothek), a river separates the divine world (Christ) from the world of the patron (a certain Johannes) (Ill. 7).[21] This is less true of the *Bladelin Triptych* of roughly 1445-1448 by Rogier van der Weyden (Berlin, Staatliche Museen zu Berlin, Preussischer Kulturbesitz) probably destined for the church of Middelburg in the Netherlands (Ill. 8).[22] Pieter Bladelin is shown in black, kneeling in devotion and without demonstrable visual separation from the newborn child. At the same time, he is accorded no specific function within the scene. 'En outre, le modèle ne 'voit' pas vraiment la ... scène religieuse qui se déroule devant lui; il a les yeux baissés ..., comme s'il ne contemplait cette scène qu'en esprit'.[23] The viewer continues to see him as a devoted patron who, it is true, has been granted unusually close proximity to the holy space.

b. The 'implicit' portrait or 'le portrait travesti'[24]

In contrast, implicit portraits of patrons are frequently found in South Netherlandish paintings. Unlike the explicit portraits, they portray the patrons in a hidden way. They have a particular function in the panel (appearing, for instance, as one of the Three Kings or as a bystander at the Crucifixion) and do not immediately attract attention to themselves. Only their individualized facial features reveal such representations as portraits.[25] In this way, the artists and their patrons were able to sidestep the Church's reticence to allow historical and (especially) secular figures

---

[19] Martens, 'Portrait explicite', p. 13.
[20] De Vos, *Rogier Van der Weyden*, pp. 370-371, nr. B12 (with references to the literature).
[21] M. Smeyers, *Dirk Bouts, schilder van de stilte* (Louvain, 1998), pp. 91-93.
[22] De Vos, *Rogier Van der Weyden*, pp. 242-248, nr. 15 (with references to the literature).
[23] Martens, 'Portrait explicite', p. 13.
[24] See note 14.
[25] 'De prime abord, le portrait 'implicite' ... passe inaperçu. Dans la majorité des cas, il sera toutefois reconnu comme tel, en raison de l'individualité marquée des traits, une individualité qui, dans les représentations à sujet sacré, tranche sur les physionomies de répertoire des autres figures'. See Martens, 'Portrait explicite', p. 15. On the implicit portrait, see also F.B. Polleross, *Das sakrale Identifikationsporträt. Ein höfischer Bildtypus*

to take an active part in depictions of sacred events.

In the *Columba Altarpiece* by Rogier van der Weyden (Munich, Alte Pinakothek), probably intended for the Columba church in Cologne, both types are combined: a man with a rosary appears on the central panel to the left behind a wall (= the explicit portrait), while to the right stands Charles the Bold in a brilliant gold brocade outfit, 'disguised' as one of the kings honouring Christ (= the implicit portrait) (Ill. 9).[26]

Another well-known example of the implicit portrait is the *Last Supper* by Dirk Bouts, intended for the altar of St Peter in St Peter's church, Louvain (Ill. 10). In contrast with most patrons, the members of the Confraternity of the Sacrament, Raese van Bausele, Laureyse van Wynghe, Reyner Stoep and Stas Roelofs, who took part in the negotiations concerning the *Last Supper*, are not really separated from the rest of the scene, but participate in it. However, as representatives of the Confraternity, they do not reveal their identities. Without the publication of the contract for the *Last Supper* by Edward Van Even in 1898, they would have remained forever anonymous.[27] The same goes for the theologians shown above on the left-hand panel together with the Meeting of Abraham and Melchisedech. In their contemporary clothes – Varenacker in his black robe and the younger Bailluwel in a more cheerful blue garment with a fur collar – they seem in dialogue and almost teaching, as they take in the scene, thus accentuating the initial gesture by Christ. Nevertheless, even in this exceptional painting, there remains a sense of distance between the divine and the fifteenth-century world. Varenacker and Bailluwel are placed in the upper left-hand corner of the triptych and remain detached from the events. In addition, the members of the Confraternity do not truly participate in the meal. Their eyes are cast down or stare blankly. They are present as 'extras' or servants in the room and the adjacent building.

The particular importance attached by the artists to such hidden portraits is very clearly evident in the above-mentioned *Triptych of the Last Judgement* by Hans Memling (Gdansk, Museum Narodowe), which includes not only recognizable portraits of the patrons on the outer pan-

---

vom 13. bis zum 20. Jahrhundert, Manuskripte zur Kunstwissenschaft, vol. 18 (Worms, 1988); E. Heller, *Das altniederländische Stifterbild*, Tuduv Studien. Reihe Kunstwissenschaften, vol. 6 (Munich, 1976), pp. 51-53.

[26] De Vos, *Rogier Van der Weyden*, pp. 276-284, nr. 21 (with references to the literature).

[27] M. Comblen-Sonkes, *The Collegiale Church of Saint Peter. Louvain*, Corpus of Fifteenth-Century Painting in the Southern Netherlands and the Principality of Liège (Brussels, 1996), pp. 1-84, nr. 185, esp. pp. 45-48.

els, but also the implicit portraits of Tommaso Portinari and Charles the Bold (Ill. 1).[28] The former kneels devoutly in the scale held on St Michael's hand in the central panel;[29] the latter appears probably as one of the Apostles (third Apostle on the left side of Christ) and looks down, 'a suitable attitude for a mortal at the heavenly tribunal'.[30] In this way, Memling has united different contemporary figures in his altarpiece: Angelo Tani, patron and, from 1455, chief agent of the Bruges branch of the Medici bank; Tommaso Portinari, his successor; and Charles the Bold, the Burgundian duke who owed his financial support to the Medici bank.

Such concealed portraits have naturally led to speculation concerning the identity of various figures, such as, for instance the figure of Nicodemus in the *Descent from the Cross* by Rogier van der Weyden (Madrid, Museo del Prado) (Ill. 11). According to one researcher, he may be identified with Robert de Masmines, an important official at the Burgundian court,[31] while others argue that the similarity is coincidental and thus not certifiable[32] or that it was not Rogier van der Weyden's intention to paint an explicit portrait of de Masmines. The argument goes that Van der Weyden found inspiration for his portrayal of Nicodemus in a work by his teacher, Robert Campin, drawing on the facial expression from Campin's *Portrait of Robert de Masmines* (copy by Rogier van der Weyden in Berlin, Staatliche Museen zu Berlin, Preussischer Kulturbesitz, Gemäldegalerie, Kulturforum) (Ill. 12).[33]

II. The Background to the Representation of Secular Patrons in South Netherlandish Altarpieces

The tendency to depict patrons on altarpieces did not arise suddenly, but enjoyed a long tradition in painting, including illuminations. This

---

[28] De Vos, *Hans Memling*, pp. 82-89.
[29] This is an old repainting dating from before 1473, when the painting was transported and ended up in Gdansk.
[30] De Vos, *Rogier van der Weyden*, p. 85.
[31] On that painting, see A. Châtelet, *Robert Campin. De Meester van Flémalle* (Antwerp, 1996), pp. 148-151, 302 (nr. 12a) (with references to the literature).
[32] H. Belting & Ch. Kruse e. a., *Die Erfindung des Gemäldes. Das erste Jahrhundert der niederländischen Malerei* (Munich, 1994), pp. 172-173, nr. 78; Martens, 'Portrait explicite', p. 15 (note 19).
[33] A. Châtelet, 'Rogier van der Weyden: el Descendimiento de la Cruz', in: A. Kinoshita & F. Checa Cremades (eds.), *Obras maestras del Museo del Prado*, exh. cat. (Tokyo, National Museum of Western Art) (Madrid, 1996), p. 76.

tradition went back to the twelfth century, a period of great change, characterized as a 'Renaissance in plurality'.[34] The revival of arts and sciences and the renewed interest in Classical Antiquity were no longer linked to the aspirations of a particular emperor or dynasty, as they had been in the Carolingian or Ottonian periods, but reached further, pervading a larger segment of the population that at first included just the clergy and later spread to intellectual, learned lay circles. Moreover, this renewed interest now formed part of a general process of vitality and expansion in Europe, a result of political dynamism and economic expansion. This period also saw the rise of the concept of 'individuality' – and this is of course crucial in the present context – which led directly to depictions of patrons. Research has shown that frequent and extensive inquiries were made into the notion of the self in the twelfth century. John F. Benton refers, for instance, to Guido, Prior of the Chartreuse of Grenoble, who as early as the twelfth century wrote about the importance of the self and its inner drive.[35] It is in this context that works of art were created in which the patron is present in one form or another. Such representations are not true-to-life portraits, but rather standard representations in which convention and symbolism predominate and the primary task is to underline the patron's rank and social standing.

In the Carolingian period (eighth-ninth century), patrons were generally not depicted in manuscripts. The few such depictions were exclusively of the emperor; the first such example is found in the *First Bible of Charles the Bald*, better known as the *Count Vivianus Bible* (Paris, Bibliothèque nationale de France, Ms. lat. 1, fol. 423), a gift to Charles the Bald in 851 on the occasion of his visit to Tours.[36] Monks from Tours Abbey (shown at the left), led by their lay abbot, Count Vivianus, offer the Bible to Charles the Bald. The emperor is idealized and clearly resembles King David, radiant among his musicians (Asaph, Heman, Ethan and Jeduthun), imperial guards, and embodiments of the imperial virtues (wisdom, justice, perseverance and moderation). This creates an interrelation

---

[34] Cited from J. Janssens & C. Matheeusen, *Renaissance in meervoud. Als dwergen op de schouders van reuzen? (8ste-16de eeuw)* (Louvain, 1995), p. 30.

[35] J.F. Benton, 'Consciousness of Self and Perceptions of Individuality', in: R.L. Benson & G. Constable (eds.), *Renaissance and Renewal in the Twelfth Century* (Cambridge (Mass.), 1982), p. 263.

[36] P.E. Dutton & H.L. Kessler, *The Poetry and Paintings of the First Bible of Charles the Bald* (Ann Arbor, 1997); I. Marchesin, 'Temps et espaces dans le frontispice du Psautier de la Première Bible de Charles le Chauve', in: A. von Hülsen-Esch & J.-C. Schmitt (eds.), *Die Methodik der Bildinterpretation. Les méthodes de l'interprétation de l'image. Deutsch-französische Kolloquien 1998-2000* (Göttingen, 2002), pp. 317-353 (with references to recent literature).

between Charles the Bald and David, whose kingship has an exemplary function and is linked to the emperor who, like Charlemagne before him, was seen as the *novus David*. The emperor is surrounded by two subservient kings and sits enthroned above the representatives of Church and state. Above him appears the hand of God, the direct source of the emperor's authority.

The emperor was also regularly depicted in the Ottonian period. An illumination from the *Second Gospels of Otto III* (Aachen, Cathedral Treasury, s.n., fol. 16; ca. 1000), for example, depicts him in a mandorla supported by the earth and surrounded by the symbols of the Evangelists.[37] The hand of God appears from above, placing the crown on the emperor's head. Otto III seems Christ-like in his majesty and here clearly pays tribute to a mystical conception of the relation between the secular and the spiritual order. The emperor is *christomimetes*: he is the embodiment and representative of Christ – or indeed, Christ himself on earth.[38]

Besides their depictions in dedication miniatures, patrons were not represented in Carolingian and Ottonian manuscripts. The composition scheme of the imperial dedication illuminations was, however, preserved in the many presentation scenes from the Pre-Romanesque and Romanesque periods, in which a monk or an author presents his book to Christ, a saint or a Church worthy. In the *Codex Egberti* (Trier, Stadtsbibliothek, Cod. 24, fol. 2; ca. 985) the diminutive monks Keraldus and Heribertus offer their codex to Egbert, Archbishop of Trier, while in a manuscript from the Meuse region preserved in the Royal Library in Brussels (Ms. II 2570, fol. 3; 1020-1030) the author Gregorius of Nazianze and the monk that transcribed the text offer their manuscript to Christ.[39] Like the emperor, Christ is depicted larger than the figures below. He is sitting on a double mandorla, a symbol of heaven and earth. In the *Collationes Patrum* (Valenciennes, Bibliothèque-Médiathèque municipale, Ms. 169, fol. 2; ca. 1050), which differs in its composition – the patron saint of the abbey of St Amand, for which the manuscript was created, is seated not in the centre but to the left in the uppermost register – two small monks offer the completed book to St Amand. Cas-

---

[37] On Ottonian book illumination, see H.M.R.E. Mayr-Harting, *Ottonian Book Illumination. An Historical Study* (London, 1991).

[38] On this evolution, see P. Leupen, *Gods stad op aarde. Eenheid van kerk en staat in het eerste millennium na Christus. Een kerkelijke ideologie* (Amsterdam, 1996) and Idem, *Keizer in zijn eigen rijk. De geboorte van de nationale staat* (Amsterdam, 1998).

[39] *Medieval Mastery. Book Illumination from Charlemagne to Charles the Bold, 800-1475*, exh. cat. (Leuven, Museum Vander Kelen-Mertens) (Louvain, 2002), pp. 140-141 (with references to the literature and ill.).

sianus, the author, stands to the extreme right in the upper register, while the copyist is represented below.[40] The same approach is taken in the *Confessions of Augustine* (Arras, Bibliothèque municipale, Ms. 616, fol. 1v; second half of the eleventh century). St Alard, the copyist and illuminator, kneels humbly in the lowest register before St Vedast.[41] He takes on the same attitude as St Augustine, depicted in the upper register offering the codex to Christ. Whatever the representation, the setting is always the same: Christ, Mary, the saint, the emperor, the archbishop or the abbot are enthroned in the centre or to one side, but always in the spiritual centre of the composition, and receive the book from the hands of a much smaller figure. In this way the hierarchical distinction is made clear.

In addition, there are of course representations with different settings, such as that in the *Odbert Gospels* (New York, The Pierpont Morgan Library, Ms. M. 333; ca. 1000). Odbert was the most important Abbot of St Bertin's Abbey (Saint Omer, Northern France) and responsible for the illumination of some twenty codices.[42] In the *Q* of *quoniam*, the miniaturist illustrates the first story of St Luke's Gospel: an angel announces to Zacharias the birth of his son, John the Baptist. Their gestures and their attitudes are written intimately within the letter. The gazes are directed to the altar on which Zacharias is offering up incense. To the right, in the tail of the initial, Mary and the Christ Child are represented together with the ox and the ass. Abbot Odbert is probably shown kneeling in the bottom of the initial. The promise of the Nativity seems to have left such a deep impression that the abbot has prostrated himself, thereby fitting perfectly into the initial. The rest of the opening words of the text are painted in golden letters against a red background. The representation of the patron is thoroughly Romanesque, since the patron is present without drawing attention to himself. He kneels before the divine apparition and adapts his form completely to that of the letter Q in which he has been depicted. The same procedure is seen in the *Gospels* of Liessies Abbey (Avesnes, Musée de la Société d'Archéologic et d'Art de l'Arrondissement d'Avesnes, separate page; 1146),[43] where the golden centre is dominated by St John the Evangelist, whose body exudes a spiritual, supernatural strength. In the central medallion to the right of John is Wedricus, Abbot of Liessies Abbey. In a symbolic gesture he holds out the inkpot

---

[40] M. Smeyers, *Vlaamse miniaturen van de 8ste tot het midden van de 16de eeuw. De middeleeuwse wereld op perkament* (Louvain, 1998), p. 43 (ill. 31).

[41] *Ibidem*, p. 42 (ill. 28).

[42] *Medieval Mastery*, pp. 138-139, cat. nr. 13 (with references to the literature and ill.).

[43] *Ibidem*, pp. 152-153, cat. nr. 20 (with references to the literature and ill.).

to John, feeling perhaps small but nonetheless satisfied with his material contribution. Surpassing the borders of time, in the spiritual space created by the illumination, he has come face to face with John. The other medallions show scenes from the life of St John the Evangelist. The presence of the eagle, with its talons on a parchment banderole, confirms his identity. There is no question here of individualization in the sense of a naturalistic representation of the patron, inspired by reality. As historical figures, Odbert and Wedricus declare an oath in the name of the monastery community and, as in a manuscript from St Trudo's Abbey (now in Liège, Bibliothèque universitaire, Ms. 26, fol. 1), ask Christ and Mary to intercede for them and their community (the precise text is: *Fili* (Son), *Quid Mater* (What is it, mother?), *Miserere Mei Deus* (God have mercy on me)).[44]

The historical figures depicted in these representations were limited to members of the clergy. It was only from the twelfth century, in the Gothic period, that secular patrons began to appear in manuscripts. The rise of the cities and the creation of lay ateliers led to a significant lay public which from the beginning sought to have itself represented in manuscripts. The representations of patrons in fifteenth-century panel paintings was a continuation of this trend.

Secular figures were initially represented in manuscripts in the same way that monk-patrons of the Romanesque period had previously been visualized. In *Le livre d'images de Madame Marie* (Paris, Bibliothèque nationale de France, Ms. n.a. fr. 16251; ca. 1285) the patroness kneels together with a number of pilgrims before a much larger representation of St James the Greater (Ill. 13).[45] Her attitude is comparable to that of the Romanesque monks, but she is clearly more self-assured, less submissive, and her gaze falls explicitly on the saint. However, there is here no question of a strict individualization, with *Madame Marie's* characterization based on natural resemblances (= *mimesis*). The portrait is, as was the custom in that period, abstract and generalizing. Patrons in manuscripts are only identifiable on the basis of texts and/or documents, coats of arms and emblems.

With the advent of marginal decoration in the Gothic period, patrons' positions in the composition gradually shifted. Instead of placing them in the central composition, they were increasingly portrayed in the margins. They were usually shown kneeling at the edge, beholding the scene taking place in front of them, and were now depicted in the same propor-

---

[44] *Ibidem*, pp. 158-159, cat. nr. 23 (with references to the literature and ill.).
[45] *Ibidem*, pp. 214-216, cat. nr. 44 (with references to the literature and ill.).

tions as the other personages. In a *Bible historiale* (Paris, Bibliothèque nationale de France, Ms. fr. 152, fol. XI; 1347), a man and a woman kneel on the two sides of the seven days of creation. They are literally standing at the edge, in the margin, and thus in a certain sense in the shadow of the religious representation in the centre of the composition.[46] Likewise, in the *Beaupré Antiphonary* (Baltimore, Walters Art Gallery, Ms. W. 759, fol. 3 v°; 1290), the illuminator creates balanced pages in which music and representation support one another.[47] At the foot of the large initial depicting the Resurrection of Christ and the Holy Women at the empty grave, the noble Maria de Boraing kneels in her private chapel, while at the very bottom another lady from her family kneels devoutly. A comparable composition is found in the *Hours of Margaret of Beaujeu* (New York, The Pierpont Morgan Library, Ms. M. 754, fol. 114; second quarter of the fourteenth century) (Ill. 14).[48] She too kneels in prayer in the margin, gazing up at the Ascension that is shown in the initial *A(près)*, the beginning of the commemoration of the Ascension.

Until the fourteenth century, the number of personalized manuscripts was still relatively limited, and the patrons were generally members of the nobility. Only gradually and after a centuries-long process did members of the affluent bourgeoisie also commission manuscripts and have themselves depicted in them. In Pre-Eyckian book illumination of the 1380-1420 period, many examples of patrons from the bourgeoisie are found in manuscripts. In contrast to patrons from the nobility, who had their own coat of arms and could partly be identified in this way, this new class of patrons often did not possess identifying coats of arms. As a result they often remain anonymous for us. A prime example of this can be found in the *Psalter Hours* from London (The British Library, Royal Ms. 2.A.XVIII, fol. 23 v°; beginning of the fifteenth century), where a man and a woman are shown kneeling on the two sides of the Annunciation while they themselves have taken their places before a prie-dieu on which an open book is placed (Ill. 15).[49] In iconographical terms, little has changed from the High-Gothic period: the patrons kneel in the margin and look upwards towards the religious scene taking place in front of

---

[46] *Ibidem*, pp. 214-216, cat. nr. 44 (with references to the literature and ill.).
[47] *Ibidem*, pp. 217-219, cat. nr. 45a+b (with references to the literature).
[48] Smeyers, *Vlaamse miniaturen*, p. 134 (ill. 33).
[49] M. Smeyers (ed.), *Vlaamse miniaturen voor Van Eyck (ca. 1380-ca. 1420)*, Corpus of Illuminated Manuscripts, vol. 6, Low Countries Series, vol. 4, exh. cat. (Leuven, Cultureel Centrum Romaanse Poort) (Louvain, 1993), pp. 40-45, cat. nr. 14 (with references to the literature and ills.).

them. The events thus seem to be unfolding in the minds of the patrons. The relation to fifteenth-century panel painting in which the patrons are very often depicted on the side panels is very clear.

Yet another image of the patron begins to be seen in Pre-Eyckian illuminations: the patron in the presence of his or her patron saint, as in the *Prayerbook* in Frankfurt-am-Main in which the patron kneels facing St Bernard (Museum für Kunsthandwerk, Ms. Linel. 11, fol. 114 v°; beginning of the fifteenth century) (Ill. 16)[50] or in the *Hours* preserved in Rouen (Bibliothèque municipale, Ms. 3024, fol. 12 v°-13; 1400-1415).[51] Once again, the relation to fifteenth-century panel painting is manifest, for there too the patron is often depicted in the company of his or her patron saint. Moreover, in late fourteenth- and early fifteenth-century illumination there is a tendency toward individualization comparable to that found in fifteenth-century panel painting. Such figures were no longer deemed exchangeable or replaceable. The portraits sometimes had their own inalienable characteristics and those portrayed were identifiable on the basis of natural resemblance. An early example of this, with a strong artistic impact, is found in the *Bible Historiale* of Jan Baudolf (The Hague, Museum Meermanno-Westreenianum, Ms. 10 B 23, fol. 2; 1372) in which Jean de Vaudetar presents the manuscript to Charles V of France.[52] Instead of the nice, even-featured, and somewhat doll-like and unearthly face, the king's features impart a very real, corporeal quality. His face, in three-quarter profile and with a decidedly long nose – it seems almost a symbol for the nosing-about in books for which he was well known – makes a lasting and almost emotional impression. The man is completely present in the events in a psychological sense, and not simply a typecast monarch in gaudy pomp.

As the fifteenth century progressed and the number of preserved manuscripts increased, patrons continued to be omnipresent. They came from different strata in society (dukes, nobility and courtiers, rich bourgeoisie, middle class and of course the clergy, of both high and more moderate birth) and were systematically depicted in the margins, from top to bottom. With the passing of time they were increasingly identifiable by means of resemblance based on objective characteristics, observable by all.

---

[50] Smeyers, *Vlaamse miniaturen*, p. 197 (ill. 27).
[51] *Vlaamse miniaturen voor Van Eyck*, pp. 99-104, cat. nr. 33 (with references to the literature and ills.).
[52] *Medieval Mastery*, pp. 256-257, cat. nr. 64 (with references to the literature and ill.).

It was particularly the Burgundian dukes and their coterie that considered themselves privileged protagonists. Philip the Good, for instance, is depicted numerous times in books of hours, prayer books and religious treatises, as well as manuscripts with political implications (Ill. 17).[53] He is always recognizable on the basis of a number of inalienable characteristics: his black attire, pointed, elongated footwear, the chain of the Golden Fleece, his long, lean build, and especially his typical facial features. He often appears in the middle of the compositions and not in the margins (cf. the examples from panel painting). He takes his place as an actor in both religious and non-religious scenes. In this he remains in the Carolingian and Ottonian tradition in which the emperor was always portrayed in the centre the composition. Now, of course, he no longer has such divine status. In the Burgundian period, the indivisible link between Church and State was no longer as prominent, as each of the two poles tended towards a relatively independent existence.

Conclusion

The fifteenth-century manner of representing secular patrons in South Netherlandish altarpieces did not arise suddenly but developed out of a long tradition. Since the twelfth century, patrons had been regularly depicted in book illumination in two specific ways: either they were included (incognito or not) in the religious scene or they stood or kneeled in the margins. Deep in devout thought, they meditated on the scene before them. This well-established approach was taken over by fifteenth-century panel painters. The manner in which they were represented did not change unequivocally over time. Various systems of representation existed concurrently, often combined with one another. A number of trends can be identified.

To start with, most patrons were depicted not on the outer panels of commemorative works, but on the inner ones. This has the effect of visually placing them as close as possible to the divine world to which they aspire. Secondly, there is a tendency to integrate them as much as

---

[53] Examples: *Traité sur l'oraison dominicale,* Brussels, Royal Library of Belgium, Ms. 9092, fol. 9 (after 1457); *Hours of Philip the Bold,* Cambridge, Fitzwilliam Museum, Ms. 3-1954, fol. 253 v° (1450-1455) (Ill. 17); *Roman de Girart de Roussillon,* Vienna, Österreichische Nationalbibliothek, Cod. 2549, fol. 6 (after 1448). His successors and their contemporaries are also regularly depicted. See e.g. Pierre de Vaux, *Vie de Sainte Colette,* Ghent, Arme Claren-Coletienen, Ms. 8, fol. 40 v° (ca. 1470): Charles the Bold and Margaret of York; *Vie de Saint-Adrien,* Vienna, Österreichische Nationalbibliothek, Cod. s.n. 2619, fol. 3 v° (ca. 1480): Louis XI of France and his wife Charlotte of Savoy.

possible into the religious scene itself. If in the work of Robert Campin they are explicitly left to one side of the action, with access to the religious space only by means of an open door or portico, the later South Netherlandish painters tended to include them more in the sacred events. By allowing a landscape or a row of houses to continue from the middle panel to the side panels an immediate connection is created. The relation becomes stronger – although this is not a clear evolution over time – when the patrons themselves are represented on the central panel. This creates not only the illusion of a spatial proximity, but also of a temporal presence. In other words, the patron and the Biblical events seem to be linked across time. Nevertheless, despite this connection, a distinction always remains between the world of the patron and that of the Biblical figures, sometimes because the patrons keep their distance from the religious scene, sometimes because a crevice or a stream separates them from the protagonists. In this way the panel painters, albeit often in a subtle way, made clear the continuing distinction between the *Diesseits* (the world of the patrons) and the *Jenseits* (the religious world).

Illuminare – Centre for the Study of the Illuminated Manuscript (K.U.-Leuven)

ILLUSTRATIONS 89

Ill. 1. – Hans Memling, *Triptych of the Last Judgement*, panel painting, Bruges, 1467. – Gdansk, Muzeum Narodowe.

Ill. 2. – Rogier van der Weyden?, *Abegg Triptych*, panel painting, Brussels, 1438-1440. – Riggisberg, Abegg-Stiftung.

Ill. 3. – Robert Campin, *Mérode Triptych*, panel painting, Tournai, ca. 1422. – New York, The Metropolitan Museum of Art, The Cloisters Collection.

ILLUSTRATIONS 91

Ill. 4. – Master of Moulins, *Triptych of the Dukes of Bourbon*, panel painting, Brussels?, end of the fifteenth century. – Moulins, Cathedral.

Ill. 5. – Gerard David, *The Baptism of Christ*, panel painting, Bruges, 1502-1508. – Bruges, Groeningemuseum.

Ill. 6. – Rogier van der Weyden, *Triptych with the Crucifixion*, panel painting, Brussels, 1443-1445. – Vienna, Kunsthistorisches Museum.

Ill. 7. – Dirk Bouts, *Ecce Agnus Dei*, panel painting, Louvain, ca. 1460-1470.
– Munich, Bayerische Staatsgemäldesammlungen, Alte Pinakothek.

Ill. 8. – Rogier van der Weyden, *Bladelin Triptych*, panel painting, Brussels, 1445-1448. – Berlin, Staatliche Museen zu Berlin, Preussischer Kulturbesitz.

Ill. 9. – Rogier van der Weyden, *Columba Altarpiece*, panel painting, Brussels, ca. 1450-1465. – Munich, Alte Pinakothek.

Ill. 10. – Dirk Bouts, *Last Supper*, panel painting, Louvain, 1464. – Louvain, St Peter's church.

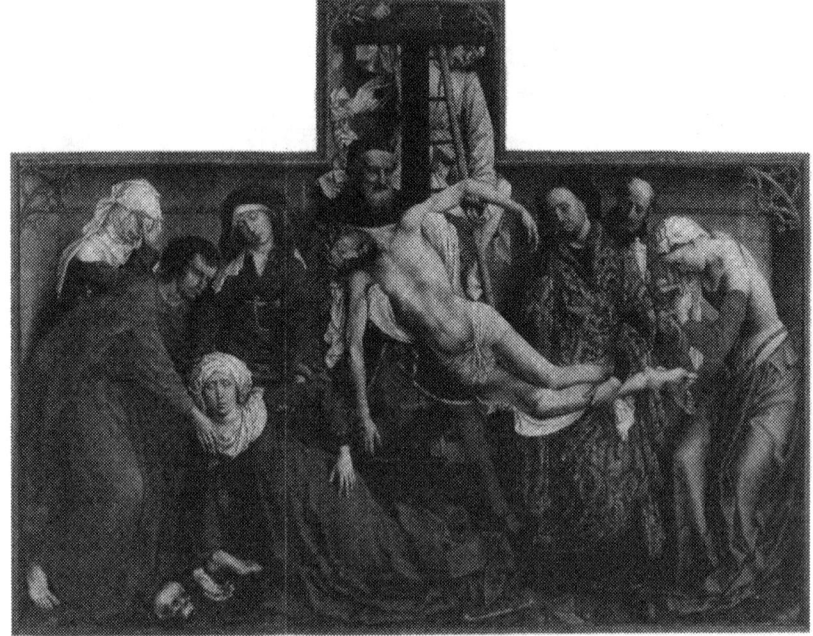

Ill. 11. – Rogier van der Weyden, *Descent from the Cross*, panel painting, Brussels, ca. 1430-1435. – Madrid, Museo del Prado.

Ill. 12. – Rogier van der Weyden, *Portrait of Robert de Masmines*, panel painting, Tournai, ca. 1430-1435 (?). – Berlin, Staatliche Museen zu Berlin, Preussischer Kulturbesitz, Gemäldegalerie, Kulturforum.

Ill. 13. – *Madame Marie and Pilgrims Kneeling before James the Great*, miniature from *Le livre d'images de Madame Marie*, Hainaut, ca. 1285. – Paris, Bibliothèque nationale de France, Ms. n.a. fr. 16251, fol. 66.

Ill. 14. – *Ascension*, miniature from the *Hours of Margaret of Beaujeu*, Arras or Saint Omer, second quarter of the fourteenth century. - New York, The Pierpont Morgan Library, Ms. M. 754, fol. 114.

Ill. 15. – *Annunciation*, miniature from a *Psalter Hours*, London (Herman Scheerre), beginning of the fifteenth century. – London, The British Library, Royal Ms. 2.A.XVIII, fol. 23v°.

Ill. 16. – *Saint Bernard Adorated by an Anonymous Patron*, miniature from a *Prayerbook*, Bruges, beginning of the fifteenth century. – Frankfurt-am-Main, Museum für Kunsthandwerk, Ms. Linel. 11, fol. 114 v°.

Ill. 17. – *Mass of Saint Gregory*, inserted miniature from the *Hours of Philip the Bold*, Brussels, 1450-1455. – Cambridge, Fitzwilliam Museum, Ms. 3-1954, fol. 253 v°.

Jenny Rahel OESTERLE

THE LITURGICAL DIMENSION OF ROYAL REPRESENTATION

The tenth and eleventh centuries, the time of the Ottonian and Salian rulers, are often described as a period of sacred, divine kingship, expressed in German as 'Sakralkönigtum'.[1] The king in the Early Middle Ages represented himself as 'vicarius Christi', as the vicegerent of Christ on earth. Through his coronation and in particular his anointment, he ensured the status which Ernst Kantorowicz described as the 'king's two bodies':[2] he was the ruler on earth and the future heavenly co-ruler. The king was therefore a half-sacred and half-political person, with no definite limit between his political and sacred roles.

For Ottonian times a process of sacralization[3] can be noticed. The rituals and ceremonies of the king's representation[4] became more and

---

[1] See, e.g., G. Althoff, *Die Ottonen. Königsherrschaft ohne Staat* (Stuttgart, 2000); A. Angenendt, '*Rex et Sacerdos*. Zur Genese der Königssalbung', in: N. Kamp & J. Wollasch (eds.), *Tradition als historische Kraft. Interdisziplinäre Forschungen zur Geschichte des frühen Mittelalters* (Berlin / New York, 1982), pp. 100-118; J.I. Engels, 'Das 'Wesen' der Monarchie? Kritische Anmerkungen zum 'Sakralkönigtum' in der Geschichtswissenschaft', *Majestas*, 7 (1999), pp. 3-39; F.-R. Erkens, *Die Sakralität von Herrschaft. Herrschaftslegitimierung im Wechsel der Zeiten und Räume. Fünfzehn interdisziplinäre Beiträge zu einem weltweiten und epochenübergreifenden Phänomen* (Berlin, 2002); Idem, '*Vicarius Christi – sacratissime legislator – sacra majestas*. Religiöse Herrschaftslegitimierung im Mittelalter', *Zeitschrift der Savigny-Stiftung für Rechtsgeschichte, Kan. Abt.*, 120 (2003), pp. 1-55; G. Feeley-Harnik, 'Herrscherkunst und Herrschaft: Neuere Forschungen zum sakralen Königtum', in: A. Lüdtke (ed.), *Herrschaft als soziale Praxis. Historische und sozial-anthropologische Studien*, Veröffentlichungen des Max-Planck-Instituts für Geschichte, vol. 91 (Göttingen, 1991), pp. 195-253; H. Fichtenau, *Lebensordnungen des 10. Jahrhunderts. Studien über Denkart und Existenz im einstigen Karolingerreich* (Stuttgart, 1984); H. Keller, 'Die Investitur. Ein Beitrag zum Problem der 'Staatssymbolik' im Hochmittelalter', *Frühmittelalterliche Studien*, 27 (1993), pp. 51-86; Idem, 'Ritual, Symbolik und Visualisierung in der Kultur des ottonischen Reiches', *Frühmittelalterliche Studien*, 35 (2001), pp. 23-59; P. Linehan, 'The King's Touch and the Dean's Ministrations: Aspects of Sacral Monarchy', in: M. Rubin (ed.), *The Work of Jacques Le Goff and the Challenges of Medieval History* (Woodbridge, 1997), pp. 189-206; S. Weinfurter, 'Idee und Funktion des 'Sakralkönigtums' bei den ottonischen und salischen Herrschern (10. und 11. Jahrhundert)', in: R. Gundlach & H.Weber (eds.), *Legitimation und Funktion des Herrschers. Vom ägyptischen Pharao zum neuzeitlichen Diktator* (Stuttgart, 1992), pp. 99-127.

[2] E. Kantorowicz, *The King's Two Bodies: A Study in Medieval Political Theology* (Princeton, 1957).

[3] See Weinfurter, 'Idee und Funktion', pp. 99-127.

[4] For definitions of 'Herrschaftsrepräsentation', see H. Hofmann, *Repräsentation. Studien zur Wort- und Begriffsgeschichte von der Antike bis ins 19. Jahrhundert*, Schrif-

more integrated into a religious or sacred sphere. They had to *show* the sacral base of power, to *confirm* it and *remind* their subjects of it again and again.⁵ The liturgical dimension is part of the visualization, confirmation and remembrance of sacred power. It brings a certain quality into the representation of power: the specific element of a dynamic enactment by *all* the participants. Major aspects in the representation rituals and ceremonies were the use of sacred space, places and time, the performance of mass, the 'öffentliche, 'multimediale', performative Inszenierung des 'Gottesdienstes' einer großen Gemeinde'.⁶ The sacral time was extremely important for religious settings. The principal religious feasts, *viz.* Christmas, Easter and Whitsun, became increasingly integrated into the ruler's representation: festival coronations and councils of kings frequently took place on holy days.⁷

The process of sacralization was accompanied by chains of rituals.⁸ Signs, symbols, symbolic acts, symbolic times and places were connected to a sacral setting, which was literally 'begehbar'. These chains of rituals structured royal representation during holy days. An example of such a chain of rituals is the festive coronation of the Ottonian and Salian kings.

This contribution concentrates on a certain aspect of this early medieval divine kingship: the liturgical dimension of royal representation. I want to emphasize that the king's representation within a sacral sphere was *not* an act that happened 'on stage', performed by actors and viewed by spectators. It was a dynamic enactment. Everyone – the king, the clergy, the aristocracy, the populace (who saw the king as he proceeded) – was a participant in the event, and they all were equally important for the *effect* of the king's representation.

---

ten zur Verfassungsgeschichte, vol. 22 (Berlin, 1974); H. Keller, 'Herrschaftsrepräsentation im ottonischen Sachsen. Ergebnisse und Fragen', in: G. Althoff & E. Schubert (eds.), *Herrschaftsrepräsentation im ottonischen Sachsen* (Sigmaringen, 1998), pp. 431-452; A. Zimmermann (ed.), *Der Begriff der Repräsentation im Mittelalter. Stellvertretung, Symbol, Zeichen, Bild,* Miscellanea Medievalia, vol. 8 (Cologne, 1971).

⁵ See H. Keller, 'Herrscherbild und Herrschaftslegitimation. Zur Deutung der ottonischen Denkmäler', *Frühmittelalterliche Studien,* 19 (1985), pp. 290-311, 297: 'Die Repräsentation der Königsherrschaft entwickelte sich ganz in den liturgischen Bereich hinein, nicht nur um den sakralen Grund der Königsherrschaft immer neu sichtbar zu machen, sondern vor allem um ihn immer neu zu festigen, d.h. sich des Fundaments der Königsherrschaft, der Gnade und Hilfe Gottes, immer wieder neu zu versichern'.

⁶ Keller, 'Ritual', p. 53.

⁷ For political acts on holy days, see H.-M. Schaller, 'Der heilige Tag als Termin mittelalterlicher Staatsakte', *Deutsches Archiv,* 31 (1974), pp. 1-25.

Three central aspects of the following will be: 1. the Ottonian and early Salian kings' use of liturgical settings for political purposes and the reasons for selecting a sacral setting for a certain political activity; 2. the role and function of ecclesiastical buildings and holy days in the framework of royal representation in particular; 3. the role of the public.

I have deliberately chosen three sources that present us with conflicts, problems, forgeries and the exploitation of sacral settings for royal representation. The focus on texts indicating a lack of well-organized liturgical settings for the king's celebration may help to adjust our view of the necessity of sacral settings for political purposes in the Early Middle Ages.

Royal Representation without the Use of Ecclesiastical Buildings

During Whitsun of the year 1081, Henry IV found himself in an extremely difficult political situation. He had planned to celebrate Whitsun in Rome, but was unable to enter the city. As a consequence, he found himself in a place where the local conditions did not allow him to celebrate Whitsun with a festival coronation, since there were not two churches, one to be crowned in and another to celebrate mass. A Gregorian historian ironically notes: the king celebrated with 'Lanzen statt Wachslichtern, Bewaffneten statt der Chöre der Geistlichen... Schmähungen statt der Lobsprüche, wildes Geschrei statt der Beifallsbekundungen'.[9]

This situation resulted in an intensive debate between the ruler and his bishops, which came down to us in a description by Benzo, Bishop of Alba: 'Quid hodie, fratres, faciemus, quia hic duas aecclesias non habemus?'[10] Could it be possible to celebrate a festival coronation without two churches? He and his bishops decided: it would be better to celebrate only the Holy Mass of Whitsun and to refrain from the coronation, rather than to proceed with the coronation without the availability of two churches ('ut in una dominus noster rex vestiatur et coronetur, et in alteram vadens coronatus ubi missa celebretur. Ista est vetus consuetudo regalis coronae... Si non possumus agere quod volumus, velimus ut quimus. Et si removet nos ab obsequio regiae coronae locus inconveniens,

---

[8] Keller, 'Ritual', p. 24.

[9] G. Meyer von Knonau (ed.), *Jahrbücher des deutschen Reiches*, vol. 3: *Heinrich IV. und Heinrich V.* (Berlin, 1965), p. 390.

[10] Benzo of Alba, *Ad Heinricum IV imperatorem libri VII*, G. H. Pertz (ed.), Monumenta Germaniae Historica. Scriptores, vol. 11 (Hannover, 1854 (Stuttgart, 1963)), pp. 581-691, 656.

celebremus tamen debita devotione missam, quam postulat sollempnitas presens'[11]). However, also according to Benzo of Alba, the ruler did not have a choice: he *had* to use the *mysterium* of the crown ('debet cesar uti mysterio regalis coronae') as a symbol for a transpersonal kingship. The final outcome of the debate was that two tents were pitched. The ruler was crowned in the first one. Then he marched in a festive procession from the first tent to the second, where he celebrated the Holy Mass of Whitsun ('Preparentur itaque duo tabernacula, in uno coronatus cesar processionaliter ad alterum eat tabernaculum, eritque angelis et hominibus delectabile spectaculum'[12]).

Although the topographic preconditions for a festival coronation were not present[13] due to the absence of two churches, and although the political circumstances of the ruler were extremely difficult, he did not refrain from a representation under the crown. The problem was overcome through the construction of a sacred setting for a festival coronation by the ruler and the bishops.

The source gives information about 1. the topographic precondition for a festival coronation; 2. the importance of ecclesiastical buildings; 3. the variability of the chains of rituals.

1. The source shows the construction of a sacral setting in a difficult political situation. The setting is far from how it should be, and not even the basic necessity of two churches has been complied with. The description of this extraordinary situation informs us about the usual procedure for a festival coronation with two churches and a procession in 'public' between these. The ruler was crowned in the first church by a bishop or an archbishop. Under the crown he marched through the town in a procession, accompanied by the clergy and the aristocracy and various symbols and signs of power, until he arrived at the second church, where the festive mass was celebrated.

2. The debate whether a coronation is possible *without* two churches and the initial conclusion *that it is not* emphasized the importance of ecclesiastical buildings and sacral space during festival coronations. In a second step, the focus of the debate changed and the celebration, *viz.* the sacral time of the high feast, came to the fore. The emphasis was shifted from the problem of sacred space to the problem of sacred time. The central question for the consideration of the ruler and the bishops became the

---

[11] Benzo, *Ad Heinricum*, p. 657.

[12] *Ibidem*, p. 657.

[13] Also other examples, such as the festival coronation of Friedrich Barbarossa in 1184, show the necessity of two churches for a festival coronation ceremony.

procedure of the mass, the liturgical celebration and the traditions of the celebration. It can be concluded that buildings and space were changeable, even ecclesiastical buildings, but the liturgical constellation of two places and two different liturgical and symbolic acts remained fixed.

3. This leads us to the question of variability in the chains of rituals. The lack of two churches – a topographical precondition – caused other changes in the ritual chain. With regard to our question concerning the political use of sacred settings, it is remarkable that, obviously, some elements – even important elements such as churches – could be replaced and changed, as long as the liturgical constellations remained the same and the ensemble of symbols and signs, symbolic acts, participation of aristocracy, clergy and 'public' guaranteed the effect of the representation. With regard to the ecclesiastical buildings, variation was possible.

The Exploitation of a Liturgical Setting

At Easter 984, Henry II came to Quedlinburg to celebrate the high feast with the aristocracy, clergy and the people of the town. Thietmar of Merseburg records that many important delegates of the *Reich* came together for this event.[14] The celebration was well-organized and splendid. Henry of Bavaria was publicly greeted as the new king; liturgical acclamations, the *laudes regiae,* were sung for him.[15]

This example is particularly striking because Henry of Bavaria was the rival of Otto III. Henry II was announced as the king during a political gathering at the holy day of Easter, in a public-political as well in a liturgical way. He used the religious setting of Easter and the liturgical acclamations to legitimize his claim to the throne in public in the town of Quedlinburg, which at the time was one of the most popular festival places of the Ottonian rulers.

In the context of the study how liturgical settings, and ecclesiastical buildings in particular, were used for political purposes the liturgical chants for the ruler, the *laudes regiae,* which were mentioned in the source, are an important example of the connecting integration of mass, the liturgy and the king's representation. In the case of Henry II of Bava-

---

[14] See Thietmar of Merseburg, 'Chronik', in: W. Trillmich (ed.), *Ausgewählte Quellen zur Geschichte des deutschen Mittelalters*, Freiherr-vom-Stein-Gedächtnisausgabe, 9 vols. (Darmstadt, 1957⁶), vol. 4, p. 2: 'Quo magnus regni primatus colligitur, a quibusdam autem venire illo nolentibus ad omnia diligenter inquirenda nuntius mittitur'.

[15] Thietmar, 'Chronik', vol. 4, p. 2: 'Hac in festivitate idem a suis publice rex appellatur laudibusque divinis attollitur'.

ria, they had 'certainly constitutive'[16] and also representative functions. The *laudes regiae* were presented to both the ruler in heaven and the (crowned) ruler on earth during the holy mass. The chants and prayers for the ruler were integrated in the liturgy of mass, usually between the first Collect and the Epistle, and could not start before the archbishop or bishop was present.[17] To praise the ruler in a liturgical song means, to 'create a new ruler and to recognize him publicly in his new dignity'.[18] Henry II of Bavaria made use of this effect of the liturgical chants: he represented himself as the new, sacred king.

Additionally, the *laudes regiae* were 'ein staatssymbolisches Spiegelbild des frühen Mittelalters'[19] and in 'the acclamation not only for the visible Church, but also for the invisible one ... the images of king and Christ had been brought together as close as possible'.[20] The performance of Henry II during Easter caused him to move closer to Christ and thus emphasized for the subjects the righteousness of his claim to the throne, in preference to Otto.

The Avoidance of Humiliation

Extensive preparations were necessary for a dignified and representative celebration of a high feast. If the liturgical and representative setting was not well-prepared and well-organized, this might endanger the honourable representation of the king and of his rule. An effective representation could strengthen the king's power whereas an unsuccessful one could lead to the destabilization of power. It was unthinkable that the ruler should celebrate the high feast with his status impaired or diminished.

Otto I celebrated Easter 953 in Dortmund. He had planned to spend Easter in Aachen, but since that city failed to prepare properly for an honorable celebration, he avoided humiliation by going to Dortmund.

---

[16] E. Kantorowicz, *Laudes Regiae. A Study in Liturgical Acclamations and Medieval Ruler Worship* (Los Angeles, 1958), p. 77, n. 38. See also A. Eckenberg, *Cur cantatur? Die Funktionen des liturgischen Gesangs nach den Autoren der Karolingerzeit*, Bibliotheca Theologiae Practicae, vol. 41 (Stockholm, 1987) and R. Elze, 'Die Herrscherlaudes im Mittelalter', *Zeitschrift der Savigny-Stiftung für Rechtsgeschichte. Kanonistische Abteilung*, 84 (1954), pp. 201-223.

[17] Contrary to the ruler acclamations of Antiquity, the *laudes regiae* were not spoken or shouted, they were sung by the clergy. This chanting for the ruler in heaven and the ruler on earth gave the *laudes regiae* a special sacred quality, role and function during mass.

[18] Kantorowicz, *Laudes*, p. 76.

[19] B. Opfermann, *Die liturgischen Herrscherakklamationen im Sacrum Imperium des Mittelalters* (Weimar, 1953), p. 60.

[20] Kantorowicz, *Laudes*, p. 81.

Otto had been 'in danger of 'losing the king', of losing his own identity as king, particularly because at a key point he would not have been able to behave and to be seen in a manner which a modern German-speaker might term *repräsentativ*'.[21] Finally, as Widukind describes, he found in his 'patria' Dortmund the dignity which befitted his station, and which he might have lost in Aachen.[22]

During the feast days, he also held a council with his nobles and with the clergy. The coincidence of the council with Easter served to stress the importance of the king's honorable representation. He needed to present an aura of glory and to use this representation in the setting of Easter specifically for political purposes. In the case under discussion, he succeeded: the *Continuatio Reginonis* states that he gained strength and returned to Cologne with a great crowd of followers.[23]

It has to be emphasized here that royal councils were – statistically – mostly planned to coincide with major religious feasts. The itineraries of the Ottonian and Salian rulers show that they used numerous feasts for political gatherings. However, why did the ruler specifically choose holy days such as Christmas, Easter or Whitsun for his political gatherings?

The ruler, his nobles and the clergy usually spent the first day of the council celebrating the holy day. It should be noted that the holy mass and the ceremonies connected with mass were an integral and irreplaceable element of the council. Hagen Keller even speaks of a performative production of the holy mass,[24] which took place in the centre of the council. The council and the religious feast were sometimes even connected with a festival coronation.

The religious celebrations made it possible for the ruler to emphasize his sacral position among the aristocracy and the clergy *before* the political considerations of the council took place. Only the second day was reserved for political and 'secular' activities. This means that the structure of the council was mainly determined by the religious celebrations.

---

[21] T. Reuther, '*Regemque, quem in Francia pene perdidit, in patria magnifice recepit*: Ottonian Ruler Representation in Synchronic and Diachronic Comparison', in: Althoff & Schubert (eds.), *Herrschaftsrepräsentation*, pp. 363-380, 364.

[22] Widukind of Corvey, 'Die Sachsengeschichte des Widukind von Corvey', in: A. Bauer & R. Rau (transls.), *Quellen zur Geschichte der sächsischen Kaiserzeit*, Freiherr-vom-Stein-Gedächtnisausgabe, 8 vols. (Darmstadt, 1990³), vol. 3, p. 137.

[23] Adalbert of Magdeburg, *Adalberti Continuatio Reginonis*, F. Kurze (ed.), Monumenta Germaniae Historica, Scriptores rerum Germanicarum in usum scholarum separatim editi, vol. 50 (Hannover, 1980), p. 166: '... navigio Coloniam attigit indeque progrediens Drotmanni vico pascha celebravit. Post pascha coadunata fidelium suorum multitudine Coloniam iterum rediit'.

[24] Keller, 'Ritual', p. 53.

Thietmar of Merseburg even described how the political component of a council was transferred in its entirety to another place and time, because the intensive liturgical and representative celebrations of the feast did not allow space for political considerations.[25]

The legitimization, confirmation and remembrance of sacral kingship and power are three reasons for selecting religious feasts for a political gathering. Another is the pacification of all participants. The framework of a religious feast guaranteed a considerable degree of peace, at least during the holy day, but it may also have had effects on the political considerations of the council.

Festival Coronations and the Topography of Sacral Space

After the discussion of three cases in which sacral time was used and a sacral setting created for the king's representation, we will now concentrate on the topography of sacral space, using the example of festival coronations. Throughout the course of the sacralization process, the number of festival coronations increased in the tenth century.[26]

The Ottonian and Salian kings changed their venue for celebrations and councils from *Pfalzen* to bishop's towns.[27] While the major religious feasts fixed the date and the temporal structure of the festival coronations, the bishop's towns offered special topographic conditions for a liturgical celebration. The *civitas* which was chosen for a festival coronation had to create the following specific topographic preconditions: adjacent to the two churches, processional routes were built and established for a festival procession which ideally marched through the city

---

[25] In this example, most emphasis was put on the religious celebrations during that day: 'Das Palmfest feierte der König in Mainz, Ostern in Ingelheim und niemals ging es in dieser Gegend prächtiger und glänzernder her. Weil nun aber wegen des hohen Festes die wichtigsten Verhandlungen dort keinen Abschluß hatten finden können, wurde eine Fürstenversammlung in Aachen anberaumt'. Thietmar, 'Chronik', vol. 7, p. 54: 'Palmas rex celebrat Magoncia et in Ingilnemen pascha et in his partibus magis honorifice ac potestative numquam fuit. Et quia ob tantam sollempnitatem maxima ibidem finiri non poterant, ad Aquasgrani ponitur conventus'.

[26] For festival coronations, see C. Brühl, 'Kronen und Krönungsbrauch im Mittelalter', *Historische Zeitschrift*, 234 (1982), pp. 1-31; H.-U. Jäschke, 'Frühmittelalterliche Festkrönungen? Überlegungen zur Terminologie und Methode', *Historische Zeitschrift*, 211 (1970), pp. 556-588; H.-W. Klewitz, 'Die Festkrönungen der deutschen Könige', *Zeitschrift der Savigny-Stiftung für Rechtsgeschichte. Kanonistische Abteilung*, 28 (1939), pp. 48-96.

[27] C. Brühl, *Fodrum, Gistum, Servitium regis. Studien zu den wirtschaftlichen Grundlagen des Königtums im Frankenreich und den fränkischen Nachfolgestaaten Deutschland, Frankreich und Italien vom 6. bis zur Mitte des 14. Jahrhunderts* (Graz, 1968), p. 129.

from one church to the other. The sacral kingship was represented in the public space of the town.

Integrated within the liturgical setting of the holy day, the king's procession moved through the *civitas* from one church to another, accompanied by prayers, songs, symbols and signs. The coronator (a bishop or an archbishop) re-crowned the king with the quasi-liturgical symbol of the crown in the first church. The second part of the ceremony was the public procession: the crowned and adorned ruler walked from the coronation church to the second church, where holy mass was celebrated; he was accompanied by the archbishop or bishop, the aristocracy and the clergy. During the service, the *laudes regiae* were chanted for him.

At the outset of this paper, I have referred to the debate of the two churches during Whitsun of the year 1081. The same source describes the procession of Henry IV from the tent in which he was crowned to the tent where he attended mass. The procession was not just a performance of the crowned king, but rather of all persons who were involved. Furthermore, as Benzo of Alba writes, the procession was joyful for both humans *and* angels. This double dimension of the procession, earth and heaven, corresponds to the king's two natures. The idea that the angels were watching the crowned king, full of joy, might have been in the minds of everyone who took part in the procession: the king, the clergy, the aristocracy, the crowd and last but not least Benzo of Alba, the author of the description. The source provides an insight into a double imagination and dimension of space: earthly and heavenly space were related to each other, even heavenly spectators were viewing the performance of the king's representation from above.

The procession after the coronation was a highly important act in the context of the king's liturgical representation. While the coronation inside the church could be witnessed only by a small selected group of people, both the population of the bishop's town and all who came to celebrate the holy day could see the crowned and adorned ruler when his procession moved through the streets of town. All present were able to participate in the representation of power. In this particular ensemble, the *witnesses* were just as important as those who *took part* in the procession.

The king's procession reminded the viewers of the king's first coronation and of his future as a heavenly co-ruler. Through visualization, memory and imagination everybody (the king, the clergy, the aristocracy and the people of the town) participated in the procession and in a kingship based on the grace of God. The early medieval king chose the liturgical setting for his coronation ceremony. This was done not only to stress the relationship between political and sacral power; but the ruler also used it for the legitimization, presentation and visualization of his position as vicegerent of Christ, king by the grace of God and future heavenly co-ruler.

What was true for space can be also be mentioned with regard to sacred time. The 'terrestrial kingship appeared all the more transparent against the background of the kingship of Christ'[28] as he chose a feast day for his coronation.

The impressive changes in the plans of the medieval towns which took part in the sacralization movement of the tenth and eleventh centuries can be seen e.g. in the bishop's city of Augsburg.[29]

In 1012, King Henry II and his brother, Bishop Bruno of Augsburg, founded the monastery of SS Ulrich and Afra. In 1019, they also founded the chapter of St Moritz, which was located directly on the border between the old city and the new Ottonian-Salian constructions. The extension of Maximilian Street dates back to the early eleventh century. This street, which linked SS Ulrich and Afra with St Moritz, was built as a procession street with a length of 600 meters.[30]

Bamberg and Paderborn are other examples of extraordinary changes in relation to royal representation in a bishop's town. The new bishop's city of Bamberg, founded by Henry II, was like a 'capital of the *Reich*'. In reference to Rome, the bishop's town was called the city of the seven hills with a cathedral which was built after the example of St Peter's in Rome. The king equipped Bamberg not only with a representative cathedral, but also with monasteries and chapters. These ecclesiastical buildings were arranged in an ensemble which unified 'Kirchenlandschaft und Repräsentationsraum' in the town of Bamberg.[31]

In Paderborn, Bishop Meinwerk vigorously championed the construction of the cathedral and furthermore he built a *Kaiserpfalz*, a palace for the bishop and two monasteries. One of the monasteries was built after the

---

[28] Kantorowicz, *Laudes*, p. 92.

[29] See W. Noack, 'Stadtbaukunst und geistlich-weltliche Repräsentation im 11. Jahrhundert', in: B. Hackelsberger & G. Himmelheber (eds.), *Festschrift für Kurt Bauch. Kunstgeschichtliche Beiträge zum 25. November 1957* (S.l., 1957), pp. 29-49.

[30] See E. Herzog, *Die ottonische Stadt. Die Anfänge der mittelalterlichen Stadtbaukunst in Deutschland*, Frankfurter Forschungen zur Architekturgeschichte, vol. 2 (Berlin, 1964), p. 193.

[31] See B. Schneidmüller, 'Die einzigartig geliebte Stadt – Heinrich II. und Bamberg', in: J. Kirmeier, B. Schneidmüller & S. Weinfurter (eds.), *Kaiser Heinrich II. 1002-1024. Begleitband zur bayerischen Landesausstellung 2002* (Stuttgart, 2002), pp. 30-52, p. 45.

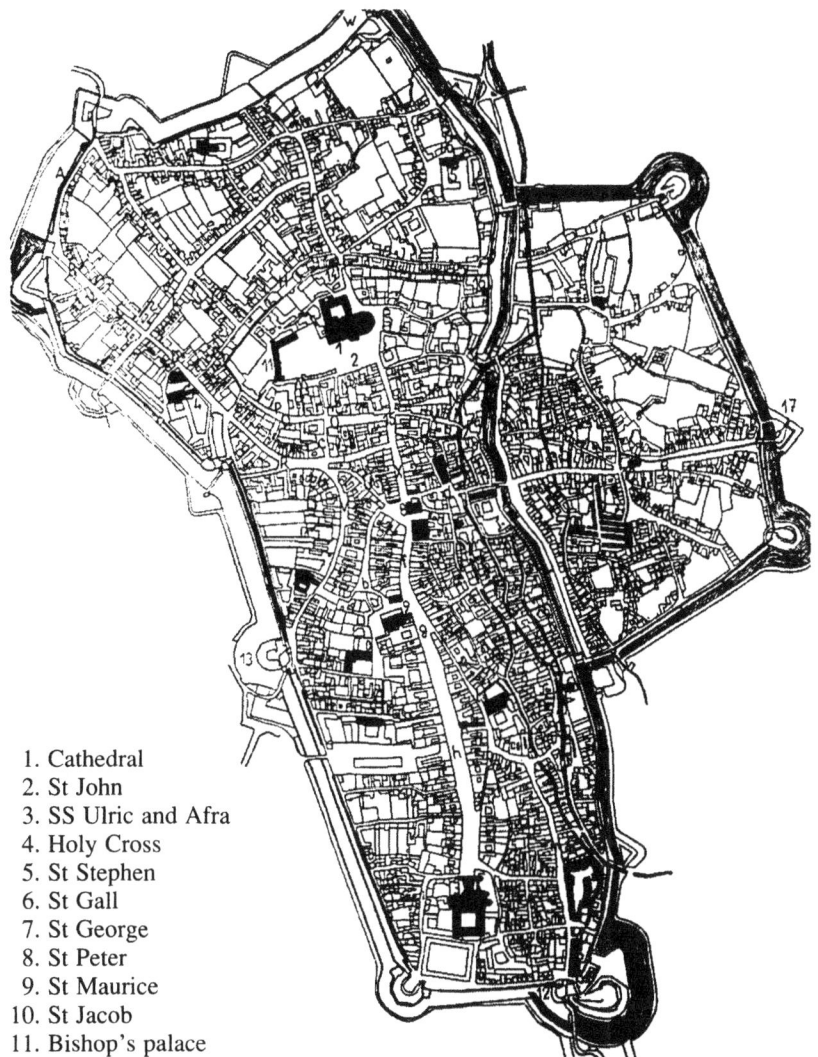

1. Cathedral
2. St John
3. SS Ulric and Afra
4. Holy Cross
5. St Stephen
6. St Gall
7. St George
8. St Peter
9. St Maurice
10. St Jacob
11. Bishop's palace

Map: E. Herzog, *Die ottonische Stadt. Die Anfänge der mittelalterlichen Baukunst in Deutschland* (Berlin, 1964), p. 187.

model of Jerusalem's Church of the Holy Sepulchre, the other after a Roman example. 'Sakrale Erinnerungslandschaften' and the royal use of representative space were connected in urban planning and architecture.

A double development can be observed: not only did the king begin to choose bishop's towns, bishops also started to develop and change the topography and architecture of their towns for festival coronations and for the purpose of royal representation. The towns' structures were shaped by the *king's and bishop's* need for representation. Here, we can observe the interaction of 'political' and 'liturgical' representation, which Hagen Keller describes as an impulse of visualization.[32] It found its expression in the architecture and topography of the Ottonian and early Salian bishop's towns.

Final Considerations

This paper has focused on the interdependencies of sacral and political power and their representation in the Early Middle Ages. Through the example of festival coronations and councils on holy days, I have intended to show that within the framework of sacralization in the tenth and eleventh centuries, the liturgical dimension of royal representation became a foundation of kingship. The ruler *needed* a sacred setting for the representation of his kingship by the grace of God, and of his political purposes.

Ecclesiastical buildings were essential for representational ceremonies. The interior of the church building was not only used for the purpose of representation, but also to establish the connection between the church in question to the other churches during festival processions.

The festival coronations of medieval kings were both highly political and highly religious acts. They were, within the framework of the feast days and with all their ritual elements – the processions, the celebration of mass, the *laudes regiae* etc. - an opportunity to show everybody the interdependence of sacral and political power. A festival coronation is an important example of the combined use of sacred space, buildings and times for the purpose of the king's representation.

I would furthermore like to emphasize that the increasing integration of sacral elements in the king's representation implied a double strategy and that this was not only in the ruler's interest. The clergy and also the bishop's towns wished to persuade the ruler to spend his feasts in their town, since this increased their importance and influence in the *Reich*. The bishops of Paderborn, Bamberg, Augsburg and Speyer for example changed the topography and architecture of their towns for such representative occasions and simultaneously incorporated into their towns features borrowed from the examples of Jerusalem or Rome.

---

[32] Keller, 'Ritual', p. 24.

It is obvious that certain elements of the king's representation during feast days, such as *adventus* ceremonies for the ruler, processions, the attending of mass, banquets and others were present frequently, during festival coronations as well as during councils. There was a development of 'vielgliedriger Ritualketten'[33] in the tenth and eleventh centuries. The 'main' rituals are part of a chain of rituals, which can be embellished and completed by further rituals, depending on the occasion.

The liturgical dimension of royal representation raises the question whether these rituals placed more emphasis on the liturgical aspects or on the aspects of royalty. In Ottonian times, there seems to have been a fragile balance between both, with a noticeable tendency towards the sacralization of kingship and its rituals. That balance was disturbed in the late eleventh century by the conflict between the church and the ruler.

To conclude this discussion of the liturgical dimension of royal representation, which manifests itself in the urban development and architecture, I would like to refer back to our primary source: the debate concerning the two churches and the construction of a sacred space for the festival coronation of Henry IV in 1081. During the tenth and eleventh centuries, the 'chains of rituals' in general and the festival coronations in particular became more and more complex and filled with symbolic meaning and understanding. However, it is obvious that certain situations could lead to a reduction of the complexity of the ritual, such as political dangers and exceptional situations. If necessary, it was possible to refrain from representative places and sacral space, but it was not possible to refrain from the liturgical and representative celebration of the high feast as a framework and structure. On the contrary, the high feast overcame difficult and dangerous situations and occasioned strength, steadiness and constancy. It confirmed the legitimacy of the sacral kingship during a sacral time that was not contestable. The high feast could not be occupied or usurped. However, this did not imply protection against abuse and annoyances, as the description of the council of Henry II of Bavaria in Quedlinburg demonstrates. These attempts emphasize the attractiveness of the ensemble of liturgy and royal representation in Ottonian and Salian times.

Westfälische Wilhelms-Universität Münster

---

[33] *Ibidem.*

Gabriela SIGNORI

SAKRAL ODER PROFAN?
DER KOMMUNIKATIONSRAUM KIRCHE

'Und Jesus ging in den Tempel hinein und trieb heraus alle Verkäufer und Käufer im Tempel und stieß die Tische der Geldwechsel um und die Stände der Taubenhändler und sprach zu ihnen: Es steht geschrieben (Jes. 56, 7): 'Mein Haus soll ein Bethaus heißen'; ihr aber macht eine Räuberhöhle daraus'.
(Matt. 21, 12-16; Luk. 19, 45 f.)

Wenig menschliche Tätigkeiten sind religionsübergreifend so eindeutig als profan zu erkennen, wie Geldwechsel oder Handel. Sie stehen unverkennbar in Widerspruch zur Dignität, zur Sakralität des Kirchenraums, den Christus dem Lukas- und Matthäusevangelium zufolge als Gebethaus begriff.[1]

Mircea Eliade geht davon aus, dass die Unterscheidung zwischen profan und heilig zum Wesen des Religiösen gehört. Es seien zwei streng von einander getrennte Welten, zwei verschiedene Arten des In-der-Welt-Seins, die mit unterschiedlichen Raumkonzeptionen verbunden seien. Das Profane sei homogen, das Sakrale hingegen basiere auf der Erfahrung der räumlichen Heterogenität. Für den Menschen fassbar, sichtbar und erkennbar werde das Heilige erst mittels Zeichen. Später hätten die Menschen über dem heiligen Ort mit göttlichem Plan oder, wäre Mircea Eliade zu ergänzen, mit dem Zauberstab der Weihe heilige Gebäude errichtet, Tempel, Kirchen, Kathedralen, deren Mauern die eine Welt von der anderen trennten, deren Funktion es war, das Heilige zu schützen. Türen ermöglichten es den Menschen, von der einen in die andere Welt zu wechseln, gewissermaßen zu transzendieren.[2]

Die Welt in sakrale und profane Räume zu ordnen, fällt Ethnologen und Theologen leicht. Im Wechsel vom Mythos zur Geschichte bzw. vom Ideal zur Praxis verlieren die Grenzlinien jedoch zumeist ihre ursprüng-

---

[1] Nach dem Johannesevangelium schalt Christus die Taubenverkäufer: 'Tragt das weg und macht nicht meines Vaters Haus zum Kaufhaus' (Joh. 2, 16).
[2] Mircea Eliade, *Das Heilige und das Profane. Vom Wesen des Religiösen* (Frankfurt, 1984). Vgl. auch Berndt Hamm, ''Heiligkeit im Mittelalter'. Theoretische Annäherung an ein interdisziplinäres Forschungsvorhaben', in: Nine Miedema & Rudolf Suntrup (Hgg.), *Literatur – Geschichte – Literaturgeschichte. Festschrift für Volker Honemann zum 60. Geburtstag* (Frankfurt u. a., 2003), S. 627-645.

liche Schärfe. Geldwechsler und Taubenhändler als Metaphern für die Welt dringen in den Kircheninnenraum. Nicht immer werden sie vertrieben. Die Rezeptionsgeschichte der evangelischen 'Tempelreinigung' ist aber erst in Ansätzen erschlossen.[3]

Der Sakralraum Kirche fasziniert bis heute vornehmlich in seiner idealen Gestalt, als paradiesische Vorschau, als himmlisches Jerusalem.[4] Im Verlauf der Jahrhunderte hatte sich das Kircheninnere jedoch schrittweise in Zonen unterschiedlicher Heiligkeitsdichte ausdifferenziert. Es entstanden Teilräume mit unterschiedlichem Öffentlichkeitsgrad und unterschiedlichen Funktionen für den Klerus und die Gemeinde.[5] Die Frage, was sakral und was profan ist, erhob sich mit wachsender Differenzierung immer klarer zu einer *Standortfrage* mit zwei, manchmal auch drei Fixpunkten im Chor bzw. in der Apsis und im Langhaus der Kirche.[6] Die Grenzlinien, welche das Profane vom Sakralen trennten, verschoben sich und verloren, wie angedeutet, zugleich an Schärfe. Sakral und profan vermischten sich zusehends. Um dieses 'Gemisch', diesen 'Zwischenraum' im metaphorischen Wortsinn zu bezeichnen, fehlen uns jedoch die passenden Worte. Unsere Sprache tradiert und zementiert Jahrtausende alte Dichotomien, welche die 'Realität' eigentlich längst überwunden hat.

Gebrauch

Die meisten 'profanen' Nutzungsmöglichkeiten des mittelalterlichen Kirchenraums gründen in der Sakralität des Ortes bzw. des Gebäudes.[7] Sind sie darob überhaupt noch als profan zu verstehen? Und was genau

---

[3] C. M. Kauffmann, 'Art and Popular Culture: New Themes in the Holkham Bible Picture Book', in: David Buckton & T. A. Heslop (Hgg.), *Studies in Medieval Art and Architecture presented to Peter Lasko* (Phoenix Mill, 1994), S. 46-70. Im hohen Mittelalter sei die Episode unter dem Oberthema Simonie behandelt worden, im späten Mittelalter im Kontext des Wucherverbotes.

[4] Vgl. u. a. Joseph Sauer, *Symbolik des Kirchengebäudes und seiner Ausstattung in der Auffassung des Mittelalters. Mit Berücksichtigung von Honorius Augustodunensis, Sicardus und Durandus* (Freiburg im Breisgau, 1924²); Friedrich Ohly, 'Die Kathedrale als Zeitenram. Zum Dom von Siena', *Frühmittelalterliche Studien*, 6 (1972), S. 94-158; Ders., 'Die Säulen des salomonischen Tempels und die Doppelturmfassade. Materialien zum Nachleben biblischer Architektur im christlichen Sakralbau', ebd., 32 (1998), S. 1-27.

[5] Brigitte Bedos-Rezak, 'Form as Social Process', in: Virginia Chieffo Raguin u. a. (Hgg.), *Artistic Integration in Gothic Buildings* (Toronto, 1995), S. 236-245.

[6] Zur Kanzel als dritten Mittelpunkt vgl. Gabriela Signori, *Räume, Gesten, Andachtsformen. Geschlecht, Konflikt und religiöse Kultur im europäischen Spätmittelalter* (Ostfildern, 2005).

[7] J. G. Davies, *The Secular Use of Church Buildings* (London, 1968); Hartmut Boockmann, *Die Stadt im späten Mittelalter* (München, 1986), S. 191-218.

heißt in diesem Zusammenhang eigentlich profan? Ist für die mittelalterliche Weltsicht nicht gerade das Ineinandergreifen der beiden Arten des In-der-Welt-Seins charakteristisch? Seit frühester Zeit wählte man den Sakralraum, um Herrscher zu krönen[8] oder um Ritter zu weihen.[9] Aber sind Krönung und Ritterweihe wirklich profane Rituale? Sind sie nicht primär Riten, sakrale Handlungen?

Sakrales und Profanes vermischen sich auch im Kirchenasyl, das Schutz vor Fehden und, auf bestimmte Delikte begrenzt, Schutz vor dem Zugriff der Gerichtsknechte bot.[10] Spätmittelalterliche Gerichtsquellen bezeichnen den Akt der Asylsuche verheißungsvoll als Flucht in die Freiheit.[11] Diese Freiheit aber besaß nicht jede Kirche. Sie wurde verliehen.[12] Das päpstliche Privileg aber respektierte die weltliche Obrigkeit nicht immer, wie wir den 21 Artikeln (1501) des Straßburger Münsterpredigers Geiler von Kaysersberg († 1510) entnehmen. Geiler rekapituliert das geltende Kirchenrecht. In Kirche und Kirchhof dürfe niemand belangt werden. Der Freiheitsraum dehne sich bei einer Hauptkirche auf einen Umkreis von vierzig, bei allen anderen Kirchen auf einen Umkreis von dreißig Fuß aus:

> Der Tempel (die Kirche) hat gemäß eines kaiserlichen Privilegs Asylrecht (Freiheit), desgleichen der Kirchhof, so dass man niemanden daraus vertreiben darf. Dies gilt nicht allein für den Tempel und den Kirchhof, sondern vierzig Schritt darüber hinaus bei einer Hauptkirche, dreißig jede andere Kirche. Soweit darf man gehen, um seine Notdurft zu erledigen und nicht wegen anderen Dingen.[13]

[8] Vgl. u. a. Jean-Pierre Bayard, *Sacres et couronnements royaux* (Paris, 1984); *Krönungen. Könige in Aachen – Geschichte und Mythos*, 2 Bde. (Mainz, 2000).

[9] Jean Flori, 'Chevalerie et liturgie. Remise des armes et vocabulaire 'chevaleresque' dans les sources liturgiques du IXe au XIVe siècle', *Le Moyen Âge*, 84 (1978), S. 247-278 und 409-442.

[10] Peter Landau, 'Art. 'Asylrecht' III', *Theologische Realenzyklopädie*, Bd. 4 (1979), S. 319-327.

[11] Staatsarchiv Basel-Stadt, Gerichtsarchiv D (= Kundschaften), Bd. 11, fol. 84 r°: 'Jtem Stoffel Propst hat geseit, wie sich vor Wyhenechten vngeuerlich gemacht, dz Hannß Swijcz Knopffen zu Núwenburg gestochen vnd da von in die /fryheit/ gewichen, da selbs er vnd ander mit im geredt vnd gemeint, in uß der fryheit zu tedingen'.

[12] Zur spätmittelalterlichen Rechtspraxis vgl. u. a. Hermann Schmid, 'Das Asylrecht der Deutschherren und ihres Hauses', *Zeitschrift für die Geschichte des Oberrheins*, 133 (1985), S. 179-207; Kathryn L. Reyerson, 'Flight from Prosecution: The Search for Religious Asylum in Medieval Montpellier', *French Historical Studies*, 17 (1992), 603-626.

[13] Geiler von Kaysersberg, '21. Artikel', in: Ders., *Sämtliche Werke, I: Die deutschen Schriften. Erste Abteilung: Die zu Geilers Lebzeiten erschienen Schriften*, Gerhard Bauer (Hg.), 3 Bde. (Berlin / New York, 1989-1995), Bd. 1, S. 189: 'Der tempel hat friheit, des glichen der kilchhoff / das man daruß niemans sol mit bescheid / und noch inhalt keiserlicher frijheit. Und nit allein der tempel und kilchhoff / sunder ouch viertzig schrit witer die houbtkilch, als unser munster / aber ein ander kirch xxx / So wijt mag eyner gon, sin

War die profane Nutzung anfänglich situationsbedingt, verwandelte sie sich im Spätmittelalter zur Institution. Vielerorts, sowohl in der Stadt als auch auf dem Land, diente das Langhaus, also der Laienteil der Kirche, als Rathaus oder als Gerichtsstätte.[14] Der Befund ist für einzelne Städte bekannt, die Belege aber sind noch nicht systematisch erschlossen.[15] Ungleich mehr Interesse erwecken seit längerem die Rathäuser, profane Gebäude, teilweise mit sakralem Kern. Auch die Nutzung der Kirche als Rathaus hängt wesentlich mit der Sakralität, partiell aber auch mit der Größe des Gebäudes zusammen. Selbst nach dem Bau eines Rathauses verzichtete die Obrigkeit selten auf ihren angestammten Platz im Inneren der Kirche, sei der in Gestalt hoher, Maßwerk verzierter, herrschaftlicher Stallen[16] und/oder in Gestalt einer eigenen Ratskapelle.[17] Wie der Fürst oder der Monarch verstand sich auch das Stadtregiment als ein von Gott bestimmtes Gremium im Dienste des Gemeinwohls.[18] Das Gemeinwohl

notturft zu thun / und nit umb ander sachen willen'. Vgl. Léon Dacheux, *Un réformateur catholique à la fin du XVe siècle. Jean Geiler de Kaysersberg, prédicateur à la cathédrale de Strasbourg, 1478-1510. Étude sur sa vie et son temps* (Paris / Straßburg, 1876), p. 92; Uwe Israel, *Johannes Geiler von Kaysersberg (1445-1510). Der Straßburger Münsterprediger als Rechtsreformer*, Berliner Historische Studien, Bd. 27 (Berlin, 1997), S. 250.

[14] Nikolaus Zaske, *Die gotischen Kirchen Stralsunds und ihre Kunstwerke. Kirchliche Kunstgeschichte von 1250 bis zur Gegenwart* (Berlin, 1964), S. 53: 'Dieser Raum (das Westwerk) ersetzte das Rathaus, denn noch im vierzehnten Jahrhundert tätigten die Ratsherren verschiedene Rechtsgeschäfte in ihrem Amtssitz unter den hohen Gewölben der Kirche. Hier empfingen sie auswärtige Gesandtschaften, fassten Beschlüsse und hielten ihre Sitzungen zuweilen auch während des Gottesdienstes ab, ohne diesen jedoch zu stören'. Zu Bern und Lausanne, wo die Sitzungen im Refektorium stattfanden, vgl. Petra Zimmer & Brigitte Degler-Spengler (Hgg.), *Die Dominikaner und Dominikanerinnen in der Schweiz*, Helvetia Sacra. Abt. IV, Bd. 5, Teil 1-2, Bd. 1 (Basel, 1999), S. 290 und 428. Zu den Dorfkirchen Karl Siegfried Bader, *Dorfgenossenschaft und Dorfgemeinde* (Weimar, 1962), S. 402-408; Gabriela Signori, 'Umstrittene Stühle. Spätmittelalterliches Kirchengestühl als soziales, politisches und religiöses Kommunikationsmedium', *Zeitschrift für Historische Forschung*, 29 (2002), S. 189-213.

[15] Cord Meckseper geht davon aus, dass die meisten Rathäuser ursprünglich Kaufhäuser gewesen und häufig bewusst unmittelbar neben Kirche bzw. Dombezirk errichtet worden seien. Cord Meckseper, 'Das Rathaus im Stadtbaugeschichtlichen Kontext', in: Ursula Schädler-Saub & Angela Weyer (Hgg.), *Mittelalterliche Rathäuser in Niedersachsen und Bremen. Geschichte, Kunst, Erhaltung*, Schriften des Hornemann Instituts, Bd. 6 (Petersberg, 2002), S. 19-24, 19.

[16] Dietrich W. Poeck, 'Zahl, Tag und Stuhl. Zur Semiotik der Ratswahl', *Frühmittelalterliche Studien*, 33 (1999), S. 396-427; Ders., *Rituale der Ratswahl. Zeichen und Zeremoniell der Ratssetzung in Europa (12.-18. Jahrhundert)*, Städteforschung, Bd. A/60 (Köln u. a., 2003).

[17] Vgl. Uwe Heckert, *Die Ratskapelle als religiöses und politisches Zentrum der Ratsherrschaft in deutschen Städten des späten Mittelalters* (Bielefeld: Diss., 1997).

[18] Vgl. u. a. Winfried Eberhard, "Gemeiner Nutzen' als oppositionelle Leitvorstellung im Spätmittelalter', in: Manfred Gerwing & Godehard Ruppert (Hgg.), *Renovatio und Reformatio: wider das Bild vom 'finsteren' Mittelalter. Festschrift für Ludwig Hödl zum 60. Geburtstag* (Münster, 1985), S. 194-214; Peter Hibst, *Utilitas publica – Gemeiner*

wiederum beinhaltete spätestens seit dem 14. Jahrhundert auch die Sorge um Sittlichkeit und Zucht, dazu wiederum gehörte das Wohlverhalten auf dem Kirchhof und in der Kirche.

Regelmäßig für profane bzw. größtenteils für politische Zwecke genutzt wurde auch die Kirchentür, der Lettner oder die Kanzel.[19] Von ihnen aus wurden der Öffentlichkeit bzw. der Gemeinde, der Stadtgemeinde, Dorfgemeinde oder dem Kirchspiel, Ratsbeschlüsse oder Mandate unterbreitet, auch solche, welche die Kirchenzucht betreffen. Dennoch, profan ist nicht gleich politisch. Die Heiligkeit des Ortes führte dazu, dass im Kircheninneren bevorzugt, nicht nur Friedensverträge abgeschlossen und gefeiert wurden, sondern auch andere 'private' Schwüre abgelegt wurden, wie eine Episode aus dem berühmten Kölner 'Buch Weinsberg' zeigt. Weinsbergs Magd behauptete, er habe sie geschwängert, was er auf Anhieb nicht glauben wollte. In der Kirche musste sie ihm feierlich schwören, dass er wirklich der Vater des Kindes war, mit dem sie schwanger ging.[20] Dagegen war nichts mehr einzuwenden.

Häufig wurden in oder vor der Kirche Geschäfte abgeschlossen und Verträge aufgesetzt. So beginnt ein Basler Testament aus dem Jahr 1490 mit den Worten:

> Im Namen Gottes. Amen. Allen und jedem, der dieses vorliegende, offene Instrument sieht oder hört, sei kund und offenbar, dass im Jahr nach der Geburt Christi, unserer Herren, als man das Jahr tausend und neunzig zählte… auf Mittwoch, den 16. Tag des Monats Juni, *in der Stadt Basel und auf dem Kirchhof zu Sankt Peter und da vor der Kirche und vor der großen Türe, wovor man gewöhnlich das Sakrament der heiligen Ehe vollzieht*, vor mir, einem öffentlichen Notar und in Gegenwart von Zeugen, die unten genannt werden, persönlich erschienen ist die ehrbare Frau Anna Seitenma-

---

Nutzen – Gemeinwohl: Untersuchungen zur Idee eines politischen Leitbegriffs von der Antike bis zum späten Mittelalter, Europäische Hochschulschriften, Bd. III/497 (Frankfurt/M., 1991); Pierangelo Schiera, '*Bonum commune* zwischen Mittelalter und Neuzeit. Überlegungen zur substanziellen Grundlage der modernen Politik', *Archiv für Kulturgeschichte*, 81 (1999), S. 283-303.

[19] Max Seidel, 'Die Kanzel als Bühne. Zur Funktion der Pisani-Kanzeln', in: Klaus Güthlein & Franz Matsche (Hgg.), *Begegnungen. Festschrift für Peter Anselm Riedl zum 60. Geburtstag*, Heidelberger Kunstgeschichtliche Abhandlungen, Bd. 20 (Worms, 1993), S. 18-34; Gabriela Signori, 'Ritual und Ereignis: Die Straßburger Bittgänge zur Zeit der Burgunderkriege (1474-1477)', *Historische Zeitschrift*, 264 (1997), S. 281-328; Ralph Melcher, *Die mittelalterlichen Kanzeln der Toscana*, Manuskripte zur Kunstwissenschaft, Bd. 56 (Worms, 2000), S. 101-234; Falk Eisermann, 'Typographie und öffentliche Kommunikation im 15. Jahrhundert', in: Miedema & Suntrup (Hgg.), *Literatur*, S. 481-502.

[20] *Das Buch Weinsberg. Kölner Denkwürdigkeiten aus dem 16. Jahrhundert*, Konstantin Höhlbaum (Hg.), Bd. 1 (Leipzig, 1886), S. 257f.

cherin, die eheliche und verlassene Witwe des verstorbenen Klaus Seitenmachers, ehedem Scherer und Bürger der Stadt Basel...'[21]

Noch häufiger diente das Kirchengebäude als Depot für Wertpapiere, ein Phänomen, das sich über die Jahrhunderte hindurch beobachten lässt.[22] Bekannt ist die Trese in der Lübecker Marienkirche, ein Raum über der Rats- bzw. Herrenkapelle, in dem der Rat bis weit in das 19. Jahrhundert seine Freiheiten und Privilegien aufzubewahren pflegte.[23] Ähnliches ist aus Braunschweig und Bremen[24] sowie aus Lausanne,[25] Padua, Perugia,

---

[21] Staatsarchiv Basel-Stadt, Klosterarchiv, St. Peter, Urkunden, Nr. 1165: 'Im namen gottes Amen. Allen vnnd jeglichen, so dis gegenwùrttig offen jnstrument sehennd oder hoᵉrend lesen, sig kundt vnnd offembar, das jm jor nach der gepurt Cristi vnnsers herren, alß man zalt thusent vierhundert vnnd nunzig jore... vff mitwuchen, der do was vnnd ist der sechzehende tag des monatz juny, jn der statt Basel vnnd vff dem kylchoff zů sannt Petter vnnd doselben vor der kilchen vnnd der grossen thúren, dauor mann gewonlichen das sacrament der heyligen ee verfuᵉget, vor mir, offenen notarien, vnnd jngegenwurttigkeit der gezugen, hie vnnde geschriben, personlichen erschynnen ist die ersam frow Anna Seittenmacherin, eelichen vnnd verlassen wytwe wylent Clauß Seittenmachers, des scherers vnnd burgers ze Basel seligen...'
[22] Ernst Posner, *Archives in the Ancient World* (Cambridge, 1972), S. 44-46, 115f.; William C. West, 'The Public Archives in Fourth-Century Athens', *Greek, Roman and Byzantine Studies*, 30 (1989), S. 529-543.
[23] Ernst Pitz, *Schrift und Aktenwesen der städtischen Verwaltung im Spätmittelalter. Köln – Nürnberg – Lübeck. Beitrag zur vergleichenden Städteforschung*, Mitteilungen aus den Stadtarchiv Köln, Bd. 45 (Köln, 1959), S. 415-424. Die Bürgerschaft hatte sich in einer speziellen Kammer der Marienkirche, in der Trese, ihr Urkundenarchiv eingerichtet. Dies war noch im Jahr 1843 der Fall, als der erste Band der Lübecker Urkundenbücher erschien. Damals nämlich kommentierten die Herausgeber (*Lübeckisches Urkundenbuch. 1. Abtheilung: Urkundenbuch der Stadt Lübeck* (Lübeck, 1843), S. X): 'Die Trese ist ein geräumiges festes Gewölbe in der Marienkirche über der Bürgermeister- oder Ratscapelle, in der sich in älteren Zeiten der Senat, bevor er sich auf das nahe Rathhaus begab, zu versammeln pflegte, belegen, und von dieser aus vermittelst einer steinernen Wendeltreppe zugänglich. Dieses Local kommt schon sehr früh unter dem Namen *treselaria consilii*, *Tresecamere*, vor und scheint, wie aus dem Namen und manchen äußeren Vorrichtungen hervorgeht, in ältester Zeit nicht bloß ausschließlich zur Aufbewahrung der Urkunden, sondern auch als Schatzkammer gedient zu haben. Noch jetzt befinden sich daselbst nicht nur fast alle älteren Urkunden der Stadt, sondern auch neuere Staatsverträge und wichtige Documente werden daselbst deponirt'. So lautet der Eschatokoll einer Urkunde aus dem Jahr 1321 (*Ebd.*, Theil 2, Nr. 404, 355): 'Litere ciuitatum predictarum super istis arbitriis destinate in ecclesia beate Marie in camera dominorum consulum sunt deposite et seruate'. Die mittelniederdeutsche Übersetzung der Urkunde spricht von *treserie* (Trese), worin der Rat seine *breve*, seine Urkunden bzw. Privilegien aufbewahre. Nicht nur der Rat, auch geistliche Gemeinschaften wie das Brigittenkloster zu Marienword pflegten in der städtischen Trese ihre Privilegien in eigenen *laden* zu verwahren (*Urkunden-Buch der Stadt Lübeck*, Bd. 5 (Lübeck, 1877), Nr. 522, 566f.
[24] Adolf Brenneke, *Archivkunde. Ein Beitrag zur Theorie und Geschichte des europäischen Archivwesens* (Leipzig, 1953), S. 129.
[25] Zimmer & Degler-Spengler (Hgg.), *Die Dominikaner*, Bd. I, S. 428.

Orvieto, Sezze und anderen oberitalienischen Städten bekannt. Petra Koch bilanziert: 'Die zahlreichen und vielfältigen Quellenbelege zeigen, dass die Kommunen parallel zur Entwicklung eigener Institutionen für die Archivierung bis ins 14. Jahrhundert und darüber hinaus kirchliche Räumlichkeiten zur Aufbewahrung von Teilen ihres Schriftgutes nutzten'.[26]

Weniger bekannt sind hingegen die unzähligen Privaturkunden, welche die Gläubigen in Kathedralen, Mendikanten- oder Gemeindekirchen aufbewahrten. Die Frage, wem man seine Papiere anvertraute bzw. wo man sie deponierte, hatte sich im 15. Jahrhundert von der Empfängerfrage losgelöst. Jede Art Handänderung wurde fortan in Gerichts- oder Stadtbüchern mit unterschiedlichen Namen (Schreinsbücher, Fertigungsbücher *etc.*) eingetragen. Wer es sich leisten konnte, ließ sich jedoch weiterhin bald mehr, bald weniger kostbare Urkunden ausstellen. Wem man diese anvertraute, darüber entschieden fortan immer häufiger persönliche Bindungen. Das heißt, Rechtsansprüche bzw. Besitztitel traten in den Hintergrund. Um ihr Testament oder andere Wertpapiere (Eheverträge, Erbverzichte, Schenkungen) aufzubewahren, wählten die einen spezielle Orte in der Kirche, die anderen die Zunftstube. Das Zunfthaus war sozusagen das Konkurrenzmodell zum Kirchengebäude.[27] Egal ob Kirche oder Zunftstube, die Praxis weist zahlreiche Parallelen zum Amt des Testamentsvollstreckers auf. In beiden Fällen geht es in erster Linie um Vertrauen. Häufig überschneiden sich die beiden 'Institutionen' auch. Das heißt, als Testamentsvollstrecker wählten viele Erblasser Angehörige derjenigen Institutionen, denen sie auch ihre Wertpapiere anvertrauten.

Die Basler Achtburgerin Adelheid von Laufen beispielsweise hinterlegte ihre erste Testamentsfassung aus dem Jahr 1471 'hinter dem *Liebfrauenbau*'.[28] Unter dem 'Bau', dem 'Werk' oder der 'Fabrik' einer Kir-

---

[26] Petra Koch, 'Die Archivierung kommunaler Bücher in den ober- und mittelitalienischen Städten im 13. und frühen 14. Jahrhundert', in: Hagen Keller & Thomas Behrmann (Hgg.), *Kommunales Schriftgut in Oberitalien. Formen – Funktionen – Überlieferung*, Münstersche Mittelalter-Schriften, Bd. 68 (München, 1995), S. 19-69, hier 24ff. Auffallend oft würden Bettelordenskirchen erwähnt, beobachtet die Autorin.
[27] Zunftgenossen wie der Basler Bäckermeister Hans Sperrer, genannt Brüglinger, zogen es vor, ihre Nachlassregelungen in den entsprechenden Räumlichkeiten ihrer Zunftstuben, in seinem Fall 'hinder der brotbecken zunfft', zu hinterlegen. Staatsarchiv Basel-Stadt, Gerichtsarchiv B, Bd. 9, 169-174 (1471). Es handelt sich um eine Pfründstiftung in der Elisabethenkirche.
[28] Staatsarchiv Basel-Stadt, Gerichtsarchiv B, Bd. 9, 195: 'alles nach lut vnd jnnhalt eins papirenen zedels von jrer eigenen hand geschriben vnd mit jrem jngesigel besiglett vnd beslossen, so sy, als sy redt, hinder den bŭw vnser lieben frowen stifft vnd münster zu Basel als zŭᵉ gemeinen getruwen handen geleit hett'.

che versteht man im Spätmittelalter die meist von der Stadt verwalteten Einnahmen und Ausgaben für den Kirchenbau, häufig mit entsprechender Örtlichkeit in oder in der Nähe des Kirchengebäudes.[29] In Basel blieb das Amt des Werkmeisters über die Jahrhunderte hinweg fest in geistlicher Hand.[30] In Straßburg war die Verwaltung des Liebfrauenwerks schon im 13. Jahrhundert in städtische Hände gelangt. Geiler von Kaysersberg beschwerte sich um 1500 bitter darüber, dass die Stadt die Einnahmen häufig zweckentfremdete und für weltliche Zwecke benutzte. Das Geld sei allein 'zum Gebrauch für den Tempel (die Kirche) und zur Vergrößerung und Vermehrung der Ehre und des Dienstes an Gott und Maria, seiner würdigen Mutter' zu verwenden.[31]

Zurück zu Adelheid von Laufen. 1479, also acht Jahre später, sah sie sich gezwungen, ihren letzten Willen zu ändern. Kurz zuvor war ihre Vater gestorben, der gemäß Stadtrecht ihr nächster Erbe gewesen wäre. Den immensen Geldbeträgen entsprechend, die in ihrem Testament den Besitzer wechselten, dauerte die Prozedur mehr als vier Monate. Am Dienstag, den 20. April 1479 widerrief sie vor dem Basler Schultheißengericht zunächst feierlich ihr erstes Testament und ließ sich von demselben Gericht darauf die handgeschriebene Neufassung bestätigen. Am Donnerstag, den 22. April legte sie die vom Schöffengericht ausgestellte und besiegelte Urkunde zur wortgetreuen Abschrift und abermaligen Beglaubigung dem bischöflichen Gericht vor.[32] Ins Gerichts- bzw. 'Fertigungsbuch' nachgetragen, eine vom Stadtrecht vorgegebene Pflicht, wurde die Testamentsänderung allerdings erst am 4. Mai. Darin kündigte Adelheid an, dass sie dieses Mal gedenke, die handgeschriebene Version der *Domküsterei* zur Aufbewahrung zu übergeben.[33] Die feierliche Über-

---

[29] Zu ähnlichen Beschwerden siehe Sebastian Schröcker, *Die Kirchenpflegschaft. Die Verwaltung des Niederkirchenvermögens durch Laien seit dem ausgehenden Mittelalter*, Görres-Gesellschaft, Bd. 67 (Paderborn, 1934), S. 147-156.

[30] *Ebd.*, S. 89-94.

[31] Geiler von Kaysersberg, '21. Artikel', S. 182, vgl. Dacheux, *Un réformateur catholique*, S. 88: 'zu handhabung des tempels und uffgang und merung der er und dienst vor ab gots und Marie siner wurdigen muter', sowie Barbara Schock-Werner, 'L'Œuvre Notre-Dame, histoire et organisation de la fabrique de la cathédrale de Strasbourg', in: Roland Recht (Hg.), *Les bâtisseurs des cathédrales gothiques* (Straßburg, 1989), S. 133-138.

[32] Staatsarchiv Basel-Stadt, Klosterarchiv, Kartäuser Urkunde Nr. 308.

[33] Staatsarchiv Basel-Stadt, Gerichtsarchiv B, Bd. 10, fol. 355 v°: 'Es was vnd ist och ir ernstlich will, meynung vnd begeren, das diß /ir/ testament och die usteilung <wie man die in ettlichen bestimpten stuken fúrhannd nemen, ordnen vnd teilen solte vnd sy dann> /aller vorgeschribnen stuken, wie sy die/ mit ir eignen hantgeschrifft uffgeschriben vnd underzeichet hät /oder furo hin vorzeichnen wirt/ <damit> hinder die custerij der megemelten hohen stifft flyssiglich behalten vnd bewaren solte biß nach irem abgang vnd dannathin zü hannden nemen, damit hanndeln vnd thon nach lut diß testamentz /vnd innhaltung irer eignen hantgeschrifft/ alles getrúwlich vnd vngeuerlich'.

gabe des Briefs fand aber erst am 11. September statt.³⁴ Zwei Tage später, am 13. September, ließ sie dann wiederum vor dem Offizial für die Kartäuser einen eigenen Stiftungsbrief ausstellen. Von eigener Hand bestätigte sie die Urkunde dieses Mal links unten neben der Signatur des bischöflichen Notars:

> Ich, obengenannte Adelheid Waltenheim, Witwe, bekenne mit dieser, meiner Handschrift, dass ich alles, was oben geschrieben steht, durch mich und kraft meines Testamentes geschehen und mein unwiderruflicher Wille ist.³⁵

Als Testamentsvollstrecker wählte Adelheid zunächst ihren Vater, dazu den alten Oberzunftmeister der Stadt und den Domdekan Wilhelm von Aachen. Nach dem Tod ihres Vaters gehörten sämtliche drei Testamentsvollstrecker demselben Domstift an, dem sie auch ihre Papiere anvertraute, darunter befand sich der neue Domdekan sowie der 'Baumeister' bzw. Bauverwalter des Münsters.³⁶

Missbrauch

Soweit die Geschäfte, im breitesten Wortsinn. Andere nutzten die Kirche am Sonntag zum Balzen und Kokettieren, sei es mit einem Hund oder einem standesgemäßen Falken. Das Thema ist uns aus den älteren Kultur- und Sittengeschichten geläufig. Das passt nun entschieden nicht zur Heiligkeit des Ortes. Was diese Heiligkeit im Spätmittelalter konstituiert, daran lassen die Quellen nicht zweifeln, ist aber nicht der Ort, der Raum oder das Gebäude, sondern die Weihe. Der Kirchenraum ist die 'geweihte stett' bzw. die 'wigede stede' (in mittelniederländischer Begrifflichkeit). Von 'sakral' ist in diesem Kontext nicht die Rede. Ebenso selten wird der Begriff 'profan' benutzt. Peter Schott (1460-1490), Canonicus am Straßburger Jung-St.-Peterstift, bezeichnet mit dem Epitheton die Lieder, die der 'Roraffe' an Pfingsten im Straßburger Münster sang.³⁷ Geiler von

---

[34] Staatsarchiv Basel-Stadt, Klosterarchiv, Domstift Urkunde Nr. 386 (samt Beilage).
[35] Staatsarchiv Basel-Stadt, Klosterarchiv, Kartäuser Urkunde Nr. 308 (mit Beilage): 'Ich Adelheit Valtenheymyn, wittwe, obgenant, bekenn mit diser myner hantgeschrifft, dz solichs alles, wie vorstat, durch mich in krafft myns testaments beschehen vnd myn vnwiderrvᵉflicher wille ist'.
[36] Gabriela Signori, *Vorsorgen – Vererben – Erinnern. Kinder- und familienlose Erblasser in der städtischen Gesellschaft des Spätmittelalters*, Veröffentlichungen des Max-Planck-Instituts für Geschichte, Bd. 160 (Göttingen, 2001), S. 25.
[37] Peter Schott, *The Works of Peter Schott (1460-1490)*, A. Murray & Marian L. Cowie (Hgg.), Bd. 1 (Chapel Hill, 1961), Nr. 186, S. 204-207; A. Murray & Marian L. Cowie, 'Geiler von Kaysersberg and Abuses in Fifteenth Century Straßburg', *Studies in Philology*, 58 (1961), S. 483-493, hier 490.

Kaysersberg übersetzt Schotts 'prophana et indecora cantica' mit 'weltlicher ouch etwan schandbarer und spotlicher lieder'.[38]

Der Aufruf, sich in der Kirche 'ziemlich', d.h. züchtig zu verhalten, erhallte in den Kirchen nördlich der Alpen ausgesprochen häufig und bemerkenswert multimedial. Predigt, Dekalogauslegung zum dritten Gebot, Gedicht, Flugblatt, Holztafel, Gestühlsbrüstung oder Wange, Wandbild oder städtisches Mandat ergänzen sich und geben, zusammengenommen, der Forderung nach 'Kirchenzucht' ein überraschend modernes Profil. Zuweilen wird dabei auch explizit auf das Evangelium verwiesen, wie Geiler von Kaysersberg in seinen *21 Artikeln*: 'Es sprach der Herr, mein Haus ist ein Gebetshaus, und er hat es nicht gestattet, dass man Geräte durch den Tempel trug'.[39]

Der Lärm in der Kirche ist ein sehr altes Problem. Doch seit dem 15. Jahrhundert beschäftigten sich immer mehr Kreise in Kirche und Welt mit den vielen Gebet und Gottesdienst störenden Geräuschen. Die Reformationsgeschichtsschreibung verlieh der Diskussion später den strengen Titel 'Kirchenzucht'.[40] Für die Kirchenzucht verantwortlich fühlte sich seit dem ausgehenden 14. Jahrhundert nicht mehr nur der Ordens- oder Pfarrklerus, sondern immer häufiger auch das Stadtregiment. Wenn Klerus und Rat vom Lärm in der Kirche sprachen, meinten sie aber nicht dasselbe. Was profan und was sakral ist, hängt eben wesentlich vom Standort des Betrachters bzw. vom Standort des Zuhörers ab.

Der Straßburger Rat nahm den Wortlaut des Matthäus-Evangelium sehr ernst. Seit 1454 intensivierten sich seine Bemühungen, das weltliche, den Gottesdienst störende Treiben aus dem Langhaus der Liebfrauenkirche zu verbannen. Zunächst versuchte er, das 'Sponzieren', das Hin- und Her-

---

[38] Geiler von Kaysersberg, '21. Artikel', S. 190. Zum Roraffen vgl. Dacheux, *Un réformateur catholique*, S. 92f.; Otto Winckelmann, 'Zur Kulturgeschichte des Straßburger Münsters', *Zeitschrift für die Geschichte des Oberrheins*, 61/NF 22 (1907), S. 247-290; Hermann Köpcke, *Johannes Geiler von Kaisersberg. Ein Beitrag zur religiösen Volkskunde des Mittelalters* (Breslau: Diss., 1926); Israel, *Johannes Geiler von Kaysersberg*, S. 232-236.

[39] Geiler von Kaysersberg, '21. Artikel', S. 182: 'Sprach der her Myn huß ist ein bethuß / und hat nit gestattet. ouch das man ein geschir durch den tempel trug'.

[40] Zum Begriff vgl. Olaf Kuhr, *'Die Macht des Bannes und der Buße'. Kirchenzucht und Erneuerung der Kirche bei Johannes Oekolompad (1482-1531)*, Basler und Berner Studien zur historischen und systematischen Theologie, Bd. 68 (Bern u. a., 1999), S. 20f. In Konstanz benutzte man den Begriff 'Zucht' (*disciplina*) ursprünglich allein in bezug auf den Klerus vgl. Wolfgang Dobras, *Ratsregiment, Sittenpolizei und Kirchenzucht in der Reichsstadt Konstanz 1531-1548. Ein Beitrag zur Geschichte der oberdeutsch-schweizerischen Reformation*, Veröffentlichungen des Vereins für Kirchengeschichte in der Evangelischen Landeskirche in Baden, Bd. 47 (Karlsruhe, 1993), S. 168.

spazieren in der Kirche zu unterbinden. 1469 galt seine Aufmerksamkeit neben dem 'Sponzieren' den Käufen und anderen Geschäften in der Kirche und auf dem Kirchhof.[41] 1470 schränkte der Rat das Verbot dann auf das Kircheninnere ein. Fortan richtete sich die Spitze des Mandats vor allem gegen Handwerker und Gerichtsleute. Die anfänglich sehr hohen Strafgelder wurden im Verlauf der Jahre auf einen Schilling Pfennig reduziert. Das war zwar nicht viel, aber das Strafgeld summierte sich schnell, wenn man sich aus Gewohnheit nicht an das Mandat hielt. Gemahnt werden die Gerichtsbeamten, namentlich die Fürsprecher, Vögte, Richterboten und Schöffen.[42] Sie sollten ihre Gespräche im Gericht und nicht in der Kirche führen. Bevor die Stadt über ein eigenes Gerichtsgebäude verfügte, hatte das Gericht auch in Straßburg zuweilen vor, zuweilen in der Liebfrauenkirche getagt.[43] Von dieser Gewohnheit trennten sich offenbar nicht alle gleich gern. Das aber war nicht der Hauptgrund. Wichtiger war wohl, dass der Sakralraum Kirche den Befragten mehr Ehrfurcht einflösste als das Gerichtsgebäude. Ich zitiere im folgenden nach der Druckfassung aus dem Jahr 1514:

> Desgleichen sollen alle Fürsprecher, Vögte, Gerichtsboten und andere Gerichtsleute im Münster keine Gespräche oder Reden halten, die vor das Gericht, nicht in das Münster gehören, bei dem oben genannten Bußgeld, sondern sie sollen mit den Leuten aus dem Münster an die genannten Orte oder anderswohin gehen, wo der Gottesdienst nicht gestört wird, bei dem oben genannten Bußgeld von einem Schilling. Das Strafgeld dürfen die Siebenzüchter, wenn es ihnen angezeigt wird, niemandem erlassen bei ihrem Amtseid. Anzeigen sollen es bei ihrem Amtseid auch die Münsterknechte, die Ammeisterknechte, die Turmhüter und die Siebenerknechte, auch die beiden Bote des Stadtgerichts. Die, die es zur Anzeige bringen, sollen jeden dritten Pfennig vom Bußgeld erhalten, das übrige Geld soll zum einen dem Frauenwerk, zum andern der Stadt zugute kommen.[44]

---

[41] Winckelmann, 'Zur Kulturgeschichte', S. 280.
[42] Zum Gerichtspersonal vgl. Gernot Kocher, *Zeichen und Symbole des Rechts. Eine historische Ikonographie* (München, 1992), S. 138-147, sowie Jürgen Weitzel, 'Gerichtsöffentlichkeit im hoch- und spätmittelalterlichen Deutschland', in: Alfred Haverkamp & Elisabeth Müller-Luckner (Hgg.), *Information, Kommunikation und Selbstdarstellung in mittelalterlichen Gemeinden*, Schriften des Historischen Kollegs, Bd. 40 (München, 1998), S. 71-84.
[43] Adalbert Erler, *Das Straßburger Münster im Rechtsleben des Mittelalters*, Frankfurter wissenschaftliche Beiträge. Rechts- und Wirtschaftsgeschichtliche Reihe, Bd. 9 (Frankfurt, 1954).
[44] Stadtarchiv Straßburg, Mandate und Ordnungen III, eingeklebter Einblattdruck vom 27. Februar 1514 mit dem Titel 'Spatzierens halb jm Münster': 'Deßglichen sollent alle Fürsprechen / Voͤgte / Richters botten / noch ander Gerichtzlüte jm Münster ouch nit habenn dhein gespreche / oder rede / die an die gericht / vnd nit jnn das Münster geho͡e-rent / Ouch by der egemelten *pene* / Sonder mit den lüten vß dem Münster an die *egemelten*

Überwachen bzw. beim 'Siebenzüchter', dem Straßburger Sittengericht, anzeigen mussten die Mandatsüberschreitungen die Stadtknechte:⁴⁵ der Münsterknecht, der Ammeisterknecht, die Turmhüter, die zwei Gerichtsboten und die Knechte des 'Sübenzüchters', ein stattliches Aufgebot an Überwachungspersonal! Ein Drittel der Einnahmen sollte an die Knechte, ein Drittel an die Stadt und das letzte Drittel an den Liebfrauenbau gehen. Kirchenzucht war im Straßburg des ausgehenden 15. Jahrhunderts demnach zu einer durch und durch weltlichen Angelegenheit geworden. Namenslisten sind leider keine erhalten.

Auch Lohnherren, Maurer und Zimmerleute 'sollten jnn dem Münster kein gespreche me haben / ouch kein gedinge darjnn machen', das heißt 'im Münster nicht sprechen und keine Verträge abschließen'. Als Alternative stünden ihnen, räumten die Reformer ein, der Kreuzgang offen. Die Handwerksleute könnten auch 'vff die graᵉte [auf die Treppen] / oder vff die Steinhütte' oder vor das Münster unter das Dach gehen, wo man Töpfe verkaufe, und ihre Geschäfte dort abwickeln.⁴⁶ Die Liebfrauenkirche bzw. die im ganzen Land bekannte Münsterbauhütte (neben Wien und Köln einer der drei Haupthütten) war ein günstiger Standort für das Baugewerbe, für Lohnherren, Maurer und Zimmerleute. Denn er war einer der wichtigsten Arbeitgeber.⁴⁷

Ähnliche Bestimmungen sind u. a. aus Braunschweig (1420), Frankfurt (1363, 1401, 1443), Heilbronn (1507) oder Hildesheim (1445, 1451)

---

ende / oder anderswohin gon, all do der Gots dienst nit geirret werde / by der egeruᵉrten pene nemlich j ß pfen[nig], die ouch die *Sübenzüchter*, so es jnnen *geruᵉget* würt, nyeman faren lossen sollent by jren eyden / vnd sollent es nemlich by jren eyden *ruᵉgen* die Münsterknecht / Ammeisterknecht / die Thurnhuᵉtter / vnd die *Sübenerknecht* / vnnd dotzů die zwen botten an der statgericht / vnd sol den, die es ruᵉgent, der dritte pfennig werden von der besserunge / vnd die übrigen zweyteil Vnser frowen werck / vnd der Stat jedem teyl das halbe'. Vgl. Winckelmann, 'Zur Kulturgeschichte', S. 279ff.

⁴⁵ Die Siebenzüchter bildeten eine Art Sittengericht mit sieben Schöffen. Das Gremium wurde 1433 eingerichtet und beschäftigte sich neben Verstößen gegen die Kirchenzucht auch mit den 'Delikten' Konkubinat und Ehebruch. Auch andere oberrheinische Städte richteten sich im 15. Jahrhundert solche Sittengerichte ein. Vgl. Hans-Rudolf Hagemann, *Basler Rechtsleben im Mittelalter*, Bd. 1 (Basel / Frankfurt, 1981), S. 70-82, sowie allgemein Pirmin Spiess, *Rüge und Einung, dargestellt anhand süddeutscher Stadtrechtsquellen aus dem Mittelalter und der frühen Neuzeit*, Veröffentlichungen der pfälzischen Gesellschaft zur Förderung der Wissenschaften, Bd. 82 (Speyer, 1988), S. 10ff.

⁴⁶ Stadtarchiv Straßburg, Mandate und Ordnungen III.

⁴⁷ Lucien Sittler, 'Les associations artisanales en Alsace au Moyen Âge et sous l'Ancien Régime', *Revue d'Alsace*, 97 (1958), S. 36-80, hier 51-55; Anselme Schimpf, 'Les tailleurs de pierre strasbourgeois', in: *Artisans et ouvriers d'Alsace*, Publications de la Société savante d'Alsace et des régions de l'est, Bd. 9 (Straßburg, 1965), S. 97-126.

bekannt.⁴⁸ Im November 1445 verbot der Stadtrat von Hildesheim seinen Bürgern und Untertanen, in der Kirche oder auf dem Kirchhof Handel zu treiben. Dies störe, heißt es in Anlehnung an das Matthäusevangelium, das' Gebet der Gläubigen:

> Zum ersten, dass keiner unserer Bürger und Bürgerinnen, dingpflichtig oder unsere Untertanen, hier auf dem Kirchhof oder an anderen geweihten Stätten, für die wir zuständig sind, etwas kaufen oder verkaufen darf bei einem Pfund Strafgeld, damit ein jeder Christenmensch ebenda nicht an seinem innigen Gebet gestört werde.⁴⁹

Die Kirchenordnung von Heilbronn verordnet:

> dass künftig, wer immer es sei, niemand davon ausgenommen, während des Frühamts oder der Frühmesse und anderen göttlichen Ämter in der Kirche schwatzen darf. Das gilt auch für den Kirchhof, auf dem niemand einen Vertrag mit Tagelöhnern aufsetzen oder andere Dinge machen, verabreden oder beschließen darf.⁵⁰

Verboten wird zunächst das Geschwätz während des Gottesdienstes, dann die Geschäfte auf dem Kirchhof abzuwickeln. In Heilbronn scheint allein der Kirchhof als Stellenbörse fungiert zu haben. Hier, auf den Kirchhof, ging man, wenn man eine ungelernte Hilfskraft, einen Tagelöhner, brauchte. Jede Stadt hatte ihr eigenes System verschiedener wirtschaftlicher und politischer Öffentlichkeiten, die sich da überschnitten, wo Kirche, Rathaus und Mark unmittelbar aneinander stießen.

Der Rat von Heilbronn beklagte sich außerdem, dass 'die frowenbilder, jungfrowen und ander, ganz an die altar hinan steend, dardurch den priestern an dem gottlichen dienst merklich verhinderung entsten mecht'.⁵¹ Jung und Alt forderte der Rat schließlich nachdrücklich auf,

---

⁴⁸ Rainer Driever, *Obrigkeitliche Normierung sozialer Wirklichkeit*, Göttinger Forschungen zur Landesgeschichte, Bd. 2 (Bielefeld, 1999), S. 234-236.
⁴⁹ *Urkundenbuch der Stadt Hildesheim im Auftrag des Magistrats zu Hildesheim. Teil IV: 1428-1450*, Richard Doebner (Hg.) (Hildesheim, 1890), Nr. 598, S. 505: 'Tom ersten, dat numer neyn unser borgere, borgerschen, dingpflichtigen eder der unser, der wii mechtich sin, hir up neynem kerkhove eder anderen wigeden steden, da wii des mechtich sin, neynewisz schal kopen eder vorkopen by eynem nyen punde, uppe dat eyn islik gud cristenmynsche darsulves an sinem innigen bede darmede nicht vorhindert enwerde'.
⁵⁰ *Urkundenbuch der Stadt Heilbronn*, Bd. 2 (1476-1500), Moriz von Rauch (Hg.), Württembergische Geschichtsquellen, Bd. 15 (Stuttgart, 1913), Nr. 1661, S. 532: 'das furohin, wer der sey, niemans außgenommen, under dem frueampt oder fruemeß auch ander gotlichen empter in der kirchen geschwez treyben, desgleichen auff dem kirchhoff ainicherley geding mit taglonern oder ander weg treyben, bestellen, machen, abreden oder beschließen'.
⁵¹ *Ebd.*, S. 532f.

'an ir gepurliche statt [zu] steen'.⁵² In Straßburg hatte man an den 'leichtfertigen' Frauen Anstoß genommen, die mit dem Rücken zum Chor vorne auf den Altartreppen säßen und sich benähmen, als seien sie auf dem 'Grümpelmarkt'. Sehen und gesehen werden, lautete hier wie dort offenbar die Devise:

> Auch weil einige leichtfertige Frauen bisher im Münster auf der Treppe vor dem Altar gesessen sind, dem Altar und dem Gottesdienst den Rücken zugewandt, und die Leute angeschaut haben, als ob sie den Gottesdienst nicht beachteten, sondern auf dem Gerümpelmarkt säßen, um sich umzusehen, welcher Kauf ihnen der liebste wäre. Dies ist im Münster an den geweihten Stätten unbillig und nicht zu dulden. Deswegen ist auch verordnet worden, dass, wenn eine solch leichtfertige Frau dies wieder täte, auf die solle man warten, bis sie das Münster verlasse, sie fragen, wie sie heiße und ihren Namen aufschreiben und den den Siebener übergeben, die darauf das Strafgeld bestimmen müssen. Das aber darf einen Schilling nicht unterschreiten. Das Geld soll so geteilt werden, wie oben geschrieben. Verhängen die Siebener über ein solches Vergehen, das ihnen angezeigt wird, kein Bußgeld, dann müssen die Fünfzehnerherren die Sieben vorladen und bestrafen.⁵³

Derartige Ausschreitungen zu ahnden fiel in den Zuständigkeitsbereich der Siebener, also des Sittengerichts. Sollten die Siebener ihrer Aufgabe nicht nachkommen, hätten sie sich vor dem Fünfzehnergericht zu verantworten. Das Fünfzehnergericht wiederum war u. a. für Korruption sowie für Verstöße gegen die Ammeisterordnung und Vergehen von Amtleuten zuständig.⁵⁴

Regelmäßig vom Redeverbot in der Kirche ausgenommen war in der Sichtweise des Magistrats allein der Stett- und der Ammeister, also der

---

⁵² *Ebd.*
⁵³ Stadtarchiv Straßburg, Mandate und Ordnungen III (Anm. 46): 'Ouch als ettliche lichtuertige frowen bitzhar jnn dem Münster vff die Staffelen für die Altar gesessen sint / dem Altar / vnd dem Gots dienst den Rucken gekeᵒrt / vnd die lüte angeschouwet haben / als obe sie Gots dienst nit achtetent / Sonder vff dem Gümppelmarckt sehssent, vmb sich zůsehen / welcher kouff jnen der liebste were / das doch jnn dem Münster an den gewichten enden vnbillich / vnd nit zů liden ist / Darumb so ist ouch geordent, wellich sollich lichtuertige frowe semlichs me taᵉte, vff die soll man wattern / so sie vß dem Münster gaᵉt / sie frogen, wie sie heisse / vnnd jrenn namen geschryben geben den Sübenen / besserunge vff sie zů erkennen / Also das die mynste besserunge nit sy vnder j ß pfen[nig], ouch zů teilen, als vor gemelt ist. Wo ouch die Süben sollichs, so jnenn geruᵉget würt, nit fürderlich bessern / so sollent die herren die fünfftzehen darumb die Süben für nemmen / vnd stoffen'.
⁵⁴ Zum Gremium der Fünfzehner vgl. Otto Winckelmann, 'Straßburgs Verfassung und Verwaltung im 16. Jahrhunderts', *Zeitschrift für die Geschichte des Oberrheins*, Bd. 18 (1903), S. 493-537, hier 526ff.; Martin Alioth, *Gruppen an der Macht. Zünfte und Patriziat in Straßburg im 14. und 15. Jahrhundert. Untersuchungen zu Verfassung, Wirtschaftsgefüge und Sozialstruktur*, Bd. 1, Basler Beiträge zur Geschichtswissenschaft, Bd. 156 (Basel, 1988), S. 144f.

Bürgermeister, nach Martin Alioth geradezu die Personifikation des Straßburger Stadtregiments.⁵⁵ Die beiden Stadthäupter durften, so es die Sachlage gebot, wie ehedem in der Kirche tagen, Leute verhören, Befehle erteilen und ähnliches mehr.⁵⁶ Darauf reagierte der Straßburger Klerus umgehend und heftig. Um 1485 beschwerte sich erstmals Canonicus Schott in seinem Brief an den päpstlichen Nuntius Emerich Kemel über ebendiesen Ammeisterstuhl im Münster, eine Herd von Unruhe und Lärm, der die Messe störe.⁵⁷ Seine Beschwerde führte dazu, dass der Ammeister zumindest vorübergehend die Audienzen im Münster einstellte. In diesen Jahren war Schotts Vater, Peter Schott (1427-1504), wiederholt Ammeister der Stadt Straßburg (1470, 1476, 1482 und 1488).⁵⁸ Das dürfte die Durchsetzung der Reformen maßgeblich erleichtert haben.

Rund zwanzig Jahre später scheint es aber wieder zur Gewohnheit geworden zu sein, im Münster zu tagen. So schimpfte Geiler von Kaysersberg von der Kanzel des Straßburger Münster hinunter, die Herren, also die Ratsherren, seien alle des Teufels. Der schickte unverzüglich zwei Boten zum Münsterprediger mit der Bitte um sofortige Klärung.⁵⁹ Darauf schrieb Geiler seine '21 Artikel'. Als Vorlage diente ihm Schotts Brief an Emerich Kemel. In Artikel 18 präzisiert er:

> Der Ammeister schwatzt zur Zeit der heiligen Ämter in der Vesper, auch wenn man neben seinem Stuhl die heilige Messe zelebriert. Sie setzten auch den Leutetag auf diesen Termin, wie man sagt. Das ist unchristlich und nach päpstlichem, also nach kanonischem Recht verboten.⁶⁰

Der Ammeister störte den Münstergottesdienst anscheinend um so mehr, als sich sein Stuhl ganz vorne, neben dem Hauptaltar befand. Nicht

---

⁵⁵ Alioth, *Gruppen an der Macht*, S. 465.
⁵⁶ *Straßburger Zunft- und Polizei-Verordnungen des 14. und 15. Jahrhunderts. Aus den Orginalen des Stadtarchivs*, Johann Karl Brucker (Hg.) (Straßburg, 1889): 'Es söllent ouch alle ander lüte dhein tage, stunde oder gespreche in dem münster... haben noch halten... doch sol dis den stetmeister und den ammeister nit berüren; die mögent lüte verhören und usrichten als von alter herkommen ist'.
⁵⁷ Cowie, 'Geiler von Kaysersberg', S. 490f.: 'Item magister ciuium locum suum habet in ecclesia maiori: in quo passim responsa dare: et partes coram se vocatas audire: item illic cim alijs confabulari consueuit: eciam tempore quo in proximo per sacerdotes misse celebrantur: qui tanto murmure et strepitu turbantur'.
⁵⁸ Marcel Mathis, 'Un grand Ammeister strasbourgeois du XVᵉ siècle: Pierre Schott (1427-1504)', *Annuaire de la Société des Amis du Vieux-Strasbourg (ASAVStr)*, Bd. 20 (1990), S. 15-35.
⁵⁹ Geiler von Kaysersberg, '21. Artikel', S. 155.
⁶⁰ Ebd., S. 188f.: 'Es haltet der ammeister ein geschwaͤtz zu den ziten der heiligen aͤmpter under der vesper / ouch so man by synem stul aller nest die heiligen messen macht / und setzent ouch den luten tag do hin als man seit / ist unchristlich und verbotten in christlichen bebstlichen rechten'.

klären ließ sich indessen die Frage, was Geiler genau mit dem 'Leutetag' meinte. Den Schwörtag? Die Gemeinde? Das Rathaus befand sich seit Beginn des 14. Jahrhundert auf der Pfalz mit Öffnung auf den Martinsplatz.[61] Darin hatten der Dreizehnerrat, der Fünfzehnerrat, der Große und der Kleine Rat ihre je eigenen Räumlichkeiten. Geschworen aber wurde in Straßburg nicht vor dem Rathaus, sondern vor der Liebfrauenkirche.[62]

Die meisten um die Kirchenzucht besorgten geistlichen Autoren beschäftigten sich jedoch mit anderen 'Dingen', als mit ratsherrlichen Verstößen gegen die Kirchenzucht. Wie Theoderich Engelhusen († 1434) beklagten viele das Mitbringen von Hunden, Falken und kleinen Kindern:

> Ich mahne alle Leute, dass sie weder Hund noch Vogel noch kleine Kinder in die Kirche bringen, die weder schweigen, noch still sitzen können, weil dies die Leute daran hindert, ihr Gebet zu sprechen.[63]

Sebastian Brant († 1521) schimpft: 'Man braucht nicht fragen, wer die seien / Bei denen die Hund' in der Kirche schreien, / Während man Messe hält, predigt und singt, / Oder bei denen der Habicht schwingt'.[64] Auf dem Straßburger Schrotschnitt erscheinen Falke und Hund als Attribut der beiden adligen Jünglinge, die den Reigen der vier 'Sündenpaare' im unteren Bildfeld schließen.[65] Mit den Straßburger Verhältnissen im ausgehenden 15. Jahrhundert selbst hat der Schrottschnitt wenig gemein. Es

---

[61] Roland Oberle, 'La Pfalz: cœur et symbole de la vieille République de Strasbourg', *ASAVStr*, Bd. 2 (1971), S. 39-55.

[62] Georges Livet & Jean Rott, 'En commémoration d'un demi-millénaire. La Constitution de 1482. Aperçu sur l'histoire constitutionnelle de Strasbourg jusqu'à la Révolution', *ASAVStr*, Bd. 12 (1982), S. 17-22.

[63] 'Leyen regulen', in: Rudolf Langenberg (Hg.), *Quellen und Forschungen zur Geschichte der deutschen Mystik* (Bonn, 1902), S. 88: 'Ick vormane allen luden, dat se neyne hunde noch vogele noch cleyne kinder to der kercken brengen, de nicht swigen noch stille sitten en willen, wante men hindert dar de lude mede an eren beede'. Zu Engelhus vgl. die verschiedenen Beiträge in Volker Honemann (Hg.), *Dietrich Engelhus. Beiträge zu Leben und Werk*, Mitteldeutsche Forschungen, Bd. 105 (Köln u. a., 1991).

[64] Sebastian Brant, *Das Narrenschiff. Nach der Erstausgabe (Basel 1494) mit Zusätzen der Ausgaben von 1495 und 1499 sowie den Holzschnitten der deutschen Originalausgaben*, Manfred Lemmer (Hg.) (Tübingen, 1968²), S. 107 (Kap. 44): 'Gebracht in der kirchen': 'Man darff nit fragen, wer die sygen / By den die hund jnn kylchen schrygen / So man meß hat, predigt, vnd singt / Oder by den der habich schwyngt'.

[65] Unordnung in der Kirche, Einblattdruck o. J. und o. O., vermutlich aus Straßburg, ausgehendes 15. Jahrhundert, abgedruckt in: Boockmann, *Die Stadt im späten Mittelalter*, S. 202f., vgl. W. L. Schreiber, *Handbuch der Holz- und Metallschnitte des XV. Jahrhunderts*. Bd. 5: *Metallschnitte <Schrotblätter>. Mit Darstellungen religiösen und profanen Inhalts* (Stuttgart, 1928), Nr. 2761, S. 209.
Ein zweiter Hund befindet sich auf dem Schoß einer der beiden im Gespräch vertieften Frauen, die auf Schemeln vor der Kanzel Platz genommen haben.

geht allein um die Aufdeckung zeitgenössischer Missbräuche: die Konkurrenz zwischen Welt- und Ordensklerus in der Predigt, der Polyzentrismus sowie die Omnipräsenz schwatzender Frauen und Handwerker, die in der Kirche Verträge abschließen etc.

Über das Mitbringen von Hunden und Falken hatte sich schon Bernardino da Siena († 1444) in einer seiner auf der Piazza del Campo in Siena gehaltenen Predigten beschwert: 'Mit schulterlanger Pagenfrisur', gemeint sind wiederum die jungen, adligen Galane, 'in kurzem Rock und langen geschlitzten Strumpfhosen... wetzen sie die Kirchenbänke mit ihren Falken und Hunden an der Leine entlang'.[66]

Im letzten Viertel des 15. Jahrhunderts beauftragte Siena mehrere Künstler, das Wirken ihres seit 1450 heilig gesprochenen Mitbürgers auf Tafelbilder festzuhalten. Die Gemälde sind, wie Sanos di Pietro († 1481) Darstellung der Predigt des Heiligen auf der Piazza del Campo, ausgesprochen didaktische Kompositionen.[67] Sie entwerfen das Bild der idealen Gemeinde, die gemäß Phil. 2, 10 ehrfürchtig niederkniet, und gemäß 1 Kor. 11, 4-16 züchtig ihr Haupt ver- bzw. enthüllt und ihren Blick konzentriert auf den Prediger bzw. das Christusmonogramm richtet. Darin unterscheidet sich die Version, die Neroccio di Bartolomeo Landi († 1500) für die Stadt anfertigt, markant von seinem Vorgänger. Bei Neroccio schweifen die Blicke umher, gleiten in den hinteren, von Jugendlichen besetzten Reihen über das Tuch hinweg, kreuzt sich, was sich eigentlich nicht kreuzen dürfte, der Blick, das Einfallstor der Sünde.[68]

In seiner 73. Homelie zum Matthäus-Evangelium fordert Johannes Chrysostomus († 407), auf Deutsch Johannes mit dem goldenen Mund:

> Im Innern solltet ihr eine Mauer haben, die euch von den Weibern trennt; da dem aber nicht so ist, so erachteten es eure Väter für notwendig, euch wenigstens durch die Gitter hier von ihnen zu scheiden. Wie ich von älteren Leuten höre, gab es früher keine solchen Schranken, 'den in Christus Jesus ist weder Mann noch Weib' [Gal. 3, 28]. Auch zu den Zeiten der Apostel waren Männer und Frauen miteinander beisammen, denn die Männer waren eben Männer und die Frauen waren wirklich Frauen. Jetzt aber ist es

---

[66] Iris Origo, *Der Heilige der Toskana. Leben und Zeit des Bernardino von Siena* (München, 1989), S. 43.

[67] Keith Christiansen, Laurence B. Kanter & Carl Brandon Strehlke, *La pittura senese nel Rinascimento (1420-1500)* (Siena / New York, 1988/1989), S. 152-181. Vgl. auch Chiara Frugoni, 'L'immagine del predicatore nell'iconografia medioevale', *Medioevo e rinascimento*, Bd. 3 (1989), S. 287-299 (mit falschen Datierungen); Roberto Rusconi, 'Le pouvoir de la parole. Représentation des prédicateurs dans l'art de la Renaissance en Italie', in: Rosa Maria Dessi & Michel Lauwers (Hgg.), *La parole du prédicateur (V^e-XVe siècle)*, Collection du centre d'études médiévales de Nice, Bd. 1 (Nizza, 1997), S. 445-456.

[68] Christiansen, Kanter & Strehlke, *La pittura senese*, S. 342-348.

ganz anders geworden. Die Weiber haben die Art von Buhlerinnen angenommen und die Männer sind wie brünstige Hengste.⁶⁹

Die kontrastreichen Gemälde, die spätmittelalterliche Bußprediger wie Bernardino da Siena von den Sitten bzw. Unsitten ihrer Zeitgenossen entwarfen, inspirierten sich gerne bei diesen spätantiken Sittenbildern. Die Kirche als Hurenhaus zu beschimpfen war rhetorisch wirkungsvoller, als von einem Kaufhaus zu reden. In diesem Punkt waren sich Klerus und Stadtregiment einig. Mit vereinten Kräften versuchten sie, die Kirche von dieser Art Profanierung zu säubern. In anderen Belangen gingen die Ansichten von Kirche und Welt indessen weit auseinander. Jeder zog andere bzw. eigene Grenzlinien zwischen dem Heiligen und dem Profanen, und jeder glaubte für sich, nur er dürfe darüber entscheiden, wo sie entlang liefen. Sakral und profan waren keine scharf von einander getrennten Räume bzw. Welten mehr. Das Problem hatte sich relativiert, es war standortabhängig geworden.

Westfälische Wilhelms-Universität Münster

---

⁶⁹ *Des heiligen Kirchenlehrers Johannes Chrysostomus, Erzbischofs von Konstantinopel Kommentar zum Evangelium des hl. Matthäus*, aus dem Griechischen übersetzt von P. Joh. Chrysostomus Baur, Bibliothek der Kirchenväter, Bd. 27 (Kempten / München, 1916), S. 20. Vgl. Gabriela Signori, 'Links oder rechts? Zum 'Platz der Frau' in der mittelalterlichen Kirche', in: Susanna Rau & Gerd Schwerhoff (Hgg.), *Zwischen Gotteshaus und Taverne. Öffentliche Räume in Spätmittelalter und Früher Neuzeit*, Norm und Struktur, Bd. 21 (Köln, 2004), S. 339-382.

Jens RÖHRKASTEN

SECULAR USES OF THE MENDICANT PRIORIES OF MEDIEVAL LONDON

The secular use of mendicant convents in the Middle Ages was not unusual.[1] Examples from different European regions show that friary precincts were made available to urban authorities for a variety of purposes and that secular rulers would on occasion also make use of the buildings and the space provided by a mendicant priory, occupying convents with their household or providing accommodation for guests. Mendicant houses were used to store records or to serve as a venue for political and diplomatic negotiations. The German royal election of 1292 was held in the Dominican convent of Frankfurt, the Franciscan convent of Reggio served as a political centre where the town's population assembled for meetings and the town council of Mâcon held its assemblies in the Dominican priory. In the Later Middle Ages the rector of the university of Cologne was elected in one of the city's mendicant houses. The extent of secular use has led Stüdeli to ask whether there may have been a deliberate connection between the spiritual aims of the Franciscans and the secular purposes for which many of their convents were repeatedly used.[2] Mendicant houses were well-suited for such

---

[1] B. Stüdeli, *Minoritenniederlassungen und mittelalterliche Stadt. Beiträge zur Bedeutung von Minoriten- und anderen Mendikantenanlagen im öffentlichen Leben der mittelalterlichen Stadtgemeinde, insbesondere der deutschen Schweiz*, Franziskanische Forschungen, vol. 21 (Werl, 1969), p. 22, states that a 'regelmäßige und ständige Benutzung für nichtkirchliche Zwecke' can be demonstrated for mendicant convents, cf. O. Schmucki, 'Conventus Francescani et medii aevi urbes', *Collectanea Franciscana*, 40 (1970), pp. 153-168. The question 'L'église du couvent est-elle utilisée pour des réunions par les pouvoirs civils?' was added to a checklist by A. Vauchez, 'Introduction', in: 'Les Ordres mendiants et la ville en Italie centrale', *Mélanges de l'École Française de Rome, Moyen Age-Temps Modernes*, 89 (1977), pp. 557-562, at p. 562.

[2] *Ibidem*, pp. 23, 84-108; T. Berger, *Die Bettelorden in der Erzdiözese Mainz und in den Diözesen Speyer und Worms im 13. Jahrhundert*, Quellen und Abhandlungen zur mittelrheinischen Kirchengeschichte, vol. 69 (Mainz, 1995), p. 27; Idem, 'Die Ausbreitung der Minoriten in der Erzdiözese Mainz und und den Diözesen Speyer und Worms in 13. Jahrhundert', in: D. Berg (ed.), *Könige, Landesherren und Bettelorden*, Saxonia Franciscana, vol. 10 (Werl, 1998), pp. 37-59, at p. 44-5; F. Fossier, 'La ville dans l'historiographie franciscaine de la fin du XIIIe et du début du XIVe siècle', *Mélanges de l'École Française de Rome*, 89 (1977), pp. 641-55, at p. 648; A. Guerrau, 'Rentes des ordres mendiants à Macon au XIVe siècle', *Annales. Economie, Société, Civilisation*, 25 (1970), pp. 956-65, at p. 960; G.M. Löhr, *Beiträge zur Geschichte des Kölner Dominikanerklosters im Mittelalter*, 2 vols. (Leipzig, 1920-22), vol. 1, p. 76.

use. They were most commonly located in towns, they were not always formally owned by the Orders and their inmates did not shy away from contact with the public. They offered space in churches, chapter houses and other buildings as well as in their churchyards – the cemetery of the Cologne Carmelites was used to store the goods of an exiled woodmonger[3] – and in some instances they may have provided a neutral ground where parties involved in delicate negotiations may have preferred to meet. In some instances, e.g. in Bern, their location seems to have been strategically planned with the intention of strengthening the town's defences. Here, there was no question that town council and officials had to be given free access even to the church.[4]

The English mendicant provinces were no exception to this pattern. The Oxford Black Friars were the venue of the 'Mad Parliament' of 1258.[5] When King Edward I spent Christmas at Exeter in 1285 at least one of his noble companions, the Earl of Hereford, lodged with the Franciscans where he noticed the poor quality of their living conditions. In 1309 King Edward II was staying in his chamber in the Dominican priory of Stamford. The Exeter Dominicans were entrusted with a sum of money by Gilbert de Knovill, Sheriff of Devon, towards the end of the thirteenth century.[6] The convent also occasionally served as venue for meetings between representatives of the town and the Earl of Devon.[7] A legal agreement concerning an annual rent made in 1307 stipulated that the money was to be regularly handed over in the Carmelite church of Winchester.[8] Ten years later the warden of the Franciscans at Lincoln was safeguarding private legal documents of a crown vassal.[9] That the secular demands made on mendicant houses could even spill over on adjacent private properties is shown by a document obtained by the owner of such a house in Northampton who wanted his property exempted from the 'livery' of royal ministers.[10]

---

[3] W. Herborn, *Die politische Führungsschicht der Stadt Köln im Spätmittelalter*, Rheinisches Archiv, vol. 100 (Bonn, 1977), pp. 276-7.

[4] Stüdeli, *Minoritenniederlassungen*, pp. 36-7, 74; J.B. Freed, *The Friars and German Society in the Thirteenth Century*, The Mediaeval Academy of America, vol. 86 (Cambridge (Mass.), 1977), p. 50.

[5] E. Barker, *The Dominican Order and Convocation* (Oxford, 1913), pp. 29, 58.

[6] A.G. Little & R. Easterling, *The Franciscans and Dominicans of Exeter*, History of Exeter Research Group, vol. 3 (Exeter, 1927), p. 15, 46; *Calendar of Patent Rolls, 1301-7*, p. 376; *Calendar of Close Rolls, 1307-13*, pp. 225-6.

[7] Little & Easterling, *Franciscans and Dominicans*, p. 39.

[8] *Calendar of Close Rolls, 1307-13*, pp. 47-8.

[9] *Calendar of Close Rolls, 1313-18*, p. 562.

[10] *Calendar of Patent Rolls, 1307-13*, p. 402.

Although such references abound no systematic assessment of this aspect of mendicant-lay relations has yet been made. This is at least partly caused by the fact that the friars in different regions and even towns were faced with different political structures and constellations as well as different topographical conditions. It has not yet been possible to set the wealth of available detail in its context. There is no doubt that a systematic discussion of the subject would be desirable because it would add a further dimension to the known rôles and functions of the mendicants in their urban environment. Even though the time for an extensive survey has not yet come, it is possible to study the friaries of one of Western Europe's great medieval centres, London.

The early development of London's mendicant houses partly coincides with the process during which the city and its immediate vicinity became the centre of administration and the kingdom's capital. The city's economic and political pre-eminence can be traced back to the eleventh century and beyond. The location of the key elements of royal government, the Exchequer, Chancery and the central law courts, in nearby Westminster marked the transformation of the city into a capital in the thirteenth and fourteenth centuries. In addition to housing the administration and increasingly also the royal household, the city and its immediate environment emerged ever more clearly in their exalted rôle because not only bishops and the heads of religious houses but members of the aristocracy established urban residences on the banks of the Thames. This new manifestation of the city's political dominance coincided with the arrival of the new Orders in the thirteenth century.[11] There were eight mendicant houses in medieval London. The first to arrive were the Dominicans, who developed their first priory near the Fleet river in Holborn. Two general chapters of the order were celebrated here in 1250 and 1263. Although the convent was situated on one of the western approaches to the city leading towards Newgate, the location was deemed unsuitable and the priory was moved to a site south-west of St Paul's

---

[11] F.M. Stenton, 'Norman London', in: D.M. Stenton (ed.), *Preparatory to Anglo-Saxon England* (Oxford, 1970), pp. 23-47; S. Reynolds, 'The Rulers of London in the Twelfth Century', in: Eadem, *Ideas and Solidarities of the Medieval Laity* (London, 1995); D. Keene, 'Medieval London and Its Region', *The London Journal*, 14 (1989), pp. 99-111; Idem, 'Wardrobes in the City: Houses of Consumption, Finance and Power', in: M. Prestwich, R. Britnell & R. Frame (eds.), *Thirteenth-Century England VII* (Woodbridge, 1999), pp. 61-79; T.F. Tout, 'The Beginnings of a Modern Capital: London and Westminster in the Fourteenth Century', *Proceedings of the British Academy*, 10 (1921-23), pp. 487-511; G. Rosser, *Medieval Westminster 1200-1540* (Oxford, 1989), pp. 35-41; C.M. Barron, 'Centres of Conspicuous Consumption: The Aristocratic Town House in London 1200-1550', *The London Journal*, 20 (1995), pp. 1-16.

from 1275. Here it was directly approachable from the city's main way of communication, the Thames. The Franciscans, who arrived at the most three years after the Dominicans, were given a site within the city walls, inside Newgate. Though distant from the Thames this area was close to the cathedral and to Cheapside, one of the city's key commercial centres. The Carmelites were located in Fleet Street in the city's western suburbs. The church and the other priory buildings were on the southern side of the street and during the completion of the convent in the fourteenth century the precinct expanded towards the Thames. The Carmelites and the Dominicans were the two mendicant priories with direct river access in the fourteenth century. The Friars of the Cross to the north-west of the Tower and the Austin Friars near Bishopsgate were less centrally placed and the monastery of the Franciscan nuns to the east of the city was equally neither on a major throughfare nor near the river.[12]

My investigation will concentrate on two aspects: firstly, the relative frequency of secular use affecting the different mendicant houses and secondly its nature and purpose. The intention is to identify the phases in the convents' history during which secular use was most common, to see which other than religious rôles they played in the late medieval city and to assess the extent to which secular use interfered with religious observance. This approach has the potential to reveal another dimension of the mendicants' relations with different secular groups and authorities. Measuring the levels of secular demand on religious space may also help to clarify the process of London's development as an administrative centre. Although there were phases in the fourteenth century when parts of the administration were removed from the London region to the north of England, this did not stop the city's development as a capital. Its proximity to Westminster, where the royal administration gradually settled – the Court of Common Pleas and the Exchequer being permanently located here from 1339 and the Court of King's Bench from the mid-1360s – still enhanced its already established dominance.[13] The city's importance found an expression in its topography. From the late twelfth century onwards English bishops as well as heads of religious houses began to established their town houses in London and its suburbs. Early examples are the house of the Abbot of Ramsey, dating from the second decade of

---

[12] J. Röhrkasten, 'The Origin and Early Development of the London Mendicant Houses', in: T.R. Slater & G. Rosser (eds.), *The Church in the Medieval Town* (Aldershot, 1998), pp. 76-99.

[13] Rosser, *Medieval Westminister*, p. 36.

the twelfth century and Abbot's Inn, the town house of the Abbots of Waltham near Billingsgate, established before 1200. A preferred location were sites near the Thames where e.g. the Priors of Ogbourne, the Abbots of Faversham and the Bishops of Salisbury had their urban residences. From the thirteenth century onwards they were joined by secular lords who established town houses in the city as well as near the river bank between London and Westminster where they were staying with their retinues during Parliaments or when they were pursuing other political and legal interests.[14] The Dominicans became involved in this process when they sold their first convent to Henry de Lacy, Earl of Lincoln, who established his town house here in 1286.[15] The old royal palace at Westminster, the Tower and London's thirteenth-century Guildhall as well as the large ecclesiastical precincts of the Temple, the priories of St Martin-le-Grand, St Bartholomew and Holy Trinity were other landmarks shaping the city's topography, able to offer space on request. However, this extensive and developing infrastructure was not deemed to be sufficient.

The first Dominican priory on the western approaches to the city only appears as venue for one transaction. This was an agreement between private parties, made in 1269 when the English Baron John of Musgrove undertook to pay 400 Marks Sterling to the Viscount of Périgord. Musgrove, a supporter of Henry III in the civil war earlier in the reign, promised to repay the sum by 20 October 1269 in the London Blackfriars, offering estates in Suffolk and Wiltshire as surety.[16] The sheer scale of this arrangement led to the creation of a record, and it is likely that other transactions of this nature were made in the convent. Occasional later references relate to the Dominicans' new site near Ludgate. In 1317 a physician made an agreement with what appears to have been his sister-in-law concerning lands in Essex,[17] in 1359 three London citizens and their two business partners chose the Dominican church as a venue for the repayment of a loan,[18] a tenurial relationship was acknowledged in the convent in 1367 before the Royal Chancellor, the Treasurer and the

---

[14] Barron, 'Centres of Conspicuous Consumption', pp. 4-9; H.A. Harben, *A Dictionary of London* (London, 1918), pp. 1, 444, 516

[15] *Calendar of Close Rolls, 1279-88*, p. 428; Corporation of London Record Office (CLRO) HR 16 (51); Public Record Office (PRO) DL 27/62. W. Hinnebusch, *The Early English Friars Preachers* (Rome, 1951), pp. 37-8.

[16] *Calendar of Close Rolls, 1268-72*, p. 114; R.F. Treharne, *The Baronial Plan of Reform 1258-1263* (Manchester, 1932), p. 335; F.M. Powicke, *King Henry III and the Lord Edward*, 2 vols. (Oxford, 1947), vol. 2, 486.

[17] *Calendar of Close Rolls, 1313-18*, p. 471.

[18] *Calendar of Close Rolls 1354-60*, p. 618.

Keeper of the Privy Seal.[19] In 1390 the Dominican convent was again used as a venue for a legal agreement between private parties when a grant of an estate in Lincolnshire was acknowledged here.[20] A similar process concerning estates in Herefordshire and Shropshire was brought to a conclusion in the convent in 1409, again an instance of secular use of convent buildings. These occasions were probably not uncommon although it has to be emphasized that they left few traces in the records. The only remarkable aspect on this occasion was the fact that the prominent Lollard knight Sir John Oldcastle was one of the parties.[21]

While the convent's use by private parties is only sporadically revealed in the sources, the long-term use of the London Dominican priory by the royal administration and the government has left clearer traces. They fall into two categories: 1. the holding of political assemblies – including Parliaments – in the priory precinct; 2. the occupation of convent buildings by the Royal Chancery. Although most English Parliaments met in the royal palace at Westminster, there were alternative venues in the London region. The first recorded Parliament in the Dominican house was convened in August 1311. On this occasion Edward II was forced to assent to the 'Ordinances', a list of baronial demands designed to deal with weaknesses in royal government and finance. The confirmation and publication of the Ordinances caused a stir in the city and there is a brief report on proceedings according to which the Parliament lasted fifteen days. The text of the new legislation was read out to an assembly of the city's population in the cemetery of St Paul's close to the Dominican priory by the Bishop of Salisbury. While the king was staying in the priory he also received and confirmed Richer de Refham, London's newly elected mayor. The friars received £33-6-8 from Edward II in alms as well as 'pro dampnis que sustinuerunt in domibus gardinis, et aliis rebus suis occasione more dicti regis ibidem'.[22] Another Parliament in the priory was called for

---

[19] *Calendar of Close Rolls 1364-68*, p. 404.
[20] *Calendar of Close Rolls, 1389-92*, p. 106.
[21] *Calendar of Close Rolls, 1405-9*, p. 481.
[22] British Library (BL) MS Cotton Nero C VIII fol. 51 r°; R.R. Sharpe (ed.), *Calendar of Letter Books of the City of London*, A-L, 11 vols. (London, 1899-1912), Letter Book D, p. 17; T. Stapleton (ed.), *De Antiquis Legibus Liber. Cronica maiorum et vicecomitum Londoniarum*, Camden Society, vol. 34 (London, 1846), pp. 251-2; *Rotuli Parliamentorum*, vol. 1, pp. 281-6; M. McKisack, *The Fourteenth Century 1307-1399*, The Oxford History of England vol. 5 (Oxford, 1959), pp. 10-21. Given the attention paid to aspects like the fiscal and legislative powers of Parliament, its development, composition and political rôle, the question of the venues has been neglected. An exception is: I.M. Cooper, 'The Meeting Places of Parliament in the Ancient Palace of Westminster', *Journal of the British Archaeological Association*, Third series, 3 (1938), pp. 97-138. As general background: G.L. Harriss, *King, Parliament and Public Finance in Medieval England to 1369* (Oxford, 1975); R.G. Davies & J.H. Denton (eds.), *The English Parliament in the Middle Ages* (Manchester, 1981) (with bibliography).

January 1515, however, the assembly only met in February and it is not clear whether the Dominican convent was actually involved.[23] The Black Friars were mentioned again in connection with the only Parliament assembled during the government of Cardinal Wolsey, summoned in 1523. This Parliament actually convened in the great chamber of the convent on 14 April in the presence of Henry VIII; speaker of the Commons was Sir Thomas More.[24] Although the convent was only used on a very few occasions as a venue for Parliament, by 1529 the occasion had provided a name, 'Parliament Chamber' for a room in the priory. In November of the same year the next Parliament assembled, again in the presence of the king and again in the presence of Sir Thomas More who had now become Chancellor.[25]

While only a few Parliaments were called to meet in the mendicant priory near Ludgate, the Dominican house was much more frequently used as a venue for deliberations of the Royal Council. The Council, usually consisting of some prelates, lay magnates and senior members of the royal administration, also commonly met in the royal palace at Westminister, however, some of the city's mendicant houses became alternatives, most prominent among them the Dominican convent. The earliest recorded event concerns a financial agreement between the Council and the firm of the Bardi and Peruzzi on 6 March 1341.[26] This single reference must stand for many unrecorded meetings in the priory because only a few years later, in June 1349, there was a 'chamber of the council' in the Dominican convent. On this particular occasion, at the height of the Black Death, the brother of the recently deceased Chancellor handed over the great seal to the royal Chamberlain.[27] In 1375 the Council met in the friars' chapter house, the precise location of other meetings in 1378 and 1382, when the prior of the English Hospitallers did fealty to the king, is not known.[28] The choice of different venues offered a high degree of flexibility to the government and the proximity of other branches of the administration could be of advantage.[29]

---

[23] R. Brodie (ed.), *Letters and Papers, Foreign and Domestic of the Reign of Henry VIII*, vol. 1, 3 parts (London, 1920), part 2, n°. 2590.

[24] J.S. Brewer (ed.), *Letters and Papers, Foreign and Domestic of the Reign of Henry VIII*, vol. 3, 2 parts (London, 1867), part 2, p. 1244; J.S. Roskell, *The Commons and Their Speakers in English Parliaments 1376-1523* (Manchester, 1965), pp. 324-7.

[25] J.S. Brewer (ed.), *Letters and Papers, Foreign and Domestic of the Reign of Henry VIII*, vol. 4, 3 parts (London, 1870-1876), p. 2581; *Ibidem*, n°. 6043.

[26] *Calendar of Close Rolls, 1341-43*, p. 117.

[27] *Calendar of Close Rolls, 1349-54*, p. 84.

[28] *Calendar of Close Rolls, 1374-77*, pp. 210-1; *Calendar of Close Rolls, 1377-81*, pp. 222-3; *Calendar of Close Rolls, 1381-85*, p. 208.

[29] Sharpe (ed.), *Calendar*, Letter Book H, pp. 301-2. *Calendar of Close Rolls 1389-92*, pp. 229-30. PRO E28/4/4; J.F. Baldwin, *The King's Council in England during the Middle Ages* (Oxford, 1913), pp. 517-20.

Unlike Parliament, meetings of the Council did not interfere with the convent's internal routine because space was only required for a small group of people. On 9 March 1401 the Earls of Northumberland and Worcester, the Chancellor, Treasurer as well as the Clerk of the Council and one further official held a meeting, on 17 March the Clerk was joined by the Treasurer, three other officials and the Earls of Salisbury and Oxford. On 22 March the Council held another meeting in the priory when it was attended by the Chancellor, the Bishops of Durham, Hereford and Bangor, the Earl of Worcester, the Treasurer, the Keeper of the Privy Seal, the Clerk of the Council and five other people.[30] A similar pattern emerges for other Council meetings in the Dominican priory which are documented until 1438.[31] In August 1420 only the Bishops of Winchester and Bath and the Treasurer's deputy met, on 5 March 1423 the Dukes of Gloucester and Exeter, the Bishops of London and Winchester, the Chancellor, the Treasurer, the Keeper of the Privy Seal and one other official assembled in the priory, on the next day they were joined by the Earl of Warwick.[32] In May 1423 there were three Council meetings in the Black Friars, attended by between ten and twelve men.[33] It is true that the councillors were attended by servants who would e.g. provide food but this was still a manageable group. Exceptional were those occasions when individuals or groups were summoned to appear before the Council. This happened in the summer of 1416 when all captains and leaders of the expedition planned for this year were ordered to attend the Council in the Dominican convent to receive their instructions there. A similar order had been given to knights of Henry IV's retinue in 1407 when a foreign expedition had been planned.[34] On other occasions the Council issued summons in its legal capacity, turning a part of the priory into a venue for litigants.[35]

A much more constant presence in the Dominican priory was the Royal Chancery which is first mentioned in this location in March 1315.[36] Although it is not possible to say precisely which departments of the Chancery were lodged in the priory, operations must have been substan-

---

[30] PRO E28/7/50; E28/11/13; *Calendar of Patent Rolls, 1399-1401*, 470.
[31] *Calendar of Patent Rolls, 1436-41*, pp. 166-7.
[32] PRO E28/33/48; E28/39/65; E28/39/78.
[33] PRO E28/41/29; E28/41/54; E28/41/111. A meeting in 1426: ten members present in the priory, E28/47/73.
[34] Sharpe (ed.), *Calendar*, Letter Book I, p. 152, 162, 175-6; C. Allmand, *Henry V* (London, 1992), pp. 102-105; *Calendar of Close Rolls, 1405-9*, p. 257.
[35] *Calendar of Close Rolls, 1385-89*, pp. 586-7.
[36] *Calendar of Close Rolls, 1313-18*, p. 216.

tial because letters were issued here and the convent buildings were also used to store records and documents.[37] It is highly likely that the priory was frequented not only by Chancery clerks and officials but also by suitors who needed royal writs. This – rather than occasional meetings of the royal government – will have had an impact on the character of the priory and its internal life because the presence of at least parts of the Chancery meant daily interference by members of the laity who arrived in the priory to pursue their legal and political interests. This interference seems to have lasted from the 1320s to the 1340s – the Chancery can still be found in the priory in March 1345[38] – and throughout the 1370s. The work of the Chancery was conducted in at least two locations, the church and the chapter house, often it is not known which space within the convent was required by the royal clerks.[39] The nave of the large Dominican church near Ludgate may have accommodated a government department over long periods of time in the fourteenth century. This was made possible by the architectural transformation of small oratories into mendicant churches with extended naves in the thirteenth century, a space generally designated for the laity and used not just for worship but for business transactions, negotiation and even arbitration. This area was physically separated from the choir which was reserved for the friars.[40]

The Dominican priory was extensively used for secular purposes over extended periods of time but it was not the city's only mendicant precinct to be used in this way. The Carmelites also hosted the Royal Council on several occasions, in 1313, 1338, 1340 and 1364. On the first of these occasions, in early January 1313, London's mayor and aldermen were summoned and informed of the Council's decision to impose a tax on the city. This set off a negotiation process about the city's privileges and different options of assessment which lasted throughout the day. A settlement was found five days later at another meeting of the Council and the city's government. In the meantime the royal government had applied

---

[37] BL MS Stowe 553 fol. 33 r°; *Calendar of Close Rolls, 1318-23*, p. 313; *Calendar of Close Rolls, 1323-27*, p. 411; *Calendar of Patent Rolls, 1321-24*, p. 191.

[38] *Calendar of Close Rolls, 1343-46*, p. 547.

[39] Chancery use of the chapter house: *Calendar of Close Rolls, 1333-37*, pp. 309, 327; the Chancery in the Dominican church: *Calendar of Close Rolls, 1339-41*, pp. 448, 453; *Calendar of Close Rolls, 1341-43*, p. 112. Unknown location: *Ibidem*, p. 125; *Calendar of Close Rolls, 1343-46*, pp. 107; 125; *Calendar of Close Rolls, 1468-76*, p. 35.

[40] L. Barbaglia, 'Mendicanti, ordini (architettura)', in: *Dizionario degli Istituti di Perfezione*, vol. 5 (Rome, 1978), col. 1189-1212. The architectural development of Dominican churches has been investigated by G. Meersseman, 'L'architecture dominicaine au XIIIe siècle. Législation et pratique', *Archivum Fratrum Praedicatorum*, 16 (1946), pp. 136-190.

pressure by sending royal justices to the Guildhall while it is possible that the city offered bribes to a royal official in return for assistance.[41] The Chancery equally made long-term use of the buildings, again we find the royal clerks occupying parts of the church and the chapter house. This use extended from the 1320s into the 1350s. In August 1381, after the great revolt, the Chancery was again active in the White Friars.[42] Both mendicant houses were used, sometimes at the same time. When the Custodian of the Great Seal died in August 1343, the matrix was taken to the Dominican church in a sealed bag and used there; on the following day documents were sealed with it in the Carmelite priory.[43] In June 1321 an official request was sent to the Dominican prior to find a safe place for the rolls of the Chancery which were at the moment being kept in the Carmelite house. In the event the records were not taken to the Dominicans but to the Tower, where they were kept in greater safety during the armed rebellion against royal government at this time.[44]

To a lesser extent the Dominican priory was also used for a range of other secular purposes. Given the large demands made by the royal administration there was surprisingly little use of priory buildings by the civic authorities. In 1326 the election of a mayor of the staple of wool as well as other commodities was to be held in the priory before the mayor of London but this was an event authorized by royal command.[45] From the thirteenth century onwards London had its own guildhall which could be used both by the city's administration as well as for ceremonial and political functions. At least some of the wards appear to have had meeting places for their wardmotes, e.g. the wardmote of Cripplegate Ward meeting in the brewers' hall, while royal justices were using the guildhall in the early years of the fourteenth century, moving later to the more neutral liberty of St Martin-le-Grand close to Newgate.[46]

---

[41] Sharpe (ed.), *Calendar*, Letter Book D, pp. 305-6; on 10 January 1313 a man who had accused a clerk of Chancery of accepting bribes in this matter was committed to prison because he failed to provide detailed information, *Calendar of Close Rolls, 1307-13*, p. 563. A.H. Thomas & P.E. Jones (eds.), *Calendar of Plea and Memoranda Rolls Preserved among the Archives of the Corporation of the City of London A.D. 1323-1482*, 6 vols. (Cambridge, 1926-61), vol. 1323-1364, pp. 120, 147; *Calendar of Close Rolls, 1364-68*, p. 61.

[42] *Calendar of Close Rolls, 1323-27*, p. 324; *Calendar of Close Rolls, 1337-39*, p. 284; *Calendar of Close Rolls, 1339-41*, p. 336; *Calendar of Close Rolls, 1349-54*, p. 619.

[43] *Calendar of Close Rolls, 1343-46*, pp. 225-6.

[44] *Calendar of Close Rolls, 1318-23*, p. 313; McKisack, *Fourteenth Century*, pp. 58-70.

[45] Sharpe (ed.), *Calendar*, Letter Book E, p. 211; *Calendar of Close Rolls, 1323-27*, p. 564.

[46] C.M. Barron, *London in the Later Middle Ages. Government and People 1200-1500* (Oxford, 2004), p. 27, 123.

On some occasions the priory was used as accommodation for foreign visitors and for diplomatic negotiations. This happened in 1411 after the Burgundian Duke John the Fearless had approached King Henry IV for assistance against the Dukes of Orléans and Berry. The duke's ambassadors were housed in the priory and the Custodian of the Royal Wardrobe, Sir Thomas Bromflet, was ordered to pay their expenses.[47] A peace agreement between Louis XI and Edward IV was sealed in a room of the Dominican priory in 1478 and the priory served again as a venue for Anglo-French negotiations in 1528[48] but by now significant changes had occurred. Ever since the Black Death the number of Dominicans had dwindled. While eighty and more friars resided in the convent in the early fourteenth century, by the late fifteenth century the community probably only had half that number. The precinct, however, had not diminished in size and it was still attractive for court and government. King Henry VIII entertained here in 1511, Cardinal Wolsey was staying in the priory in 1523 and from 1529 the proceedings of the king's divorce were conducted here.[49]

The friars seem to have become increasingly aware of the precinct's value as a commercial asset. Here was another form of secular use: economic exploitation of the priory precinct initiated by the friars themselves. A house with a garden in the Dominican priory was first leased to a member of the laity in 1373;[50] by the sixteenth century it was quite common for lay parties to rent or lease a building in the convent. Whereas the Dominicans had not been in a position to object to requests for the use of their buildings made by kings like Edward II or Edward III who were prominent supporters of their convent, they made a deliberate choice to accept lay interference in their priory in return for economic benefits.[51]

---

[47] PRO E403/608 m 12; E.F. Jacob, *The Fifteenth Century 1399-1485*, The Oxford History of England, vol. 6 (Oxford, 1961), p. 111.

[48] Brodie (ed.), *Letters and Papers*, vol. 1, part 2, p. 1354; Brewer (ed.), *Letters and Papers*, vol. 4, part 2, n°. 4340.

[49] J.S. Brewer (ed.), *Letters and Papers, Foreign and Domestic of the Reign of Henry VIII*, vol. 2, 2 parts (London, 1864), part 2, p. 1494-5; Idem (ed.), *Letters and Papers*, vol. 3, part 2, p. 1330; BL MS Cotton Vitellius B XII fol. 48 r°.

[50] Corporation of London Record Office HR 101 (42); the same tenant, Robert Pypot, was still living in the Dominican priory in 1378, HR 106 (111).

[51] Brodie (ed.), *Letters and Papers*, vol. 1, part 2, n°. 3017(2); Brewer (ed.), *Letters and Papers*, vol. 4, part 1, n°. 1083; J. Gairdner (ed.), *Letters and Papers, Foreign and Domestic of the Reign of Henry VIII*, vol. 5 (London, 1880), n°. 1478; Idem (ed.), *Letters and Papers, Foreign and Domestic of the Reign of Henry VIII*, vol. 11 (London, 1888), n°. 1344; J. Gairdner (ed.), *Letters and Papers, Foreign and Domestic of the Reign of Henry VIII*, vol. 13, 2 parts (London 1892-3), part 1, n°. 296.

The atmosphere in the priory if not the whole character of the convent is likely to have been transformed by these changes. The disruption caused by business deals and political meetings, legal proceedings and even royal visits in the decades before the dissolution must have had its own impact on the friars' religious life.[52]

It has already been indicated that church and chapter house of the Carmelite priory in Fleet Street were also used by the Royal Chancery and – to a lesser extent – by the Council.[53] A few other official demands were made on the friars: in 1423 French ambassadors were given lodgings in the convent[54] and in the summer of 1538, a few months before the end of the community, the precinct was used to store some arms of Henry VIII's bodyguard.[55] The priory was occasionally also used by private parties for different purposes. In 1289 charters as well as other goods belonging to a local landholder were found 'in quadam cista' in the priory.[56] The storage of a large sum of money in the convent in the early fourteenth century even led to a serious crime in which one of the friars was implicated and another killed.[57] It may have been common for private parties to make business transactions in the church, fourteenth-century sources refer to the repayment of loans, specifically in the Carmelite church, or the conclusion of private contracts.[58] Since there was a constant business traffic to the offices of the Chancery in addition to other types of secular use by members of the laity this is likely to have interfered with the life of a community which repeatedly complained about the disruption caused by prostitution in its vicinity in the mid-fourteenth century.[59] A reduction in the number of friars in the house in the years before the dissolution the Carmelites also began to make commercial use of their precinct.

---

[52] *Letters and Papers, Foreign and Domestic of the Reign of Henry VIII*, Addenda, vol. 1, 2 parts (London, 1929-32), part 1, n°. 832; Brewer (ed.), *Letters and Papers*, vol. 4, part 3, n°. 5813; J. Gairdner (ed.), *Letters and Papers, Foreign and Domestic of the Reign of Henry VIII*, vol. 7, 2 parts (London, 1883), part 2, n°. 1338; Idem (ed.), *Letters and Papers, Foreign and Domestic of the Reign of Henry VIII*, vol. 12, 2 parts (London, 1890-91), part 2, n°. 1136.

[53] BL MS Cotton Vespasian D XVI fol. 23 v°.

[54] PRO E364/57 m 7.

[55] Gairdner (ed.), *Letters and Papers*, vol. 13, part 2, n°. 1280.

[56] PRO E159/62 m 6.

[57] J. Röhrkasten, *Die englischen Kronzeugen 1130-1330*, Berliner Historische Studien, vol. 16 (Berlin, 1990), pp. 348-9.

[58] *Calendar of Close Rolls, 1343-46*, p. 231; *Calendar of Close Rolls, 1346-49*, p. 590; *Calendar of Close Rolls, 1349-54*, pp. 234-5.

[59] *Calendar of Close Rolls, 1333-37*, p. 734; *Calendar of Close Rolls, 1343-46*, p. 544; *Calendar of Close Rolls, 1346-49*, p. 37.

While heavy royal demand was made on the priories of the Dominicans and the Carmelites the precinct of the Franciscans was largely free of this burden. A meeting of the Royal Council is only recorded in February 1475.[60] In 1529 the Franciscans also provided the venue for the ecclesiastical tribunal which was to hear the case of the king's divorce and the papal nuntio lodged in the priory in 1531 but there are few other references of this nature.[61] A few months before the dissolution of the house the Order of the Garter held a chapter in the convent where a few friars, led by a guardian who had already decided to abandon his vocation, were still holding out.[62] Private use of the convent precinct is already documented in the thirteenth century, before the construction of the large Franciscan church. In 1279 and in 1285 the convent was the venue for the repayment of loans, transactions sufficiently significant to be entered into the memoranda rolls of the Exchequer. According to a complicated marriage settlement involving a contract between the Countess of Norfolk and the Archbishop of Canterbury made in 1388, annual payments of 500 Marks Sterling were to be made in the Franciscan church.[63] Queen Blanche of Navarre, the wife of Edward I's brother Edmund, deposited a large amount of money in the priory before she left the kingdom after her husband's death. After the death of his sister-in-law the English king repeatedly sent officials to the priory to remove large amounts from this treasure, leaving either jewels or his letters as pledges for restitution.[64] Just like the Carmelites the Grey Friars were prepared to let their convent be used as a site for the safe deposit of valuables. In addition the Franciscan chapter house was the scene of arbitration between physicians, surgeons and a complainant who wanted to be compensated after an alleged medical error. This one case, heard in September 1424, is documented; there may have been more.[65] The Franciscans began to make commercial use of priory property in the fifteenth century, they had already agreed to cede part of their priory to the city in the mid-fourteenth century when the funding of the maintenance for London Bridge was consolidated.

---

[60] PRO E163/8/36.
[61] Gairdner (ed.), *Letters and Papers*, vol. 5, n°. 614; Idem (ed.), *Letters and Papers, Foreign and Domestic of the Reign of Henry VIII*, vol. 6 (London, 1882), n°. 5774.
[62] Gairdner (ed.), *Letters and Papers*, vol. 13, part 1, n°. 1127.
[63] PRO E159/52 m 2; E159/58 m 17; *Calendar of Close Rolls, 1385-89*, p. 472.
[64] *Calendar of Patent Rolls, 1301-1307*, p. 108; PRO E101/364/13 fol. 34 r°; E101/365/6 m 19d. The money had not yet been fully repaid by 1331, *Calendar of Patent Rolls, 1330-34*, p. 53.
[65] Thomas & Jones (eds.), *Calendar of Plea and Memoranda Rolls*, 1413-37, p. 175.

Even less demand was made on the other mendicant houses. Only one meeting of the Royal Council is recorded in the Austin Friars' priory, held in 1533, perhaps because it was convenient for Thomas Cromwell, whose house was adjacent to the convent.[66] As in the case of the other three great male mendicant houses in the city, the Austin Friars' church was appointed as the place for the repayment of debts or the payment of annuities on a few occasions, the level of the surviving entries in the Chancery records matching that of the other priories.[67] When the Papal Ambassador Spinelli came to London in 1514 he also visited the Austin Friars but he does not seem to have lodged in the priory.[68] In the early sixteenth century the Company of Pewterers met in the convent for a few times before their own hall was completed.[69] The conclusion of only one legal agreement in the monastery of the Franciscan nuns survives, the transaction with a volume of £200 was enrolled in the Chancery in 1384; however, the nuns had admitted members of the aristocracy as lay residents into their precincts since the middle of the fourteenth century, the Austin Friars only took this step in the 1520s. The Friars of the Cross had lay residents from the 1370s onwards; apart from this particular type of function their convent does not seem to have been used at all.[70]

There were significant differences in the level of demand made by secular users on the priories. The Dominicans clearly bore the brunt throughout the fourteenth and fifteenth centuries, sharing their role with the Carmelites. The priories of the Franciscans and the Austin Friars played a different role. The overall demand on them was at a much lower level and no part of the royal administration or government was present for

---

[66] *Letters and Papers*, Addenda, vol. 1, n°. 843. It is possible that Cromwell was sent a letter in which a transfer of part of the priory precinct was offered: 'In the gardyn at the Austen friars London Sir yt shalbe a gret plessur for you to have your wall goo strayt it shall make your gardyn square sir ye have nonother plasse to make your bowlyng alle in sane only ther for your Plessur you maye have this grounde and it shalbe no hourte to no man for if longes unto the bryge hows and the other unto you sadelards hall Sir I dyd speke with my lorde mayer and the shreuys on my none mynde to know what that the wold saye to it and the mayde me this ansur that you shold have it with all ther hartys iff that it had byn a greter mater then that'. PRO E36/153 fol. 42 r° (21 r°); however, neither the recipient nor the property in question is clearly identified.

[67] *Calendar of Close Rolls, 1349-54*, p. 78; *Calendar of Close Rolls, 1419-22*, pp. 41, 234.

[68] Brodie (ed.), *Letters and Papers*, vol. 1, part 2, n°. 2929.

[69] C. Welch, *History of the Worshipful Company of Pewterers of the City of London*, 2 vols. (London, 1902), vol. 1, p. 90.

[70] Brewer (ed.), *Letters and Papers*, vol. 3, part 1, n°. 952; *Calendar of Close Rolls, 1369-74*, p. 187.

any length of time. The other mendicant houses hardly feature. There were also variations and differences in the type of secular use. These differences need to be explained.

The location and convenience of access may have been important factors. The priory most in demand, the Dominicans, was inside the city walls offering convenient river access. The Dominicans had received the largest share of royal support during the early phase of their London priories, they also offered the most suitable location for use by different government departments. The Carmelite priory could also easily be approached from the walled area of the city and from Westminister via the Thames. None of the other priories had river access, the priory of the Austin Friars was not even situated on a main thoroughfare near a gate. The location was certainly a major factor but there were other reasons for giving preference to a particular convent. It is striking that the civic authorities hardly made any use of the mendicant priories. In November 1441 the mayor held a hearing in the Franciscan church after a riot in the Guildhall which had led to the arrest of a number of men. This was clearly an exception.[71] Another meeting, held in the church of the Friars of the Penance of Jesus Christ in November 1298 had been summoned by the beadles of three wards. Their purpose is not clear but a few days after the event the officials had to explain to the mayor on what authority they had assembled the 'honest men'.[72] Other urban assemblies in the city's mendicant precincts were even associated with riots or political opposition or were at least viewed with suspicion. In the summer of 1387 three serving men of the Company of Cordwainers were accused by the surveyors of their guild to have formed an illegal assembly in the Dominican church. The three admitted not only that but added that they had collected money and handed it to one of the friars, William Bartone, who had undertaken to obtain a papal confirmation of their association. Their efforts were regarded as prejudicial to the civic authorities and the three were sent to prison. There is no further reference to the Dominican friar involved, who was outside the city's jurisdiction.[73] This may, in fact, have been the core of the problem and the cause for the absence of official urban meetings in the mendicant convents: the precincts were outside the city's jurisdiction. Although all houses received constant material support

---

[71] CLRO Journal 3, fol. 103 v°.
[72] A.H. Thomas (ed.), *Calendar of Early Mayor's Court Rolls 1298-1307* (Cambridge, 1926), pp. 18-9.
[73] Sharpe (ed.), *Calendar*, Letter Book H, pp. 311-2.

from individual citizens, London's government had no direct claim over property and buildings. This affected even the Franciscans. While their real estate was still thought to be formally owned by the city in the early fourteenth century this legal fiction was no longer maintained five decades later. When in 1368 the city wanted to use a part of the precinct, property on the streetfront, to build shops, the mayor had to enter into negotiations with the friars. The Franciscans were happy to give up land and buildings they did not require but they laid down a number of conditions concerning access to their church and the possible obstruction of their church windows.[74] After a riot in the Carmelite precinct in 1376 the city's authorities could only make an arrest after they had received a royal authorisation.[75] The churches of the Austin Friars, the Franciscans and the Carmelites served as assembly points in the political disputes between the party around John of Northampton and the established aldermen which threatened to erupt into violence in the autumn and winter of 1383-84. On 26 January there was an armed standoff between Northampton's armed followers and the city's government led by the mayor who ordered the rebels not to proceed to the Carmelite church.[76] Discontent with the urban government is supposed to have led to the preparation of another rebellion in 1443. Men from the Tailors', Brewers', Sadlers' and other companies were alleged to have had clandestine meetings in the Franciscan church.[77]

While the city of London had no immediate control over the mendicant precincts, the Crown did and in the case of the Carmelites and the Dominicans it made good use of these assets. Being associated with an unpopular king led to problems for the Dominicans in 1326 when Edward II's protégé Hamo de Chigwell sought refuge in the priory which was subsequently attacked by a crowd.[78] The convent features again in the faction fighting of 1449-51. The Dominican house was chosen as temporary residence by Edmund Beaufort, Duke of Somerset after his return from France in August 1450.[79]

---

[74] CLRO, Bridge House, Large Register of Deeds, fol. 9 v°-10 r°, 13 r°- 14 r°.
[75] Sharpe (ed.), *Calendar*, Letter Book H, p. 44.
[76] R. Bird, *The Turbulent London of Richard II* (London, 1949), pp. 82-3, 138.
[77] C. Barron, 'Ralph Holland and the London Radicals, 1438-1444', in: R. Holt & G. Rosser, *The Medieval Town 1200-1500* (London, 1990), pp. 160-83, p.176.
[78] Thomas & Jones (eds.), *Calendar of Plea and Memoranda Rolls, 1323-64*, p. 46.
[79] On 2 December he was attacked in the priory and his treasure was looted; BL MS Egerton 1995, fol. 194 r°; R. Griffiths, *Henry VI* (Berkeley (USA), 1981), pp. 284-9.

The secular uses of the churches, chapters houses and other conventual buildings of the London priories reveal another dimension of mendicant life in a wider context. They are a reflection of the relations between the various groups including the royal government and the civic authorities and the mendicants. They reveal parallels to mendicant houses in other European towns, where secular use of religious precincts was equally common. However, they also show differences, in particular the London mendicants' independence of the urban government and their close relations with the Crown. The survey could be expanded to include other outside use, e.g. the Blackfriars' Council of 1382 and other meetings of clerics and prelates. Seen in a wider context the observations made for medieval London show the influence of outside factors on the mendicants, they reveal strategies to cope or make use of them, e.g. economically. These outside factors created the conditions for the activities with which the mendicants are commonly associated. They will also help to explain why the Orders, large international structures, were highly sensitive to local influences.

University of Birmingham

Emilia JAMROZIAK

ST. MARY GRACES:
A CISTERCIAN HOUSE IN LATE MEDIEVAL LONDON

The Cistercian house of St Mary Graces, the last foundation belonging to that order in England has not received much scholarly attention despite its intriguing history and its role in the city of London in the late Middle Ages.[1] The results of the extensive excavations conducted in the 1980s by the Museum of London also have not been utilized by historians. St Mary Graces was an unusual monastery in two ways. Not just because of its location, but also because it was founded at the time when the Cistercian order was decidedly unfashionable and eclipsed, certainly in terms of the number of new foundations and appeal to the laity, by the mendicant orders.

It was the only Cistercian house in Britain and one of very few across Europe, which was located in a city.[2] The stereotype of the Cistercian order as far removed, both physically and socially, from the lay world has been successfully challenged recently. The old image of remote monasteries, removed as far as possible from society, has been abandoned and replaced by a more balanced perspective incorporating a large variety of possible interactions between the communities of white monks and wider

---

[1] This contribution benefited from the generous advice and comments of Prof. Derek Keene, who also allowed me access to the unpublished material collected during the project 'Social and Economic Study of Medieval London, Stage 2', based at the Institute of Historical Research and funded by the Economic and Social Research Council (ref. D0023 2027). The work was undertaken by Martha Carlin, Vanessa Harding, Derek Keene and Joanna Maltinghley. Dr Cordelia Beattie very kindly corrected problems of the English expressions in my article.

[2] Most examples of Cistercian houses located in cities or in their immediate vicinity come from Italy: SS. Vincenzo ed Anastasio alle Tre Fontane, S. Sebastiano *ad Catacumbas* (near Rome), S. Nicola (near Agrigento, Sicily), S. Spirito (outside the walls of Palermo), SS. Trinitá (inside the walls of Palermo). K. Białoskórska, 'Czy o wyborze miejsca na założenia opactwa cysterskiego decydowały zawsze wskazania reguły? Między teorią i rzeczywistością', in: J. Strzelczyk (ed.), *Cystersi w kulturze średniowiecznej Europy* (Poznań, 1992), pp. 151-152; for regional studies of the relationship between Cistercian houses and the cities see: W. Bender, *Zisterzienser und Städte: Studien zu den Beziehungen zwischen den Zisterzienserklöstern und den grossen urbanen Zentren des mittleren Moselraumes (12.-14. Jahrhundert)* (Trier, 1992); K. Brigljevic, 'The Cistercian Monastery and the Medieval Urban Development of Zagreb', *Annual of Medieval Studies at Central European University Budapest*, vol. 1 (1993-94), pp. 100-107.

society.³ Nevertheless, it is a well recognized fact that Cistercian houses never became established in any significant numbers in the urban environment. Although many of them owned properties in towns, often to facilitate their trading interests, their natural habitat was predominantly rural.

St Mary Graces was founded by King Edward III in 1350 as a daughter house of an earlier royal foundation in Beaulieu in Hampshire. Beaulieu was established by King John in 1204 and was later particularly favoured by King Henry III and Edward I. The founder of St Mary Graces, King Edward III, was also a recurring visitor there.[4] The new house was located just outside the city walls of London, in the parish of St Botolph, on the site of a Black Death cemetery in East Smithfield, near the Tower of London. The Tower at that time was not so much a royal residence, but an important seat of power, a stronghold and administrative centre. It was also used for receiving important guests.[5] However, the new abbey was located not so far from other royal residences along the Thames River in Baynard's Castle, Kennington, Rotherhithe, and Sheen in Surrey.[6]

The site for the abbey itself was bought by Edward III from John Corey, royal clerk and trusted servant, the founder of the plague cemetery and a chapel.[7] The cemetery was established in 1349 for the victims of the Black Death. It consisted of a chapel and two trenches of mass

---

[3] Most recently: C. Bouchard, *Holy Entrepreneurs: Cistercians, Knights, and Economic Exchange in Twelfth-Century Burgundy* (Ithaca, 1991); J. Burton, *The Monastic Order in Yorkshire, 1069-1215* (Cambridge, 1999); C. Berman, *The Cistercian Evolution: The Invention of a Religious Order in Twelfth-Century Europe* (Philadelphia, 2000).

[4] *Calendar of the Close Rolls*, vol. 7, *Edward III, 1343-46* (London, 1896), pp. 70-162, 219.

[5] D. Carpenter, 'King Henry III and the Tower of London', *London Journal*, 19 (1994), pp. 95-107; S. Thurley, 'Royal Lodgings at the Tower of London, 1216-1327', *Architectural History*, 38 (1995), pp. 36-57.

[6] For the royal residences along the Thames River see: H.M. Colvin (ed.), *The History of the King's Works*, vol. 2: *The Middle Ages* (London, 1963), pp. 980, 967-969, 989, 994-1002.

[7] *Calendar of the Patent Rolls*, vol. 1, *Henry VI, 1422-1429* (London, 1901), p. 89. London, British Library (BL), Additional Charter 39405. John Corey was in June 1341 called 'King's clerk', in 1344-5 he was called 'clerk of the [Black Prince's] exchequer or the clerk of the [Black Prince's] receipt'; in 1349 he was the 'prince's attorney-general'. T.F. Tout, *Chapters in Administrative History of Medieval England* (Manchester, 1920-1933), vol. 4, p. 267 and vol. 5, pp. 326, 334, n. 10. John Corey was later involved (in 1361), by royal order, in appointing craftsman to work on the abbey precincts. *Calendar of Patent Rolls*, vol. 11, *Edward III, 1358-61* (London, 1891), p. 567.

burials with up to five layers of bodies in them. The archaeological excavations revealed that the building of the monastic precinct did not disturb the burials, but the chapel became incorporated into the Cistercian church.[8] Some of the older publications on the subject of St Mary Graces' location suggested that it was a remote place, a swamp, fulfilling the qualities of the Cistercian ideal of isolation.[9] This is, I believe, a completely misplaced argument. The site for the new house was chosen not for its allegedly Cistercian qualities, but rather because it was close to the plague cemetery, similar to the another contemporary foundation of Charter House in 1370 (Carthusians) in West Smithfield on the site of another Black Death cemetery.[10] The monarch selected the Cistercian order for his new foundation partly as a commemoration of the tragic events. For St Mary Graces the connection with the king and its location proved to be vital for later material success and for securing important benefactors. At the same time, the abbey is a good example of the abilities of the Cistercian model to adopt itself to a very different environment and very different socio-economic conditions.

The motivations surrounding the foundation of St Mary Graces are expressed by some contemporary sources. The charter of agreement between the Prior of Holy Trinity London, who was in charge of the chapel and cemetery, and the newly founded Cistercian house, said that St Mary Graces was established to further religious cults and pious works in connection with the Black Death cemetery.[11] An entry in the Close Roll in 1351 contains a letter to the Abbot of Beaulieu stating that the new foundation was a thanksgiving to God and the Virgin Mary for the king's recovery and was to be an assistance in battles and other perils.[12] The later *inspeximus* of the foundation charter states that the foundation was a thanksgiving of Edward III to the Virgin Mary for saving him from

---

[8] I. Grainger, D. Hawkins, P. Falcini & P. Mills, 'Excavations at the Royal Mint Site 1986-1988', *London Archaeologist*, 5 (1988), pp. 429-431.

[9] M. B. Honeybourne, 'Two Plans of the Precinct and Adjoining Property of St Mary Graces', *Transactions of the London and Middlesex Archaeological Society*, New Series, 6 (1927-31), pp. 19-23.

[10] B. Barber, C. Thomas, *The London Charterhouse* (London, 2002).

[11] London, Public Record Office (PRO), E42/447. The document, dated 20 March 1365, carefully outlines any possible areas of dispute between both religious houses and lists the properties of St Mary Graces. The common seal of the abbey is attached, showing a kneeling king-founder.

[12] *Calendar of Close Rolls*, vol. 9, *Edward III, 1349-54* (London, 1896), p. 283.

death at sea.[13] Regardless of the precise details, this information indicates that the foundation was an act of personal significance and that the location allowed for regular contact with the royal court. Edward III had a history of spectacular religious acts with high public impact. He founded a college of secular canons of St Stephen, Westminster (1348) and a chivalric Order of the Garter at St George's Chapel in Windsor; he also went on several pilgrimages. All these acts were in tune with the fashion of the day and differed, in that sense, from his distinctively unfashionable Cistercian foundation.

The endowment of St Mary Graces was relatively small and at first consisted of £20 yearly paid out of the Exchequer until better sustenance was provided for the new foundation.[14] Soon after, in August 1353, the new house was given some lands and tenements in East Smithfield and Tower Hill and the king paid for the initial work on the buildings of the precinct.[15] This being insufficient, Edward III added in 1358 an annual grant of 40 marks paid from the Exchequer.[16] This was followed by other smaller, mainly monetary, grants from the founder and patron and his mother Isabel.[17] The initial group of five monks came from Beaulieu Abbey and William of Holy Cross was appointed as the first abbot.[18] By the late 1360s St Mary Graces' property in London was worth around 60 marks a year and included an advowson of three churches.[19] Its properties in London were diverse and included a brewing tenement with shops and gardens adjoining in the parish of St Botolph and a garden in East Smithfield.[20] Later the king added several manors further away. By the

---

[13] BL, Add. Charter 39405. The story of near ship-wreck in 1347 has been cited by the contemporary chronicles. F. Brie (ed.), *The Brut*, Early English Text Society, vol. 2 (London, 1908), pp. 295-6; Thomas Walsingham, *Historia Anglicana*, Rolls Series, vol. 1 (London, 1863), pp. 271-272.

[14] Given in March 1250. *Calendar of Patent Rolls*, vol. 8, *Edward III, 1348-1350* (London, 1891), p. 560.

[15] The appointment of John de Tiryngton to take carpenters, masons and other workers to work on the 'free chapel of St Mary Graces by the Tower of London' dated 8 June 1353. *Calendar of Patent Rolls*, vol. 9, *Edward III, 1350-4* (London, 1891), p. 465.

[16] BL, Additional MS 15664, fol. 138.

[17] A freedom from paying rent of 16 s p.a. for a particular plot near the Tower in August 1359. PRO, E326/12493. Isabel, the Queen Mother, left in her will £100 to the abbey (March 1361). *Calendar of Close Rolls*, vol. 11, *Edward III, 1360-1364* (London, 1896), p. 179; *Inspeximus* of Edward III grants in *Calendar of Patent Rolls*, vol. 1, *Henry IV, 1399-1401* (London, 1903), p. 327.

[18] D. M. Smith & V.C.M. London (eds.), *Heads of Religious Houses, 1216-1377* (Cambridge, 2001), p. 290.

[19] W. Page, *The Victoria History of London*, vol. 1 (London, 1909), p. 461.

[20] PRO, E 156/28/30; *Calendar of Patent Rolls*, vol. 13, *Edward III, 1364-1367* (London, 1891), p. 393

end of the fifteenth century the abbey had a number of prominent benefactors including the Countess Marie de St Pol, (widow of Aymer de Valence, Countess of Pembroke), Mary, Countess of Derby (wife of Henry IV) and King Richard III.[21] A number of wills of citizens of London show that the abbey became an element of the religious landscape of the city, but attracted only a limited number of donations, chantries and burial requests. The bequests in the wills are evidence of connections between these people and St Mary Graces during their lifetime, but the abbey never gained greater popularity as a focal point of religious practices of lay Londoners in the fourteenth and fifteenth centuries.

Table 1. Bequests to St Mary Graces

Person	Type of donation	Burial	Date	Source
Johannna Cros, widow of Henry	Bequest for building works	No	30 November 1352	*Calendar of Wills*, vol. 1, p. 665[22]
Henry de Yerdelee	Provision for chantry in the Holy Trinity chapel	No	18 October 1369	*Calendar of Wills*, vol. 2 (1), p. 131
John Shirbourne	Bequest on the altar	Yes (church or churchyard)	10 August 1375	*Calendar of Wills*, vol. 2 (1), p. 182
Richard Rothyng, stockfishmonger	A tenement for a perpetual chantry priest	No	5 October 1379	*Calendar of Wills*, vol. 2 (1), p. 213
Simon de Mordon, stockfishmonger	Bequest	No	7 April 1383	*Calendar of Wills*, vol. 2 (1), p. 243
William de Lincoln, saddler	Bequest	No	1 November 1393	*Calendar of Wills*, vol. 2 (1), pp. 301-2.
Robert Somersete, draper	Bequest	No	18 July 1400	*Calendar of Wills*, vol. 2 (1), p. 249
Robert Fitz, grocer	All his lands and tenements in Dowegate (parish of All Hallows) for celebrating divine service within the said monastery; also an annual rent of 10 s. from certain tenements as a pittance	No	26 December 1422	*Calendar of Wills*, vol. 2 (2), p. 437.

[21] Page, *Victoria County History*, p. 462; A.W. Clapham, 'On the Topography of the Cistercian Abbey of Tower Hill', *Archaeologia*, 66 (1915), p. 354; R.R. Sharpe (ed.), *Cal-*

Person	Type of donation	Burial	Date	Source
Matilda Aston, widow of John fishmonger	Certain tenements in Holbornstreet to be sold for pious uses and the abbey has the right of pre-emption	No	15 October 1436	*Calendar of Wills*, vol. 2 (2), p. 502.
Thomas Chynnore, fishmonger	Release of a portion due to him from the abbot and convent, on condition that they maintain a chantry in their chapel of St Anne	Yes (in the monastery)	6 January 1442	*Calendar of Wills*, vol. 2 (2), p. 539
John Norman, alderman of Castle Baynard Ward, citizen and draper	A certain annual rent from houses and wharf in the parish of St Michael at Queenwhite or 10 s. if the rent payments are in arrear	No	10 September 1467	*Calendar of Wills*, vol. 2 (2), p. 564.
Elizabeth Rollysley	Pittance for each monk to pray for her soul	Yes (in the church)	1513	*Formulare Anglicanum*, p. 440.[23]

The citizens of London also showed an interest in the abbey by means of chantries, a typical late medieval act of piety and not practised widely by the Cistercian order. There are at least four documented cases of chantries – from 1379, 1380, 1422 and 1442 – established by stockfishmongers and a grocer.[24] This is again a rather low number, which suggests that the abbey never attained the level of popularity which other religious houses enjoyed in late medieval London.[25] The most obvious reason for

endar of Wills Proved and Enrolled in the Court of Husting, London: Preserved Among the Archives of the Corporation of the City of London, at the Guildhall (London, 1889-1890), vol. 2 (1), p. 195. Mary, the wife of Henry IV, had her name written in the martyrology of the abbey and the monks were obliged to say a mass on the anniversary of her death, likewise for John, Duke of Lancaster. *Calendar of Close Rolls*, vol. 1, *Henry IV, 1399-1402*, pp. 325-6.

[22] R. R. Sharpe (ed.), *Calendar of Wills*, vols. 1-2 (London, 1890).

[23] T. Madox (ed.), *Formulare Anglicanum: or, A Collection of Ancient Charters and Instruments of Divers Kinds, Taken from the Originals, Placed under Several Heads, and Deduced (in a Series According to the Order of Time) from the Norman Conquest, to the End of the Reign of King Henry the VIII* (London, 1702).

[24] Clapham, 'On the Topography', p. 356.

[25] J.A.F. Thomson, 'Piety and Charity in Late Medieval London', *Journal of Ecclesiastical History*, 16 (1965), pp. 178-95; J. Röhrkasten, 'Mendicants in the Metropolis: The Londoners and the Development of the London Friaries', in: M. Prestwich, R.H. Britnell & R. Frame (eds.), *Thirteenth-Century England. VI: Proceedings of the Durham Conference 1995* (Woodbridge, 1997), pp. 61-76.

the relatively low number of bequests from the citizens of London to the abbey is its location. The parish of St Botolph was already well served by a number of religious institutions pre-dating St Mary Graces, namely the Augustinian priory of Holy Trinity (a royal foundation of Queen Matilda in 1107 or 1108), the house of Franciscan Minoresses (founded by Edmund, Earl of Lancaster in 1293) and the parish church itself.[26]

The building of the monastic precinct was a slow process and accelerated only by the late fourteenth century when the financial condition of the abbey improved. The accounts from 1391 show that the church was almost completed and the abbot's residence and infirmary were under way.[27] Not much was known about the form and layout of the abbey until the excavations twenty years ago, although some seventeenth-century maps allowed identification of the main part of the precinct. The excavations of the site between 1986 and 1988 revealed the layout of the abbey and many important and unusual features of it. It was distinctively non-Cistercian, close to the Dominican or Franciscan model with a string of chapels to the north and south of the presbytery and choir. Moreover the buildings had to fit in the relatively small space between other plots along Tower Hill and East Smithfield. There was also an unusually long frater, which, as it has been recently suggested, might have been used to feed a large number of poor.[28] Although, as I have explained earlier, St Mary Graces was not a particularly popular destination for the bequests of London citizens, its charitable activities became an important element in interactions between the Cistercian house and the city.

The excavations by the archaeologist from the Museum of London, revealed a lay cemetery on the north side of the church. As many as 133 burials (45% of them in coffins) and remnants of some tombs indicate that the abbey was a popular burial destination for lay people, with some high-rank burials. A completely unique feature of the church is the Lady Chapel built before 1492 by Sir Thomas Montgomery. He was a councillor of King Richard III, often travelling on diplomatic missions to the Continent, clearly a person acquainted with the latest fashions, yet he had chosen the Cistercian house to be the necropolis of his family. The excavations uncovered some indents of brasses, probably associated with the burial chapel of Montgomery dated to the late fifteenth or early sixteenth

---

[26] A.G.B. Atkinson, *St Botolph Aldgate: The Story of a City Parish* (London, 1898), pp. 22-41, 60-79.

[27] Transcript of the bursar's accounts in: Clapham, 'On the Topography', p. 364; PRO, SC6/1258/1.

[28] P. Mills, 'The Royal Mint: First Results', *London Archaeologist*, 5 (1985), p. 74

century, indicating a high status monumental burial decoration.[29] Thomas Montgomery's will dated 28 July 1489 gives further information as to the extent of his involvement in the abbey. He requested to be buried in the Our Lady Chapel of the abbey, which he built, and provided a further £20 for decorating it. Moreover he gave some land in Essex called Bowre Hall. The income from it should be used to keep 'oure Lady masse dayly by note' in that chapel to pray for him, his two deceased wives, maternal grandmother, brother John, uncle Thomas and his friends; in addition *de profundis* should be done next to his tomb. Further, he added bequests of vestments, a chalice, a candlestick, and money for singing masses for the souls of the above, and those of King Edward IV, his uncles, Lord Sudeley and Thomas Montgomery, and his sister Ann.[30] The range and scale of the donations indicate a particular attachment of Sir Thomas to the abbey, but his burial and that of his relatives were not the only high-status interments in the church. A record of visitation of the church in 1530, by Thomas Benolt Clarencieux records a great number of burials of members of the high aristocracy and courtiers.[31] A record of another visitation in March 1533 lists several tombs of aristocrats and royal officials in close proximity to the high altar and adjoining chapels.[32] This information appears in striking contrast to the rather limited number of bequests from the citizens of London, which indicates that St Mary Graces was particularly favoured by aristocrats associated with the royal court and became an important location for high-status funerals for that group. This is undoubtedly a result of the royal patronage of the house, which helped to create these links between the Cistercian house and members of the court.

---

[29] *Ibidem*, pp. 76-77.

[30] PRO, PROB 11/10, ff. 175 v° – 178 v°.

[31] Printed in: A.R. Wagner, *Heralds and Heraldry in the Middle Age: An Inquiry into the Growth of the Armorial Function of Heralds* (Oxford, 1956), pp. 143-144.

[32] C. L. Kingford (ed.), *A Survey of London by John Stow: Reprinted from the Text of 1603* (Oxford, 1908), pp. 287-288. Burials in the chapel of Our Lady: T. Montgomery and his wives, William Belknap, Montgomery's daughter, Alice Spice. To the south side of the quire Nicholas Loveyn, Lord of East Smithfield, and his wife. North side: Lewes John and his wife and their daughter Eleanor. In front of the altar: Elizabeth, daughter of Edward, Duke of Buckingham, her son and her husband, Earl of Essex, and his brother George Ratclyff; to the right of the altar Jane Stafford, daughter of the Duke of Buckingham; in the chapel within the quire sir Thomas Charles, Lieutenant of the Tower, Walter Hayward, secretary to the Lord Treasurer, Elizabeth Rowley. In the St Anne Chapel: John Montgomery, brother of Thomas, Andrew Cavendish and his wife Rose, Richard or John Walden and his wife Elisabeth.

Further clues as to the contact of the abbey with the royal court can be found in the abbot's residence. Because St Mary Graces was a royal foundation, the king could ask the abbey to accommodate his guests there or even to use it himself.[33] Again, there was a precedent for this, as travelling monarchs in the thirteenth and fourteenth centuries sometimes stayed in the Cistercian houses, with Beaulieu Abbey being the most favourite.[34] Nevertheless, the physical closeness of St Mary Graces to the Tower and many royal residences provided opportunity for regular visits by the monarch and also encouraged the king to use abbey buildings to accommodate his guests. There were also high-status people living temporarily on the precinct in the late fifteenth century, including Louis John and his pregnant wife, a daughter of the Earl of Oxford.[35] As much as the dead aristocrats needed splendid tombs, the living high-status guests needed a comfortable and fashionable environment, whilst the abbot wanted to emphasize connections with the royal patrons and powerful benefactors. The 1980s excavations revealed remnants of late fifteenth or early sixteenth century continental stove-tiles, discovered in the layers contemporary to the suppression of the abbey, but the original location of the stove is not certain. The analysis of the tine-glazed and lead-glazed tiles suggests strong stylistic connections with the Lower Rhineland, but the neutron-activated analysis indicates its possible origin from Bruges or Antwerp.[36] The presence of the stove can be connected with the post-Dissolution use of the abbey as a private residence, but it could well be evidence of the Continental links of St Mary Graces. Besides, as is attested independently, the abbey was, at the Dissolution in 1535, the third wealthiest Cistercian house in Britain with an income of over £602.[37] Its powerful benefactor, the earlier mentioned Thomas Montgomery, had often travelled to the Continent. The stove could have been commissioned by one of the last three abbots, John Langton (c. 1483-1514), Richard Prehest or Pest (1514-16) and Henry More (1516-38).[38] Above all, the

---

[33] P. Mills, 'The Cistercians and their London House', *London Archaeologist*, 4 (1982), p. 219.

[34] D. H. Williams, 'Layfolk within Cistercian Precincts', in: J. Loades (ed.), *Monastic Studies: The Continuity of Tradition*, vol. 2 (Bangor, 1990), pp. 97-98.

[35] G.A.J. Hodgett (ed.), *The Cartulary of Holy Trinity Aldgate* (London, 1971), nr. 995.

[36] D. Gaimster, R. Goffin & L. Blackmore, 'The Continental Stove Tile Fragments from St Mary Graces, London, in their British and European Contexts', *Post-Medieval Archaeology*, 24 (1990), pp. 16-33, 40-44.

[37] J. Caley (ed.), *Valor ecclesiasticus temp. Henr. VIII. auctoritate Regia institutus*, vol. 1 (London, 1810), pp. 398-9.

[38] Gaimster, Goffin & Blackmore, 'The Continental Stove', pp. 35-6.

presence of such high-status furnishings within the abbey adds another argument that the space was used for important meetings and hosting guests, which could encompass both lay members of the court, important London citizens and high ecclesiastics.

An important visual source attesting to the connection between the abbey, city and the royal court are seals: two from the fourteenth century, one from the fifteenth century, and two from the sixteenth.[39] The seals of the abbey show iconography indicating attachment both to the memory of the royal founder and, more unusually, to the city of London. The fourteenth-century seals contain the figure of Edward III, kneeling in adoration, and his coat of arms respectively.[40] The fifteenth-century seal of Abbot Paschal (dated 1420-1421) incorporates the coats of arms of both Edward III and the city of London.[41]

The most lasting and socially significant element of the contacts between the abbey and the city were, as mentioned earlier, charitable works. Charity, particularly helping the poor, was an important element of monastic ideology and Cistercian houses were actively engaged in it. The poor were often housed and fed in the separate purpose-built hospitals near the gate, within the precinct of the monastery, whereas high-status guests were received in a separate guest-house and often ate with the abbot. In fact, by the Late Middle Ages, lay people often formed a significant proportion of the individuals living within the monastic precinct.[42] However, the charitable works were usually conducted in the rural settings of the majority of Cistercian houses. St Mary Graces' case was different due to its urban location. The charitable works of the abbey were commented upon positively by the Bishop of London in 1368, only 18 years after its foundation, in the charter giving permission for the abbey to appropriate All Hallows church, Staining, in the city of London. The document states that the extra income from that church was necessary for the abbey to continue its valuable charity work in the city.[43] Of course this can be dismissed as a formulaic justification for the appropriation of the church, but much later sources attest that St Mary Graces was indeed providing vital help. In September 1538, during the suppression of the remaining religious houses in London, Richard Gresham, the mayor of the

---

[39] W. de Gray Birch, *Catalogue of Seals in the Department of Manuscripts in the British Museum* (London, 1887-1900), vol. 1, pp. 6421-642.

[40] Gray Birch, *Catalogue of Seals*, nrs. 3549, 3552.

[41] Gray Birch, *Catalogue of Seals*, nr. 3553.

[42] Williams, 'Layfolk', pp. 88-98, 116.

[43] R.C. Fowler (ed.), *Registrum Simonis de Sudbiria Diocesis Londoniensis, A.D. 1362-1375* (Oxford, 1927-1938), vol. 1, pp. 83-86.

city, sent a letter to King Henry VIII in which he singled out three hospitals – that of St Mary, St Bartholomew and St Thomas and the abbey of St Mary Graces – as the institutions which were founded and run primarily to care for the sick and poor who had no other means of sustenance. The aim of the letter was not to save these religious institutions from closure, but to secure the control of their assets by the city authority to continue the charitable work and keep the poor off the street. However, the concern of Richard Gresham indicates that the monastery had been providing an important social service for the city and was widely perceived to do vital work in that field.[44]

The case of St Mary Graces abbey remains as a unique case of an urban, late medieval and royal foundation among Cistercian houses. Despite it unusual setting, or rather because of it, the monastery successfully built its material success on the close links with the court. Its royal patronage continued beyond the lifetime of the founder and helped to foster connections with prominent aristocrats. In fact, the presence of high-status burials from the fifteenth and early sixteenth century in the abbey's church shows that this was a long-standing association between the Cistercian house and members of the political and social elite. The citizens of London never became such an important group for St Mary Graces. The number of burials, chantries and other bequests by merchants and artisans from London remained low in comparison with other religious houses in the area. The parish church of St Botolph was the major recipient of the chantry banquets and burials in that part of the city.[45] Donations from the citizens of London were surely welcomed, but they never formed an important support group in the same way as the aristocrats and courtiers did. The important links between the city and St Mary Graces were built predominantly on charitable works, mainly feeding the poor, which is attested by both written sources and archaeological evidence. This is, in itself, a rather standard occurrence, but what differentiates St Mary Graces from dozens of other religious houses in late medieval London, is the fact that it was a Cistercian house established at a time when

---

[44] The letter is published from BL Cotton, MS Cleopatra E, IV, f. 222, in J. W. Burgon, *The Life and Times of Sir Thomas Gresham, Knight, Founder of the Royal Exchange* (London, 1839), vol. 1, pp. 26-29. The abbey is incorrectly identified there as St Clare (Minories). For more information about Thomas Gresham, see: V. Harding, 'Citizen and Mercer: Sir Thomas Gresham and the Social and Political World of the City of London', in: F. Ames-Lewis (ed.), *Sir Thomas Gresham and Gresham College: Studies in the Intellectual History of London in the Sixteenth and Seventeenth Centuries* (Aldershot, 1999), pp. 24-37.

[45] Atkinson, *St Botolph Aldgate*, pp. 81-101.

this order was rather unfashionable. Not only was the layout of the precinct significantly remodelled to fit into the urban space, but the expectations of its benefactors were also taken into the account. Providing them with high-status burials gave the abbey, in return, significant donations and useful associations with powerful individuals. The influence of Edward III is visible in the location of the abbey close to the Tower, its sustained contacts with the royal court and even the iconography of seals evoking the patron, but St Mary Graces' involvement in charitable acts summarizes its successful interaction with the urban environment.

University of Leeds

Sheila SWEETINBURGH

MAYOR-MAKING AND OTHER CEREMONIES: SHARED USES OF SACRED SPACE AMONG THE KENTISH CINQUE PORTS

Introduction

Churches were ubiquitous in medieval England, their buildings and grounds used for a multiplicity of purposes by different groups and individuals. Urban churches might provide sites for civic ceremonies, possibly large-scale pageants and processions, like those in the cities of London, Coventry, Bristol and York, but equally in small towns, at the sole parish church, perhaps.[1] This essay examines the role and place of such rituals in the small Kentish towns of Hythe, New Romney, Sandwich and Dover. Together these towns comprise four of the five head ports (the fifth, Hastings, is in Sussex) of the Cinque Ports Federation, an ancient organization which was constituted to provide ship service for the Crown in exchange for rights and privileges in common.[2] Though remaining distinct, the ports, through their shared responsibilities, favoured status and close network of communications, developed certain similar features, making them an especially interesting group. Moreover, such features – the civic ceremonies of mayor-making, court proceedings, processions and pilgrimages, which are the subject of this article – are recorded in the towns' custumals, with further references in the various chamberlains' accounts, fraternity accounts and the Black and White Books of the Cinque Ports.[3] Dating the custumals is difficult but the preface in the Sandwich custumal states that it was produced in 1301 by Adam Champney, town clerk, its writing a response to Edward the First's attempt to

---

[1] A comprehensive study of civic ceremonies in medieval Germany, with other examples from France and England, has recently been produced; D.W. Poeck, *Rituale der Ratswahl. Zeichen und Zeremoniell der Ratssetzung in Europa (12.-18. Jahrhundert)* (Cologne, 2003).

[2] K.M.E. Murray, *Constitutional History of the Cinque Ports* (Manchester, 1935), pp. 12, 14-15, 28-9.

[3] For a list and brief description of the Cinque Port custumals; J.P. Croft, *The Custumals of the Cinque Ports c. 1290-c. 1500. Studies in the Cultural Production of the Urban Record* (Kent: University of Kent (Ph.D. thesis), 1997), pp. 324-39.

gain greater sovereignty over the town.[4] Even though this custumal does not survive, a late fourteenth-century edition is thought to resemble very closely the original.[5] Thus it seems appropriate to consider the civic rituals (elections, courts) recorded in the custumal as belonging to the fourteenth century. The impetus for writing was probably not confined to Sandwich, and it appears likely other Cinque Ports had developed similar customary practices by the same period. The first extant custumal for New Romney is fourteenth-century (a later edition in English is fuller and annotated) but the earliest surviving copy from Hythe is late fifteenth- and the one from Dover dates from the sixteenth century.[6] Another development of the fourteenth century was the Brodhull, the Cinque Ports own court, which began to meet on a regular basis from 1357, though the proceedings only survive from the fifteenth century onwards.[7] Of the other evidence used here, the chamberlains' accounts date from the fourteenth and fifteenth centuries, and the fraternity accounts from the fifteenth. With regard to thinking about these different civic ceremonies in terms of timing, the fourteenth century would seem appropriate except for the two fraternities, which may be considered to be part of fifteenth-century Kentish society. The heavy reliance on the town custumals has important implications for the study of these civic rituals because even though they became enshrined through their writing up in the fourteenth century, the customary practices they describe may be far older and it is often unclear how these practices developed over time. Thus the discussion in this paper prioritizes the ideal over the real, that is specific occasions in any particular year cannot be recovered for scrutiny. Yet it may still be useful to consider these ceremonies as events, thereby retaining an awareness of the interrelationship of time and space, while remaining aware of certain caveats. Firstly each ceremonial event was unique, and though the ritual process was constrained, within these boundaries the potential for variation was considerable. Secondly, the actors were not a homogeneous

[4] J.P. Croft, 'An Assault on the Royal Justices at Ash and the Making of the Sandwich Custumal', *Archaeologia Cantiana*, 117 (1997), pp. 13-36.

[5] Whitfield, East Kent Archives (EKAW): Sa/LC 1. Croft, 'Custumals', pp. 67-8, 104, 106.

[6] K.M.E. Murray (trans. & ed., with an introd.), *Register of Daniel Rough, Common Clerk of Romney 1353-1380*, Kent Records, vol. 16 (Ashford, 1945), pp. 1-27. EKAW, NR/LC 1. J.P. Croft, *Hythe MS. 1061. The Making of an Urban Register* (Kent: University of Kent (M.A. diss.), 1992), pp. 45-59, 118-23. London, British Library (BLL): Stowe MS 850 ff. 133-142. I should like to thank Dr Justin Croft for kindly allowing me to use his transcription.

[7] Murray, *Cinque Ports*, pp. 152-5. F. Hull (ed.), *A Calendar of the White and Black Books of the Cinque Ports*, Kent Records, vol. 19 (London, 1966).

group, instead they comprised a gathering of individuals whose perceptions and uses of space were dependent on their own personal circumstances, which they might modify with regard to the ideas of others, the dynamics of interaction potentially producing/enhancing/enforcing the formation of sub-groups. However, before looking specifically at these urban rituals, it is worth drawing out certain ideas about space which may aid the subsequent analysis.

Thinking about Space

As Edward Soja, the eminent cultural geographer, acknowledges, the development of ideas about space over the last forty years owes much to the writings of the Marxist, Henri Lefebvre.[8] Even though many were only available in French until relatively recently – his book *La Production de l'espace* published in 1974 was not translated into English until 1991 – his work has had a profound effect on contemporary theoretical discourses concerning spatial issues. He was one of the first to highlight the importance of thinking about space, the need to consider what is meant by space, how to define it, because although it could be described – a 'room', a 'marketplace' – terms relating to use, this added little or nothing to notions about its production.[9] Though he conceded that 'an already produced space can be decoded, can be *read* ... [that] there may have existed specific codes, established at specific historical periods and varying in their effects ... [whereby] interested 'subjects', as members of a particular society, would have acceded by this means at once to *their* space and to their status as 'subjects', acting within that space and (in the broadest sense of the word) comprehending it', this was only part of the question/answer.[10] Rather he wished to put forward the proposition that 'every society ... produces a space, its own space. The city of the ancient world [for example] cannot be understood as a collection of people and things in space; nor can it be visualized solely on the basis of a number of texts and treatises on the subject of space ... For the ancient city had its own spatial practice: it forged its own-appropriated-space. Whence the need for a study of that space which is able to apprehend it as such, in its genesis and its form, with its own specific time or times (the rhythm

---

[8] E.W. Soja, *Thirdspace. Journeys to Los Angeles and Other Real-and-Imagined Places* (Oxford, 1996), pp. 6-12, 26-82.

[9] H. Lefebvre, *The Production of Space*, D. Nicholson-Smith (transl.) (Oxford, 1991 [1974]), p. 16.

[10] *Ibidem*, p. 17.

of daily life), and its particular centres and polycentrism (agora, temple, stadium, etc.)'.[11] As a result, 'each society offers up its own peculiar space, as it were, as an 'object' for analysis and overall theoretical explication'.[12] However, this was neither easy nor straightforward, according to Lefebvre, 'because of the real and formal complexity that it connotes' and the necessity of envisaging space 'not [as] a thing but rather a set of relations between things (objects and products)', its production the result of processes of human intervention.[13] To overcome some of these difficulties, he put forward the idea of 'a conceptual triad ... of spatial practice, representations of space, representational spaces' as a way of thinking about the production of space.[14] This 'trialectics of spatiality', space as 'perceived, conceived, lived' is at the heart of his discourse, though for the purposes of discussion here the third part of the triad would seem to be the most fruitful, not least, because it encompasses the other two, allowing human beings to access 'symbols which we can readily conceive and intuit' which are 'inaccessible as such to our abstract knowledge' derived from conceived space.[15] Lefebvre defined 'representational spaces' as space 'directly lived through its associated images and symbols, and hence the space of 'inhabitants' and 'users' .... The dominated – and hence passively experienced – space which the imagination seeks to change and appropriate. It overlays physical space, making symbolic use of its objects. Thus 'representational spaces' may be said, though again with certain exceptions, to tend towards more or less coherent systems of non-verbal symbols and signs'.[16]

The second concept which would appear to be especially valuable is Lefebvre's notion of 'absolute space', a spatiality he believed dominated western medieval Europe.[17] For Lefebvre, as absolute space 'it has no place because it embodies *all* places, and has a strictly symbolic existence'.[18] Furthermore, being at once religious and political, absolute space was within the power of the ecclesiastical authorities, who could assign markers of identification, like crosses, so actually and metaphysically identifying 'any space with fundamentally holy space'.[19] Originating in

---

[11] *Ibidem*, p. 31.
[12] *Ibidem*, pp. 31-2.
[13] *Ibidem*, pp. 32, 83.
[14] *Ibidem*, pp. 33, 38-9.
[15] *Ibidem*, pp. 40-3.
[16] *Ibidem*, p. 39.
[17] *Ibidem*, p. 254.
[18] *Ibidem*, p. 236.
[19] *Ibidem*, pp. 236-7.

natural space, sacred places like springs and caves often became the sites of churches where rites associated with life and death were performed, which set them up as religious and civil foci. The socio-political forces that used this space (these places) to 'organize social production and reproduction' were personified as 'priests, warriors, scribes and princes', who were seen possessing, through appropriation, the space which had been produced by other social groups.[20]

Such ideas Lefebvre felt were appropriate for the period before 1100, the twelfth century marking the beginning of a time of change as space was conceived of in new ways, though absolute space retained its dominance. Church architecture exemplified this shift, seeing a move from Romanesque to Gothic forms, which Lefebvre considered was 'an emancipation from the crypt and from cryptic space', the space of a religion which revolved around death.[21] Other conceptual changes included the space of the market place, where commerce and the processes of accumulation took place. This is not to say religious space disappeared with the arrival of 'commercial space', instead 'alongside religious space, and even within it, there were places, there was room, for other spaces – for the space of exchange, for the space of power', symptomatic of its complexity and multifaceted nature.[22] Yet he did see such changes as having important implications, for him the church 'lost' the symbols of power and knowledge when the town built its freestanding bell tower and town hall, the chronology of this development differing widely across Western Europe.[23] Nor was this a straightforward change because townsmen might provide themselves with a common hall while still continuing to use a local church for civic activities (see below).

In introducing this idea of change in 'medieval space', Lefebvre introduces the significance of time, of history.[24] For him the transition from medieval (feudal) space to capitalist space was a time of mediation when the town, which had long dominated and controlled the countryside, began to distance itself, a position he called 'duality in unity'.[25] As a consequence the merchant sought to take power from the feudal lord, a desire that was articulated symbolically through ceremonies and festivals.[26] Such rituals were 'lived' in Lefebvre's terms, which meant that the actors,

[20] *Ibidem*, p. 48.
[21] *Ibidem*, p. 254, 256.
[22] *Ibidem*, p. 266.
[23] *Ibidem*, pp. 264-5.
[24] *Ibidem*, pp. 20-1.
[25] *Ibidem*, pp. 268-9.
[26] *Ibidem*, pp. 267-8.

whether individuals or groups, were involved in this relationship between time and space because the pre-existence of space conditioned their presence and actions. Thus the actors were inhabiting contemporary space. The way they lived it was the product of their discourse with its history.[27] By pointing to the idea of the multi-layering of space through time, it seems useful to envisage the space/time dynamic as a series of palimpsests in which what has gone before is not totally eroded. Instead, on occasion, the actors may seek to retain only vestiges of the earlier forms, structures, functions of the space they now inhabit, whereas at other times these aspects are merely subject to minor modifications. Taking these ideas as a starting point, the next step is to consider them in terms of the evidence from the Kentish Cinque Ports.

Mayor-Making and Other Elections

Though somewhat of a misnomer in that only Sandwich and Dover had mayors from the thirteenth century, each of the ports did have an elected body of twelve jurats who, together with the bailiff (and mayor), attended to administrative and judicial matters. Hythe and New Romney each received the privilege of a mayoralty from Queen Elizabeth, Romney's royal charter (1564) stipulating that henceforth the mayor and jurats were to be elected in St Nicholas' church as heretofore the jurats had been.[28] At Dover and Sandwich the bailiff was a royal appointee, while Hythe and New Romney were under the jurisdiction of the Archbishop of Canterbury, who likewise sent his nominee under warrant to the town concerned. Although the day appointed for civic elections differed among the four ports (Sandwich used Monday and Thursday after the feast of St Andrew the Apostle; Dover the feast day of the Nativity of Our Lady; Hythe Candlemas and New Romney the Annunciation of Our Lady), there were a number of similar elements, like the sounding of the common horn at designated places throughout the town to summon the freemen or commonalty to gather at one of the town's parish churches.[29] Those at Hythe assembled at the largest church, St Leonard's, which was uphill of the town centre; at New Romney, St Nicholas's church was near to the old harbour; the men of Dover met at St Peter's church, adjoining the

---

[27] *Ibidem*, p. 57.

[28] Murray, *Cinque Ports*, pp. 73, 163. W. Somers, *The Story of the Church of St Nicholas New Romney. A Personal View* (Romney, 1994), p. 33.

[29] At Sandwich, for example, the horn was sounded at fourteen places, at New Romney it was sounded at every corner of the town; EKAW, Sa/LC 1, f. 1 v°; NR/LC 1, f. 1 v°.

market place, and close to the minster church of St Martin-le-Grand; and at Sandwich the commonalty used St Peter's church, the most central, and St Clement's, possibly the town's oldest parish church.

Looking in detail at elections in Dover and Sandwich, at Dover the commonalty were called to join the outgoing mayor and jurats in St Peter's church, to which the accoutrements of office including the common chest and the town seal had been brought.[30] Once the new mayor had been selected, if present he swore to uphold the town and its people, the wording of the oath apparently very similar to that used at Sandwich, and then kissed the Bible. Next the jurats were chosen, and they too swore to uphold the town's interests. Finally the three keys to the common chest were distributed, keys were given to senior jurats, the third held by the mayor, who also received the chest and other muniments into his safe keeping for the following year.

The situation at Sandwich was more complicated, mayor-making taking place at St Clement's church following the summoning of the freemen, jurats and out-going mayor.[31] Having taken the common horn from the town sergeant and the keys of the common chest from two of the jurats, the old mayor put these with his wand and the third key, and then called upon the commonalty to proceed to the new election. After naming three other reputable candidates, he was asked to withdraw, leaving the symbols of office behind. According to the custumal, the freemen were party to the discussion, but the views of the jurats were heard first, and once one of the candidates had been chosen he was recalled into the church to take his oath and to receive the wand and key, taking delivery of the common chest that afternoon or the next day. The jurats were also sworn in and the ceremony concluded with a procession to the new mayor's house. On the following Thursday the new mayor instructed his sergeant to summon the jurats and commons to meet him at St Peter's church. There the election of the other town officers took place, possibly in the north aisle, surrounded by the tombs of notable predecessors.

Even though the level of detail contained within these fourteenth-century descriptions of the election procedures is far less than that included in Ricart's *Kalendar* for Bristol, where matters such as the clothing worn by the town officers at the ceremony is listed, it is still possible to say something about this use of ecclesiastical space in the Cinque Ports.[32]

---

[30] BLL, Stowe MS. 850, f. 133.
[31] EKAW, Sa/LC 1, ff. 1 v° – 3. W. Boys, *Collections for an History of Sandwich in Kent, with notices of the other Cinque Ports and Members and of Richborough* (Canterbury, 1792), pp. 429-31.
[32] L.T. Smith (ed.), *The maire of Bristowe is kalendar by Robert Ricart*, Camden Society New Series, vol. 5 (London, 1872), pp. 70-1.

Parish churches, as foci in the unbounded space of absolute space, which is by its very nature sacred and political, were presumably seen as the only places where the election process should take place, their use demonstrating the sanctity of the election procedure. Nonetheless, some towns and cities by this period were conducting elections and other civic business in town halls, though, as at New Romney, the citizens might return/continue to use the parish church for such activities well into modern times.[33] For these townsmen, the election was being conducted in the sight of God, in His house, the commonalty guided by His unseen presence, surrounded by signs and symbols of His omnipotence. Thus their choice of the new jurats and mayor was a divinely guided process which should make the successful candidates acceptable to the freemen and others, and also to important authorities outside the town, especially the king and archbishop, their bailiffs and the Crown's officer, the Warden of the Cinque Ports. Yet this use of ecclesiastical space was probably more complex, the actors aware of the multiple layering of jurisdiction and 'ownership', where use and meaning were matters of negotiation, co-operation and/or appropriation, affected by changing circumstances over time. Such matters were similarly associated with issues of power and authority concerning the town itself, the exclusion of the bailiff from the ceremony, as representative of outside lordship, a public reminder of the port's privileged status. Though at Hythe the use of St Leonard's church added to this complexity because the church was the daughter foundation of the neighbouring parish church at Saltwood, the advowson of each belonging to the archbishop, who also had authority over Hythe.[34] Consequently, the men of Hythe may have seen their use of the town's largest parish church for the election of the jurats as a political act of appropriation.[35]

For the leading citizens of Dover St Peter's church was probably chosen for its central position; like the other town churches it may be Anglo-Saxon in origin, but the extent of the parish is difficult to ascertain. Perhaps from the beginning each of the churches paid a pension to the local minster church, an act of tribute that was transferred to St Martin's Priory when the monastic house was refounded in the early

---

[33] Murray, *Daniel Rough*, p. 2. Civil meetings at St Nicholas' church in New Romney were not stopped until 1886; Somers, *New Romney*, pp. 33-4.

[34] E. Hasted, *The History and Topographical Survey of the County of Kent*, vol. 7 (Canterbury, 1972 [1799]), p. 253.

[35] Sponsler, in her essay on theorizing cultural appropriation, notes that appropriation is 'a key event in the creation of meaning'; C. Sponsler, 'In Transit: Theorizing Cultural Appropriation in Medieval Europe', *Journal of Medieval and Early Modern Studies*, 32 (2002), p. 18.

twelfth century.³⁶ This hierarchical relationship between Dover's parish churches and the priory was reinforced in the 1270s when the priory acquired the advowson of St Peter's church from the Archbishop of Canterbury.³⁷ By conducting town elections in one of the ancient parish churches where the incumbent was a client of the local Benedictine priory, the civic authorities were presumably required to acknowledge their role in the relationship of benefactor and beneficiary. As the receiver of this monastic largesse, the mayor and jurats were expected to be grateful recipients, the interdependency of church and town witnessed by the commonalty annually on 8 September. It is not clear where in the church the election took place but the spatial dynamics of the process might have been used to underline this relationship, though they may also have indicated a greater complexity, in part due to the linking of various areas within the church to different groups, the nave the financial responsibility of the parishioners, the chancel the clergy, this latter space a place where notions of inclusion/exclusion could be expressed.

Turning to Sandwich, the sounding of the common horn at assigned places to summon the commonalty was also part of the spatial dynamics of the election process, and even though it occurred outside the church it was an integral aspect of the ritual. By drawing the freemen to the church for the election, the leading citizens were highlighting the inclusiveness of the procedure, together they, with the commonalty, had the right to conduct the election. Furthermore, the calling of the townsmen from throughout the town (the sound of the horn would have been heard over a considerable distance at each of the designated places), might be thought of as applying an aural boundary to the town by binding those who heard and responded, whose consequent presence in St Clement's church brought the town into the building. They and the church, for the time of the election, were the town, a special relationship that was underscored by the active participation of the freemen in the election process. Consequently, the civic authorities in St Clement's church through their use of ecclesiastical space demonstrated their position vis-à-vis the church, nonetheless the relationship in this instance was different in some respects in terms of lordship and power. Unlike Dover, there were no local monastic institutions in Sandwich and by the fourteenth century Canterbury

---

³⁶ Lambeth, Palace Library (PLL): MS 241, f. 48.
³⁷ S. Statham, *The History of the Castle, Town and Port of Dover* (London, 1899), p. 205. C. Haines, *Dover Priory, A History of the Priory of St Mary the Virgin, and St Martin of the New Work* (Cambridge, 1930), p. 236 citing Archbishop Pecham's Register, f. 40 v°.

Christchurch Priory, the town's earlier overlord, had few interests there.[38] The Crown's overlordship in Sandwich did not extend to any of its three parish churches, and the advowson of St Clement's, like St Mary's, was in the hands of the Archdeacon of Canterbury.[39] There is little to indicate the relationship between this ecclesiastical official and the town officers but the potential for conflict was presumably less than that at Dover.

In considering the inter-relationship between space and time, the custumal's description of the election process also highlighted the ancient nature of the ceremony, the idea that procedures had been done 'time out of mind' draws on notions of authenticity and antiquity, which were in a sense corroborated by the design and location of the church building. Mayor-making at Sandwich took place in possibly the town's oldest parish church, sited on higher ground away from the town centre, its great church tower and steeple seemingly an ancient beacon which had acted as a guide for centuries for the town's seamen and others off Kent's east coast.[40] As a consequence, the process received legitimacy. The senior townsmen could see themselves as upholding the ancient laws and privileges of their community-rights that had been theirs since the time of the Anglo-Saxon kings who had been the first to assign a special status to the ports. This time-depth relationship was reinforced by the timing of election, those at Dover and Sandwich apparently tied to the beginning and end of the herring season, and those at Hythe and New Romney taking place during the spring when local, coastal fishing took place.[41] In addition, the continuity of use of such procedures and spaces reinforced the links between new office holders and their predecessors. These men, having inherited responsibility for the good governance of the port which they were called upon to discharge as their ancestors had done, were aware that their election had been 'witnessed' by these same ancestors from beyond the grave, their tombs acting as a tangible reminder of their ongoing guardianship. And conversely, it seems likely that the Stuppeny tomb had been set into the place where elections were traditionally held

---

[38] Though still holding some property adjoining the harbour, the priory had relinquished overlordship to the Crown in exchange for sixty librates of land in 1290; D. Gardiner, *Historic Haven: The Story of Sandwich* (Derby, 1954), p. 38.

[39] Hasted, *Kent*, vol. 10, p. 210. Boys, *History of Sandwich*, p. 312.

[40] H. Clarke & S. Pearson, personal communication.

[41] The duration of the North Sea herring season can be gauged from a clause in Domesday which states that 'from the Feast of St Michael until the Feast of St Andrew the King's truce, that is peace, was in the town [Dover]'; P. Morgan (ed.), *Domesday Book: Kent* (Chichester, 1983), p. 4.

in New Romney. For Richard Stuppeny, a leading townsman and jurat, his physical presence in the midst of his fellow jurats and their successors placed death at the town's centre. This space was understood as a place where the living and the dead came together to celebrate the town's and their immortality. A further development of these ideas may be envisaged by the actions of Richard's great-grandson.[42] Clement Stuppeny had the tomb rebuilt in 1622, a brass plaque commemorating his generous action which had enhanced the citizens' ancient election place, a fitting memorial for these important members of the Stuppeny family whose links with New Romney encompassed the past, the present and the future.

The taking of the oath and the accepting of the symbols of office were similarly witnessed by God and these silent observers, as well as the living, such actions intended and presumably continuing to make the recipients acutely aware of the gravity of the ceremony, and their new role in the government of the town. Oath-taking was particularly important, and the apparent use of the Bible rather than a reliquary on which to swear seems to highlight the connection between God as Logos and the set form of the mayor's and jurat's oaths, these too, like the word of God having special, though not sacred meaning. Yet words were only part of the process and objects played significant roles, both with regard to their type and number. The lockable chest kept the town's documents secure, enshrining a high degree of exclusivity whereby only those who had held senior civic office in the past were privy to exactly what was contained therein. Such documents, like the town books, were not for display, instead it was their container which was seen by the commonalty, and as in the case of some reliquaries the imagination filled the chest with precious objects. These tokens of civic power and authority were safeguarded by the three keys, a prudent system but one which was equally pregnant with religious symbolism. Like the keys, the town seal, wand and horn were important symbols of office and their placement at the centre of the election process may have been intended to underline notions of continuity, authority and tradition. For the leading citizens, therefore, mayor-making was directed towards a number of audiences, the structures and processes outlined in the various custumals intended to reinforce the connection between religion and politics as the space of power and authority, speech and knowledge. These audiences were not necessarily physically present but were expected to comprehend the symbolic meanings

[42] Somers, *New Romney*, pp. 32-3.

underpinning this use of religious space, leading them as a result, it was hoped, to respect those elected. Yet this remains the 'ideal', mayor-making as it was envisaged by the writer of the custumal, because the event, reality, cannot be retrieved, which might provide ideas about the 'cultural consumption' of such rituals.[43] Instead, the only references in the various civic archives are the names of the newly appointed officials as they were recorded in the town books and customary payments of money for livery and expenses to the town clerk and other officers.

The Dispensing of Justice

Before (and perhaps after) the building of guildhalls in the Late Middle Ages at Hythe, Sandwich and probably New Romney, all the head ports had employed ecclesiastical spaces to conduct judicial proceedings, including both the town's own court and the bailiff's (hundred) court, the latter presided over by the bailiff with the civic officers. Courts were held in St Peter's church at Sandwich, possibly in the wide north aisle (and at St Clement's church); at New Romney either in the chancel or in the south aisle of St Stephen's chapel, close to the site of the later Stuppeny tomb; and in Hythe at St Edmund's chapel, on the south side of the high altar. The portsmen of Dover may similarly have used St Peter's church, but at some point after 1200 decided to opt for the old chapter house of St Martin-le-Grand, and thereafter an annual expense was the rent paid to St Martin's Priory, the local Benedictine house which at its foundation had been the beneficiary of the minster and its property.[44] Through its association and position vis-à-vis the minster, the old chapter house may also have been seen as a religious space, its suitability enhanced by Dover's relationship with St Martin, who was depicted on the reverse of the town seal.[45] However, this use of ecclesiastical space by the various town officers might be seen as an act of appropriation, the timing of court sessions tied to civic and commercial rhythms not the liturgy or church calendar. At New Romney this led to a supplanting of sacred time, the civic officers holding sessions when divine service was taking place, and in 1407 the incumbent sought to persuade them to alter their timetable

---

[43] Sponsler, 'In Transit', p. 26, citing M. de Certeau, *The Practice of Everyday Life*, S.F. Randall (transl.) (Berkeley, 1984).

[44] For example, in 1367/8 the chamberlains paid 4 s. to the priory; BLL, Add. MS. 29615, f. 7.

[45] On the reverse are St Martin of Tours and a three-towered gateway; J. M. Steane, *The Archaeology of Power* (Stroud, 2001), p. 227.

through a gift of 3s. 4d.⁴⁶ His role in the gift exchange would seem to illustrate Lefebvre's theories about changing spatial dynamics and the 'forces of history', an example of the idea of the palimpsest where what had gone before was significantly eroded.⁴⁷ Nevertheless, even though the belfry, Lefebvre's symbol of such changes in the later Middle Ages, was still an integral part of these churches, responsibility for time and time-keeping at Dover, in the form of the clock at St Martin-le-Grand, was in the hands of the civic authorities.⁴⁸

Such courts were not the only ones held in ecclesiastical spaces because the Lord Warden of the Cinque Ports presided over his court at St James' church, Dover, following the abandonment of the ancient outdoor meeting place at Shepway and, from 1357, the Federation's own court was held in St Nicholas's church, New Romney.⁴⁹ St James' church was within the liberty of Dover, primarily serving the port's fishing community in the twelfth and thirteenth centuries, but in what might be termed the suburbs, about equidistant between the town centre and the royal castle.⁵⁰ St Nicholas's church at New Romney provided the setting for the Court of Brodhull, where the head ports and their subsidiaries met to hear cases of infringements brought against individual ports or portsmen, to organize their regulation and overseeing of the herring fair at Great Yarmouth and to discuss disputes with the Exchequer over allowances relating to royal taxation.⁵¹ In addition, it is important to remember that these Cinque Port churches were also used by the ecclesiastical authorities for church court proceedings, hearing cases relating to religious and moral issues, the latter at times construed by the civic authorities as falling under their jurisdiction.⁵² Thus flexibility and negotiability would seem to be the hallmark of ecclesiastical spaces,

---

⁴⁶ *Royal Commission on Historic Manuscripts, 5ᵗʰ Report and Appendix* (London, 1876), p. 537.

⁴⁷ Lefebvre, *Space*, pp. 48-9.

⁴⁸ *Ibidem*, p. 265. In 1428/9 the Dover chamberlains paid 13 s. 4 d. to William Goldsmith for looking after the clock; BLL, Add. MS. 29615, f. 147 v°. For the introduction of the public clock as an indicator of modernity; G. Dohrn-Van Rossum, *History of the Hour. Clocks and Modern Temporal Orders*, T. Dunlap (transl.) (Chicago / London, 1996), p. 171.

⁴⁹ With the transfer of most of its business to St James', sessions of the Court of Shepway became more formal and were led less frequently; Murray, *Cinque Ports*, pp. 73, 106.

⁵⁰ Some cases at the Court of Shepway had been referred to the 'Court of the [Dover] Castle Gate' during the late thirteenth and early fourteenth centuries, but being outside the liberties of the Cinque Ports was deemed unsuitable by the portsmen and from *c*. 1350 St James' church was used; *Ibidem*, pp. 103-5.

⁵¹ Hull, *Black and White Books*, pp. xii-xiii.

⁵² From the mid-fifteenth century, the mayor and senior jurats at Sandwich seem increasingly to have tried such cases, women comprising the majority of defendants; S.

their various producers, both secular and religious authorities, demarcating 'ownership' through use and the placing of objects.

Moreover, for the mayor and jurats, the keeping of good order and the dispensing of justice were necessary for the correct functioning of the ports, both individually and collectively, especially during the later Middle Ages when the special status of the Federation was considered to be under threat from the growing competition of the West Country ports, Southampton, Bristol, those of Devon and Cornwall, and the continuing threat of invasion and civil unrest.[53] For the bailiffs, too, their role as the representatives of higher authority meant that it was advantageous for them to act in concert with the town officers, their position strengthened by their ecclesiastical surroundings. The circumstances of the town and bailiff's court, therefore, allowed them, as judges of temporal affairs, to emulate the actions of God, whose impartiality made him the supreme judge, and Christ, who would select the sheep from the goats on the Day of Doom, a familiar scene in numerous wall paintings. Yet even though the mayor, senior jurats and bailiff presumably wished to see themselves and to be seen in this way, any public disagreement within this sacred space resulting from a conflict of interests, either within the civic judiciary or between the senior town officers and the bailiff, had the potential to be especially damaging to their authority, their conduct compared unfavourably to that of celestial judges. The representatives of the ports at the Brodhull seated in St Nicholas's church could similarly draw on biblical connections between the weighing of souls and the dispensing of more prosaic forms of justice. They too were aware of the need to maintain this fictive comparison, which may help to explain why the head ports having built 'communi domo nostro' at New Romney still conducted their judicial sessions in the chancel of St Nicholas's church.[54] For the senior officials such notions were extremely valuable because they were called upon to arbitrate between individual ports concerning trade disputes, or between the ports and the Crown, an at times difficult process requiring negotiation to try to overcome animosity, so permitting them to present a united stance against outside authority, including the Lord Warden. Thus the leading portsmen favoured the bring-

---

Sweetinburgh, 'Care in the Community: Local Responses to the Poor in Late Medieval Sandwich' (paper given at an international conference on medieval poverty, University of Kent, 1996).

[53] M. Kowaleski, 'The Expansion of the South-Western Fisheries in Late Medieval England', *Economic History Review*, 53 (2000), pp. 441, 450-1.

[54] Murray, *Cinque Ports*, p. 163; Somers, *New Romney*, p. 3.

ing of cases before the Court of Brodhull in New Romney, rather than resorting to St James' at Dover.[55]

By holding his court at this Dover church, the Lord Warden was apparently addressing a number of issues concerning his relationship with the Federation. The church was located in what might be termed a border area, neither of the royal castle, nor of the semi-autonomous town, requiring those who attended to enter a marginal space but still within the liberty of Dover. Yet by its use as a court of law, the church had come under the authority of the Lord Warden, those pleading before him possibly unlikely to see this as a shared space, instead royal power and authority had been extended, encroaching into an area that had once housed Dover's fishing community. Even though the town's fishing industry was in a state of decline by the Late Middle Ages, historically the industry had been of major importance, recognized through the giving of the town's fish tithes to St Martin's altar and the strength of its relationship with the Crown, based on ship service and the formation of the Federation.[56] Thus the appropriation of what had been the fishermen's church by the Crown to allow it to regulate the conduct of Dover citizens and their fellow portsmen may have been deeply resented, especially when the king's interests (or those of the Warden) did not intersect with those of the leading townsmen. For the men of Dover, as for the other head ports, this use of God's space for the administration of the king's law, though somewhat modified by customary practices, may, on occasion, have been extremely irksome (ideologically and practically). Some apparently sought to resist through absence, while for those who did attend the spatial dynamics within the church, as at the other courts, was presumably intended to demonstrate the power of the magistracy. Unfortunately there is nothing to indicate how this court was arranged but it seems likely height (a dais, steps were used to place the judges above those pleading) and direction (placing the judges towards the east) would have been significant factors.[57]

Pilgrimages, Processions and Other Performances

Parish fraternities were ubiquitous in late medieval England, and at the Cinque Ports, too, they were a significant element in local society, but there was one exception. For Dover, there is very little evidence

[55] Hull, *Black and White Books*, pp. xii-xiii; Murray, *Cinque Ports*, pp. 158-9.
[56] PLL, MS. 241, f. 2 v°. Statham, *Dover*, pp. 64-6.
[57] There is a plan of the Court of Shepway but whether a similar arrangement was used at St James' church is uncertain; Murray, *Cinque Ports*, p. 76.

concerning such groups beyond a single reference to one at St Mary's church and another called St John's Bothe, in the same parish.[58] As an alternative, the 'trendyll' or great candle of Dover, measuring the length of the circumference of the town, may have provided a symbol of civic fraternity for the mayor and jurats. Donations for the making of the candle were collected by the wife of the mayor 'of the devotion of the people', and after it had been wound on its great reel, it was offered every three years at the shrine of St Thomas of Canterbury on the eve (6 July) of the feast of the saint's translation.[59] The town's four porters carried Dover's votive offering to Canterbury Cathedral, a civic pilgrimage of thanksgiving or supplication (the result, perhaps, of a specific event in the thirteenth century) that may have begun with a blessing of the candle at St Martin's altar in the ancient minster church, a gift from one patron saint of Dover to the other.[60]

Sandwich, too, organized a town pilgrimage, though unlike Dover its maintenance appears to have been exclusively in the hands of the mayor and jurats, but the commonalty did have a part to play in the procession. To commemorate the town's deliverance from the French by St Bartholomew in 1217, the townspeople had erected a hospital on the outskirts of Sandwich, under the patronage of the civic authorities, and every year the mayor and jurats led a pilgrimage from St Peter's church to the hospital chapel to lay unlit tapers before St Bartholomew.[61] These senior town officers, who carried the town's votive offering, were accompanied by members of the commonalty, some playing musical instruments, and by the clergy from St Peter's church, the parish priest expected to say high mass at the hospital chapel. Occasionally the procession was joined by certain local knights, especially those of the de Sandwich family, who were similarly allowed to bring unlit tapers for the saint.

At Hythe and Sandwich there were several parish fraternities of which two of the most important were the fraternity of the Assumption of the Blessed Virgin Mary at St Leonard's church, Hythe, and the St George fraternity in St Clement's church, Sandwich. Open to men and women, this Hythe fraternity was not exclusively the domain of the leading

---

[58] Maidstone, Centre for Kentish Studies (CKSM): PRC 32/17, f. 35. EKAW, Do/ZZ 02/01 15.

[59] Certain details concerning the trendyll were recorded by the shrine keepers in the early fifteenth-century customary of the shrine of St Thomas; BLL, Add. MS 59616 f. 9.

[60] Similar great candle rituals occurred in France and the Southern Netherlands from the late twelfth century; H. Van Der Velden, *The Donor's Image. Gerard Loyet and the Votive Portraits of Charles the Bold* (Turnhout, 2000), pp. 240-1.

[61] EKAW, Sa/LC 1, f. 15 v°.

citizens and their wives, and in 1471 membership stood at 102 persons.[62] The brotherhood seems to have had its own priest, who officiated at fraternal gatherings, and was also available to members to provide various intercessory services, including the sounding of the knell. His main duty was to officiate at the high mass held on the principal feast day, the brothers and sisters presumably processing into the chapel, possibly dressed in cassocks, where they offered wax candles to burn before the image of their chosen saint. Afterwards they enjoyed a communal feast, comprising bread, meat, spices and ale, apparently held in a room over the south porch.[63] Far more exclusive was the St George fraternity at Sandwich, which seems to have drawn its membership solely from among the leading townsmen. The fraternity met in the mayor's church of St Clement, the brothers, as prominent local citizens, taking their places in the chancel of St George from whence they witnessed high mass at 'their' altar.[64] As at Hythe, the fraternity may have had its own chaplain because Nicholas Burton, a former mayor, intended Sir Thomas Bland should also celebrate at the same altar as part of his perpetual chantry; and another wealthy citizen instructed his executors to make provision for boys to be instructed in pricksong so that they could also take part in the St George mass services.[65] In 1481 connections between the civic authorities and this fraternity became more explicit when the mayor and jurats agreed to donate 6s. 8d. towards the St George's day procession, and thereafter this was an annual payment in the Sandwich accounts.[66]

Looking first at the two civic pilgrimages, it seems advisable to focus on how the mayor and senior jurats might have envisaged them in terms of the spatial issues involved at the two churches, during the journey and at the final destination. In terms of Lefebvre's 'absolute space', the churches of St Peter and St Martin-le-Grand were complex places, at once religious and political (and communal). For those taking part in the St Bartholomew's day procession and the ritual of Dover's great candle, their varying roles in the performance of these ceremonies was symptomatic of the multiple use and perception of sacred space. At Sandwich, the town's involvement in the multi-faceted life of the church may have

---

[62] EKAW, Hy/Z4/4.
[63] In the eighteenth century this room was used as the town hall and mayoral elections were conducted there; Hasted, *Kent*, vol. 8, p. 250.
[64] Hasted, *Kent*, vol. 10, p. 210.
[65] CKSM, PRC 32/3, f. 368; 17/6, f. 291.
[66] EKAW, Sa/AC 1, f. 262 v°.

meant that the mayor and jurats saw St Peter's as shared, their involvement in its spatial production more a matter of use than of the placement of objects, though presumably the trappings of justice provided materials that at least for a time joined (possibly obscured) their religious counterparts (see above). The north aisle may have been especially significant in this respect because it was the place where the town officers dispensed justice and commemorated their honoured predecessors, its political and communal uses intertwined with its role as a religious space. Consequently, as guardians of this important space with the parish clergy and churchwardens, the senior town officials may have believed it was a particularly appropriate place to begin the procession because the pilgrimage demonstrated their commitment to the spiritual and temporal welfare of the town and its citizens. Yet St Peter's church was also a hierarchical space, the various groups concerned with different spatial production, though at times overlapping and intersecting, which seems to have meant that in 1532, for example, the parish priest's refusal to take part saw the mayor and senior jurats acting as protectors of the St Bartholomew's day procession and St Peter's church.[67] Furthermore, as noted above, matters of hierarchy articulated through spatial dynamics at meetings of the town court and during election time were similarly significant, where precedence and standing could be indicated by the places taken by members of the civic authorities, the bailiff (king's nominee) and the freemen who gathered there.

For the mayor and jurats at St Martin-le-Grand, Dover, the spatial dynamics were apparently different, though probably equally complex. This religious space of the old minster church had come under the power and authority of the local Benedictine priory, a religious house which, like the town's two hospitals, was sited outside Dover. However, the mayor, on behalf of the commonalty, seems to have had some involvement in the appointment of the Archipresbyter to St Martin's church, and did undertake the presentment of the fish tithes on the high altar there.[68] Such actions were significant in terms of the perception of the place of St Martin-le-Grand in the town and this sense of its belonging to Dover was symbolized, as noted earlier, by the image of the saint on the reverse of the town seal. Thus there was an important relationship between the mayor and jurats and St Martin's church, which was reinforced by their use of the church as the place of departure for the town's votive offering

---

[67] S. Sweetinburgh, *The Role of the Hospital in Medieval England. Gift-Giving and the Spiritual Economy* (Dublin, 2004), pp. 232-3.

[68] Haines, *Dover Priory*, p. 48. Cambridge, Corpus Christi College: MS. 59, f. 27.

to St Thomas, an opponent of royal authority. By so doing they, through their presence, action and discourse, saw St Martin's church as a religious, political and communal space, their actions on behalf of the commonalty a demonstration of the idea of corporate responsibility. Yet, as at Sandwich, the picture was more complicated and matters like hierarchy, and the sanctioning or forbidding of the involvement of others – foreigners, resident non-freemen – in the ritual raised issues about how absolute space was deployed.

With regard to the journey both sets of pilgrims travelled from the centres of their respective towns to places outside the walls. For the mayor and jurats, they were leaving the churchyard, a multivalent possibly ambiguous space, produced by the ecclesiastical and civic authorities, parishioners, and townspeople, to enter what Lefebvre called 'commercial space', places within the town over which they exercised a degree of power and authority.[69] However, like the perceptions and uses of space at the churches, the commercial (civic) spaces of Sandwich/Dover were similarly complex, products of the interactions between the actors at the event, the pilgrimage, and the multi-layering of these spaces over time. Thus as the procession/candle passed through the market place and along the streets, public places frequently used for the exchange of goods and knowledge, the senior town officers may have considered that they, through the ritual process, were transforming such spaces for a time. By association, while they carried or oversaw the carriage of the votive offering, a gift that symbolically reaffirmed the town authorities' concern for the well-being of the urban inhabitants, commercial space might be said to have been transformed, being 'lived' as sacred in the eyes of the actors and those witnessing the event, who together produced the space.[70] This deployment of absolute space was important because the Crown and the Church, in addition to the civic authorities were involved in the control of different aspects of town life. Furthermore, during the fifteenth century at Sandwich in particular, such ambiguities over jurisdiction had become increasingly apparent when the mayor and jurats sought to extend their authority over the moral conduct of the townsfolk.[71]

---

[69] At Dover, the fair that began on the feast day of St Martin was held in the churchyard of St Martin-le-Grand, the royal grant dating from *c.* 1160; Haines, *Dover Priory*, p. 57. PLL, MS. 241, f. 59 v°.

[70] Although concerned with understanding ritual rather than spatial dynamics, Baumann's work seems appropriate here; G. Baumann, 'Ritual Implicates 'Others': Rereading Durkheim in a Plural Society', in: D. de Coppet (ed.), *Understanding Rituals*, European Association of Social Anthropologists (London, 1992), pp. 97-116.

[71] See note 52.

Once outside the town walls, the procession/candle passed through another marginal space, the town suburbs, and though at Sandwich the procession's destination was the nearby hospital, at Dover the candle was taken through the countryside before arriving at Canterbury. For the Dover authorities this may have been seen in terms of Christ's journey to and into Jerusalem, the candle's triumphal entry into Canterbury marked by its passage along the processional way and its entry into the ecclesiastical heart of the city. It is not clear how this event was perceived by the Canterbury citizens and the city authorities, but as at Dover the absolute space of the city was multi-layered, its production open to ambiguity, negotiation and appropriation. For example, the streets through which the candle passed were the city's principal market areas, this commercial space possibly seen as transformed, however briefly, for the porters (and others in Canterbury) by their actions, the timing in relation to the feast day heightening the general awareness of the singularity of the occasion.

At the culmination of the two pilgrimages: Becket's shrine and the high altar in the hospital chapel, the participants sought to demonstrate ideas about hierarchy and inclusiveness/exclusiveness, highlighting again the complexity of these ecclesiastical spaces. For the mayor and jurats of Sandwich, their pilgrimage to the town's saint in his chapel offered them an annual opportunity to commemorate symbolically their reciprocal relationship with St Bartholomew. During high mass the senior town officials presumably stood nearer to their saint than others among the procession, a privileged position they continued to hold when they placed the tapers on the high altar, thereby allowing them into the most sacred area of the chapel. This deployment of place within the chapel was important in terms of the civic authorities' relationship with the commonalty, but also with certain local knightly families. Members of the local knightly de Sandwich family, in particular, may have believed they should be foremost among the leading group because their ancestor had been involved in the first foundation of the hospital, an idea reinforced by the presence of his tomb close to the high altar.

Like the Sandwich tapers, the great candle was offered to Dover's saintly protector, a symbolic gesture which commemorated the saint's deliverance of the town and the belief that he would continue to protect Dover from 'outsiders'. Furthermore, the gift of the candle signified the interdependency of the town officers and commonalty, a relationship that the mayor and jurats intended to demonstrate by fulfilling their social duty to the commonalty, a duty that their predecessors had discharged successfully and their successors would continue to do. For the civic authorities this sense of continuity was presumably important, and the placing of their candle close to Becket's shrine where it could be used daily to illuminate the Eucharist there was a symbolic endorsement of Dover's relationship with their saint. Consequently, even though the great candle was surrounded by the gifts of others, including various kings, for the mayor and jurats their gift, with the town's sanction, was extremely conspicuous, its presence signifying their multiple use of this sacred space.[72]

Turning finally to the two fraternities, at Sandwich during the second half of the fifteenth century, the public linking of town government to St George, a saint associated with English nationhood, and the church where the mayor was elected, may have been intended to reinforce ideas about sovereignty and good governance. Thus, in a sense the members of the fraternity may have seen themselves as standing apart from their fellow townsmen, forming an elect group, who through birth and/or service had become the guardians of their town at a time when the ability of the Crown to protect Sandwich had apparently receded. Serious factional disputes in the town mirrored those at the national level, a situation that some in the judiciary may have wished to surmount through membership of a fraternity which was supposed to appeal to English nationhood. Though conversely, membership may have followed factional lines but such ideas cannot be tested because of the lack of evidence. Yet, even if this occurred, it seems likely the founders of the fraternity saw the merit in seeking to draw together the leading citizens spiritually as well as temporally, their commitment to the moral well-being of the townsfolk demonstrated through such fraternal activities and their actions in the town court. These involved the use of ecclesiastical buildings, in particular St Clement's church when members attended the St George mass, and probably services of commemoration for deceased brothers, like Nicholas Burton, but also during the procession on the saint's feast day when the statue of St George was paraded through the streets of Sandwich, to be followed by a fraternal feast. Such events took place outside the church, where the use of the market place as the focus of commer-

---

[72] These civic gift exchanges seen as conveying a rich symbolism that was constructed in social, political and spiritual terms; J. Davis, *Exchange*, Concepts in the Social Sciences (Buckingham, 1992), pp. 1-4; I. Kopytoff, 'The Cultural Biography of Things: Commoditization as Process', in: A. Appadural (ed.), *The Social Life of Things* (Cambridge, 1986), pp. 87-90.

cial space was suspended for a time, those involved transforming the spatial dynamics so that, like the civic pilgrimages, the saint and his followers travelled along what had become a sacred way. Thus, for the members of the St George fraternity, St Clement's church and the commercial space of the town had the potential to intersect, at least for a set time, being aspects of absolute space (religious and political and communal).

Having a less exclusive membership, yet still appealing to the 'better sort' at Hythe, the fraternity of Our Lady may too have been seen as having a part to play in the governance of the town. For the jurats and their wives, their devotion to the Virgin provided a communal setting in which they might articulate ideas about the humanity of Christ and the love of a mother for her son, aspects of the holy family that were increasingly favoured by late medieval townspeople in their pursuit of salvation, giving added meaning to the lives of those in Hythe. Even though economically the town was relatively buoyant during the last decades of the century, national problems of dynastic conflict continued to affect local politics. Political instability, and the uncertainties of living on the Channel coast where the possibility of French raids was an ever present threat, may have meant the leading citizens and other prosperous townsfolk were drawn to this major town fraternity, its annual ceremonial rhythm providing a sense of continuity and stability for the living and comfort for the dying. Consequently the use and control of the Lady chapel, their sacred space, could have given the warden and the senior brothers and sisters an arena where they might aim to control morally and socially, as well as spiritually, the conduct of their fellows, and the certainty that after their death they would be commemorated, the living and the dead bound together in absolute space for eternity.

To conclude, for the leading townsmen in the Kentish Cinque Ports, many of whom were civic officers, churches were extremely important, not merely as sacred places for the liturgical life of the town but as sites where other issues – communal and political – might be negotiated. Consequently, Lefebvre's concept of absolute space seems a useful construct to try to understand the production of this space, especially in terms of how it was 'lived'. The inter-play of the living and the dead through commemoration and remembrance at places of religious and civil importance to the urban community offered opportunities for continuity, but was still open to change. Such complex uses of absolute space also take account of ideas about time, the actors using and seeking to control these spaces for a range of different reasons, the symbolic meanings given objects and actions as part of the process of negotiation and appropriation. Many of these activities were integral to the work of civic governance, whether it was the election of town officers, the working of the court or the performance of civic pilgrimages and other festivals, which meant that as well as the mayor and jurats others, like the bailiff, local clerics and knights, members of the commonalty and foreigners, were participants (including as witnesses, bystanders). Furthermore, even though the ports developed their own individual ways of employing these spaces, the leading portsmen had many aims in common, not least the desire for greater autonomy, which seems to have resulted in a number of shared ideas and practices. Thus each generation of civic officers at Sandwich, Dover, Hythe and New Romney was obliged or found it necessary to modify its deployment of absolute space in the form of ecclesiastical places to meet changing circumstances, its renegotiation a complex response which took due regard of what had gone before and what successors would inherit for the future.

Acknowledgements

The conference on 'The role of ecclesiastical places with regard to secular authorities', held in December 2003 at the University of Leuven, Campus Kortrijk, was a stimulating environment, and I should like to thank the organizers and my fellow delegates, especially Dr Jacqueline van Leeuwen, for their willingness to discuss this fascinating topic. My continuing interest in thinking about space for the medieval period owes much to the work of Dr Catherine Richardson and Dr Jessica Malay, and I am also extremely grateful for their comments and suggestions regarding this essay. Similarly, I am grateful to Dr Justin Croft for allowing me to cite his unpublished Masters dissertation and doctoral thesis on the custumals of the Cinque Ports.

University of Kent, Canterbury

Karen STÖBER

THE ROLE OF LATE MEDIEVAL ENGLISH MONASTERIES AS EXPRESSIONS OF PATRONAL AUTHORITY: SOME CASE STUDIES

Monasteries and nunneries were an integral part of the medieval landscape of Christian Europe, and of medieval society. In England, as in the rest of western Christendom, the local lay community was involved with the communities of religious men and women on several levels and in many ways, which varied from mere trading contacts to frequent, close and personal relationships. The contacts which arose between the lay party on the one hand, and the religious community on the other inevitably raise the question whether, and to what extent, different forms of behaviour were compatible with the religious life: there is ample evidence for correspondence, meetings and other types of involvement between secular patrons and benefactors and the heads of monasteries and nunneries.[1]

Besides the communities of monks, canons or nuns, however, the physical buildings of the English abbeys and priories were in themselves important expressions of their patrons' and benefactors' status and authority, and it is this aspect of monastic patronage which deserves some closer attention.

The Patrons of English Religious Houses

The earliest English monastic foundations were financed and maintained by the Crown and by the very wealthiest of the Anglo-Saxon nobility. Many of these were large, prosperous Benedictine houses, like Peterborough Abbey in Northamptonshire, St Swithun's Priory in Winchester (Hampshire), or Ely Priory in Cambridgeshire, all substantial, impressive, wealthy foundations, and all still in use as cathedral churches today. Following the Norman Conquest in the eleventh century, the pattern of monastic foundations and of monastic founders was changing. From the

---

[1] Note, for instance, J. Burton, *Monastic and Religious Orders in Britain, 1000-1300* (Cambridge, 1994), pp. 210-232; K. Stöber, *Late Medieval Monasteries and their Patrons: England and Wales, c. 1300 – 1540* (Woodbridge, forthcoming).

twelfth century onwards the men and women responsible for founding religious houses in England and Wales, apart from bishops and kings, were predominantly members of the new Anglo-Norman aristocracy, many of whom had been granted lands and estates by William I as reward for their participation in the Conquest.[2] It was thanks to the initiative of these new nobles that monasteries came to be founded in such abundance in England during this period. The wave of lay foundations of abbeys and priories coincided with the arrival of the new religious orders in England from the twelfth century: Cistercian monks and Augustinian canons in particular found great popularity among the laity, who were responsible for the foundation of no less than 60 out of a total of 76 Cistercian abbeys, and over 170 Augustinian abbeys and priories between the first half of the twelfth century and the middle of the fourteenth. These new religious communities offered hitherto unknown opportunities to lower levels of the laity: due to the fact that they were, in comparison with houses of Benedictine or Cluniac monks, relatively cheap to establish, the foundation of a monastery or nunnery was suddenly a viable option also for men and women among the lesser nobility.[3]

One consequence of the foundation of religious houses by pious lay patrons was the initial personal involvement of the founder, often resulting in high levels of contact between monasteries and their patrons. These contacts were expressed in many ways: the lay community provided the recruits for the many and multiplying communities of monks, canons and nuns, they endowed them with lands, property and rents, and they traded with them. The religious, on the other hand, provided essential services for the lay community: they buried their dead and prayed for their souls, and they provided acceptable careers for their younger sons and for their unmarriageable daughters. Patrons can be seen to fulfil their roles of protectors and advocates, of supporters and lords of their religious houses. They endowed and visited the monasteries and nunneries under their patronage, they confirmed newly elected heads of their abbeys and priories, and they chose their own houses for their family mausolea. They, their sons or their daughters frequently enough took the habit themselves and entered their abbeys and priories as members of the religious communities. They had custody over the house and its estates during vacancies. The religious communities, on the other hand, spoke of them as their

---

[2] Note E. Cownie, *Religious Patronage in Anglo-Norman England, 1066-1135* (Woodbridge, 1998).

[3] See also S. Wood, *English Monasteries and their Patrons in the Thirteenth Century* (Oxford, 1955).

fundator, their *advocatus* or their *patronatus*. The patron was recognized in canon law and he (or she) was aware of the benefits to which the patronage of a monastery entitled him. By the fourteenth century, over a thousand monasteries had been founded in England and Wales. Many of them had been short-lived and had already failed by this time. With the exception of houses of the Carthusian order, very few religious houses at all were to be established after the year 1300. By this time, the situation of patronage had changed as the advowsons of monasteries had passed from the hands of the original founders and their successors into those of their heirs, ideally the direct male heir of the current patron, but more frequently a more distant relative, or a member of a different family who had acquired the advowson of the house by marriage, inheritance, purchase or royal grant. And in many *more* cases the advowson of the monastery had passed to the Crown. With the passage of the centuries, the ties between the monasteries and their patrons weakened and often became purely formal, but they never completely disappeared. Every monastery and every nunnery still had a patron, right up until the Dissolution of the Monasteries in the sixteenth century, but the role which these patrons played for their religious communities varied from house to house and also from religious order to religious order.[4]

There is one very important difference between benefactors of religious houses in general, and their actual patrons: benefactors chose of their own free will to maintain a connection, or to strengthen existing ties between themselves and their families and the monastery or nunnery they decided to support or endow. Consequently, they might be held in great esteem by the religious community; they might even be styled 'patrons' by them in their documents. Hereditary patrons, on the other hand, as the word implies, were just that. They had inherited the title of patron of a religious house, or of several religious houses, and with it they had inherited the rights and duties of a monastic patron. They had not in fact chosen to be patrons of the monastery or nunnery whose advowson they had inherited.

Lay Patrons as Figures of Authority

Hereditary patrons of religious houses had a number of recognized rights and duties. Theirs was the right to give assent to elections of abbots and priors, as well as to appoint a – usually specified – number of persons to the religious community. In the context of elections they can occa-

---

[4] On these developments, see Stöber, *Monasteries and their Patrons*.

sionally be seen as acting as mediators between their monastery or nunnery and a third party.[5] Moreover, patrons had the pleasant and popular right to enjoy the hospitality of the monks or nuns under their patronage, to stay in the house and dine with the abbot or prior.[6] Among the most important rights of a lay patron was that of burial in the precinct of his monastery. All these types of contact between the lay and the religious community had an impact of some sort on the monastery or nunnery.

There were situations which required the patron, or a representative, to fulfil his duty as advocate of the religious house under his patronage. Among these were elections of heads of houses. Normally the patron of a monastery or nunnery gave his assent to the election of a new abbot or abbess, prior or prioress, and confirmed the appointment.[7] There were instances, however, when the patron might disagree with the proposed candidate and oppose the appointment. He or she might then suggest an alternative candidate of his or her own choosing instead. So in 1335, when Pope Benedict XII confirmed the appointment of one Simon to be abbot of the Augustinian monastery of St Peter and Paul of Bourne, in Lincolnshire, he stated that 'the election was opposed by Thomas Wake, Lord of Liddell, knight, on the ground that he was patron of the said monastery'.[8] The abbot elect, one Simon, appealed to the pope for support, who caused the case to be heard by the bishop, with the result that the patron was reprimanded by the bishop and Simon's appointment was duly confirmed.

Patrons might appear in an authoritative position in the context of elections of heads of houses also in a slightly different manner, i.e. in the attempt to protect their house from an imposed appointment against the will of the religious community. Patrons were in this case acting as mediators between their houses and a third party, usually ecclesiastical, occasionally royal authority. In 1301, during the pontificate of Boniface VIII, the pope issued a mandate to the Prior of the Benedictine priory of Holy Trinity in York, ordering them to make an inquiry into 'the cause relating to the Cluniac priory of Thetford in the diocese of Norwich'.[9] The abbot and convent of the mother-house of the order in Cluny, to which Thetford Priory was subject, enjoyed the privilege of appointing the house's priors.

---

[5] Bishops' registers, in particular, bear witness to patronal involvement in monastic elections.

[6] See for instance Wood, *English Monasteries*, pp. 122-135.

[7] See also Wood, *English Monasteries*, pp. 40-74.

[8] *Calendar of Entries in the Papal Registers Relating to Great Britain and Ireland: Papal Letters*, W.H. Bliss (ed.), 15 vols. (London, 1893-1960), vol. 2, p. 523

[9] *Papal Letters*, vol. 1, p. 594

However, the monks of Thetford were aggrieved about this arrangement and they explained to the pope that they wished to 'withdraw themselves from the jurisdiction of the said abbot [of Cluny]'.[10] With the support of the Bishop of Norwich and the patron of the house, Roger Bigod, Earl Marshal, and his brother, John Bigod, the monks of Thetford proceeded to elect a new prior of their own choice. This was much to the displeasure of the community at Cluny who, failing to call the monks at Thetford to order, involved the pope, who disciplined the rebellious monks at Thetford. The prior chosen by the community, moreover, allegedly 'imprisoned and ill-treated' monks sent from Cluny. Roger Bigod, as patron of the priory, received a warning from the pope to 'desist from interference' in this matter.[11]

A wealthy and powerful patron might also be instrumental to a house's ambitions as regards building programmes. In the case of Neath Abbey in Glamorgan the patrons, the de Clare family, were at least in part responsible for organizing and providing the funding for the major building programme at the abbey in the fourteenth century.[12] Similarly at Tintern Abbey in Monmouthshire, Roger Bigod, Earl of Norfolk, patron of the house, who died in 1306, played an important part in the rebuilding of the abbey church.[13]

There were a range of other expressions of authority by lay patrons, and involvement of a somewhat different kind can be seen in the actions of the fifteenth-century patron of the Benedictine abbey of Wymondham in Norfolk. Here Sir Andrew Agard, 'a descendant of the founder', petitioned in 1448 to cause his monastery, then Wymondham Priory, to be elevated to the status of abbey.[14] The action of increasing the status of a monastery, then, was another way in which lay patrons might use their authority on behalf of the religious houses of which they were patrons.

Among the rights of a patron was that of enjoying the hospitality of his monastery or nunnery. Patrons could expect to be received as guests by the religious community and to eat with the abbot or prior in his hall. Complaints were sometimes made by heads of houses if their patrons

---

[10] *Ibidem*.
[11] *Ibidem*.
[12] The arms of the de Clare family, three chevrons, can still be seen on floor tiles in the abbey today.
[13] *Cf.* D.M. Robinson, *Tintern Abbey* (Cardiff, 2002), pp. 14-15.
[14] *Registrum Johannis Whethamstede*, H.T. Riley (ed.), 2 vols. (London, 1872), i, pp. 152-153.

took advantage of the hospitality offered to them, either by overstaying their welcome, or by imposing themselves upon their monasteries with large parties, thus considerably straining the resources of the house, as well as distracting them from their spiritual duties.[15] This, however, was generally more problematic in the case of royal, than of lay patrons, because royal parties tended to be large and expected particularly lavish hospitality. Unfortunately, evidence for this type of mundane contact is less easy to come by, especially if the visit passed off uneventfully. If the visitor was particularly important, he might be mentioned in the annals of the monastery. Just so, if the hospitality offered to him was particularly generous we are more likely to encounter records of purchases of large quantities of special or unusual foodstuffs of a kind which we might not normally expect in a monastic context.[16]

In any case, where the evidence for this type of contact between secular authorities and religious communities survives we are left with the feeling that expressions of patronal authority in monasteries had a considerable impact on the religious community, their daily routine and their resources. The presence in a religious house of members of the laity, particularly the presence of a member of the nobility accompanied by his retinue and the noise and commotion that naturally resulted from this, would have been felt among the religious men and women.

One of the most important rights of a lay patron was that of burial within the precinct of his abbey or priory.[17] Burial in a monastery was still an important issue for the late medieval lay patrons of religious houses in this country, and in connection with burial we find monuments commemorating family members, while at the same time representing a powerful reminder of the patron's presence in the house. To be interred in the conventual church or another part of the religious house (the Chapterhouse for instance) meant close physical proximity of the tomb to the prayers of the religious community and was hence considered particularly spiritually beneficial. Other factors, too, were fundamental in influencing a patron's decision regarding his choice of burial place. Particularly important among these was the issue of family tradition. The graves of their ancestors represented a crucially important incentive for the

---

[15] Numerous complaints by heads of religious houses to this effect survive in the papal registers.

[16] The accounts of Thetford Priory, for instance, bear witness to this.

[17] On monastic burial, see also B. Golding, 'Burials and Benefactions: An aspect of monastic patronage in thirteenth-century England', in: W.M. Ormrod (ed.), *England in the Thirteenth Century* (Woodbridge, 1986), pp. 64-75.

medieval aristocracy when electing their sepulchres. Family mausolea, once established, were normally used by successive generations of a family until this family either failed, or inherited or purchased a grander, better suited location for burial, or moved away. The burial of a patron in a religious house had an impact upon the house on several levels. First of all, the burial was accompanied by the funerary mass on the one hand, and by more or less elaborate funerary celebrations on the other. We get a sense of this in the wills of laymen and laywomen, in which they specify instructions for the ceremony, often in much detail.[18]

These events, apart from the impact they had on the life of the community, also, and very significantly, had an impact on the monasteries and nunneries themselves, that is on the monastic buildings. The tombs, ranging in size from relatively modest effigies, tombstones or simple to the most elaborate chantry chapels, were often positioned in prominent places, preferably, though not always, near the high altar in the eastern part of the nave.

But tombs of lay folk in conventual churches were not the only showcase for a layman's dynastic paraphernalia in a monastic church. The heraldry of the founding families, as well as of the monastery's chief benefactors, often featured prominently in the fabric of the monastic church or buildings, particularly in gatehouses of monastic complexes. The visitor would thus be confronted with the patron's presence even upon entry into the monastic precinct, leaving him in no doubt about the latter's authoritative position in the house. A magnificent example of this is the splendidly decorated gatehouse of Kirkham Priory in Yorkshire which still stands today. Upon his arrival at this Augustinian priory, the medieval traveller encountered first of all the elaborately decorated gatehouse, adorned not only with groups of figures, including the Crucifixion, St George and the dragon and David and Goliath, but also with the brightly painted arms of Walter Espec, founder of the house, as well as those of some of the chief benefactors of the community, and most prominently those of the de Ros family of Helmsley, later patrons of Kirkham. This show of force 'firmly proclaimed Kirkham as the family monastery of Ros of Helmsley'.[19] Likewise in the Premonstratensian abbey at Torre in Devon, the arms of the founding family, the Brewers, and other benefactors

---

[18] For a particularly elaborate example, see the will of John de Vere, Earl of Oxford (d. 1513) in *Archaeologia*, 66 (1915), pp. 275-348.

[19] J. Burton, *Kirkham Priory from Foundation to Dissolution*, Borthwick Paper, vol. 86 (York, 1995), p. 23; S. Harrison, *Kirkham Priory* (London, 2000), pp. 14-15

of the house were on display.[20] The monastic gatehouse was not the only place where patronal heraldry might be on show. The conventual church itself provided a more than adequate environment for the display of coats of arms and family insignia. In the case of the Cistercian abbey of Hailes in Gloucestershire, it is in the late thirteenth-century heraldic floor tiles that the arms of the patron, Richard Earl of Cornwall (d. 1272), who was also buried in the abbey, were represented.[21] Stained-glass windows were another medium for the display of heraldry or other depictions representing the patron's family and thus cementing the association between himself and his abbey or priory. Although stained glass, lamentably, less often survives! Often heraldic symbols can be seen where they might be most obviously expected, i.e. on the tombs and in the chantry chapels of aristocratic patrons, where they might be seen integrated into the architecture. An example for this is the chantry chapel of Margaret Countess of Salisbury in Christchurch Priory (Dorset), built in 1529, and without doubt one of the grandest chantries in England. The chapel, known today as the Salisbury Chantry, is an intricate and beautifully executed edifice in the north quire of the priory church which Margaret had built as a tomb for herself and her son Cardinal Reginald Pole. The chantry stands there still, with its fan vaulted ceiling, the bosses of which used to bear the Salisbury family arms before they were defaced at the orders of Henry VIII, following the countess' execution for treason in 1541. After her beheading Margaret was not buried in her magnificent chantry, but was laid to rest in the small chapel of St Peter's-ad-Vincula in the Tower of London, permission to transfer her remains to Christchurch having been refused, and the great Salisbury Chantry remains unused to this day.[22]

In this, as in many other cases, we have to rely on the documentary evidence for that which has since been destroyed or disappeared. Representations of heraldic symbols in stone are more likely to survive than those which were painted on church walls that were subsequently whitewashed, or those which were embroidered onto cloth used for curtains and wall-hangings, and which were subsequently removed or simply vanished in the Dissolution and beyond. In 1381 William, Lord Latimer, donated money for two separate building projects at Guisborough Priory in Yorkshire, one

---

[20] W. Dugdale, *Monasticon Anglicanum*, 7 vols., new ed. (London, 1849), vol. 7, p. 923.

[21] C. Platt, *The Abbeys and Priories of Medieval England* (London, 1995), p. 102, ill. 63; J. Steane, *The Archaeology of the Medieval English Monarchy* (London, 1999), p. 191, ill. 111.

[22] G.H.Cook, *Mediaeval Chantries and Chantry Chapels* (London, 1947), p. 147.

of them being the reconstruction of the steeple of the priory church. The same William, in the same year, made another donation to another two monasteries, which he claimed were under his patronage, namely the Augustinian priories of Bushmead and Caldwell, both in Bedfordshire. To these monasteries, of which, he explicitly stated, 'je suy avowe',[23] he wished to give to each canon of each house 'un cape de drap d'orre ou de sey enbroude ove mes armes en le manere come ils sont a Gisburn'.[24]

Patrons might thus make their presence felt, and thereby imply their position of authority, simply by means of their symbolic presence in the religious buildings. The monastery was in this case used as expression of the patron's status and authority and of his dynastic integrity, symbolizing the direct link between himself and his family, and the religious house.

Apart from using the monastery as a status symbol, patrons might make practical use of the grand yet normally secluded environment of the religious house for a range of other purposes. The monastery as burial place of the aristocracy has already been mentioned. Religious houses had moreover a number of convenient uses (and abuses) during a patron's lifetime.

Monasteries were used by the laity for the storage and safekeeping, as well as the production, of important documents. The secluded nature of a religious house lent itself to this purpose, together with the fact that monasteries tended to have well-maintained archives and storage chests. Some of these chests still survive today, and not infrequently they are directly associated with a particular family for the safekeeping of whose documents they were used. Not only documents, but other valuable items, too, were occasionally kept in religious houses, mostly for reasons of safety.

The Three Case Studies

In order to illustrate some of the issues discussed above in some more detail, case studies of three English monasteries shall serve as examples. The houses in question are the wealthy Benedictine abbey of Tewkesbury in Gloucestershire, the Cluniac priory at Thetford in Norfolk, and St Augustine's Abbey in Bristol, an important house of Augustinian canons. All three houses were under the patronage of members of the laity during the later Middle Ages, all three were urban monasteries, and two of them still exist today. Coincidentally, all three cases happen to be examples of intact, even amicable relationships between the two parties for at least part of their

---

[23] *Testamenta Eboracensia*, J. Raine & J. Raine jr. (eds.), Surtees Society, 6 vols. (Durham, 1836-1902), vol. 1, nr. 83.
[24] *Ibidem*.

history. It need not be stressed that this was not always the case. There is ample evidence for less than friendly relationships, even open hostility, between religious communities and their patrons. However, the most common situation, and in some ways the gravest problem as regards relationships between religious communities and their patrons during the later Middle Ages, was not abuse of authority, but rather the lack of interest and consequently the lack of involvement shown by the majority of late medieval lay patrons towards their houses of monks, canons and nuns.

Tewkesbury Abbey

The great Benedictine abbey of St Mary's at Tewkesbury was by a long way the most prosperous of all the religious houses of the Earls of Gloucester, and the focus of their pious attention.[25] Tewkesbury Abbey had been re-founded during the opening years of the twelfth century, originally as a cell of the Benedictine abbey of Cranborne (Dorset), on the site of an earlier priory, which was itself apparently a re-foundation of an eighth-century hermitage. A favourite of William Rufus, Robert FitzHamon, who received the lordship of Tewkesbury from the king, is credited with the re-establishment of the abbey, and is generally regarded as the founder of Tewkesbury Abbey. In an early sixteenth-century illustration in the abbey's book of founders and benefactors he is depicted, together with his wife Sybil, bearing the abbey in their hands and thus symbolizing their patronage of the house.[26] In this illustration Robert FitzHamon and Sybil can be seen jointly holding the abbey church, for the building of which they were responsible, accompanied by their respective arms, which also incorporate the so-called Tewkesbury Cross. Towards the end of the twelfth century, the patronage of the monastery passed from Robert FitzHamon's descendants through the marriage of his great-granddaughter Amice and Richard de Clare to the de Clare family, together with the earldom of Gloucester. During the century and a half that followed, successive generations of the de Clare family were patrons and benefactors of the abbey, a role which they evidently took very seriously, as the family's grants to, and burials in the house emphasize. In the first quarter of the fourteenth century, the de Clares, in turn, were succeeded to the patronage of Tewkesbury Abbey by the Despensers, who came to hold the advowson through the marriage of

---

[25] On the Earls of Gloucester as patrons of Tewkesbury Abbey, see also M. Hicks, 'The Early Lords: Robert Fitzhamon to the de Clares', in: R.K. Morris and R. Shoesmith (eds.), *Tewkesbury Abbey: History, Art & Architecture* (Logaston, 2003), pp. 11-18.

[26] Oxford, Bodleian Library, MS Top. Glouc. d. 2, fol. 13 r°.

Eleanor, sister of the last de Clare patron, Gilbert, to Hugh Despenser the Younger after the former's death in 1314.

The de Clares in the early fourteenth century were among the great aristocratic families in England, indeed, the head of the family was one of the greatest landholders in the British Isles, and one of the most influential noblemen. They were moreover the patrons of over a dozen monasteries and nunneries in England and Wales, and several more in Ireland. Of all their religious houses, Tewkesbury Abbey was evidently held in special esteem by the de Clares, as it had been by their ancestors and would be by their successors. From the time the de Clares first held the patronage of the abbey and the earldom of Gloucester in the early thirteenth century, it was Tewkesbury which they chose as their family mausoleum. No fewer than eleven members of the family were interred in the grand environment of the abbey church in the fourteenth century alone. The role of Tewkesbury Abbey as family sepulchre for its patrons was continued by those who succeeded the de Clares to the patronage of the house. Several members of the Despenser and the Burghersh families, later patrons of Tewkesbury, were received for burial in the abbey church during the fourteenth and fifteenth centuries. Hugh Despenser (d. 1326), patron of the abbey, was buried there, as were his widow's second husband William La Zouche (d. 1336) and their son Hugh (d. 1349).[27] The burial tradition was continued by Edward Lord Despenser (d. 1375),[28] son of the second Hugh (d. 1349), and his son Richard, Lord Despenser (d. 1414).[29] Isabel, Countess of Warwick and Warenne, Baroness Burghersh, sister of the latter, was also buried in the house when she died in 1439.[30] As late as 1476 the current patroness of the house, Isabel Duchess of Clarence, was buried in Tewkesbury Abbey,[31] and in 1478 the Duke of Clarence himself was buried in the monastery, rather than choosing either of his other mausolea. Over twenty records survive regarding the burial of patrons and their families in the monastery between 1300 and the end of the fifteenth century.

---

[27] G.E. Cokayne, *The Complete Peerage of England, Scotland, Ireland, Great Britain and the United Kingdom*, 13 vols. (London, 1910-59), vol. 4, p. 269. See also M. Hicks, 'The Later Lords: The Despensers and their Heirs', in: Morris and Shoesmith, *Tewkesbury Abbey*, pp. 19-30.
[28] *Testamenta Vetusta*, N.H. Nicolas (ed.) (London, 1826), p. 99; Cokayne, *Complete Peerage*, vol. 4, p. 269.
[29] Cokayne, *Complete Peerage*, vol. 2, p. 426; Dugdale, *Monasticon Anglicanum*, vol. 2, p. 53.
[30] Cokayne, *Complete Peerage*, vol. 2, p. 426.
[31] Dugdale, *Monasticon Anglicanum*, vol. 2, p. 53.

By choosing to be buried in Tewkesbury Abbey church, the Earls of Gloucester reinforced their bonds with the house and its community, and conspicuously so. The graves of these patrons occupied very prominent places in the house. Many of them were particularly splendid monuments. Several effigies, all grand affairs, are grouped around the presbytery. Sir Edward Despenser's Trinity Chapel of c.1380 with a statue of Despenser himself, kneeling in prayer, forms part of the south partition of the presbytery. The north partition is dominated by the effigies of Sir Hugh III Despenser and his wife Elizabeth Montacute, the so-called Founder's Chapel of Robert FitzHamon (1397), and by the fifteenth-century Warwick Chapel. These monuments could not be easily ignored or overlooked, in fact they were very powerful and constant reminders of the patrons' power and authority in the monastery and, indeed they remain so to this day.

As well as being chosen as the main family burial site, the Benedictine community at Tewkesbury was moreover the focal point of the generosity of members of the de Clare and the Despenser families, and the fortunate recipient of the greater part of their benefactions. The abbey's patrons in the fourteenth century were involved in, or perhaps even initiated, a range of building programmes at the monastery. Most prominently of these, Eleanor de Clare (d. 1337), widow of Hugh Despenser (d. 1326), and her son Hugh (d. 1349), who were among the abbey's most generous and active patrons, were responsible for the grand-scale remodelling of the house's choir and presbytery in the Decorated Style.[32] Other building work undertaken under their patronage during the 1340s included the completion of the vaulting of the nave and chancel, and, remarkably, the intricate ambulatory with its many chapels. The active relationship between the abbey and the de Clares during the fourteenth century is further illustrated by the presence of depictions of the patrons and their arms in the fabric of the house. A female figure, very possibly Eleanor de Clare (d. 1337), is depicted in the east window, kneeling 'stripped of all earthly trappings' and in prayer, below glass panels showing Christ, the Archangel Michael and the Virgin, and the twelve Apostles. Her first husband, Hugh Despenser, is portrayed in one of the choir windows, in full armour and holding his sword in his hand.[33] In addition to depictions of some of Tewkesbury's later patrons, the medieval windows include their coats of arms. These not merely represent the families of de Clare, Despenser, *etcetera*, but also indicate dynastic connections and alliances

[32] A. Porter, *Tewkesbury Abbey* (Andover, 1999).
[33] On the stained glass in Tewkesbury Abbey, note S. Brown, 'The Medieval Stained Glass', in: Morris and Shoesmith, *Tewkesbury Abbey*, pp. 183-196.

with other families and thus express very secular concerns indeed at the very heart of the religious building.

As well as being depicted in the windows of the abbey, the remains of masonry found in the abbey indicate the former presence of some small statues depicting some of Tewkesbury's lay patrons. Moreover, the arms of the Despenser family are clearly visible, even today, in the stone screen of the fourteenth-century St Margaret's Chapel. Floor tiles were another popular vehicle for the representation of heraldry. The fourteenth- and fifteenth-century tiles that survive from Tewkesbury bear witness to this. Unfortunately the state of many of the surviving tiles is rather poor and our knowledge about them remains scanty.[34]

The de Clares, and the Despensers after them, clearly took their rights and duties as patrons of Tewkesbury Abbey, their 'spiritual home', seriously. The evidence for this is the range of activities in which the family were involved in connection with the abbey, and indications for which are still visible in the abbey church today. In addition to the building work undertaken by members of the family, their commemoration in the fabric of the house, and the bequests made by members of the family, they were also involved in other aspects of monastic patronage, notably the election of new abbots, as in August 1347, when Hugh Despenser, son of the last Gilbert de Clare's daughter Eleanor (d. 1337), granted to the prior and convent of the abbey his licence to elect a successor for the recently deceased abbot of the house.[35] The range of contacts between the monastery and its patrons during the later Middle Ages clearly went beyond the mere fulfilment of patronal duty. Tewkesbury Abbey's lay patrons were present in their conventual church, and visibly so, in life as well as in death.

St Augustine's Abbey, Bristol, now Bristol Cathedral

Like Tewkesbury Abbey, and indeed like Thetford Priory, St Augustine's Abbey in Bristol, too, dates back to the twelfth century. Like the other two houses a lay foundation, the house was established at the instigation of Robert FitzHarding, merchant of Bristol, whom the biographer John Smyth styles 'the devout' in the Berkeley Manuscripts.[36] Robert

---

[34] See A. Vince, 'The Medieval Floor Tiles', in Morris and Shoesmith, *Tewkesbury Abbey*, pp. 197-204.

[35] R.M. Haines (ed.), *A Calendar of the Register of Wolstan de Bransford, Bishop of Worcester 1339-49* (London, 1966), n° 928.

[36] John Smyth of Nibley, *The Berkeley Manuscripts*, J. MacLean (ed.) (Gloucester, 1883-85).

FitzHarding was subsequently granted the castle and honour of Berkeley and was thereby created Lord Berkeley.[37] The patronage of St Augustine's Abbey remained with the Berkeleys throughout the Middle Ages and up until the sixteenth century. Fortunately the abbey church continued in use and was not destroyed during the Dissolution of the Monasteries in the sixteenth century.

By the later Middle Ages the patrons of St Augustine's, according to contemporary opinion, were active, engaged, even generous patrons of at least half a dozen religious houses in southern and central England. St Augustine's Abbey was, and indeed still is, a particularly splendid, cathedralesque foundation, and hence much more prestigious than the other monasteries of which the Berkeleys were patrons. Of all their religious houses, the Augustinian abbey at Bristol was evidently the favourite monastery of the Berkeley family, and the house which attracted the patronage of several generations of family members more than any other of their religious houses. The preferential treatment shown by the Berkeleys to St Augustine's Abbey, not unlike the de Clares and Tewkesbury, was reflected in the family's burial preferences. Building upon the tradition of their ancestors in the twelfth and thirteenth century, at least five members of the family sought burial in the abbey during the fourteenth century. Their tombs are still there today, located mainly in the south choir aisle of the abbey church. The graves of Thomas Lord Berkeley (d. 1321) and his wife Joan (d. 1309) are situated in a beautifully carved star-shaped niche in the north wall of the fourteenth-century Berkeley Chapel. The tomb and well-preserved effigy of Maurice Lord Berkeley, who died in 1326, can also still be seen close to that of his parents in the south choir aisle, next to the tomb of his thirteenth-century ancestors Thomas Lord Berkeley (d. 1243) and his wife Joan.[38]

The contacts between St Augustine's Abbey and the Berkeley family remained close until ties weakened temporarily and the family neglected the abbey as their burial place for around 120 years and turned their attention elsewhere. Between the burial of Sir James Berkeley (whose will is dated 1405) and the burial of Thomas Lord Berkeley's first wife Eleanor in 1525 no other burials of family members are recorded to have taken place in the abbey. Instead the Berkeleys chose their Cistercian abbey of Kingswood (Gloucestershire), the London house of Austin Friars, and Berkeley Church. However, shortly before the Dissolution, the family returned their attention to this, their grandest monastery, and there is

---

[37] Cokayne, *Complete Peerage*, vol. 2, p. 124.
[38] *Ibidem*, pp. 127-130.

evidence for at least three more burials in the abbey church during the sixteenth century.[39]

For the Berkeleys the splendid environment of St Augustine's Abbey clearly served the purpose of a magnificent status symbol, and a most impressive family mausoleum. Just like the patrons of Tewkesbury Abbey, successive generations of St Augustine's patrons demonstrated their authority in the house. As well as being active and generous patrons of the monastery during their lifetimes, they continued to play an authoritative role in the monastery after their deaths. Their tombs are in prominent locations within the abbey church, and their effigies constant reminders of their presence in the house to this day.

Thetford Priory

The third and final example is a particularly interesting case in point. The Cluniac priory of Thetford had been founded around the year 1104 by Roger Bigod, and the patronage of the house was with his heirs, the Earls, later the Dukes of Norfolk right up until the Dissolution of the monastery in 1540.[40]

Today nearly nothing remains of the monastery beyond its gatehouse. However, fortunately there is a relative wealth of evidence regarding the later history of Thetford Priory, thanks to the surviving accounts of the house, known as the *Thetford Register*.[41] The accounts in this register grant an insight into the day-to-day affairs of the priory and thus illuminate the types of contact which we find between the religious community and the house's later lay patrons and benefactors. The evidence provided by the *Thetford Register* more than compensates for the absence of any physical remains of the priory church or buildings. Fortunately, additional documentary evidence from the wills of Thetford's later medieval patrons, relating to the period not covered by the *Register*, contains copious information regarding the burial preferences of successive generations of the patronal family. Following the dissolution of Thetford Priory in 1540, and the eventual destruction of its buildings, later generations of the Howard family moved the graves of their ancestors to a safer place, choosing the parish church at Framlingham for their new family mau-

---

[39] *Ibidem*, p. 136.
[40] D. Knowles and R.N. Hadcock, *Medieval Religious Houses: England and Wales* (London, 1971), p. 103.
[41] D. Dymond (ed.), *The Register of Thetford Priory*, 2 vols. (Oxford, 1995-6).

soleum.[42] Throughout the later Middle Ages, however, and right up to the closure of the monastery, the Howards and their predecessors, the Bigods and the Mowbrays, had chosen Thetford Priory as their family burial place. Their tombs in the priory church were numerous and must have been a prominent presence in the building, as were those of the Berkeleys in St Augustine's Abbey and those of the de Clares and the Despensers in Tewkesbury Abbey.[43]

Of particular interest in relation to the issue of the religious house as an expression of its patron's authority during the later Middle Ages are the last patrons of Thetford Priory, the Howards, Dukes of Norfolk, very active, engaged and indeed protective patrons of Thetford.

From the *Register* we get the impression that fairly regular contact between the monks, and in particular the prior, and the Howards was maintained. The Dukes of Norfolk, quite apart from entertaining and being entertained repeatedly in the priory, can be seen to use the house for such purposes as the deposition of valuables and documents. In a letter to the Duchess of Norfolk, written shortly before the suppression of Thetford Priory, William Ixworth, the prior of the house requested his patroness's counsel concerning 'such ornamentes & juelles as ye have leffte here in thys howse'.[44] At least one entry in the *Register* bears witness to the fact that written correspondence between the prior and the patrons was exchanged on more than one occasion: 'Richardo Spendlowe of Norwyc' pro le cariyng of letterys to London \to the Duches of Norff' at Lambeth/: 4d'.[45]

There are also references to other letters written by William Ixworth, the prior, to the Duke of Norfolk and his wife, one of them referring very explicitly to the prior's anxiety regarding the imminent dissolution of the monastery.[46] This Prior Ixworth left some particularly insightful evidence for maintaining more or less regular contact with the patrons of the house. In 1527 he gave for them 'an elaborate dinner', which, judging by the long and extravagant list of expenses for this dinner, this was an elaborate affair indeed. Under the heading 'Pro expensis Domini Ducis Norff' & Domini Ducis Suff' quando prandebat cum priore', the expenses included 1s 4d and 1s 8d for big, and 1s 9d for small eels, generous quantities of dates, figs, almonds and raisins at between 4d and 10d, two

---

[42] Cokayne, *Complete Peerage*, vol. 9, p. 619.
[43] See also J. Weever (ed.), *Antient Funeral Monuments* (London, 1767), p. 827.
[44] Dymond, *The Register of Thetford Priory*, vol. 2, p. 735.
[45] *Ibidem*, vol. 2, p. 504.
[46] *Ibidem*, vol. 2, p. 735.

pounds of prunes worth 8*d*, and wine worth 1*s* 2*d*. The cost for the meal totalhing no less than £22 9*s* 8*d*.[47] The prior's generosity towards his patrons did not stop there. The *Register* bears evidence to several occasions on which the Dukes of Norfolk and other members of the Howard family, often together with other magnates, visited Thetford Priory, dined with Prior Ixworth and not seldom received 'refreshments, gifts, and other favours' from him.[48] On those occasions, particularly when along with the Duke of Norfolk other important laymen were received, there is clear indication of the patron of the house holding court in the monastery and thus using the house, a suitably grand setting for such receptions, for his own secular purposes.

The Duke of Norfolk and his family were enthusiastic and fairly frequent visitors of their Cluniac monks at Thetford. Theirs was, however, by all indication a comparatively balanced, successfully reciprocal relationship. At the event of the dissolution of the priory the Howards were to demonstrate for the last time their part in the symbiotic nature of the relationship. Thomas Howard, Duke of Norfolk, was a powerful and influential patron with close connections to the Crown. A few years before the suppression of Thetford Priory in 1540, Thomas Howard wrote a series of letters to Henry VIII. In one letter, written around the year 1536, he petitioned the king to spare Thetford Priory from the Dissolution and turn the house, of which his ancestors had been patrons for many generations, and in which many of them, as well as some of the king's own family, including a son of his, lay buried, into 'a very honest parish church'.[49] Prior William Ixworth composed a letter to the Duchess of Norfolk, a draft of which survives in the latest of Thetford Priory's registers. In this undated letter the prior thanked the duchess for her support whereby, he wrote, she 'sett me in a synguler comfort in that [she] certefyed me that I shuld nott nede to fere the suppression of your howse here of Thetford, nor of myn' own' puttynge owte of the same'.[50] Despite the royal connections of the priory, the duke's petition and the duchess's efforts came to nothing: Thetford Priory was dissolved on 16 February 1540.

Thanks to the documentary evidence some of the activities of the patrons of Thetford Priory are known to us. The Howards in particular used the house not only as their family mausoleum, but also as a suitably impressive environment to hold court and as a secure and appropriate location for the storage of valuables.

---

[47] *Ibidem*, vol. 2, p. 522.
[48] *Ibidem*, vol. 1, p. 37.
[49] *Ibidem*, vol. 1, p. 56.
[50] *Ibidem*, vol. 2, p. 735.

Compared with Tewkesbury and St Augustine's Abbey, both particularly large, splendid, cathedralesque foundations, the much more modest priory of Thetford was in many ways different. Perhaps the reasons for the apparent closeness of the house's patrons and its religious community has to be sought on a somewhat more personal level. The location of the priory was certainly an important factor in their choice of patronage, as was the presence in the priory church of numerous graves of the family's ancestors, linking the Howards in all eternity with Thetford Priory.

Some Conclusions

The three examples of Tewkesbury, St Augustine's and Thetford serve to illustrate just some aspects of the range of expressions of patronal authority, and the ways in which a monastery might be instrumental in the expression of this authority. This was normally much more striking in the case of royal or episcopal houses than in that of monasteries with lay patrons, but nonetheless it seems clear that abbeys and priories might be used for a range of activities by the laity. Nor was this restricted to particular religious orders, as the examples show. Any kind of contact between lay and religious communities also meant contact between the sacred, and the profane, and some degree of tension between respect and abuse of the religious space was inevitable. Yet despite the potential for tension between the two parties, the use by lay authorities of the religious space was a mutually accepted part of lay patronage, provided that this was not abused by either party.

Monasteries, then, might be used first and foremost, and perhaps most obviously as *monuments* – both to the living and to the dead. Families promoted themselves in the representation of family heraldry in the fabric of the house, painted onto walls, carved into monuments or onto monastic gatehouses. The family arms might be embroidered onto vestments and hangings, or shown on heraldic tiles or in stained glass windows. Physical likenesses of patrons were displayed in prominent positions in the naves of conventual churches, in effigies and chapels.

Apart from the function of religious houses as symbols of their wealth, power and authority, monasteries were often used for the *storage of valuables and/or documents*. The letters of Thetford's last prior provide evidence for just one such example. In this case the choice of the monastery for the safekeeping of certain valuable items, particularly also of documents, as in the case of Tewkesbury Abbey's *Founders' Book*, is perhaps understandable. The secluded and well-guarded environment of a religious house lent itself to this purpose.

Patrons used their religious houses also to *hold court*, to receive visitors and to be received as visitors themselves. A monastery, even a more modest one, was still in most cases the most impressive available location for a lay patron to hold court. The visits of the Duke of Norfolk feature prominently in the house's accounts, hinting at just how elaborate these occasions often were. They undoubtedly involved a great deal of expense: in addition to the fine foods and wine which were consumed, frequent gifts received by the duke from the prior are mentioned in the *Register*. These occasions inevitably caused some degree of disturbance of the monastic routine, although nothing in the *Thetford Register* make reference to this.

A large and/or wealthy monastery, then, like St Augustine's Abbey in Bristol or Tewkesbury Abbey, both of them grand, imposing, cathedralesque foundations, or even a somewhat smaller, less prosperous and less immediately impressive priory like the Cluniac house at Thetford, was clearly a status symbol for a lay patron, with which he chose to be associated and in which he chose to be present. And while a wealthy and powerful patron might be a valuable asset for a religious house, just so the religious house could clearly be a valuable asset indeed for its lay patrons in late medieval England.

University of Wales, Aberystwyth

CONCLUSION

by
Koen GOUDRIAAN

'Quam terribilis est locus [...] iste. Non est hic aliud nisi domus Dei et porta caeli' ('How awesome is this place. This is none other than the house of God, and this is the gate of heaven'; Gen. 28, 17).[1] With these words the patriarch Jacob commented on the dream vision in which he saw a heavenly ladder and angels descending and ascending on it. The words have been included in the mass with which the consecration of a church is celebrated.[2] It is through consecration that church buildings receive their sacred character.[3] Basically, it is the divine presence that made a church building into a holy place. As such, it was supposed to be awe-inspiring. Profane use of the church building was precluded, because this was supposed to constitute a violation of its sacred nature.

So much for clerical theory. In practice, the consecrated character of the church proved to be compatible with multiple types of profane uses, or at least of uses considered to be 'profane' from a modern perspective. In this volume, various categories of secular users of ecclesiastical buildings passed in review, standing in different relationships to the institutions to which the buildings appertained. At the end of the volume, time has come to draw the general contours of the topic. Which features prove to be common to these eleven contributions? In what directions can research be continued in a meaningful way? A rough framework will be sketched for the interpretation of the multiple phenomena subsumed under the topic. This makes as much use as possible of the clues offered by the contributors. Because this implies a more or less static approach, it remains to be seen at the end whether general patterns can be discerned in the dynamics of changing attitudes towards sacred buildings during the Late Middle Ages. Here, some of the problems put forward by Paul Trio in his introductory remarks will be addressed. The promise of resolving them cannot be given, but in some instances it will at least be possible to reformulate them on the basis of the results of the conference.

---

[1] Quotations from the Bible are in the New Revised Standard Version.
[2] A. Angenendt, *Geschichte der Religiosität im Mittelalter* (Darmstadt, 1997), pp. 430, 436.
[3] 'Was diese Heiligkeit im Spätmittelalter konstitutiert... ist... die Weihe' (Signori, in this volume).

Throughout, the accent has been on ecclesiastical buildings and places and on the secular uses made of them, in accordance with the theme of the conference. In addition to the places and the actions (rites, ceremonies *etcetera*) taking place in them, a third factor inevitably came to the fore, *viz.* the people involved in these actions. The opposition between ecclesiastical buildings and secular uses was doubled by the one between clergy and laity, with the clergy in a more or less defensive role and the laity either encroaching on what was supposed to be the reserve of the clergy or calling in that same clergy to participate in ceremonies devised with secular intentions. At the heart of the matter lies the relationship between the sacred and the profane. But none of the dichotomies involved is as clear as they might seem to be at first sight. On all levels we come across ambiguities, gradations and nuances.

Let us first consider sacred place. Though church buildings as sacred spaces in late medieval cities cannot be missed even by a superficial observer, within Christendom the existence of such sacred places is not entirely self-evident. Did not Christ abolish the Temple, replacing it with his own body (John 2, 18-21)? And did He not give the assertion that where two or three would be gathered in His name, He would be there among them (Mt. 18, 20), which resulted in the statement 'God's temple are you' (1 Cor. 3, 17)?[4] 'You are... members of the household of God, built upon the foundation of the apostles and prophets, with Christ Jesus himself as the cornerstone. In him the whole structure is joined together and grows into a holy temple in the Lord; in whom you also are built together spiritually into a dwelling place for God' (Eph. 2, 19-22). In the spiritualized vision of the Gospels and Epistles there is no need for sacred buildings, the locus of the sacred being Christ himself as well as his 'body', the congregation. People like Bernard of Clairvaux and Peter the Chanter in the High Middle Ages objected to excessive campaigns of church building.[5] Likewise, in the Late Middle Ages Geert Grote of Deventer, the founding father of the Modern Devotion, was opposed to the building of the tower of the Utrecht Cathedral.[6] They had a point.

But dissidents like the ones I mentioned remained in the minority. Starting with the great basilicas founded by Constantine and his dynasty, the

---

[4] The point is made for instance by Angenendt, *Religiosität im Mittelalter*, p. 432, and by D.M. Hayes, *Body and Sacred Place in Medieval Europe, 1100-1389* (New York / London, 2003), pp. 7-8.

[5] Hayes, *Body and Sacred Place*, p. 10.

[6] *Gerardi Magni Contra Turrim Traiectensem*, R. Hofman (ed.) (Turnhout, 2003).

Church built churches and regarded them as indispensable. Before long, church buildings acquired sacrality. Without ever rejecting the more spiritual conception of the temple expounded in the New Testament, church leaders could easily lean upon passages from the Old Testament, like the one cited above, to underscore the sacred nature of church buildings. In a recent monograph on the cathedral of Chartres, Dawn Mary Hayes indicates two circumstances as fundamental for this development.[7] With reference to Mary Douglas, she points out that every religion, however spiritual it may be, must make the move from the interior to the exterior in order to acquire the necessary stability and continuity. Temples had to be built as shelters for worship and as the visible expression of the hierarchy (clergy) which was indispensable to lend endurance to the new religion. The second fundamental was the Christian world-view, which saw earthly life as a passage between damnation and salvation, sharing in the forces of both good and evil. 'The contentious character of worldly existence where people struggled against corruption demanded that any place to be used for worship be purified and then fortified against ever-pressing forces of evil'.[8]

Hayes then goes on to discuss several criteria for the sacrality of churches on the basis of canonistic texts dating from the High Middle Ages. There is general agreement that it is consecration that makes a church into a sacred place. In the consecration procedure, three elements can be distinguished: the separation of the church from its surroundings by going around it in procession; the purification of the sacred space, church and altars, by the sprinkling of water and hyssop, chasing out evil spirits (in fact a kind of exorcism); and the reinforcement of the place by the interment of saints' relics in the altar.[9] Interestingly, within her source material she finds two diverging interpretations of the consecration rite. The Gallican liturgy stresses the first two elements of the procedure, with the consequence that consecration is considered to 'reside in the walls'. Some Gallican authors even leave out the deposition of relics in the *sepulchra* of the altars altogether. The liturgy contained in the Roman pontificals, on the other hand, regards the presence of relics as indispensable and logically focuses on the altars as the locus for the sacred.[10] This second view probably was more widely distributed.[11] In the first book of

---

[7] Hayes, *Body and Sacred Place*, Chapter One.
[8] *Ibidem*, p. 11.
[9] *Ibidem*, pp. 11-12.
[10] *Ibidem*, p. 117 n. 67.
[11] Cf. Angenendt, *Religiosität im Mittelalter*, pp. 432-435: the sacrality of the church originally resided in the altars and then spread to the entire building.

the *Rationale divinorum officiorum* of Durandus of Mende, the most important source for learned conceptions about the church building and the rites and symbolism that surround it, both approaches are combined.[12]

Durandus also offers materials for a more refined gradation of sacrality in connection with ecclesiastical buildings.[13] Consecrated places intended for prayer – hospitals *etcetera* fall into a different category altogether – can be divided into three classes, which results in the hierarchy of the sacred (*sacra*), the holy (*sancta*) and the religious (*religiosa*). Sacred places are those that have been consecrated, mainly the churches themselves. The special character of holy places resides in privilege or immunity: churchyards, cloisters and canons' houses are cases in point. Religious space is the ground in which Christian bodies have been buried. Spaces higher in the hierarchy also possess the qualities of the categories below, but not *vice versa*. Though Durandus' system is a theoretical construction, it has the advantage of systematizing a number of approaches to holiness, all of which, no doubt, played a part in everyday practice. It might be an appropriate task for future research to uncover the dialectic between canonistic theory and practice as applied by the clergy and laity.[14] This research could extend also to the internal divisions within consecrated church buildings. Here, besides the simple binary opposition between choir (for the clergy) and nave (for the laity), the theory also applies more elaborate divisions, such as the tripartite one of sanctuary (for the altar), chancel (for the clergy) and nave (for lay people).[15] Developments in architecture, such as the appearance of the 'preaching houses' of the mendicant orders with their spacious naves (Röhrkasten), must have influenced the perception of the sacred in connection with church buildings. In the Late Middle Ages, the pulpit became an independent focal point for sacrality (Signori).

So far, this analysis of sacred space has made use of categories that were familiar to medieval people. Though the dichotomy 'sacred versus profane' is not found as such in medieval sources, the categories we do find can be translated in these terms without straining them too much. But in addition, another concept of sacrality circulated during the conference:

---

[12] William Durand, *Guillelmi Duranti Rationale Divinorum Officiorum I-IV*, A. Davril & T.M. Thibodeau (eds.), Corpus Christianorum, Continuatio Mediaevalis, vol. 140 (Turnhout, 1995).

[13] For the following cf. Hayes, *The Body and Sacred Place*, p. 17ff.

[14] Cf. the importance of the element of remembrance in the case of the tombs of predecessors figuring in the urban ritual of the Cinque Ports (Sweetinburgh).

[15] Hayes, *Body and Sacred Place*, p. 17.

'sacred space' is every space that acquires meaning in terms of religious symbolism. It is implied in several contributions and becomes explicit in particular in the contribution by Sweetinburgh. One might call this approach, without disqualification, 'anachronistic'. Concepts are tools for analysis, and if modern concepts are better equipped to explain phenomena of the past than those that were used by contemporaries, their application is justified. In this connection, the theory of space designed by H. Lefebvre might be useful, provided it is stripped of its Marxist trappings. Subsuming ecclesiastical space under the wider category of 'representational space' (alongside spatial practice and representation *of* space), considered as 'more or less coherent systems of non-verbal symbols and signs' (Sweetinburgh), has its convenience. An approach like this one, which deliberately does not take the notion of consecration as its point of departure, may reveal particularities that remain under the surface when the 'sacred' is emphasized too much. Another interesting concept is the 'multi-layering of space through time', graphically described by the metaphor of the palimpsest. Former uses of a particular space may have been eroded to a lesser or greater degree by later applications. Meanings traditionally attached to that space may or may not be alluded to in later uses, but seldom they are blotted out altogether.[16]

The second factor in the analysis of sacred places being used for worldly purposes are the people involved. Ideally, to the clergy fell the role of defining sacred space and determining the scope for activities within that space by lay people. In reality, the laity was not satisfied with this passive role and demanded a greater share. Kings and territorial lords considered the religious well-being of their subjects no less a part of their task than their material welfare. In the case of the English kings between Wycliffism and the independent Anglican Church under Henry VIII this is more than apparent. For the German territories, the church politics of the princes has by now become a familiar topic of study, mostly in connection with the Reformation and its late medieval roots.[17] On the urban level, the community of cit-

---

[16] A case could be made for treating 'time' as a separate factor in the analysis of sacred places, alongside space itself, the players involved, and rites. Lefebvre's palimpsests cover the field made accessible by Chartier's and De Certeau's concept of appropriation – to be discussed later on. This must not be confused with the Marxist idea of appropriation as applied to space by Lefebvre himself.

[17] E.g. M. Schulze, *Fürsten und Reformation* (Tübingen, 1991) and the literature mentioned in H. Schilling, 'Reformation – Umbruch oder Gipfelpunkt eines Temps des Réformes', in: B. Moeller (ed.), *Die frühe Reformation in Deutschland als Umbruch* (Gütersloh, 1998), pp. 13-34, esp. n. 7.

izens and the community of parishioners frequently coincided. This was especially the case in the large majority of smaller and younger towns in which no partitioning of the original city parish had taken place. In such circumstances, it was quite natural for the city magistrates to consider the parish church their responsibility. Lay church wardens acted as committees on behalf and under the supervision of city governments.[18] Even urban convents and monasteries were in the orbit of city magistracies, either as missionary posts from which to evangelize the growing city populations (mendicants) or as deputy institutions of sanctity on behalf of the urban community (contemplative orders). Not even the boundary between clergy and laity was always very clear. This at least is illustrated by the case of the German kings, as discussed in the contribution by Oesterle on the coronation rites in the Ottonian and Salian periods.

This having been said, it may be convenient to give an overview of the types of secular users figuring in the contributions to this volume. Royal government is prominent in a number of them (Röhrkasten, Oesterle, Jamroziak). In a more indirect manner territorial government is present as the political power imposing itself on the actions taken by municipal authorities, as in the case of the Dukes of Burgundy working through local authorities in Flanders (van Leeuwen). In other contributions urban magistracies are in the forefront in their own right (Kuys, Signori, De Smet, Sweetinburgh). Aristocratic lay patrons play a leading role in a number of contributions (Stöber, Dekeyzer). In addition, several other categories of secular users figure incidentally, such as of the board of 67 jurors prescribed by the arbitration treaty between the Counts of Holland and of Flanders concerning Zealand (Kuys), the Lord Warden and the Court of Brodhull of the Cinque Ports (Sweetinburgh), boards of dykereeves (Kuys), fraternities (Sweetinburg) and notaries (Kuys). Finally, individuals play an accessory role in several contributions. The relationships in which these actors stood to the ecclesiastical institutions concerned range from political overlordship, via the right of advowson (often deriving from the original foundation) and benefactorship to the mere status of being parishioners of the church concerned, either collectively or individually.

The third element is constituted by the activities themselves. A convenient classification of the multiple uses to which church buildings were

---

[18] H. Boockmann, *Die Stadt im späten Mittelalter* (Munich, 1987²), p. 193: 'Die weitreichende Identität zwischen Stadtregierung und Stadtgemeinde einerseits und der Pfarrkirche andererseits wurde fast überall in Gestalt der städtischen Kirchenpfleger personifiziert'.

put could start with the twin notions of 'practical' versus 'symbolic'. Practical uses range from defense in time of war, including the use of the church tower as observation post and, negatively, the demolition of church buildings in order to prevent them from becoming a sallying base for the enemy, via the storage of documents and precious objects by both authorities and individuals and of weights and measures by town governments, and via the communication of time by the clock, of danger by the bells, and of messages of general interest from the pulpit, to the offering of accommodation to all kinds of meetings: of notaries and their clients, urban boards of government, electoral bodies, aristocratic courts and various kinds of tribunals. Such uses can easily be explained by the physical characteristics of ecclesiastical buildings: their strength, their size, their location. Some tension may have existed between the opposite qualities of accessibility and safety. Practices like the 'kerkenspraak' (church announcements), the ringing of the bells in token of alarm, the meetings of the city council in the church and the location of city archives in the parish church additionally can be understood as expressions of the indivisible unity supposed to exist between the communities of citizens and of parishioners.

This last argument, however, shows how thin the line is between the practical and the symbolic. As soon as the church building is interpreted as the expression in stone of the city community and is claimed on that basis by city authorities, it receives representational meanings. Sweetinburgh made it clear that the choice of parish churches for elections and tribunals in the Kentish Cinque Ports was prompted by more than practical considerations alone: the sacred nature of the places shaded off on the administrative procedure and enhanced its value. Against this background, one might even wonder by what considerations precisely people were moved when they sought protection in the church for their papers and their precious objects: did they put their trust in the walls because of their thickness or because they enclosed a consecrated place and harboured the relics of the saints? Sacredness was supposed to be contagious: did they wish their properties to profit from the 'holy radioactivity' sent forth from the altars, the Eucharist and the relics?[19]

Whereas some hesitation is possible about the symbolic nature of these types of use, other practices leave no room whatsoever for doubt. The coronation rites described by Oesterle are replete of a symbolism in which it is difficult to separate the political from the religious, precisely because

---

[19] Hayes, *Body and Sacred Place*, p. 5 n. 11, with reference to Finucane.

German kingship itself was of a sacred nature. The same is true – apart from the elections of councillors, as noted already – for peace-proclamations (van Leeuwen). The religious and the social merge in uses in which representation of status is prominent. This is valid, for example, for the aristocratic courts discussed by Stöber, for the representation of founders and benefecators in effigie or in heraldry expounded by Dekeyzer, and for the choice of a particular church or convent as burial place by members of the aristocracy and the patriciate. Of course, remembrance is a central concern in this category of practices. A very peculiar instance of remembrance has been discussed by Jamroziak: the foundation of the Cistercian priory of St Mary Graces in London by King Edward III near a plague cemetery and in commemoration of the Black Death.

Coronations and elections illustrate perfectly a point stressed in particular by Signori, that most 'profane' uses of churches were based on the sacred nature of the building or the place. It does not follow, however, that every activity within churches partook of the same degree of sacrality. It would be worthwhile to look for some hierarchy, or perhaps several competing hierarchies, among the many rituals that were executed in churches. A convenient starting point for reconnoitring such hierarchies may be found in the analysis made by van Leeuwen of the festivities occasioned by peace-proclamations in Flanders. As she makes clear, in the profane part of the ceremonies some elements were borrowed from religious symbolic vocabulary, such as the chiming of the church bells and the lighting of candles and torches. But it was the ecclesiastical intermezzo in the celebrations in particular that was built as a whole on rituals appropriated from the liturgy: masses were said, processions held and sermons preached.

In an article about ritual and popular religion in early sixteenth-century Germany, the late Bob Scribner has proposed a tripartite classification within urban religious ritual.[20] The inner circle consists of strictly ecclesiastical liturgy, which revolves around the sacraments, is monopolized by the clergy and concedes a passive role only to the laity. The second circle is still connected with the liturgy and executed by the clergy, but it contains additions which have developed on the initiative of the laity and which allow them a more active role. To this second circle belong two specific types of ritual, the *functiones sacrae* and the sacramentals. The *functiones sacrae* refer to the 'sacred performances', which dramatize events in the liturgical year such as the washing of the feet of the

---

[20] R.W. Scribner, 'Ritual and Popular Religion in Catholic Germany at the Time of the Reformation', *Journal of Ecclesiastical History*, 35 (1984), pp. 47-77.

Apostles on Maundy Thursday or the deposition of Christ in the grave on Good Friday. Among the sacramentals are benedictions, e.g. of candles on Candlemas, of palms during Palm Sunday and of holy water in the ordinary Sunday liturgy. Holy water in its turn can be used as an ingredient for exorcisms. In addition to benedictions and exorcisms, also processions can be subsumed under this type of ritual. Both *functiones sacrae* and sacramentals could easily be appropriated by the laity, eager as they were to participate in the ritual. This gave birth to rituals that were outside the scope of the clergy and often entailed practices to which they objected. Out of the *functiones sacrae* grew mystery plays, but also folkloristic performances involving merriment, laughter and jokes and condemned as unseemly and irreverent by the clergy. Sacramentals making use of blessed objects shaded off into magic as soon as lay people applied these objects outside the official liturgy: weather processions tried to force nature into benevolence, *etcetera*. Folklorized ritual and magic together constitute Scribner's third circle of popular ritual, it being understood that the people also had their share in rituals belonging to the first and second circles. Neither between the first and the second, nor between the second and the third category was the boundary sharp; to the contrary, Scribner's model presupposes a great deal of overlap between the categories. As for sacramentals: theologians had some difficulty in evaluating them. In the sixteenth century, the formula was found that, whereas sacraments work *ex opere operato* and irrespective of the dispositions of those that used them, sacramentals were not automatically efficacious in the same way.[21]

To return to the Flemish peace-celebrations: in Scribner's terms they incorporated rituals belonging both to the strictly liturgical first circle (masses, also sermons) and to the para-liturgical second category (processions, candles, perhaps also the ringing of church bells). For the first category, secular authorities had to rely fully upon the cooperation of the clergy, but also in the second circle ecclesiastical authorities had to comply. If we generalize this approach, it might be useful to apply a tripartite scheme analogous to Scribner's to church rituals used by secular authorities and individuals with intentions which we would call secular. By having masses celebrated by the incumbents of the altars and chantries in city churches, by ordering sermons to be preached by parish priests or mendicants, but also by the foundation of council chapels and chantries, the laity could enlist the administration of the sacraments in their service.

---

[21] Scribner, 'Ritual and Popular Religion', p. 70.

Processions, oath swearing, benedictions, burials, but perhaps also the pealing of church bells and the offering of sanctuary (asylum) to fugitives could be placed in a second category, akin to Scribner's sacramentals: though not strictly liturgical, these actions are bound up with the sacred and can be detached neither from the consecrated nature of the objects and spaces they use nor from the ordained character of those that execute them. In a third category – here the analogy with Scribner's classification cannot be drawn with the same rigour – belong activities such as the placing of epitaphs and of stained glass windows, the ordering of altarpieces and of embroidery for sacerdotal vestments, and the visual representation of founders and benefactors in effigie or in heraldry. These are accretions to the liturgical and para-liturgical, and from the point of view of the clergy they may have been objectionable. Together, these three layers of interference of the laity allowed secular authorities or persons to have as big a share in church ritual as they could, but the effects were different on each level.

This classification of activities on the basis of their graded relationship to the liturgy may be supplemented by an approach that focuses on the particular types of sacred space involved. Masses, even if not prompted by the liturgical calendar but ordered by secular authorities on profane occasions, still involve consecrated altars. Burials may or may not have a spatial relationship with the relics of the saints; in some churches, but not in all, lay people are excluded from burial in the choir.[22] Processions often leave the sacred area of the church building for the streets of the town, turning them into a sacred space of a kind. Activities that are allowed in the nave may be prohibited in the chancel. Together, the dimensions of 'liturgy' and of 'space' form a framework for the evaluation of specific secular uses, their permissibility, the degree in which they encroach on the area reserved for the clergy and the risk they constitute of impairing the sacred character of the ecclesiastical building.

Throughout the analysis of secular uses of ecclesiastical places a valuable tool is the concept of 'appropriation'. It has been applied in several contributions in this volume, most explicitly by Sweetinburgh and van Leeuwen. German scholarship nowadays uses a kindred analytical concept, that of 'symbolische Kommunikation'; this approach is exemplified by the contribution of Signori. The launching of 'appropriation'

---

[22] K. Goudriaan, 'Ownership of Graves in Medieval Parish Churches in Holland', in: W. Blockmans & A. Janse (eds.), *Showing Status. Representations of Social Positions in the Late Middle Ages* (Turnhout, 1999), pp. 197-223.

as a specific approach of cultural history was the result mainly of the combined efforts of two French historians, Roger Chartier and Michel de Certeau.[23] It implies that cultural symbols and artifacts handed down by tradition are constantly being reused in a dynamic process of cultural transmission and creation. During this process, new layers of significance are added by later users, whose role is not confined to that of passive recipients, as in more traditional approaches of cultural history, but who actively engage in assigning new meanings to the 'objects' they select from tradition, without discarding the old ones. Both sides of the process are equally necessary. For cultural symbols and objects to be kept alive, it is indispensable that they be revived by each successive generation, and this can be done only by new users who attach meanings to them that are relevant in their changed circumstances. 'Appropriation becomes creation and a way of making the sign signify'.[24] On the other hand, only by relying on symbols and objects that have acquired a certain status, or at least recognizibility, through the passage of time, new users can hope to find a legitimate place for themselves. So, 'the object-code at any given historical moment served as an instrument of both change and continuity. It offers a means for a society to encourage change by helping social groups establish ways of seeing themselves that stand outside and in opposition to existing social structures, but it also provides a way for society to absorb change and limit its destabilizing potential'.[25] For us, the interpreters, this implies 'that meaning can't be fixed in the text or object itself without knowledge of its uses, which is to say, knowledge of its various appropriations'.[26]

Secular use of sacred space and church ritual is a particular field of appropriation. If a prince or an aristocrat, for instance, chooses religious symbolism to express his power, this means both that he underlines the validity of the inherited religious symbolic system and that he defines his own position with the help of that symbolic universe. New political or social meanings may be added to a ritual that in itself is religious, but that may as well have acquired political overtones already in a previous phase. The religious and the political presuppose each other: neither can func-

---

[23] For a genealogy of the concept: W.Th.M. Frijhoff, 'Toeëigening: van bezitsdrang naar betekenisgeving', *Trajecta. Tijdschrift voor de geschiedenis van het katholieke leven in de Nederlanden*, 6 (1997), pp. 99-118. For some possibilities of application on the European Middle Ages: C. Sponsler, 'In Transit: Theorizing Cultural Appropriation in Medieval Europe', *Journal of Medieval and Early Modern Studies*, 32 (2002), pp. 17-39.
[24] Sponsler, 'In Transit', p. 35.
[25] *Ibidem*, p. 29.
[26] *Ibidem*, p. 35.

tion without the other, as has been illustrated nicely by van Leeuwen in her analysis of Flemish peace-celebrations.[27]

Of course, this does not mean that everything goes. Church buildings, as cultural artefacts, have a high degree of continuity purely on the basis of their architectural solidity, but also because their sacred character is guarded jealously by a church hierarchy that has a strong stability of its own. They therefore attract the constant attention of both the clergy and of competing groups among the laity, each making its own effort at appropriation. It is here that another analytical concept, negotiation, comes in, as is exemplified by Sweetinburgh. In an ongoing process of trial and error, parties have to reach an agreement every time again about the proper use of ecclesiastical space and ritual.

Appropriation theory may also shed some light on the most extreme form of use that can be made of an ecclesiastical building, its destruction. In a thoroughly Christian society as was the late medieval one, the annihilation of churches either by 'friend' as part of defensive measures, or by offensive actions of 'enemy', seems inconceivable as long as one focuses on their consecrated character. In this connection, De Smet makes the intriguing remark that destruction not always meant desecration: this point deserves to be pursued further.[28] The advantage of applying the concept of appropriation is that it highlights the additional layers of meaning as much as the original sacral nucleus. Probably, it is on account of their wealth of additional signification – architectural, but also representational – that church buildings were destroyed, in circumstances in which their sacrality temporarily receded into the background.

The focus of the conference was on the Low Countries, though within a European context. Obviously, this raises the question whether developments in the Low Countries show characteristics peculiar to that region. In order to give a precise answer to that question, a more systematic comparison should be made of specific types of churches in the Low Countries with their counterparts in neighbouring regions: urban parish churches should be compared with parish churches elsewhere, collegiate churches with collegiate churches, monasteries with monasteries and so

---

[27] In my oral conclusion, I rejected the idea that religious symbolism is basically or properly about something else, in particular about political power. I still do, but now I think that this point can be made in a more sophisticated way by reference to the concept of 'appropriation'.

[28] Hayes, *Body and Sacred Place*, p. 16 gives a clue by pointing out that the decretals of Gregory IX restricted the need for reconsecration to a few specific cases.

on. This is a task that still awaits historical researchers. Historical investigation – it may be observed in passing – would profit also from the cross-fertilization of national traditions of research; the Kortrijk conference is a case in point. In this respect, historians of and from the Low Countries should take seriously their traditional position at the cross-roads of European scholarly traditions. The empirical research they already do should be supplemented by more thorough theoretic analysis.

It has been suggested that the high degree of urbanization characteristic of the Low Countries may have influenced the way in which urban church buildings were used. This hypothesis is not confirmed straightforwardly by the contributions in this volume. A high rate of urbanization translates itself either in the size of the cities or in their number, or in both. But neither the large cities in the German Empire (Signori), nor the cluster of the Cinque Ports in Southeast England (Sweetinburgh) offer patterns that deviate essentially from those in the Low Countries. And after all, does it make much difference for a city magistrate wishing to make use of the parish church whether the city is large or small, and whether the next city is nearby or far away? A direct link between urbanisation rate and secular use of church buildings is perhaps not what we should expect.

London, however, proved a case apart because of the preponderance of royal influence both on the churches of the mendicants (Röhrkasten) and on the lately founded Cistercian priory of St. Mary Graces (Jamroziak). This may lead to an aspect in which the Low Countries were peculiar, indeed. A general tendency in the Late Middle Ages appears to have been the effort to instrumentalize the Church as a constituent part of the State. In England, with its centralized monarchy, it was the king who profited from this development, or rather gave it its direction. The Empire, on the other hand, was politically fragmented. Large independent *Reichsstädte* had managed to remain practically sovereign alongside comital or ducal territories. Here, both the large cities and the territories, each in their turn, could be the setting of the subsumption of the ecclesiastical under the secular. In the Low Countries mighty (though not independent) cities and a strong line of territorial lords, in the persons of the (Arch)dukes of Burgundy and Habsburg, operated both in the same area. How about the long-term development of the tension between urban autonomy and ducal centralization, as expressed in religious manifestations? The peace-celebrations – again – are an example, general processions are another: though the municipalities organized them, they did so at the request of the sovereign.

Urban civic culture is another topic for which the Low Countries are supposed to stand out against other regions in Europe, although in this respect they are matched, of course, by the large Italian city-republics and by the German *Reichsstädte*. Interestingly, in contemporary research on the Low Countries this subject, too, is dominated by the rivalry between the central government and urban autonomy. One of the finest recent studies, Arnade's *Realms of Ritual*, focuses exactly on the city (one particular city, Ghent) as the setting for the ducal, Burgundian 'theater state'.[29] The striking point about this book is that the sacred (ritual and space) is hardly thematized at all. There is a thrilling chapter about the clash that occurred between the city's own ritual agenda and that of the duke when the procession of St Lieven and the Joyous Entry of Charles the Bold threatened to coincide.[30] Arnade remarks in passing that 'the city was above all without precise distinctions between sacred and profane activity'.[31] In the detailed discussion of diverse types of ritual, ecclesiastical space figures now and then. For the rest, Arnade leaves it at that. This may be because he did not consider this particular point to contribute much to his subject, which is the ritual negotiation between the prince and his citizen subjects.

But perhaps urban civic culture in the cities of the Southern Low Countries already in the fifteenth century had progressed fairly on the route towards emancipation from the ecclesiastical. If so, there is no doubt that they were ahead of the cities in the Northern Low Countries and elsewhere in Europe. Town and guild halls had become a common phenomenon in the later Middle Ages, and of course they had attracted an important part of the civic ritual. But, as is made clear by Sweetinburgh for the Kentish Cinque Ports, it did not follow that the parish church was supplanted as a focus for civic ritual. In comparison with Kent, however, the role of the parish church in Flemish cities was very much reduced. Freestanding belfries in their turn, those mighty symbols of municipal secular power, were restricted to a specific area in the Southern Netherlands. So with regard to urban civic culture, the problem can be reformulated as follows: are we entitled to conclude that at least in the Southern Low Countries church rites and sacred space no longer were the focal point for the symbolic system prevalent in local culture, to the extent that we can call it 'profane' for all practical purposes?

---

[29] P. Arnade, *Realms of Ritual. Burgundian Ceremony and Civic Life in Late Medieval Ghent* (Ithaca / London, 1996).
[30] *Ibidem*, pp. 142-158.
[31] *Ibidem*, p. 52.

Finally, can we discern any comprehensible pattern in the late medieval shifting and redefining of the boundary between the sacred and the profane? Signori ends her contribution with the observation that 'the sacred and the profane had ceased to be sharply separated spaces and areas. The problem had become relative, it had become dependent on the position of those involved'.[32] This would imply that the general tendency in the last centuries of the Middle Ages was the blurring of the distinction between the sacred and the profane. The opinion Hayes expresses about this topic is exactly the opposite. Speaking of twelfth and thirteenth century Chartres, she characterizes it as 'a world that was less concerned, I think, with compartmentalizing space and restricting activity than in the centuries that followed'.[33]

In view of such disagreements, the least one can say is that a lot of work remains to be done. The question should be asked, however, whether such an enterprise is not doomed to failure from the start. If one takes seriously the implications of the appropriation process, as it has been explained above, does this not mean that every new group assigns its own meaning to inherited symbolic systems, including those tied up with ecclesiastical buildings? If so, can the process of redefinition of the boundary between the sacred and the profane be anything but erratic?

One of the subjects discussed by Boockmann in the chapter he devotes to the parish church in his *Die Stadt des späten Mittelalters*, is the representation in effigie of benefactors. In Lubeck benefactors did not appear at altar panels at all; in Nuremberg they did, but only in a modest form. Though municipal ordinances have not been preserved, Boockman supposes, plausibly, that in both cities an official ruling governed the way benefactors were represented. But in neither of the two cities they were as prominent as in the Low Countries.[34] What counted as unseemly in one city, was permissible a couple of hundred kilometres away. Other instances of divergent principles of structuring ecclesiastical space have been investigated by Signori. Apart from conflicting views about the desirability of sessions by the Strasbourg mayor in church (this volume), the arrangement and destination of pews and the way space is allotted to the sexes prove to be very peculiar.[35] Pews were associated with the

---

[32] 'Sakral und profan waren keine scharf von einander getrennten Räume bzw. Welten mehr. Das Problem hatte sich relativiert, es war standortabhängig geworden'.
[33] Hayes, *Body and Sacred Place*, p. xx, summarizing Chapter Three on 'Earthly Uses of Heavenly Spaces'.
[34] Boockmann, *Die Stadt im späten Mittelalter*, p. 193.
[35] G. Signori, 'Umstrittene Stühle. Spätmittelalterliches Kirchengestühl als soziales, politisches und religiöses Kommunikationsmedium', *Zeitschrift für historische Forschung*,

female sex. That did not preclude them from being a highly valued symbol of status, as is made clear by pew registers preserved for the city of Basle. Decoding the system governing the placement of the pews is made difficult, however, by the intersection of various principles of arrangement, based on social rank, family membership, dependency and vicinity. Hierarchy between the two sexes made use of the opposition between 'front' and 'rear' and between 'right' and 'left', but the obvious association of the male church visitors with the best places, located in the 'front' and the 'right', did not always come true, for a variety of reasons. These examples show that divergence not only occurred between the clergy and the laity as such, but that various groups within the laity may have had different views, too.

The detection of frictions in the structuring of space in ecclesiastical buildings is very valuable, whether they concern the opposition between male and female and between patriciate and commoners, or, at a more fundamental level, the split between the sacred and the profane. As the principal shortcoming of the older standard work by Davies on the secular use of church buildings Hayes considers the fact that he took no notice of frictions between learned clerical perceptions of churches (the theory) and the practical use made of them by both clergy and laity.[36] According to Sponsler, 'moments of blockage at which appropriation across discourses is halted'[37] are revealing, precisely because they point the way to the underlying systems of thought.

So there may still have been much confusion as to where exactly the sacred and the profane had to be located. More in general, disagreements about the correct way of applying hierarchy in the distribution of space within church buildings continued. Notwithstanding all this, the hypothesis is justified that the delimitation of the fundamental categories of the sacred and the profane tended to become sharper in the Late Middle Ages and at the threshold of the Early Modern period, under the joint influence of both ecclesiastical and secular authorities. The 'moneychangers and those who sold doves' (Mt. 21, 12) who had encroached on the temple

---

29 (2002), pp. 189-213; 'Links oder Rechts? Zum 'Platz der Frau' in der mittelalterlichen Kirche', in: S. Rau & G. Schwerhoff (eds.), *Zwischen Gotteshaus und Taverne. Öffentliche Räume in Spätmittelalter und Früher Neuzeit* (Cologne / Weimar / Vienna, 2004), pp. 339-382.

[36] J.G. Davies, *The Secular Use of Church Buildings* (London, 1968). Hayes, *Body and Sacred Place*, pp. 141-142; she explains it by Davies' contemporary agenda, which was in favour of maximum secular use of the buildings.

[37] Sponsler, 'In Transit', p. 32.

in earlier periods, were finally chased out again.[38] Church furniture such as rood screens of growing height increasingly accentuated the limits between the different parts of the church.[39] In addition to and in combination with archival texts, which reflect the phenomena under investigation in a more direct way, it might be worthwhile to study the theological sources and those of Canon Law, which in their own way reflect the changes we are looking for. In the production of synodal statutes an increased activity has been observed from the middle of the fifteenth century onwards, an important concern being the purification of liturgical practices.[40] It seems probable, therefore, that these statutes offer clues for the redefinition of boundaries within ecclesiastical space. Interestingly, one of the first books to be produced by the printing press was Durandus' *Rationale divinorum officiorum*;[41] in Germany (but not in the Low Countries) it saw many reprints before the end of the century. Is it wrong to assume that this work, though it originated in the thirteenth century and despite its learned character, only now started to meet a broadly felt need?

The interests and concerns of secular authorities may have diverged on specific points from those of the clergy, but on the whole we have no reason to think that they went in a totally different direction. Urban governments, in particular, show a great concern for their parish churches. Being loath of sacerdotal absenteeism, they make every effort to provide good pastoral care, by trying to lay hold on the right of advowson themselves or by enforcing agreements on the parish clergy about the proper fulfilment of their duty. Preaching, in addition to the correct and prompt administering of the sacraments, increasingly is at the center of their concern. Maybe this is why the pulpit as a new locus of sanctity within the church building emerges at the end of the Middle Ages.[42] In the general process of disciplining, 'Kirchenzucht' (proper behaviour in church) takes an important place – to my knowledge this has so far not been investigated in a systematic way for the Low Countries in the pre-Reformation period. Throughout, city authorities manifest a heightened awareness of the improper in the face of sacred space and ritual.

---

[38] Cf. the Strasbourg print published in Boockmann, *Stadt im Mittelalter*, pp. 202-203.
[39] Hayes, *Body and Sacred Place*, p. 119 n. 79.
[40] Scribner, 'Ritual and Popular Culture', 72. For this type of source in the Low Countries see Ch. Caspers, 'The Role of the People in the Liturgy According to the Synodal Statutes of the Ancient Dioceses of Cambrai, Liège and Utrecht (c. 1300 – c. 1500)', in: Ch. Caspers & M. Schneiders (eds.), *Omnes Circumadstantes. Contributions towards a History of the Role of the People in the Liturgy* (Kampen, 1990), pp. 155-176.
[41] GW 9101: Mainz 1459 (J. Fust & P. Schoeffer).
[42] Signori, 'Links oder Rechts?', pp. 360-361.

The culmination of these developments was reached during the Reformation and the Counterreformation. The Counterreformation drew the lines between the sacred and the profane more clearly than they had ever been before. The Reformation, in its turn, declared a large proportion of the practices once considered to be compatible with the sacredness of ecclesiastical space and ritual to be 'superstitious' and forbade them. Though it also changed the theological basis on which sacrality in churches rested, this by no means entailed the abolition of the distinction between the profane and the sacred.

Vrije Universiteit Amsterdam

LIST OF CONTRIBUTORS

Paul Trio (° 1958) is currently a senior professor of Medieval History at the Katholieke Universiteit Leuven (Catholic University of Leuven) and the Katholieke Universiteit Leuven Campus Kortrijk (Catholic University of Leuven Campus Kortrijk). After having completed his PhD thesis about 'Medieval Confraternities in Ghent' (1989), which was published in two volumes in 1991 and 1993, he continued to study the confraternal system in the Low Countries and published several articles and books on this in international journals and other publications. For the past year, he has been a VNC Fellow at the Netherlands Institute for Advanced Study in the Humanities and Social Sciences in Wassenaar (the Netherlands), where he and Dr. Bram van den Hoven van Genderen did the preliminary work for a book on confraternities in the Low Countries during the Middle Ages. He furthermore wrote numerous articles with regard to ecclesiastical and urban history in the county of Flanders.

Marjan De Smet (°1974), MA, studied Germanic Philology and History at the Katholieke Universiteit Leuven. At the Katholieke Universiteit Leuven Campus Kortrijk, she is currently making an electronic inventory of the archive of the Augustinian abbey of Zonnebeke (www.kuleuven-kortrijk.be/doza). Together with dr. Paul Trio, she has written an article about the relationship between Church and town in the late medieval Low Countries, on the basis of information about interdicts (*Jaarboek voor middeleeuwse geschiedenis*, 5 (2002), pp. 247-274).

Jan Kuys (°1952) is assistant professor at the Department of Medieval History, University of Nijmegen. His research concerns the late medieval institutional history of the Eastern Netherlands, medieval ecclesiastical institutions in the bishopric of Utrecht and the relationship between Church and State in the late medieval Netherlands. Editor of *Tijdschrift voor Waterstaatsgeschiedenis* and *Biografisch Woordenboek Gelderland*. Recent publications: 'Chiesa e vita religiosa nei Paesi Bassi durante il Medioevo', in: L. Vaccaro (ed.), *Storia religiosa di Belgio, Olanda e Lussemburgo* (Gazzada, 2000); 'Zentralverwaltung und Lokalverwaltung von Grafschaft und Herzogtum Geldern bis 1543', in: J. Stinner & K.H. Tekath (eds.), *Gelre-Geldern-Gelderland. Geschichte und Kultur des Her-*

zogtums Geldern (Guelders, 2001); *Overzicht van kerkelijke instellingen in het middeleeuwse bisdom Utrecht* (Nijmegen, 2004).

Jacoba van Leeuwen (°1975) has studied history and medieval studies at the K.U.Leuven. In 2002 she finished her PhD on the ritual election and installation of the benches of aldermen in medieval Ghent, Bruges and Ypres (1379-1492). Since then she has studied the symbolic use of the written word in medieval towns and the literary discourse on the social position of aldermen. In 2005 two books dealing with these subjects were published: *De Vlaamse wetsvernieuwing. Een onderzoek naar de jaarlijkse keuze en aanstelling van het stadsbestuur in Gent, Brugge en Ieper in de Middeleeuwen*, Verhandelingen van de Koninklijke Vlaamse Academie van België voor Wetenschappen en Kunsten, Nieuwe reeks, 15 (Brusssels, 2005), and with Heike Bierschwale, *'Wie man eine Stadt regieren soll' / 'Hoemen ene stat regeren sal': Deutsche und niederländische Stadtregimentslehren des Mittelalters*, Medieval to Early Modern Culture / Kultureller Wandel vom Mittelalter zur Frühen Neuzeit, 8 (Frankfurt a.M., 2005).

Brigitte Dekeyzer (°1966) has a PhD in Art History and an MA in Philosophy. She is presently fulfilling a post-doctoral mandate at the Katholieke Universiteit Leuven and is on staff at the *Center for the Study of Flemish Illuminators*, an organ of scholarship and documentation at the K.U.Leuven. She is specialized in research into South Netherlandish panel painting and book illumination of the fifteenth and early sixteenth centuries. Most important publication: Brigitte Dekeyzer, *Layers of Illusion. The Mayer van den Bergh Breviary* (Ghent: Ludion, 2004).

Jenny Rahel Oesterle (°1978) MA, studied Medieval History, Arabic & Islamic Studies and Theology in Giessen, Jerusalem and Münster. She is a member of the 'Graduiertenkolleg Gesellschaftliche Symbolik im Mittelalter' at the University of Münster and is currently writing her PhD about 'Formen religiöser Herrschaftsrepräsentation in Christentum und Islam im Frühmittelalter'. Publications: 'Eine Investitur durch den Kalifen von Bagdad nach Hilal as-Sabis Zeremonienbuch. Zur Rolle von Religion, Ehre und Rangordnungen in der Herrschaftsrepräsentation', in: M. Steinicke & S. Weinfurter (eds.), *Investitur- und Krönungsrituale* (Cologne, 2005).

Gabriela Signori (Basle, Switserland), studied History, Romance Philology and Philosophy at the universities of Basle, Geneva, Lausanne and Paris. In 1991, she gained her PhD at the University of Basle, and in 1998 she obtained her accreditation from the Faculty of History of the University of Bielefeld. Since 2001, she has been teaching History of the Late Middle Ages and Historical Complementary Sciences as a professor at the University of Munster.

Jens Röhrkasten was assistant at the Friedrich-Meinecke-Institut of the Freie Universität Berlin and is now a lecturer at the Department of Medieval History at the University of Birmingham. He published a study of English medieval criminal law in 1990 and has since worked on the history of the mendicant friars in England. A monograph *The Mendicant Houses of Medieval London, 1221-1539*, Vita regularis – Abhandlungen, vol. 21, appeared in 2004.

Emilia Jamroziak, is currently lecturing at the School of History of the University of Leeds. Her current research concentrates on development and change of social and economic networks in medieval Britain and on the interactions between religious houses, particularly Cistercian, and the laity in the High Middle Ages in Northern England Scotland and Pomerania. Published a number of articles on the social and economic history of Rievaulx Abbey, patrons and benefactors of Polish monasteries in the twelfth century and most recently a monograph *Rievaulx Abbey and its Social Context, 1132-1300 Memory, Locality, and Networks*, Medieval Church Studies, vol. 8 (Turnhout: Brepols, in press).

Sheila Sweetinburgh gained her PhD in History at the University of Kent in 1999, where she now teaches as a sessional lecturer. She also works as a freelance documentary researcher and has been involved in numerous projects for Canterbury Archaeological Trust. Her research interests primarily relate to late medieval urban society and she has worked extensively on charity and poverty in the Middle Ages. Her recent publications include *The Role of the Hospital in Medieval England* (Dublin: Four Courts, 2004), and 'Clothing the Naked in Late Medieval East Kent', in: C.T. Richardson (ed.), *Clothing Culture, 1300-1600* (Ashgate, 2004).

Karen Stöber (MA, MPhil (Glasgow), PhD (Southampton)) is a lecturer in Medieval History at the University of Wales, Aberystwyth. Her research focuses on late medieval English and Welsh monasteries and issues of lay patronage of religious houses. She is currently working on a project which is looking at the patrons of monasteries and nunneries in late medieval Ireland. End 2006, her book *Late Medieval Monasteries and their Patrons: England and Wales, c. 1300-1540*, will be published by Boydell & Brewer.

Koen Goudriaan (°1950) studied Classical languages at the Vrije Universiteit of Amsterdam. He gained his PhD in 1989 with a study titled *Over Classicisme* (About Classicism). His field of interest shifted to the Late Middle Ages, more particularly to the history of the town of Gouda, and more generally to the cultural and religious history of the county of Holland and of the Northern Low Countries. His special interest is the Modern Devotion. He now teaches Medieval History at the VU. Among many other publications, he co-edited and contributed to *Duizend jaar Gouda. Een stadsgeschiedenis* (Hilversum, 2002).

INDEX LIBRORUM MANU SCRIPTORUM

Aachen, Cathedral Treasury, s.n.: 82
Arras, Bibliothèque municipale
  Ms. 616: 83
Avesnes, Musée de la Société d'Archéologie et d'Art, s.n.: 83

Baltimore, Walters Art Gallery
  Ms. W. 759: 85
Brussels, Royal Library
  Ms. 9092: 87
  Ms. II 2570: 82

Cambridge, Fitzwilliam Museum
  Ms. 3-1954: 87, 101

Frankfurt, Museum für Kunsthandwerk, Ms. Linel. 11: 85, 100

Ghent, Arme Claren-Coletienen
  Ms. 8: 87

Liège, Bibliothèque de l'Université
  Ms. 26: 84
London, British Library
  Royal Ms. 2.A.XVIII: 85, 99

New York, Pierpont Morgan Library
  Ms. M. 333: 83
  Ms. M. 754: 85, 98

Paris, Bibliothèque nationale de Franse
  Ms. fr. 152: 85
  Ms. lat. 1: 81
  Ms. n.a. fr. 16251: 84, 97

Rouen, Bibliothèque municipale
  Ms. 3024: 86, 98

The Hague, Museum Meermanno-Westreenianum
  Ms. 10 B 23: 86
Trier, Stadtsbibliothek
  Cod. 24: 82

Valenciennes, Bibliothèque-Médiathèque municipale
  Ms. 169: p. 82
Vienna, Österreichische Nationalbibliothek
  Cod. 2549: 87
  Cod. S.n. 2619: 87

INDEX LOCORUM

Aachen: 108-110, 125
   Cathedral: 82
Agrigento
   Nicholas, Cistercian monastery of Saint -: 153
Alba: 105, 106, 110
Alkmaar: 24
   Lawrence, Church of Saint - (= Great Church): 42
   Paul, Convent of Saint -: 9
   Town Hall: 6
Amsterdam
   Carthusians, Monastery of the -: 13, 22
   Old Church ('Oude Kerk'): 6, 30
      Iron Chapel ('IJzeren Kapel'): 6, 30
      'Librije' Chapel: 30
   Regulars, Monastery of the -: 13
   Town Hall: 30
Antwerp: 3, 12, 161
   Beguinage: 16, 20
   Carthusians, Monastery of the -: 15, 17, 18, 20
      Catherine, Chapel of Saint -: 20
      Church: 20
   Michael, Abbey of Saint -: 23
   Our Lady, Church/Cathedral of -: 4, 5, 8
   Ternonnen, Monastery of -: 16, 17, 20
   Willibrord, Church of Saint -: 17, 20, 22
Appingedam: 42
Arnhem
   Church, Main -: 40
      Town Council, Chapel of the -: 40
Arras: 49-52, 54, 57, 98
   Vaast, Cathedral of Saint -: 13
   Vaast, Monastery of Saint -: 13

Ath
   Julian, Church of Saint -: 4
Audenarde (Oudenaarde): 13, 55-57, 59-63
   Franciscans, Monastery of the -: 59
   Leper house: 15
   Sion, Monastery of -: 16
Augsburg: 112-114
   Cathedral: 113
   Cross, Holy -: 113
   Episcopal Palace: 113
   Gall, Saint -: 113
   George, Saint -: 113
   Jacob, Saint -: 113
   John, Saint -: 113
   Maurice, Chapter of Saint -: 112, 113
   Peter, Saint -: 113
   Stephen, Saint -: 113
   Ulric and Afra, Monastery of SS -: 112, 113

Bamberg: 114
   Cathedral: 112
Bangor: 142
Basle (Basel): 121-125, 224
   Carthusians, Monastery of the -: 25
   Elizabeth, Church of Saint -: 123
   Our Lady, Church/Monastery of -: 123
   Peter, Church of Saint -: 121
Bath: 142
Bavaria (Bayern): 107, 108, 115
Baynard's Castle (London): 154, 158
Beaulieu (Abbey of -): 154-161
Beaune
   Hôtel-Dieu: 72
Bedfordshire: 197
Bergen op Zoom
   Town Hall: 6

Bern: 120, 136
Berry: 145
Billingsgate (London): 139
Binche: 11
Bishopsgate (London)
  Austin Friars, Monastery of the -: 138
Bourbon: 76, 91
Bourne
  Peter and Paul, Augustinian abbey of SS -: 192
Bowre Hall (Essex): 160
Boxtel: 23
Brabant: VII, 3, 7, 14, 19, 52
Breda
  Collegiate Church: 6
  Great Church: 4
  Leper house: 21
Bremen: 122
Bristol: 165, 171, 178
  Augustine, Augustinian abbey of Saint -: 197, 201-204, 206, 207
  Cathedral: 201-203
  Berkeley Chapel: 202
Britain: 153, 161, 199
Bruges (Brugge): 50, 52-63, 66-69, 71, 80, 89, 100, 161
  Annuntiates, Monastery of the -: 16, 21
  Basil, Church of Saint -: 77
  Lawrence, Chapel of Saint -: 77
  Carthusians, Monastery of the -: 16, 21
  Catherine, Church of Saint -: 21
  Churches, Parish -: 56, 57
  Donatian, Church/Chapter of Saint -: VII, 56, 57, 59-61, 63, 66, 68, 69, 72
  Peter and Paul, Altar of SS -: 72
  Franciscans, Monastery of the -: 60
  James, Church of Saint -: 76
    Maurus and Giles, Altar of SS -: 76
  Mary Magdalen, Leper house of Saint -: 21
  Mendicant Orders, Monasteries of the -: 56, 58
  Church: 56
  Monasteries in the vicinity of Bruges: 58, 59
  Monasteries in town: 58
  Our Lady, Church of -: 61
  Saviour, Church of Saint -: 61
  Seminary, Major -: X
  Town Hall: 60, 61
  Walburga, Church of Saint -: 58
Brunswick (Braunschweig): 122, 128
Brussels (Brussel / Bruxelles): 4-12, 82, 87, 90-96, 101
  Friars of the 'Wolfsgracht', Monastery of the -: 11
  Giles, Church of Saint -: 11
  John, Hospital of Saint -: 11
  Molenbeek, Church of -: 11
  Nicholas, Church of Saint -: 4-6
  Obbrussel, Church of -: 11
  Peter, Hospital of Saint -: 11
  Rich Clares, Monastery of the -: 11, 12
Buckingham: 160
Burgundy: X, 12-14, 18, 19, 23, 25, 33, 49, 66, 69, 80, 87, 145, 214, 221, 222
Bushmead
  Augustinian priory: 197

Cadzand: 50, 55
Caldwell
  Augustinian priory: 197
Cambrai: 50, 51
Cambridge: 87, 101
Cambridgeshire: 189
Canterbury: 147, 170, 173
  Cathedral: 180
    Thomas Becket, Shrine of Saint -: 184, 185
  Christchurch Priory: 174
Chartres: 223
  Cathedral: 211
Cheapside (London): 138
Chieri
  George, Church of Saint -: 75
Chigwell: 150
Christchurch
  Priory: 196

Salisbury Chantry: 196
Cinque Ports (*see also* Hythe, New Romney, Sandwich, Dover, Hastings): 165, 166, 170-172, 177, 179, 186, 187, 212, 214, 215, 221, 222
Clairvaux: 210
Clarence: 199
Cluny: 192, 193
Cologne: 109, 121, 128
    Carmelites, Monastery of the -: 136
    Columba, Church of Saint -: 79
    Mendicants, Monasteries of the -: 135
Cornwall: 178, 196
Courtrai (Kortrijk): 221
    Groeninghe Abbey: 17, 21
    Leper house: 21
        Church: 21
    Martin, Church of Saint -: 4-6, 9
    Our Lady, Church of -: 24
Coventry: 165
Cranborne
    Benedictine abbey: 198
Crépy: 51
Cripplegate (London): 144

Damme: 50, 56, 57, 59
Delfland: 7, 33
Delft: 7
    Hippolyte, Church of Saint -: 6
    Old Church: 33, 41, 42
Derby: 157
Deventer: 7, 9, 37, 38, 210
    Lebuinus, Church of Saint -: 40
        Town Council, Chapel of the -: 40
Devon: 136, 178, 195
Dinant: 18
    Franciscans, Monastery of the -: 23
    Our Lady, Church of -: 23
Dordrecht: 37
    Church, Main -: 42, 44
    Franciscans, Monastery of the -: 7
    Town Hall: 7
Dorset: 196, 198

Dortmund: 108, 109
Douai
    Notre Dame des Près, Abbey of -: 13, 17
Dover: 165, 166, 170-187
    Hospitals: 182
    James, Church of Saint -: 177, 179
    Peter, Church of Saint -: 170-173, 176
    Martin, Benedictine priory of Saint -: 172, 173, 176, 182
    Martin-le-Grand, Minster/church of Saint -: 171, 176, 177, 179-183
        Chapter House, Old -: 176
    Churchyard: 183
        Martin, Altar of Saint -: 179, 180, 182
    Mary, Church of Saint -: 180
Dowegate (London): 157
Drenthe: 32
Durham: 142

East Smithfield (London): 159, 160
    Plague cemetery and chapel: 154-156, 216 (*see also* London: Mary Graces, Cistercian abbey of Saint -)
Edam: 42
Edinburgh: 76
Ely (Priory of-): 189
Ename (Abbey of -): 13
England: 10, 13, 50, 52, 56, 136, 138, 139, 141, 145, 147, 153, 165, 179, 185, 189-191, 196, 197, 199, 202, 207, 213, 221
    Northern England: 138
    Southeastern England: 221
    Southern and Central England: 202
Essex: 139, 160
Exeter: 142
    Franciscans, Monastery of the -: 136

Faversham (Abbey of -): 139
Flanders (Vlaanderen): VII, X, XI, 3, 35, 47, 49-57, 61, 66, 69, 74, 214,

216, 217, 220, 222
Fleet Street (London): 138, 146
Florence (Firenze)
   Badia Fiesolana, Church of -: 74
      Michael, Chapel of Saint -: 74
   Giles, Church of Saint -: 76
   Mary 'Nuova', Hospital of Saint -: 76
Framlingham: 203
France: 1, 2, 6, 11, 13, 15, 17-19, 24, 49-52, 54, 56, 58, 66, 75, 76, 83, 86, 87, 145, 146, 150, 165, 180, 186
   Northern France: 1, 6
Frankfurt: 50, 100, 128
   Dominicans, Monastery of the -: 135
French Flanders (la Flandre française): 1
Friesland: 6, 16, 27
Furnes (Veurne): 55, 61-63, 67
   Walburga, Church of Saint -: 57, 63

Gavere: 49, 56
Gdansk: 73, 79, 80, 89
   Our Lady, Church of -: 74
      George, Chapel of the Guild of Saint -: 74
Geertruidenberg
   Carthusians, Monastery of the -: 13
Germany: 38, 40, 74, 103, 113, 135, 165, 213, 214, 216, 218, 221, 222, 225
Ghent (Gent): 3, 7-10, 13, 14, 16, 49, 50, 54-57, 66, 222
   Akkergem, Church of -: 55, 56
   Bavon, Abbey of Saint - (*see also*: Ghent: Bavon, Cathedral of Saint -): 22
   Bavon, Cathedral of Saint - (*see also*: Ghent: John, Church of Saint -): X, 22, 71, 74
   Carmelites, Monastery of the -: 8
   Christ, Church of the Holy -: 55, 56
   Franciscan Nuns, Monastery of the -: 21, 87

   Franciscans, Monastery of the -: 7, 8
   James, Church of Saint -: 55, 56, 60
   John, Church of Saint - (*see also*: Ghent: Bavon, Cathedral of Saint -): 5, 22, 55, 56, 60, 74
   Michael, Church of Saint -: 55, 56, 60
   Nicholas, Church of Saint -: 4, 5, 9, 55, 56, 60
   Peter, Abbey of Saint -: 9, 10, 55
   Pharaildis, Church of Saint -: 55, 56
   Spanish Castle: 22
   Town Hall: 54, 55, 60
Glamorgan
   Neath Abbey: 193
Gloucester: 142, 198-200
Gloucestershire: 196, 197, 202
Gorinchem: 4
Gouda
   John, Church of Saint -: 42
   Regulars, Monastery of the -: 13, 21
Grammont (Geraardsbergen): 55
   Benedictines, Monastery of the -: 58
Great Yarmouth: 177
Grenoble
   Chartreuse: 81
Groningen: 32
   Franciscans, Monastery of the -: 8
   Martin, Church of Saint -: 42
   Old Convent ('Olde Convent'): 10
   Tertiaries of Mary 'ten Hoorn', Convent of the -: 24
   Town Hall: 31
   Walburga, Church of Saint -: 27
   Winsum, Monastery of -: 24
Guelders (Gelderland): 2, 3, 6, 15, 18, 19, 22
Guisborough
   Priory: 196, 197

Haarlem: 4, 7-9, 31
   Bavon, Church of Saint -: 7, 31, 42, 45

Dominicans, Monastery of the -: 9
Gangulf, Hospice of Saint -: 9
Habsburg: X, 19, 69, 221
Hailes
   Cistercian abbey: 196
Hainaut: 97
Hampshire: 154, 189
Hastings: 165
Heilbronn: 128, 129
Helmond
   Regular Nuns, Monastery of the -: 20
Helmsley: 195
Hereford: 136, 142
Herefordshire: 140
Herentals
   Waltrude, Church of Saint -: 7
Hildesheim: 128, 129
Holborn (London)
   Dominicans, Monastery of the -: 137
Holbornstreet: 158
Holland: VII, 13, 35, 214
Hoorn
   Church, Main -: 42
   Great Church: 24
Hythe: 165, 166, 174, 187
   Leonard, Church of Saint -: 170, 172, 176, 180, 186
      Edmund, Chapel of Saint -: 176
      Our Lady, Chapel of -: 186
   Town Hall: 181

Ingelheim: 110
Ireland: 199
Italy: VII, 18, 19, 22, 75, 123, 153, 222

Jerusalem: 114, 118, 184
   Sepulchre, Church of the Holy -: 113

Kaisersberg: 119, 124, 125, 131
Kampen
   Augustinian Nuns, Monastery of the -: 12
   Catherine and Mary Magdalen, Hospital of SS -: 16, 20, 21
   Chapel: 21
   Michael, Monastery of Saint -: 12
   Nicholas, Church of Saint - (= 'Bovenkerk'): 39, 42
      Town Council, Chapel of the - (= Jerusalem Chapel): 39
   Town Hall: 39
      Chapel: 39
Kaprijke: 59, 62
Kennington: 154
Kent: 165, 166, 170, 174, 186, 215, 222
Kingswood
   Cistercian abbey: 202
Kirkham
   Augustinian priory: 195
Koevorden: 27
Koksijde
   The Dunes Abbey ('Ten Duinen'): X

Lambeth (London): 204
Lancaster: 158, 159
Lausanne: 120, 122
Leeuwarden:
   Beguinage: 16
   Franciscans, Monastery of the -: 16, 22
Leyden (Leiden): 33
   Peter, Church of Saint -: 7, 31, 38
   Town Hall: 7, 31
Liddell: 192
Liège: 15, 34
   Carthusians, Monastery of the -: 14
   Cathedral: 24, 25
   Franciscans, Monastery of the -: 24
   Lawrence, Abbey of Saint -: 3, 12, 13, 14, 22
Lier
   Carthusians, Monastery of the -: 16, 17
   Gummarus, Church of Saint -: 5, 7
Liessies (Abbey of -): 83
Lincoln: 139, 157
   Franciscans, Monastery of the -: 136

Lincolnshire: 140, 192
Lo
   Peter, Church of Saint -: 61
London: 137-165, 204
   All Hallows, Church/parish of -: 157, 162
   Austin Friars, Monastery of the -: 138, 148, 150, 202
      Church: 148, 150
   Bartholomew, Hospital of Saint -: 163
   Bartholomew, Priory of Saint -: 139
   Botholph, Church/parish of Saint -: 154, 156, 159, 163
   Carmelites, Monastery of the - (= White Friars): 138, 143, 144, 146-150
      Chapter House: 144, 146
      Church: 138, 144, 146, 150
   Carthusians, Monastery of the - (*see* London: Charter House)
   Charter House: 155
   Dominicans, Monastery of the - (= Black Friars): 137, 139-151
      'Chamber of the Council': 141
      Chapter house: 141, 143,
      Church: 139, 143, 144, 149
      'Parliament Chamber': 141
   Franciscan Nuns, Monastery of the -: 138, 148, 159
   Franciscans, Monastery of the - (= Grey Friars): 138, 147-150
      Chapter house: 147
      Church: 147, 149, 150
   Friars of the Cross, Monastery of the -: 138, 148
   Friars of the Penance of Jesus Christ, Monastery of the -: 149
   Church: 149
   Martin-le-Grand, Priory of Saint -: 139, 144
   Mary, Hospital of Saint -: 163
   Mary Graces, Cistercian abbey of Saint -: 153-164, 216, 221
   Anne, Chapel of Saint -: 158, 160
   Our Lady, Chapel of -: 159, 160
   Trinity, Chapel of the Holy -: 157
   Hospital: 163
   Mendicants, Monasteries/churches of the -: 137, 221
   Michael, Church/parish of Saint -: 158
   Paul, Cathedral of Saint -: 137, 138, 140
   Peter *ad Vincula*, Chapel of Saint -: 196
   Thomas, Hospital of Saint -: 163
   Trinity, Augustinian priory of the Holy -: 139, 155, 159
Louvain (Leuven): 8, 93
   Michael, Church of Saint -: 4, 5
   Peter, Church of Saint -: 4, 5, 7, 79, 95
   Peter, Altar of Saint -: 79
   Terbank, Monastery of -: 24
   Town Hall: 7
Low Countries: VII, VIII, XI, XII, 1-3, 8, 10, 18, 19, 21, 27, 28, 32, 34, 35, 38-40, 44, 50, 71, 73, 77, 78, 80, 87, 88, 180, 220-223, 225
   Northern Low Countries: VIII, 27, 28, 32, 222
   Southern Low Countries: VIII, 71, 77, 78, 80, 87, 88, 222
Lubeck (Lübeck): 223
   Brigittines (of Marienword), Monastery of the -: 122
   Our Lady, Church of -: 122
   Town Council, Chapel of the -: 122
   Town Hall: 122
Ludgate (London): 139, 141, 143

Maastricht
   Our Lady, Church of -: 7, 31, 34, 44
   Town Hall: 31
Mâcon
   Dominicans, Monastery of the -: 135
Madrid: 51, 75, 78
Magdeburg: 109
Mainz: 110
Maximilian Street (Augsburg): 112
Mechelen: 3, 4

Beguinage: 17, 20
Bethany, Monastery of - : 20
Blijdenberg, Monastery of -: 20, 21
Franciscans, Monastery of the -: 5
Hanswijk, Monastery of -: 20
Lambert, Chapel of Saint -: 20
Muizen, Monastery of -: 20
Nekkerspoel, Church of -: 20
Nicholas, Chapel of Saint -: 20
Our Lady, Church of -: 5
Rumold, Church/Cathedral of Saint -: 5, 8
Terzieken, Monastery of -: 20
Thabor, Monastery of -: 16, 20
Mende: 212
Merseburg: 107, 110
Middelburg: 78
Milan (Milano): 51
Molenbeek: 51
Monmouthshire: 193
Montil-lez-Tours: 50, 54
Montreuil-sur-Mer
Benedictine abbey: 6
Mordon: 157
Moulins
Cathedral: 76, 91
Munster (Münster): 67

Navarre: 147
Netherlands (+ 'Dutch'): 1, 2, 19, 20, 28, 31, 78
Neuenburg: 119
Newgate (London): 137, 144
Franciscans, Monastery of the -: 138
New Romney: 165, 166, 187
Nicholas, Church of Saint -: 170, 172, 174-178
Stephen, Chapel of Saint -: 176
Stuppeny Tomb: 174, 176
Nice: 51
Nieuport (Nieuwpoort): 61, 62
Nijmegen: 32
Church, Main: 29, 30, 38, 44
Sepulchre, Chapel of the Holy -: 30
Franciscans, Monastery of the

Observant -: 18
Town Hall: 29
Nivelles: 7
Norfolk: 147, 193, 197, 203-205, 207
Norg
Church, Main -: 32
Normandy: 189, 190
Northamphire: 189
Northampton: 136, 150
Northumberland: 142
Norwich: 192, 193, 204

Ogbourne (Priory of -): 139
Orléans: 145
Aignan, Church of Saint -: 17
Orvieto: 123
Oxford: 142, 161, 195
Dominicans, Monastery of the -: 136

Paderborn: 114
Cathedral: 112
Episcopal Palace: 112
Padua (Padova): 122
Palermo
Spirit, Cistercian monastery of the Holy -: 153
Trinity, Cistercian monastery of the Holy -: 153
Paris
Denis, Abbey of Saint -: 54
Pembroke: 157
Périgord: 139
Péronne: 49, 55
Perugia: 122
Peterborough (Abbey of -): 189

Quedlinburg: 107, 115
Queenwhite (London): 158

Ramsey (Abbey of -): 138
Reggio
Franciscans, Monastery of the -: 135
Rhineland (Rheinland , Germany): 161
Lower Rhineland: 161
Rhineland (Rijnland - Nether-

lands): 33
Riggisberg: 75, 90
Roermond
   Franciscan Tertiaries, Monastery of the -: 16
Rome (Roma): 27, 105, 112-114, 153, 211
   Peter, Basilica of Saint -: 112
   Sebastian 'ad Catacumbas', Cistercian monastery of Saint -: 153
   Vincent and Anastasius 'alle Tre Fontane', Cistercian monastery of the SS -: 153
Rotherhithe: 154
Rotterdam
   Lawrence, Church of Saint -: 7, 8, 31
Roulers (Roeselare): 62

Saint Martin-le-Grand (London): 144
Saint-Omer: 98
   Bertin, Abbey of Saint -: 83
Saint-Trond (Sint-Truiden)
   Trudo, Abbey of Saint -: 84
Salisbury: 139, 140, 142, 196
Saltwood: 172
Sandwich: 165, 166, 170, 177, 180-187
   Clement, Church of Saint -: 171, 173, 174, 176, 180, 181, 185, 186
   George, Chancel of Saint - Clement: 181
   Hospital: 180, 184
   Mary, Church of Saint -: 174
   Peter, Church of Saint -: 171, 176, 180, 181, 182
Savoy (Savoye): 75, 87
Schiedam: 7
Schieland: 33
Senlis: 50, 57, 62, 67
Sezze: 123
Sheen: 154
Shepway: 177, 179
s'-Hertogenbosch
   Gulielmites, Monastery of the -: 14
   John, Church of Saint -: 7, 31, 40

Our Lady, Chapel of -: 31
   Town Hall: 7
Shropshire: 140
Sicily (Sicilia): 153
Siena: 133, 134
Sluis: 50
Somerset: 150
Southampton: 178
Spain: 11, 18-21
Speyer: 114
Staining (London)
   All Hallows, Parish/church of -: 157, 162
Stamford
   Dominicans, Monastery of the -: 136
Strasburg (Strasbourg)
   Monastery: 119, 125, 127, 130, 131
   Our Lady, Church of -: 124, 126, 128, 132, 223
   Peter, Chapter of Young Saint -: 125
   Town Hall: 132
Sudeley: 160
Suffolk: 139, 204
Surrey: 154
Sussex: 165

Temple (London): 139
Termonde (Dendermonde): 60-63
   Church, Collegiate -: 63
Tewkesbury
   Mary, Benedictine abbey of Saint -: 197-207
   Church: 199, 200, 201
   Founder's Chapel: 200
   Margaret, Chapel of Saint -: 201
   Trinity Chapel: 200
   Warwick Chapel: 200
Thetford
   Cluniac priory: 192-194, 197, 201-207
   Church: 203-206
Thielt (Tielt): 53, 55, 58, 60, 61
   Peter, Church of Saint -: 61
Tiel: 42
Tienen

Danenbroek, Monastery of -: 22
Germanus, Church of Saint -: 5
Tintern (Abbey of -): 193
Tongeren
   Our Lady, Church of -: 8
Torre
   Premonstratensian abbey: 195
Tournai: 90, 96
Tours (Abbey of -): 52, 81, 176
Tower Hill (London): 156, 159
Trente: 50

Utrecht: 4, 27, 42
   'Buurkerk': 5, 7, 8, 39
      Library: 7
      Urban Council, Chapel of the -: 39
   Carmelites, Monastery of the -: 22
   Cathedral: 210
   Catherine, Monastery of Saint -: 22
   Mary in Bethlehem, Convent of Saint -: 14
   Men's monasteries: 13
   Nicholas, Church of Saint -: 22
   Oudwijk, Monastery of -: 18
   Vredenburg Castle: 22
   Vredendaal, Monastery of -: 22
   'Vrouwenklooster': 18
   Women's monasteries: 13

Valence: 157
Valenciennes
   Amand, Abbey of Saint -: 82
Venlo: 19
Vervins: 67
Vienna (Wien): 77, 128
Vollenhove: 35

Wales: 190, 191, 199
Waltham (Abbey of -): 139
Warenne: 199
Warwick: 142, 199
Weinsberg: 121
Wervicq: 57
West Country: 178

Westminster (near London): 137-141, 149
   Stephen, Chapter of secular canons of Saint -: 156
Westrozebeke: 24
West Smithfield (London)
   Charter House (see London: Charter House):
   Plague cemetery: 155
Wetz
   Beguinage: 14
Wiltshire: 139
Winchester: 136, 142, 189
   Carmelites, Monastery of the -: 136
   Swithun, Priory of Saint -: 189
Windsor
   George, Chapel of Saint -: 156
Worcester: 142
Wymondham
   Benedictine priory/abbey: 193

York: 87, 165, 192
   Trinity, Benedictine priory of the Holy -: 192
Yorkshire: 195, 196
Ypres (Ieper): 57, 60, 67
   Dominicans, Monastery of the -: 59
   Franciscans, Monastery of the -: 10
   Martin, Church of Saint -: X
   Town Hall: 62

Zeeland: VII, 35, 214
Zoutleeuw
   Begards: 15
   Beguinage: 15, 20
   Scholars, Monastery of the -: 15, 20
Zutphen: 38
   Town Hall: 30
   Walburga, Church of Saint -: 30, 42, 43
Zwin: 74
Zwolle
   Windesheim, Monastery of -: 12, 15, 16

INDEX NOMINUM*

Aachen, Wilhelm von -: 125
Adalbert of Magdeburg: 109
Agard, Andrew: 193
Alard (Saint): 83
Alberti, Leon Battista: 19
Albert of Saxony (Duke of Saxony): 22
ALIOTH, Martin: 131
Alvarez de Toledo, Fernando (Duke of Alva): 20
Amice (Great-granddaughter of Robert FitzHamon): 198
Ann (Sister of Thomas Montgomery: 160
Anne de France (Wife of Pierre II of Bourbon): 76
ARNADE, Peter: 222
Aston, Matilda: 158
Assele, Joos van -: 57
Augustine of Hippo: 83
AUTENBOER, Eugeen VAN -: 2

Bailluwel: 79
Bardi (Family): 141
Bartone, William: 149
Baudolf, Jan: 86
Bausele, Raese van -: 79
Beaufort, Edmund (Duke of Somerset): 150
Beaujeu, Margaret of -: 85, 98
Belknap, William: 160
Benecke, Paul: 74
Benedict XII (Pope): 192
BENTON, John F.: 81
Benzo of Alba (Bishop of Alba): 105, 106, 111

Berkeley (Family; *see* FitzHarding, Robert): 202-204
Berkeley, James (Lord Berkeley): 202
Berkeley, Maurice (Lord Berkeley): 202
Berkeley, Thomas († 1243; Lord Berkeley): 202
Berkeley, Thomas († 1321; Lord Berkeley): 202
Berkeley, Thomas (16th C.; Lord Berkeley): 202
Bernard of Clairvaux (Saint): 210
Bernardine of Siena (Saint): 133, 134
Bigod (family): 204
Bigod, John (Brother of Roger Bigod): 193
Bigod, Roger (Earl Marshal; Earl of Norfolk): 193, 203
Bladelin, Pieter: 78, 94
Blanche of Navarre (Queen of Navarre): 147
Bland, Thomas: 181
Boniface VIII (Pope): 192, 193
BOOCKMANN, Hartmut: 223
Boraing, Maria de -: 85
Borluut, Elisabeth: 71, 74, 75
Bouts, Dirk: 78, 79, 93, 95
Brant, Sebastian: 132
Brewers (Family): 195
Bromflet, Thomas (Custodian of the Royal Wardrobe): 145
BROWN, Andrew: 61
Bruno of Augsburg (Bishop of Augsburg): 112
BUREN, Truus VAN -: 72
Burghersh (Family): 199

---

* All persons are alphabetically ordered by surname, except for rulers and some important lords and ecclesiastics (e.g. 'Philip the Good'), some saints (e.g. 'John Chrysostom') or persons who are specified by a toponyme (e.g. 'Galbert of Bruges'); capitals were used to indicate the surnames of modern authors.

Burton, Nicholas (Mayor of Hythe): 181, 185

Campin, Robert: 75, 80, 88, 90
Cassianus, Johannes: 82, 83
Cavendish, Andrew: 160
CERTEAU, Michel DE -: 219
Champney, Adam: 165
Charlemagne (Emperor of the Frankish Empire): 82
Charles V (Emperor of the Holy Roman Empire):17, 19, 22, 50, 51
Charles V (King of France): 86
Charles VIII (King of France): 50
Charles of Guelders (Duke of Guelders): 19
Charles the Bald (German Emperor): 81, 82
Charles the Bold (Duke of Burgundy): 22-25, 49, 66, 79, 80, 87, 222
Charles the Good (Count of Flanders): VII
Charles, Thomas: 160
Charlotte of Savoy (Queen of France): 87
CHARTIER, Roger: 219
Chigwell, Hamo de -: 150
Chynnore, Thomas: 158
Clare, de - (Family): 193, 198-204
Clare, Eleanor de -: 199-201
Clare, Gilbert de -: 199, 201
Clare, Richard de - (Earl of Gloucester): 198
Clarencieux, Thomas Benolt: 160
Constantine (Roman Emperor): 210
Corey, John: 154
CROFT, Justin: 187
Cromwell, Thomas (English statesman): 148
Cros, Johanna: 157

David, Gerard: 76, 91
DAVIES, John G.: 224
DEKEYZER, Brigitte: 214, 216
Despenser (Family): 198-204
Despenser, Edward (Lord Despenser): 199, 200
Despenser, Hugh [II] (Son of Hugh [I] Despenser and Eleanor de Clare): 199-201
Despenser, Hugh [I] - the Younger: 199, 200
Despenser, Hugh III (Lord Despenser): 200
Despenser, Richard (Lord Despenser): 199
DOUGLAS, Mary: 211
Durand, William: 212, 225

Edmund (Earl of Lancaster): 147, 159
Edward (Duke of Buckingham): 160
Edward I (King of England): 136, 147, 154, 165
Edward II (King of England): 136, 140, 145, 150
Edward III (King of England): 145, 154-156, 162, 164, 216
Edward IV (King of England): 145, 160
Egbert (Archbishop of Trier): 82
Egbert (Prefect of the bishop of Utrecht in Groningen): 27
Eleanor (Daughter of Lewes John): 160
Eleanor (Wife of Thomas Lord Berkeley, 16th C.): 202
ELIADE, Mircea: 117
Elisabeth (Wife of Richard or John Walden): 160
Elizabeth (Daughter of Edward, Duke of Buckingham): 160
Elizabeth I (Queen of England): 170
Engelhusen, Theoderich: 132
Espec, Walter: 195
EVEN, Edward VAN -: 79
Eyck, van - (Brothers): 71
Eyck, Jan van -: 71, 72, 74, 85, 86

Fitz, Robert:157
FitzHamon, Robert (Lord of Tewkesbury): 198, 200
FitzHarding, Robert (Lord Berkeley): 201, 202
Francis I (King of France): 50, 51
Francis of Cleve: 23
Frederick Barbarossa (German Emperor): 106

Galbert of Bruges: VII
Geiler von Kaysersberg: 119, 124-126, 131, 132
Ghijs, Roelant: 60
Godevaerte: 9
Goes, Hugo van der -: 76
Goldsmith, William: 177
Gregory IX (Pope): 220
Gregory of Nazianze: 82
Gresham, Richard (Mayor of London): 162, 163
Grote, Geert: 210
Guido (Prior of the Chartreuse of Grenoble): 81

Hatbert (Bishop of Utrecht): 27
HAYES, Dawn Mary: 211, 223, 224
Haynin, Jean de -: 18
Hayward, Walter: 160
Henry II (= Henry of Bavaria) (German King): 107, 108, 112, 115
Henry III (King of England): 139, 154
Henry IV (German King): 105, 111, 115
Henry IV (King of England): 142, 145, 157, 158
Henry VIII (King of England): 141, 145, 146, 163, 196, 205, 213
Henry of Vianden (Bishop of Utrecht): 18
Heribertus: 82
HERZOG, E: 113
Holy Cross, William of - (Abbot of Saint Mary Graces, London): 156
Howard (Family): 203-206
Howard, Thomas (Duke of Norfolk): 205

Isabel (Countess of Warwick and Warenne, Baroness of Burghersh): 199
Isabel (Duchess of Clarence): 199
Isabel (Mother of King Edward III): 156
Ixworth, William (Prior of Thetford Priory): 204, 205

Jacqueline of Bavaria (Countess of Holland, Zeeland and Hainaut): 24
JAMROZIAK, Emilia: 214, 216, 221
Jerome, saint: 84
Joan (Wife of Thomas Lord Berkeley, † 1243): 202
Joan (Wife of Thomas Lord Berkeley, † 1321): 202
Johannes: 78
John I (King of England): 154
John (Duke of Lancaster): 158
John Chrysostom (Saint): 133
John the Fearless (Duke of Burgundy): 145
John, Lewes/Louis: 160, 161
Juan, Don - (Military Commander): 11, 12, 20, 21

KANTOROWICZ, Ernst: 103
KELLER, Hagen: 109
Kemel, Emerich: 131
Keraldus: 82
Knovill, Gilbert de - (Sheriff of Devon): 136
KOCH, Petra: 123
KUYS, Jan: 214

Lacy, Henry de - (Earl of Lincoln): 139
Landi, Neroccio di Bartolomeo -: 133
Langton, John (Abbot of Saint Mary Graces, London): 161
Latimer, William (Lord): 196, 197
Laufen, Adelheid von - (= Adelheid Waltenheim): 123, 124
LEEUWEN, Jacqueline VAN -: 187, 214, 216, 218, 220
LEFEBVRE, Henri: 167-169, 177, 181, 183, 186, 213
Lincoln, William de -: 157
Lokeren, Boudeyn van -: 9
Louis XI (King of France): 49, 87, 145
Louis of Bourbon (Prince-Bishop of Liège): 12
Loveyn, Nicholas (Lord of East Smithfield, London): 160

MAARTENS, Maximiliaan: 72

MALAY, Jessica: 187
Margaret (Countess of Salisbury): 196
Margaret of York (Duchess of Burgundy): 87
Marie (Madame -): 84, 97
MARTENS, Didier: 77
Mary (Countess of Derby, wife of Henry IV): 157, 158
Mary of Burgundy (Duchess of Burgundy): 13, 49
Mary of Hungary (Regent of the Low Countries): 11
Masmines, Robert de -: 80, 96
Matilda (Queen of England): 159
Maximilian of Austria (Emperor of the Holy Roman Empire): 49, 50, 61, 68
Medici (Family): 76, 80
Meersch, Elisabeth van der -: 77
Meinwerk (Bishop of Paderborn): 112
Memling, Hans: 73, 75, 76, 79, 80, 89
Merode, Bernard of - (Military governor): 20
Meulere, Pieter: 57
Montacute, Elizabeth: 200
Montgomery, John (Brother of Thomas Montgomery): 160
Montgomery, Thomas (Councillor of Richard III): 159-161
Montgomery, Thomas (Uncle of Thomas Montgomery): 160
Mordon, Simon de -: 157
More, Henry (Abbot of Saint Mary Graces, London): 161
More, Thomas (Chancellor of England): 141
Moreel, Willem: 76
Moulins (Master of -): 76, 91
Mowbray (Family): 204
Musgrove, John of - (Baron): 139

Norman, John: 158
Northampton, John of -: 150
Noyelles, Pontus de - (Military governor): 20

Odbert (Abbot of Saint Bertin's abbey): 83, 84
OESTERLE, Jenny Rahel: 214, 215

OEXLE, Otto: 72
Oldcastle, John: 140
Otto I (German Emperor): 108, 109
Otto III (German Emperor): 82, 107, 108
Oudenbosch, Adrian of -: 12

Paele, Joris van der -: 71, 72
Paschal (Abbot of Saint Mary Graces, London): 162
Peruzzi (Family): 141
Peter the Chanter: 210
Philip the Bold (Duke of Burgundy): 49, 87, 101
Philip the Fair (Duke of Burgundy): 49, 50
Philip the Good (Duke of Burgundy): 13, 23, 33, 87
Pierre II of Bourbon: 76
Pietro, Sano di -: 133
Pole, Reginald (Cardinal): 196
Portinari, Tommaso: 76, 80
Pourbus, Peter: X
Prehest/Pest, Richard (Abbot of Saint Mary Graces, London): 161
Propst, Stoffel: 119
Pypot, Robert: 145

Ratclyff, George (Brother of the Earl of Essex): 160
Refham, Richer de (Mayor of London): 140
Ricart: 171
Richard (Earl of Cornwall): 196
Richard III (King of England): 157, 159
RICHARDSON, Catherine: 187
Roelofs, Stas: 79
RÖHRKASTEN, Jens: 212, 214, 221
Rolin (Chancellor): 72
Rollysley, Elizabeth: 158
Ros, de - (Family): 195
Rose (Wife of Andrew Cavendish): 160
Rossum, Maarten van - (Military commander): 3, 16, 17, 19, 20, 23
Rothyng, Richard: 157
Roussillon, Girart de -: 87

Rowley, Elizabeth: 160
Rufus, William: 198

Saint Pol, Marie de - (Countess of Pembroke): 157
Salisbury (Family):196
Sandwich, de - (Family): 80, 184
Scheerre, Herman: 99
Schott, Peter: 125, 126, 131
Schott, Peter (sr.): 131
Scorel, John: X
SCRIBNER, Robert: 216-218
Seitenmacherin, Anna: 121, 122
Seitenmachter, Klaus: 122
Shirbourne, John: 157
SIGNORI, Gabriela: 212, 214, 216, 218, 221, 223
Simon (Abbot of the Abbey of SS Peter and Paul, Bourne): 192
Sixtus IV (Pope): 18
SMET, Marjan DE -: 214, 220
Smyth, John: 201
SOJA, Edward: 167
Somersete, Robert: 157
Spendlowe, Richardo: 204
Sperrer, Hans (a.k.a. Brüglinger): 123
Spice, Alice (Daughter of Thomas Montgomery): 160
Spinelli: 148
SPONSLER, Claire: 224
Stafford, Jane (Daughter of the Duke of Buckingham): 160
STÖBER, Karen: 214, 216
Stoep, Reyner: 79
STÜDELI, Bernhard: 135
Stuppeny, Clement (Great-grandson of Richard Stuppeny): 175
Stuppeny, Richard: 174, 175
Sudeley (Uncle of Thomas Montgomery): 160
SWEETINBURGH, Sheila: 213-215, 218, 220-222
Swijcz Knopffen, Hann,: 119
Sybil (Wife of Robert FitzHamon): 198

Tanangli, Caterina di Francesco -: 74
Tani, Angelo di Jacopo - : 74, 80
Thietmar of Merseburg: 107, 110
Thomas (Uncle of Thomas Montgomery): 160
Tiryngton, John de -: 156
TRIO, Paul: 209
Trompes, Jan de -: 77

Valence, Aymer de -: 157
Varenacker: 79
Vaudetar, Jean de -: 86
Vaux, Pierre de -: 87
Vere, John de - (Earl of Oxford): 195
Vijd, Joos: 71, 74, 75
Villa, Oberto de -: 75
Vivianus (Count, Abbot of Tours): 81

Wake, Thomas (Lord of Liddell): 192
Walden, Richard or John: 160
Waltenheim, Adelheid (*see* Laufen, Adelheid von -): 125
Wedricus (Abbot of Liessies Abbey): 83, 84
Wenceslas of Brabant (Duke of Brabant): 24
Weyden, Rogier van der -: 72, 75, 77-80, 90, 92, 94-96
Widukind of Corvey: 109
William II the Rich (Duke of Guelders): 19
William of Orange, the Taciturn (Prince of Orange): 11, 12, 22
Wolsey (Cardinal): 141, 145
Wycliff, John: 213
Wynghe, Laureyse van -: 79

Yerdelee, Henry de -: 157

Zouche, William La -: 199
Zweder of Culemborg (Bishop of Utrecht): 13

INDEX OPERUM

Adalbert of Magdeburg
   Adalberti Conituatio Reginonis: 109
Alberti, Leon Battista
   De re aedificatoria: 19
Alde Caert (charter 1284): 34
Augustine
   Confessiones: 83

Beaupré Antiphonary: 85
Benzo of Alba
   Ad Heinricum IV imperatorem libri VII: 105, 106, 111
Bible: 62, 83, 117, 126, 129, 133, 171, 175, 209-211, 224
   Epistle of Paul to the Ephesians: 210
   Epistle of Paul to the Philippians: 133
   Epistle of Paul to the Galatians: 133
   First epistle of Paul to the Korinthians: 133, 210
   Genesis: 209
   Gospels: 83, 117, 126, 129, 133, 210, 224
   Gospel of Saint John: 117, 210
   Gospel of Saint Luke: 83, 117
   Gospel of Saint Matthew: 117, 126, 129, 133, 210, 224
   New Testament: 211
   Old Testament: 211
Bible historiale: 85, 86
Book of founders of Tewkesbury Abbey: 198, 207
Bouts, Dirk
   Ecce Agnus Dei (painting; Munich): 78, 93
   Last Supper (painting; Louvain): 79, 95
Brant, Sebastian
   Das Narrenschif: 132

Buch Weinsberg: 121

Campin, Robert
   Mérode Triptych (painting; New York): 75, 90
   Portrait of Robert de Masmines (painting; Berlin - copy): 80
Campin, Robert ?
   Werl Panels (painting; Madrid): 75
Cassianus, Johannes
   Collationes Patrum: 82
Charles the Bold, First Bible of - (= *Count Vivianus Bible*): 81
Chrysostom, John
   73rd Homily on the Gospel of Matthew: 133
Cinque Ports Custumals: 165, 166, 171, 176, 187
   Dover Custumal: 166
   Hythe Custumal: 166
   New Romney Custumal: 166, 176
   Sandwich Custumal: 165, 166, 171
Codex Egberti: 82

David, Gerard
   The Baptism of Christ (painting; Bruges): 76, 91
Durand, William
   Rationale divinorum officiorum: 212, 225

Eyck (Brothers Van -)
   Adoration of the Lamb (= *Ghent Altarpiece*) (painting; Ghent): 71, 74
Eyck, Jan van -
   Madonna with Canon Van der Paele (painting; Bruges): 71

Geiler von Kaysersberg
   21 Artikeln: 119, 124, 126, 131

Goes, Hugo van der -
 Bonkil Altarpiece (painting; Edinburgh): 76
 Portinari Triptych (painting; Florence): 76

Hiëronymus
 De virginitate beate Marie: 84
 Hours of Margaret of Beaujeu: 85
 Hours of Philip the Bold: 87, 101

Landi, Neroccio di Bartolomeo - (painting): 133
(Le) livre d'images de Madame Marie: 84, 97
Liessies Abbey, Gospels of -: 83

Memling, Hans
 Moreel Triptych (painting; Bruges): 76
 Triptych of the Last Judgement (painting; Gdansk): 73, 75, 79, 89
Moulin, Master of -
 Triptych of the Dukes of Bourbon (painting; Moulins): 75, 76, 91

Odbert Gospels: 83
Otto III, Second Gospels of -: 82

Pietro, Sano di-
 Sermon of Saint Bernardine (painting; Siena): 133

Quedam Narracio de Groninghe, de Thrente, de Covordia et de diversis aliis sub diversis episcopis Traiectensibus: 27

Ricart
 Kalendar: 171
(Le) Roman de Girart de Roussillon: 87

Schott, Peter
 The Works of Peter Schott: 125
Schott, Peter
 Letter to Emerich Kemel: 131
Smyth, John – of Nibley
 The Berkeley Manuscripts: 201

Thetford Register: 203-205, 207
Thietmar of Merseburg-
 Chronicon Thietmari Merseburgensis: 107, 110
(Le) Traité sur l'oraison dominicale: 87

Vaux, Pierre de -
 (La) *Vie de Sainte Colette*: 87
 (La) Vie de Saint-Adrien: 87
Vivianus Bible: 81

Weyden (Entourage of Rogier van der -)
 Pietà (painting; Madrid): 78
Weyden, Rogier van der -?
 Abegg Triptych (painting; Riggisberg): 75, 90
 Werl Panels (painting; Madrid): 75
Weyden, Rogier van der -
 Bladelin Triptych (painting; Berlin): 78, 94
 Columba Altarpiece (painting; Munich): 79, 95
 Descent from the Cross (painting; Madrid): 80, 96
 Last Judgement (painting; Beaune): 72
 Portrait of Robert de Masmines (painting - copy of Robert Campin -; Berlin): 80, 96
 Triptych with the Crucifixion (painting; Vienna): 77, 92
Widukind of Corvey
 Res gestae Saxonicae / Sachsengeschichte: 109

PRINTED ON PERMANENT PAPER • IMPRIME SUR PAPIER PERMANENT • GEDRUKT OP DUURZAAM PAPIER - ISO 9706

N.V. PEETERS S.A., WAROTSTRAAT 50, B-3020 HERENT

www.ingramcontent.com/pod-product-compliance
Lightning Source LLC
Chambersburg PA
CBHW061635040426
42446CB00010B/1428